FRITZ BENNEWITZ IN INDIA

Fritz Bennewitz in India

Intercultural Theatre with Brecht and Shakespeare

JOERG ESLEBEN
with Rolf Rohmer and David G. John

UNIVERSITY OF TORONTO PRESS
Toronto Buffalo London

Toronto Buffalo London
www.utppublishing.com

ISBN 978-1-4875-0038-2 (cloth)

Library and Archives Canada Cataloguing in Publication

Esleben, Joerg, author
Fritz Bennewitz in India : intercultural theatre with Brecht and Shakespeare / Joerg Esleben ; with Rolf Rohmer and David G. John.

Includes bibliographical references and index.
ISBN 978-1-4875-0038-2 (cloth)

1. Theater – India – History – 20th century. 2. Bennewitz, Fritz, 1926–1995 – Correspondence. 3. Mertes, Waltraut – Correspondence. 4. Theatrical producers and directors – Germany – Correspondence. 5. Theatrical producers and directors – India – Correspondence. 6. Bennewitz, Fritz, 1926–1995 – Travel – India. 7. India – Description and travel. 8. Intercultural communication in the performing arts. 9. Bennewitz, Fritz, 1926–1995 – Criticism and interpretation. I. Rohmer, Rolf, author II. John, David G. (David Gethin), 1947–, author III. Title.

PN2884.E85 2016 792.0954′0904 C2016-903843-2

This book has been published with the help of a grant from the Federation for the Humanities and Social Sciences, through the Awards to Scholarly Publications Program, using funds provided by the Social Sciences and Humanities Research Council of Canada.

University of Toronto Press acknowledges the financial assistance to its publishing program of the Canada Council for the Arts and the Ontario Arts Council, an agency of the Government of Ontario.

Canada Council for the Arts Conseil des Arts du Canada

Funded by the Government of Canada Financé par le gouvernement du Canada

To Gayatri

Contents

Illustrations

Acknowledgments

The authors would like to thank the following individuals and institutions for their help and support for this book: Akshara K.V., Amal Allana, Devendra Raj Ankur, Samik Bandyopadhyay, Uttara Baokar, Pramila Bengre, Suresh Bhardwaj, Rustom Bharucha, Prabhat Kiron Bhatnagar, Milind Brahme, Freundeskreis Fritz Bennewitz e.V. (Leipzig), Fritz Bennewitz Archiv (Leipzig), Prakash Garud, Rajini Garud, Kirti Jain, Venkatasubramanian Jayaraman, Anuradha Kapur, J.N. Kaushal, Dinesh Khanna, Belinda Kleinhans, Evelyn Mackie, Max Mueller Bhavan Chennai, Sadanand Menon, Vijaya Mehta, Natarang Pratishthan (New Delhi), National School of Drama (New Delhi), Natya Shodh Sansthan (Kolkata), Ninasam (Heggodu), B.S. Patil, Karl Pechatscheck, Prasanna, Prashanth Hiremath, Raghunandana, M.K. Raina, K.S. Rajendran, Richard Ratzlaff, Tripurari Sharma, Shastri Indo-Canadian Institute, Anju Sing, and Atul Tiwari.

Particular thanks is due to Katy Heady, Paul M. Malone, and Susan Thorne for their contributions to the translation of Fritz Bennewitz's writings.

Editorial Notes

Passages by Bennewitz are excerpts from letters to Waltraut Mertes unless noted otherwise. Elisions of original material within an excerpt are marked by three dots in square brackets: [...]. Elisions of surrounding text before and after excerpts are not marked. Emphases in UPPERCASE format are Bennewitz's own. The English translations of Bennewitz's writings are by Joerg Esleben unless noted otherwise.

FRITZ BENNEWITZ IN INDIA

Introduction

Bennewitz's Status and the Genealogy of the Documentary Project

This book provides the first comprehensive account and documentation of the work of Fritz Bennewitz (1926–95) as a theatre director in India. Bennewitz was a colourful and complex artistic personality of the German Democratic Republic (GDR). He was among that country's important interpreters of Johann Wolfgang von Goethe's drama *Faust* as well as plays by Bertolt Brecht and William Shakespeare. As a young man, while serving in the German military in the Second World War, Bennewitz was taken prisoner. After his release, Bennewitz studied and taught literature, aesthetics, and theatre in Leipzig and Weimar before taking up his profession as theatre director first at the prestigious former court theatre in Meiningen, Thuringia (1955–60) and then at the German National Theatre (Deutsches Nationaltheater, DNT) in Weimar (1960–91).[1] Bennewitz became a convinced communist after the war and remained so until his death. He was a member of the ruling communist party SED and its successor PDS until shortly after German reunification. Bennewitz was also a homosexual, an aspect of his identity that he expressed privately and cautiously, but because of which he was still subject to political reprisals in his early career. Nonetheless, the extensive travel privileges he eventually enjoyed (unlike so many other GDR citizens), in combination with his party membership and strong adherence to communist ideology, have given rise to questions

1 For further detailed information on Bennewitz's biography, see the essay by Rolf Rohmer in Part II of this volume and David G. John, *Bennewitz, Goethe, Faust*, 17–43.

whether Bennewitz was an all too willing representative of dogmatic GDR cultural policies and whether perhaps he was even implicated in the tight system of surveillance and control the East German regime attempted to maintain over the country's theatre scene. To date, no evidence has surfaced to substantiate such suspicions; on the contrary, much points to Bennewitz's early ambivalent and critical stance towards these policies and his increasing distance from them.

His role in interpretations of Goethe's *Faust*, a key text for GDR cultural authorities, offers an instructive example. With his first of three Weimar productions of both parts of the drama in 1965/7, Bennewitz had delivered a socialist interpretation of the classic that was ideologically in line with official doctrine. However, Laura Bradley in her comprehensive study of GDR theatre censorship from 1961 to 1989 shows that even then he resisted efforts on the part of the authorities to instrumentalize his production. Bradley describes how the critical production of *Faust I* by Adolf Dresen and Wolfgang Heinz at the Deutsches Theater in Berlin in 1968 countered optimistic interpretations like Bennewitz's and was therefore subjected to reprisals and censorship measures (82–91); in a culminating colloquium of the GDR Union of Theatre Practitioners, "some of the theatre practitioners present demonstrated considerable solidarity with the Deutsches Theater. Bennewitz supported the production, undermining the authorities' attempts to use his recent staging as a positive counter-example" (91). Bradley stresses his role as supporter of critical art in the debate, during which the representatives of the indicted Deutsches Theater mostly let "others like Bennewitz argue for them" (92). Moreover, David G. John has shown in his recent book *Bennewitz, Goethe, Faust* that his other two productions of the play in Weimar (in 1975 and 1981/2) grew increasingly critical of conditions in the GDR. Given Bennewitz's ambiguous positioning between ideological accordance and critical stance, the question as to why the authorities granted him such extensive travel privileges will not have a facile political answer. He certainly identified with the basic tenets of GDR cultural diplomacy, he had strong backing from the Ministry of Culture and the GDR chapter of the International Theatre Institute (ITI), and he reported regularly to both institutions on his travels and work abroad.

Bennewitz had an extraordinary international career from 1968 to 1994. In his role as cultural emissary for the GDR and through his intensive involvement with the ITI, he was able to travel and work on several continents. His travels enabled him to make unique contributions to intercultural theatre and to the cultural relations between Germany and a number of countries, especially the Philippines and India. He thereby left a mark on the national and regional theatres of these two countries and received high recognition and awards in both, including the Sangeet Natak Akademi Award in 1991, the highest award for performing artists in India. It is also only in these two countries that his intercultural contributions are still widely remembered by theatre artists, scholars, and enthusiasts. In the rest of the world, including in Germany, his name seems largely absent from theatre historiography and from discussions of the history, practice, and theory of intercultural theatre. Only over the last decade, and in particular very recently, has a significant and sustained body of scholarship on Bennewitz's intercultural contributions begun to develop.This scholarship is composed largely of publications by the contributors to the present volume.[2] This book therefore makes an important contribution to scholarly awareness of Bennewitz as a pioneer of a particular form of intercultural theatre, as well as an important figure in German-Indian cultural relations. It also widens the scope of the discussion and addresses an interested, non-specialist readership, centred as it is around Bennewitz's own voice.

The largest portion of the book is composed of English translations of Bennewitz's own writings in German about his work in India, where he directed productions and workshops of many plays by Brecht and Shakespeare as well as of Goethe's *Faust I*, Sophocles' *Antigone*, Anton Chekhov's *The Cherry Orchard*, and Volker Braun's *Great Peace*. The vast majority of these writings have never been published before in either language. They include: one of his brief articles from the leading GDR theatre journal *Theater der Zeit* (where he published with some regularity); a symposium paper Bennewitz wrote and presented in English in Mumbai; and some excerpts from his work reports and interviews. However, by far the largest share comes from letters he wrote during his sojourns in India to his life companion and confidante Waltraut Mertes.

2 The most important among these are the aforementioned book by David G. John on Bennewitz's German and intercultural productions of Goethe's *Faust* (2012), a number of earlier articles by John, essays in the 2012 *Brecht Yearbook* by John, Rohmer, and Esleben, and a chapter by Esleben in the 2014 book on *Transcultural Encounters between Germany and India* edited by Joanne Miyang Cho, Eric Kurlander, and Douglas McGetchin. See bibliography for details. For a survey of the few occurrences of Bennewitz's presence in scholarly analyses and reference works, see John, *Bennewitz, Goethe, Faust*, 17–18.

The two had met and become friends after Bennewitz's arrival at the German National Theatre in Weimar, where Mertes was secretary to artistic director Otto Lang. Their relationship reached a new level after Bennewitz suffered severe injuries, including the loss of sight in his right eye, in a car crash in 1976; Mertes nursed him back to health, and they eventually shared her house on Rembrandtweg in Weimar. Their close relationship was maintained through correspondence during Bennewitz's many journeys abroad. A particularly voluminous portion of the correspondence consists of his letters from his stays in India between 1970 and 1994. This is due to the fact that, in addition to sharing personal impressions and reflections from the country as well as discussing news, quotidian concerns, and gossip related to domestic matters with Mertes, Bennewitz increasingly used the letters as a kind of work journal where he recorded copious details and reflections about his work in many regions and languages of India and with numerous key theatre institutions, groups, and personalities of the country. It is these portions of the correspondence that form the heart of this book.

The project to publish these letters about India has a long and complicated history. Already in the 1970s, Bennewitz was aware of the potential of the letters as unique documentary material and asked Mertes to save them for such purposes. She even typed copies of many of them. Plans for a publishing endeavour began to come together in the mid-1980s, initiated by Bennewitz himself and discussed with his colleague Rolf Rohmer, then Professor at the Academy of Theatre in Leipzig. Bennewitz even began selecting passages to this end. The plans did not come to fruition, in part as a result of time constraints but likely more importantly because of growing doubts on the part of Bennewitz as to the adequacy and significance of the endeavour. (He was fond of quoting his own statement from an interview about the difficulty of documenting theatrical work: "my medium is the moment.") The plans were completely halted by the opening of the Berlin Wall and its aftermath. The idea, however, was revived after Bennewitz's death in 1995. Mertes had given the letters and a substantial amount of documentary material related to Bennewitz's life and career, which she had collected and inherited, to the newly established Fritz-Bennewitz-Freundeskreis, an association formed by his friends and colleagues to honour his memory and foster awareness of his life's work. These materials became the Fritz Bennewitz Archive, housed in Leipzig, owned by the Freundeskreis and curated by Rohmer. This time, the new round of publication plans involved Indian participation in the person of Bennewitz's long-time directing partner Vijaya Mehta. Once again, the planning did not lead to publication of the documents, but the process laid the foundation for the idea of publishing the letters in English for the benefit of an Indian readership eager to learn about Bennewitz's reflections on his work on the subcontinent.

The idea was taken up again in the early 2000s by Rohmer, David G. John of the University of Waterloo, Canada, who had by then begun researching Bennewitz's intercultural *Faust* productions, and the prominent Indian cultural critic Rustom Bharucha, who knew Bennewitz and had dedicated his book *The Politics of Cultural Practice* (2000) to him. During this phase Rohmer did extensive work on the letters, scanning the material and marking passages to be excluded from the eventual book on the basis of their personal nature or lack of relevance to Bennewitz's theatrical work in India. In the meantime, John issued a call to his colleagues in German studies in Canada for expressions of interest in order to identify scholars who would contribute to translating the letters and researching their context. Along with some other colleagues who responded, I joined the project in this capacity. Gradually, I took on larger roles within the editorial team and eventually undertook the leadership for the project.

This was greatly facilitated by a sabbatical year I spent in India in 2011–12, during which time I was able to carry out a number of tasks to move the project forward. As a first step, I completed the stage of further narrowing down the selections from the letters to the most relevant passages, in consultation with the other members of the editorial team at the time, Rohmer, John, and Bharucha. I then translated most of these passages into English, with some support from my colleagues Paul M. Malone, Katy Heady, and Susan Thorne, a generous volunteer effort on their part which I would like to acknowledge here most gratefully. During my stay in India, I was able to find a few more documentary sources in Indian archives, but more importantly I was able to interview former actors, co-directors, and academic contacts of Bennewitz in various parts of the country. Armed with this invaluable input and the archival sources from Leipzig and India, I was able to annotate the translated letter passages and write a contextual frame for them, providing information about the theatre productions they pertain to – including sites, issues, and personalities – and, for some of these productions, the critical response to them. The results are presented in the first part of the book with the translated papers and letter passages by Bennewitz along with extensive historical-critical notes and contextual commentary. This is complemented by a second part, in essay style, which provides different views on Bennewitz in India. A number of perspectives are presented, first, through a previously published character sketch of and interview with Bennewitz by his friend and collaborator, the theatre personality K.V. Subbanna, and then through excerpts from several of the interviews I conducted with other key partners of Bennewitz in India. These are followed by a biographical sketch and an outline of Bennewitz's intercultural work by Rohmer, and an essay by John on Bennewitz's politics and Brechtian aesthetics. Finally, the two main parts of the book are supplemented by a bibliography of all sources used or consulted as well as two appendices: a chronological overview of all of Bennewitz's stays in South Asia with detailed information (where available) about the productions he directed there, and a glossary of pertinent theatre terms, names of institutions, and cultural references.

The Source Material and Its Selection and Translation

Most of the source material for this book is found in the Fritz Bennewitz Archive, which is currently housed in a large room of the private dwelling of curator Rolf Rohmer in Leipzig, who generously grants access to interested scholars. This is a solution owed to practicality but also to financial exigency since the archive receives no public financial support. Instead it is (meagerly) financed by donations from members of the Fritz-Bennewitz-Freundeskreis and others. The archive contains a wealth of materials from Bennewitz's life and career, including playbooks, director's notes, posters, reviews, and, most crucially for this book, what is extant of his correspondance. John's *Bennewitz, Goethe, Faust* contains a detailed description and inventory of the holdings of the archive (285–8), so I will not reiterate the same information here. Instead, I would like to focus on the nature of Bennewitz's correspondance with Waltraut Mertes, from which the vast majority of material for this book has been selected.

We only have one side of the correspondance; unfortunately, Mertes' letters to Bennewitz have not been preserved, though at times he summarizes or refers to them in his replies. His letters to her from India alone amount to several thousand pages and fill the majority of nineteen thick binders containing his entire India correspondence. Of this corpus of letters to Mertes, approximately five per cent has been excerpted and translated into English here. Bennewitz typed most of the letters on typewriters he brought with him or borrowed from trusted persons in

India, but some he wrote by hand in a reasonably legible though by no means tidy or beautiful script. In long passages, the tone of the letters is casual and conversational, but it often becomes more technical in terms of theatrical discourse, or more philosophical and literary, in passages where Bennewitz documents and reflects on his work and on the texts and contexts which informed it. Most of the letters are a blend of both these registers, encompassing a great variety of styles, and a vast number of topics pertaining to realities both at home and abroad. The topics range from the most extraordinary to the most quotidian of experiences; the letters include not only descriptions of his work processes but also impressions of places and people in India, political commentary and news summaries, recountings of conversations and discussions, reviews of performances and films he had seen, scenes witnessed in the street or on social or official occasions, reminiscences of past experiences, details of travel plans, reports on bureaucratic procedures, expressions of concern for or gossip about family members, friends, colleagues and acquaintances at home, and plans for renovations in the house he and Mertes shared; the list could be extended still further.

This wildly heterogeneous content is presented in an equally unbounded writing style. Bennewitz far exceeds the already pronounced German penchant for long, complex sentence structures with multiple dependent clauses. His style consists of an impressionistic technique of inserting ever new side clauses, parentheses, and phrases between dashes, so that his sentences grow into many-headed albeit often beautiful hydras. Add to that the fact that he uses many puns and self-coined neologisms, quotations from high and popular culture, and personal references shared with Mertes, and it becomes clear that this style presented a considerable challenge both in selecting relevant passages (the selection criteria will be discussed below) and in translating them into an English that is comprehensible but retains some of Bennewitz's personal and personable tone.

An example will be instructive here. I have selected a passage, included in chapter 1 below (pages 79–80), from a letter Bennewitz wrote on 10 December 1979 towards the end of a stay at the National School of Drama in New Delhi. The passage recounts a farewell ceremony held for Bennewitz. The following table contains the original German text (with passages omitted from the eventual selection struck through) in the left column, a close English translation in the middle column approximating the syntax and literal word choices of the original, and in the right column the final translation as incorporated in chapter 1.

Fig. 1 Fritz Bennewitz with letters, 1993. Courtesy of Fritz-Bennewitz-Archiv, Leipzig.

German original text

[…] – also um 9 Uhr gestern früh in der YOGA-Hall waren Alle und ich mußt auf den Teppich auf der Estrade und die Reden waren – was ich auch schön und ehrenvoll fand, weil es ALLE DISTANZ von ihnen zu mir aufhob, weil sie mit Selbstverständlichkeit zeigten, daß kein FREMDER unter ihnen war und weil es so ganz herzlich war, war es auch KURZ – und was Schönem in so immer neu schön Traurigem (weil wir auch unsere Sentimentalitäten oder sogar richtige tiefen Emotionen in zumindest dieser Situation dann haben – denn natürlich wissen wir, daß es vornehmlich und fast ausschließlich die ARBEIT war, deren aufregend schöne Erlebnisse miteinander verbunden haben und nicht HERZ/SCHMERZ oder Nettigkeit zueinander – und wissen gleichzeitig um unsere/meine grundsätzlichen TREULOSIGKEITEN, d.h. daß sich im andern Land – wenn die Arbeit und ihre LEBENSBEDINGUNGEN und LERN- und WIRKUNGSBEDINGUNGEN ähnlich sind – sich das emotional wiederholt oder ähnlich dagewesen – ~~denk an die ausgerupften Barthaare auf dem Bahnhof in IASI~~ – na ja, wenn es aber immer wieder neu ist, dann ist nicht nur die auch sicher dann wieder neue TREULOSIGKEIT im HERZ/SCHMERZ-Sinn, das, was zählt wirklich, sondern es zählt – ERMUTIGEND – auch, daß meine Energien, meine Fähigkeiten nicht nachgelassen

Close translation

[…] – so at 9 o'clock yesterday morning everyone was in the Yoga Hall and I had to go on the carpet on the dais and the speeches were – which I found beautiful and an honour because it lifted ANY DISTANCE between them and me, because they showed naturally that no FOREIGNER was among them and because it was so very heartfelt, it was also SHORT – and what was beautiful within such ever newly beautiful sadness (because we then also have our sentimentalities or even truly deep emotions in at least this situation – for of course we know that it was foremost and almost exclusively the WORK, whose excitingly beautiful experiences connected with one another and not HEART/PAIN or niceness to each other – and we know at the same time about our/my basic infidelities, i.e. that in another country – if the work and its conditions for living, learning and making an impact are similar – it repeats itself emotionally or has been there similarly – ~~think of the torn-out beard hairs at the train station in IASI~~ – well, but if it is ever new again, then it is not the surely also new INFIDELITY in the sense of HEART/PAIN which counts, but what counts – ENCOURAGINGLY – is also that my energies, my abilities have not diminished (which was, after all, also the AMERICA decision after the accident, because I wanted to KNOW whether in the creative realm – ~~not in Krasser-like creation,~~

Final translation

At 9 am yesterday morning everyone was assembled in the Yoga Hall and I had to go on the carpet onto the dais. The speeches were short, which I took as a nice honour because it meant that any distance between them and me had been lifted, and because they showed naturally and with great warmth that I was not a foreigner among them. This was beautiful, even if a beautiful sadness, because at least at the time we have our sentimentalities or even truly deep emotions. But of course we know that it was foremost and almost exclusively the work that connected us with its excitingly beautiful experiences, and not some melodramatic feelings of love and bonds of friendship. At the same time, we know about our/my basic infidelity, meaning the fact that this emotional experience repeats itself in other parts of the world if the work and living conditions and the conditions for learning and making an impact are similar […]. Well, if it is true that it is always a new experience, then the infidelity in the melodramatic sense is not what counts, but rather, encouragingly, what counts is that my energies and capacities have not diminished. This was at the heart of my decision in favour of the project in America after the accident, because I wanted to know whether creatively […], in the sense of being able to both give and learn, I had lost anything. I had not – it has rather been a gain. This has repeatedly become apparent, and now, too,

German original text

haben (was ja auch die AMERIKA-Entscheidung nach dem Unfall war, weil ich WISSEN wollt, ob im Schöpferischen – ~~nicht im Krasserschen Schöpfen, sondern ich meine einfach:~~ im GEBEN- und LERNEN-KÖNNEN nichts verloren war – es war und ist nicht – es ist eher ZUWACHS, wie [s]ich auch grad jetzt so ganz UNMITTELBAR nach der einen INSZENIERUNG sich fortsetzend / wiederholend als Tiefenwirkung in die Menschen bestätigend zeigt – trotz oder auch weil der tiefen und mit Drohungen und schlimmen Worten erfüllten KRISEN in den jeweiligen späten Mitten der jeweiligen Arbeiten, aber weil es um der ARBEIT willen kriselt und nicht wegen MENSCHLICHEM-abseits-von-Arbeit sind die Krisen keine Krisen, sondern nur Unterbrechung von sonst zu harmonisch Schönem) – zurück zu gestern früh: also, was so schön, weil ganz aus den Protokollgewohnheiten, die ja auch ihre geprägten Worte und Losungen haben ~~(Du weißt – am oder zum 1. Mai stehen sie immer in aufschlußreicher Reihenfolge der Bedeutung auf der ersten Seite des ND)~~ also da war ein gemaltes großes Transparent am Eingang zur Verabschiedungshalle: DEAR FRITZ – PLEASE COME BACK SOON ! – Na ja, das geht schon – auch mit Freude unter die Haut. Und der Direktor wollt mein Versprechen that *hamare dost* (unser lieber Freund) Fritz *jaunga jera* (wiederkommen wird und muß jedes Jahr).

Close translation

~~rather I simply mean:~~ in being ABLE to GIVE and LEARN nothing had been lost – nothing had or is – rather it is GAIN, as is shown and confirmed particularly now after the one PRODUCTION in a continuous / repeated way as deep impact into the people – despite or perhaps because of the deep CRISES filled with threats and terrible words in the respective late middle phases of the respective projects, but because there's a crisis atmosphere due to WORK and not due to what is HUMAN away from work, the crises are not crises but just interruptions of what would otherwise be too harmoniously beautiful) – back to yesterday morning: so, what was so nice because outside of habits of protocol, which also have their coined words and slogans ~~(as you know – on or for the 1st of May they are always printed in revealing order of meaning on the first page of the Neues Deutschland newspaper)~~, so, there was a large painted banner at the entrance to the hall: "Dear Fritz – Please Come Back Soon!" Well, that goes – with joy, too – under one's skin. And the director wanted my promise that *hamare dost* – our dear friend – Fritz *jaunga jera* – has to come back every year.

Final translation

immediately after the production, in the deep effect my work has had on people, despite or perhaps because of the deep crises filled with threats and callous words around the middle of each respective project. Because such critical situations arise on account of work, not due to problems in the human relations outside of work, they are not crises but rather interruptions of what would otherwise be all too beautifully harmonious. So, back to yesterday morning: it was so nice because outside of the usual protocol, which has its normal expressions and slogans […] – there was a large painted banner at the entrance to the hall: "Dear Fritz – Please Come Back Soon!" Well, that was joyously thrilling. And the director wanted my promise that *hamare dost* – our dear friend – Fritz *jaunga jera*– has to come back every year.

This example illustrates the types of transformation that the source material has undergone in the process of translation. The syntax has been tamed and broken up into a larger number of shorter sentences; certain condensed, personalized references such as *Herz/Schmerz* have received an explanatory translation (a kind of "unpacking" – in this case: "melodramatic feelings of love"); Bennewitz's use of capital letters for emphasis – at times excessive – has been eliminated (but retained elsewhere in the book in places where the emphasis was deemed crucial); and a number of asides have been removed in order to minimize distractions. In the instance cited above, the asides concern: 1) an example of emotional attachment from a previous work stay in Romania; 2) a rather obscure reference to the concept of 'creation' held by a person who was likely an acquaintance shared with Mertes; and 3) a comparison of phrases used at farewell functions to slogans in the GDR official newspaper, which, although it is a somewhat irreverent political comment, is here meant merely to appeal humorously to their shared quotidian life in the socialist GDR.

Of course, this last reference could have been regarded as an interesting cross-cultural, political comparison and thus could have been left in the selection, but in this instance the editorial choice was to eliminate it based on the rather trivial function of the aside. This brings us to the question of selection criteria for the passages from Bennewitz's letters that have been included in the book. These criteria are centred upon Bennewitz's theatrical work. Considered for inclusion were letter passages that

- describe and comment on his theatre work in India, his directing style, his interaction with the actors and other partners, the process of adapting texts, the political and social contexts, and living conditions during the work, etc.
- contain interpretations of the dramatic texts he staged and commentary on their contexts.
- focus on Indian performances or performative styles, including daily life and rituals.
- reflect generally and conceptually on creating theatre across cultures.
- connect his identity and biography to the work in India.
- provide insights into his views (from his "outsider" perspective in India) on the downfall of the GDR and German reunification.

This is only a rough catalogue of themes which aided in sifting relevant passages from the topical tangle of Bennewitz's letters described above, in order to then select those among them deemed most telling and interesting. As will be seen from the eventual selections, in the process of reading the letters some unique passages were also found that did not necessarily fall under these headings but are of general interest nonetheless. Of course, such a selection process, even if in this case it was carried out or approved by several members of an editorial team with very different perspectives and approaches to the material (Rohmer, Esleben, John, Bharucha in the early phase of the project), will always remain subjective. The original source material can be consulted in its entirety by anyone interested at the Fritz Bennewitz Archive, but this presupposes knowledge of German. It is certainly our hope that this book will spark interest in further research on this material. In the meantime, the proof for most readers will be in the pudding: is there an internal coherence to the selection of passages from Bennewitz's writings and do the annotations and contextual commentary enable them to make sense?

Bennewitz and Discourses on Intercultural Theatre

A word on terminology and theoretical discourse is in order here. We have decided to retain the concept of intercultural theatre in this book, despite many misgivings about the term "intercultural" because it has come to be associated with certain kinds of Western universalizing and (arguably) neo-colonial theatre practices. This book, in part, represents a contribution to attempts to reclaim the term "intercultural" for other, more equitable theatrical exchanges.

The theoretical field concerned with intercultural theatre is highly fragmented and contested, a result of two factors: the myriad possible forms that intercultural contact can take in the theatre, and the postcolonial questioning of the ethics, politics, and economics of such contact. Contact between different cultures in the theatre can occur on multiple, overlapping levels: within the dramatic text or performance script; during the planning, design, and rehearsal of a production; within the cast and production team; during the performance, between the performance and the audience or within the audience; and in the wider reception (critical, scholarly, viral, etc.) of a project. Bennewitz's projects were characterized by intercultural contact on each of these levels, evidenced by the translation and adaptation into various Indian languages of the plays he directed, by his rehearsal and production work with Indian actors and collaborators, by the deliberate blend of Western play, Brechtian directorial approach, and Indian theatre traditions performed in front of varied audiences across India, and finally by the attention this blend elicited from Indian (and to a lesser extent German) media and intellectuals.

Intercultural theatre has been variously conceived as the transfer of theatrical elements between source and target cultures, the performative blending of cultural elements into hybrid or syncretic forms, or a mutual communicative exchange. All three definitions are applicable to Bennewitz's work to some degree. Many of the potential reasons for engaging in intercultural theatre are also reflected in Bennewitz's work. Some, however, can be ruled out from the start: unlike many Western intercultural theatre projects that import or go in search of theatrical elements and performers from non-European cultures, his adaptations of Western texts in non-European contexts were not motivated by a desire to explore or benefit from a fascination with exotic elements, by a search for performative and anthropological universals, or by an intent to create commercially successful international productions. Rather, other key motivations that have been theorized for intercultural performance are more pertinent to his work; these include the desire to bring about change in one theatre system and culture by use of elements from other cultures; the transfer of theatre from one culture to another for political or ideological purposes; the didactic purpose of encouraging cultures to learn about one another; and the negotiation of cultural differences, conflicts, and hybrid identities in contact zones.

Historically, the critical discourse about intercultural theatre has been dominated by Western practices and conceptualizations and by critical responses to these particularly from a postcolonial perspective. In his genealogy of Western approaches, Ric Knowles usefully distinguishes between a universalist, idealist strand inspired by Antonin Artaud and a materialist strand inspired by Bertolt Brecht. The idealist strand, in particular as represented by Peter Brook, Jerzy Grotowski, and Eugenio Barba, has been focused on the search for anthropological universals preceding or standing outside of historical and cultural differences. The materialist approach, conversely, focuses on specific historical and cultural contexts, particularly on their economic and ideological underpinnings (Knowles 13). It is this latter approach that has informed the postcolonial criticism of Western intercultural theatre projects as unmindful of specific cultural contexts of non-Western theatre practices, as ignoring or being complicit in representational and economic power imbalances, as exploitative, and ultimately as neocolonialist. In the wake of this critique, most recent theorizations of intercultural theatre are therefore characterized not only by aesthetic but also ethical and political considerations, stressing the importance of specific political and economic contexts, of equitableness in the intercultural exchange, and of the complex dialectic relations between identity and alterity, and universal and particular elements.

Bennewitz's work mirrors and addresses these concerns to a remarkable degree. In his two and a half decades of working in India, he sought out collaborators and developed a flexible, context-sensitive method. This method remained firmly anchored in Marxist and Brechtian aesthetics and politics, relying on the central Brechtian idea of alienation as a 'denaturalizing' of social structures in order to present them as changeable.[3] But even though as a committed communist he never ceased to regard himself as a representative of the ideas embodied by the GDR, he increasingly emancipated himself from the official lines of GDR cultural policy in favour of having an impact on struggles for social justice specific to the countries and regions in which he worked.

Bennewitz recorded numerous reflections about his work in published articles and interviews and above all in his letters from his stays abroad. Despite his characteristic modesty and abhorrence of self-promotion, he himself saw his work in India and other parts of the world as an important and rather unique contribution to intercultural theatre. At times, he contrasted his work in this field sharply with dominant Western conceptions and their prominent exponents. However, Bennewitz did not attempt (nor was he tempted) to formulate a general, fully developed theory of intercultural theatre of his own. Instead, his writings and interviews reveal musings and variations on key conceptions and ideas that stood in close reciprocal relations with his practice, arose out of that practice, and informed it in turn. Some of these were taken from his Brechtian aesthetics, others he developed "in the field" in the course of his encounters with other cultures. These reflections provide a wealth of insight into his working methods and the ideological and aesthetic assumptions underlying them.[4]

---

3 For more details on Bennewitz's relation to and uses of Brecht, see the essays by Rohmer and John in Part II of this volume.

4 See Rohmer's essay in Part II for a further perspective on Bennewitz's intercultural practices and conceptions.

The method Bennewitz developed over the course of his intercultural theatre practice is anchored by key principles that can be termed, largely based on his own designations, as integration, discovery, making offers, mutuality (in the sense of both sharing and reciprocity), and challenge. In Bennewitz's writings, these central ideas, along with other recurring concepts, form a conceptual field that is characterized by its situational specificity, by overlaps, and by dialectic movement. For Bennewitz, adaptation came to mean only a first step in transposing a foreign theatrical text into the host cultural and theatrical context, on the way to their mutually transformative integration. His aim was to help adapt the plays to the local culture and traditions, but not in order to achieve ethnic authenticity. Rather, Bennewitz saw such adaptation as a necessary initial offer of identification in a dialectic manoeuvre that would, on the one hand, make productions fit into Indian theatre and the local, particular traditions, needs, and audiences' horizons, but would, on the other hand, also confront audiences and actors with ideas that would challenge their beliefs, social attitudes, and customs.

This challenge function, however, was not to be the result of coercive imposition from without, but of a self-driven process of discovery, another key term and conception in Bennewitz's toolbox closely connected to the idea of making offers. A key component of Bennewitz's conception of integration was to react responsively to the particular cohort of actors in a production (often with immense intracultural differences) and to locally available theatrical means and styles, including music and dance. In reporting on his work with the actors, Bennewitz frequently stressed the need to challenge certain histrionic acting styles that do not connect the recited lines to meaning and communication. But he also represented this work as a mutual challenge to the preconceptions and horizons of understanding held by both Indian actors and European director. Bennewitz was aware of the dangers of imposing European ways of doing theatre and European value hierarchies onto non-European cultures, irrespective of ideological orientation. In contrast, he began to conceive of intercultural theatre as a mutual, dialectic process of discovery and negotiation that activates new critical potential.

In his reflections on this intercultural process, translation received particular attention as a collective process of active adaptation, which involved not only the authors of initial textual translations and adaptations and the director himself, but also the actors in the course of rehearsals. In this regard, Bennewitz also experienced some instructive failures that helped him clarify and further develop his conceptions. One key to these conceptions is the emphasis on the reciprocal nature of the encounter between Brecht's text and Indian folk theatre traditions. By envisioning both as enriched, Bennewitz's dialectical concept of integration represents a particular, Marxist take on the emphasis of theories of intercultural performance on non-hierarchical syncretism.

Bennewitz had strong misgivings about the degradation of genuine, vital, folk traditions into folkloristic entertainment. Indeed, one important function he came to attribute to the work he and his collaborators were doing in the Indian context was to challenge prevailing middle-class attitudes toward theatre as mere entertainment and the adoption of cinematic aesthetics in theatrical productions. His indictment gains added urgency from his conviction, expressed many times in his writings, that Indian performance traditions could uncover whole new social and aesthetic dimensions of the Brechtian text. This corresponds to recent theoretical insights into the transformative effects that intercultural productions can have on understandings of Western classical texts, which Anthony Tatlow has explored specifically for Brecht and Shakespeare productions in Asia (see Agiman 188).

In the last stage of his career, Bennewitz found a privileged organic metaphor for the intercultural theatrical encounter, arguing that "any play of some stature is a very sensitive organism of its own – dormant in the book and letter only – which meets in a given time at a given place with a group of actors who are likewise sensitive organs of their respective historical, cultural, ethnic etc. conditions and structures" (in his Mumbai seminar paper reproduced in chapter 4, page 245), and that integration "is the reciprocal challenge which may result in transformation of both" (Interview for *Theater Quarterly*). This restates his key conceptions and highlights once again his understanding of the intercultural encounter as a complex process of negotiation. While his work was necessarily and deliberately bound up with very particular historical and cultural contexts, both his practice and his conceptualizations offer a valuable contribution to thinking about intercultural performance. Bennewitz's work confirmed and enriched current theorizations of intercultural theatre that stress equitable exchange, respect for particular contexts, sensitivity to economic power imbalances and issues of social justice, and the dialectical negotiation of cultural differences. The present volume therefore contributes to the project of a critical genealogy of intercultural theatre that should help reclaim the term for the description and evaluation of a wide range of practices within, between, and across cultures.

Aims and Purposes of the Book

Just as the motivations and the history of the project to document Bennewitz's work in India are various and multifaceted, so is the book itself. In general, it is designed to create awareness of Bennewitz's unique intercultural work, among both specialist scholars of intercultural theatre and of German-Indian cultural relations, and the general public. An important related goal is to give to Indian actors, colleagues of Bennewitz, critics, and audiences, as well as scholars of Indian theatre, access to Bennewitz's thoughts about his work and life in India for the first time, allowing them to read these documents in English at first hand, as many of them have frequently urged. Key parts of Bennewitz's unpublished writings about his intercultural work in India are thereby also made accessible in English translation to a wide international audience.

As a work of scholarship, the book is intended as a catalyst for more intensive scholarly engagement with Bennewitz's work, to provide this scholarship with a solid and multifaceted basis for debate, and to spark further research on this seminal but neglected figure. The book also makes a significant contribution to Indian theatre history. Finally, it provides, with its combination of primary material, multiple perspectives, and critical scholarship, a rich sourcebook for teaching the theory and practice of intercultural theatre, Indian theatre history, the international reception of Brecht and Shakespeare, and German-Indian cultural relations.

PART I

Fritz Bennewitz on His Work in India

1 The 1970s – Brechtian Experiments

Historical Junctures

History, so favoured by Bennewitz as a central reference in his work and thought, favoured Bennewitz in creating ideal conditions for his embarcation in 1970 on the Indian adventure that would last for the rest of his life. In the late 1960s, relations between India and the GDR reached a new level (see Misra; Huber; Guenther). Trade relations between the two countries, maintained formally since the creation of trading missions in 1954, had been increasing rapidly. The declining adherence to and eventual abandonment of the West German Hallstein Doctrine, which had threatened sanctions on countries recognizing the GDR as a sovereign state, also reduced the risk that official recognition of East Germany would have posed previously to India's economic relations with the West. In India, there was growing public support and pressure for recognition, spearheaded by the All India Indo-GDR Friendship Association (INGFA), which held its first national conference in 1966. This association provided an umbrella for the many regional and state-level Indo-GDR friendship societies that had been created around the country by both communists and non-communists whose cultural and educational interests in Germany were shared by many Indian intellectuals and artists. Cultural relations were thus of great mutual interest: they allowed both sides to satisfy their curiosity about the other, as well as to pursue their respective political goals. For the GDR, these relations were an important cultural-political and propagandistic tool in support of the ultimate diplomatic prize, official recognition from India (eventually obtained in October 1972). Bennewitz's initial mission, facilitated by the signing of a two-year cultural exchange program by representatives of the Indian Ministry of Education and the GDR Trade Mission in April 1968, therefore had a very concrete political dimension.

In addition to this political context, theatre history also favoured Bennewitz's mission. A forum and resource for collaboration across national boundaries had already been established with the creation of the International Theatre Institute (ITI) by UNESCO in 1948. The National School of Drama (NSD), founded in New Delhi in 1959, provided a central institutional anchor for the theatrical dimension of the exchange agreement between the two countries. Indeed, the NSD played a key role in focusing the enormous interest demonstrated by Indian theatre artists in Bertolt Brecht's theory and practice since the 1950s. This interest was linked to the GDR from the start. While being exposed to Brecht's ideas during his studies in England in the mid-1950s, Habib Tanvir also saw some of his plays at the Berliner Ensemble (BE) in East Berlin, an experience that proved seminal for Tanvir's subsequent work (Dalmia-Lüderitz 222–3). In 1961, the contributions of the GDR delegation to the East-West theatre seminar held by the ITI in New Delhi were apparently well received (Bennewitz "Internationale Co-Operation"); in the same year, M.S. Sathyu and Shama Zaidi spent time at the BE and subsequently put on the *Caucasian Chalk Circle* in Delhi (Dalmia 180; Nathan 30). Utpal Dutt, another key theatre personality influenced by the German playwright, founded the first Indian Brecht Society in Calcutta in 1964. There was a flurry of Indian and German interaction with regard to Brecht and his work in 1968:

> Firm grounds for regular contact were created when Ebrahim Alkazi participated in the 'Brecht Dialog 1968' in East Berlin, organized by the International Theatre Institute and the Brecht Zentrum. In the same year, Goethe Institute, the West German Cultural Organization, sponsored the visit of Carl Weber, a former assistant director in Brecht's Berliner Ensemble, based in the meantime in the USA. Weber directed *The Caucasian Chalk Circle* for the National School of Drama Repertory Company. It was Weber's effort to present the play entirely in the style of the Berliner Ensemble and the model of the play created by Brecht. It was a great success and the Repertory toured the country with it. (Dalmia 180)

In turn, students of the NSD were given the opportunity to study at theatres in the GDR. Among them was Alkazi's daughter, Amal Allana, who spent much of her time in the GDR under the mentorship of Bennewitz. It was on his urging that she produced Tagore's *Post Office* at the German National Theatre in Weimar with German actors. Bennewitz had made a name for himself both at the Meiningen Theatre and in Weimar for his direction of Brecht's plays and for his application of Brechtian acting methods, and in 1968, he successfully transferred this expertise to international work when he directed the Romanian premiere of Brecht's *Life of Galileo* in Iasi. Thus, he was the logical candidate to be sent to the NSD for the production of the *Threepenny Opera* that was the object of the first theatrical concretisation of the new cultural exchange agreement, under the shared auspices of the ITI, the GDR Ministry of Culture, and the cultural section of the Indian Ministry of Education. The stage was set for Bennewitz's first work in India.

New Delhi, 1970: Brecht, *The Threepenny Opera*

In the Fritz Bennewitz Archive, there is a document whose title translates as "Directive for the stay of a directorial team from the GDR at the National School of Drama in New Delhi," dated 30 December 1969 in Berlin and presumably originating from the Ministry of Culture. This document, which still reflects the assumption that BE chief dramaturge Joachim Tenschert would accompagny Bennewitz, provides unique insights into the political context and intentions of the enterprise. Its author recounts the development of contacts with NSD director Ebrahim Alkazi and argues that in reaction to the NSD production of Brecht's *Caucasian Chalk Circle* by Carl Weber, "it seemed all the more urgent to him that now a team of people who are directly linked to the BE should also come to New Delhi in order to impart a politically more exact idea of Brecht to both students and audience there" ("Direktive"). The anonymous author draws a broader political conclusion from this:

> The main task of our team is thus clearly a political one: to help our Trade Mission in New Delhi by means of the production and through their whole demeanor to strengthen the already widespread movement for official recognition of the GDR. At the same time and for the first time, we can now battle in India's capital against the massive cultural demagoguery of the West German embassy, which attempts in its bulletins and in all its activities to usurp Brecht for its purposes as part of an "all-German culture."

The document then spells out concrete tasks for the team: directing the production in close consultation with Alkazi (including specifically the "development and exposition of a conception tailored to Indian conditions"), helping the GDR Trade Mission in its propagandistic exploitation of the event in contacts with the media and with influential individuals, holding lectures, seminars, and discussions at NSD and beyond about theatre in the GDR and about Brecht, and establishing cordial contact with the Indian ITI centre.

Armed with these orders, Bennewitz arrived in New Delhi in February 1970 to take up his work on *The Threepenny Opera* at the National School of Drama. The play was produced in a Hindustani translation by Surekha Sikri (with the songs translated by Sheila Bhatia) under the title *Teen Take Ka Swang*. Vanraj Bhatia composed the music, with assistance from Sushil Chowdury and Naima Khan. The NSD director Ebrahim Alkazi himself designed the stage set, his daughter Amal Allana was assistant director and designed the costumes for the show. The role of Macheath was played by Manohar Singh, while Peachum was double cast with M.K. Raina and S.K. Sawhney. Nadira Zaheer played Celia Peachum, Uttara Baokar was Polly, and Madhav Khadilkar, another former NSD student who had spent time in Weimar with Bennewitz, played Tiger Brown.

Bennewitz's letters from this stay, though they also record the fulfilment of his official duty to make relevant contacts, reflect above all the excitement of a first encounter with India. He describes in great detail his many experiences with all levels of Indian society, his weekend tours to Jaipur and the Taj Mahal, and his celebration of Holi. He is particularly interested in the lives and plights of the people on the lower rungs and margins of Indian society. Despite his best efforts, he regrets that he will not be able to narrate all that he sees, but even so he cannot bring himself to take photos of the people in Old Delhi, because he does not want to treat them as objects (New Delhi, 22 Feb. 1970).

Work on the production progresses very well; Bennewitz reports that it is an immense pleasure and that he feels he has more ideas here than even in his two previous productions of the *Threepenny Opera* in Germany (New Delhi, 27 Feb. 1970). The following passages from his letters show the close connection between his reflections (as yet, relatively few) about the work and about the impact his first stay in India had on him.[1]

1 Translations in this section are by Joerg Esleben and Paul M. Malone.

New Delhi, 2 March 1970

Despite the fun I am having it is an enormous exertion, of course, due to the need for concentration, above all concentration on one as yet half-foreign and one utterly foreign language. Romanian at least had similarities with Latin, but where the devil should someone like me have gotten knowledge in Sanskrit?[2] I'll just say that in the evenings I know how much I've done during the day.

New Delhi, 10 March 1970

I am on my way to myself, more than is possible under familiar circumstances: this is the most essential thing that is happening to me here, and that can happen to one in such a situation if one goes through a new, different world with open eyes (though two eyes really are too few) and with a receptive heart. It is inconceivable to me that I am here to teach – I am the one who's learning, incessantly, every hour.

[...]

It is indescribable, really [...] – and sometimes it seems as if it went faster than at home, even though much of it, almost all of it, is new for the actors. And I myself am in a constant state of discovering and am learning through teaching, including many things for back home. That is the advantage of having to find your way around in an utterly foreign language: the discovery and working out of *Gestus* receives more attention.

New Delhi, 17 March 1970

By the way, Amal's mother[3] believes (in accordance with Buddhist and Hindu beliefs) that I must have been an Indian in a previous life, because I am and feel not at all foreign here and make land and people my own in such a different manner than those who usually come here. Who knows what else I was in who knows how many previous lives, seeing as today I am neither here nor there.

[...]

2 Bennewitz is refering to English (the "half-foreign language" for him) and Hindi, the "utterly foreign language" with roots in the equally alien Sanskrit.

3 Ebrahim Alkazi's wife and Amal Allana's mother Roshan Alkazi, a costume designer and historian of Indian garments.

> The composer[4] is a miracle worker – since yesterday, three songs have already been composed and learned. [...] It sounds highly original and I like it very much. Of course, I first have to get the all too well known and firmly implanted music of Weill[5] out of my head in order to be able to judge properly. The lead roles are all cast very well, unbelievably well for a school, actually. However, one must not expect what is usual in our theatre schools. Most of them have acted for years in amateur groups in their villages, so they don't come to the school completely inexperienced. The actor playing Macheath,[6] for example, is 31 years old. But still, it is quite new what we are doing, and that's why it is so astonishing how quickly it is progressing.
>
> New Delhi, 6 April 1970
>
> I don't know (and it is too early to tell) whether my experiences here have truly changed me and if so, whether it's for good. What I'm doing here [...] is probably my greatest experience, perhaps also my best one with myself – but I won't know that until later. It really is true that a seemingly remote and different world does more to lead one to oneself or at least to question oneself in new ways.

Reportedly, the production of the *Threepenny Opera* was a success with audiences and critics in Delhi and during a 1971 tour of the NSD with several other plays (including Weber's *Caucasian Chalk Circle* and Alkazi's 1969 *Othello*) to Mumbai, Pune, Hyderabad, and Bangalore; Bennewitz accompanied this tour and supplemented the productions with lectures on Brecht and theatre in the GDR. The tour provided him with crucial exposure to the regional and theatrical diversity of India. There was also a characteristic incident involving German-German political "diversity": in Hyderabad, where the West German Max Mueller Bhavan was the host of the troupe, the *Threepenny Opera* (as the work of an East German director) had not been included in the program. Bennewitz consequently paid his own way there with some

4 Vanraj Bhatia (born 1927), an award-winning Indian composer of music for theatre and film.

5 Kurt Weill (1900–50), a German-Jewish composer who frequently collaborated with Bertolt Brecht. His music for the *Threepenny Opera* is among his best-known work.

6 Manohar Singh (1938–2002).

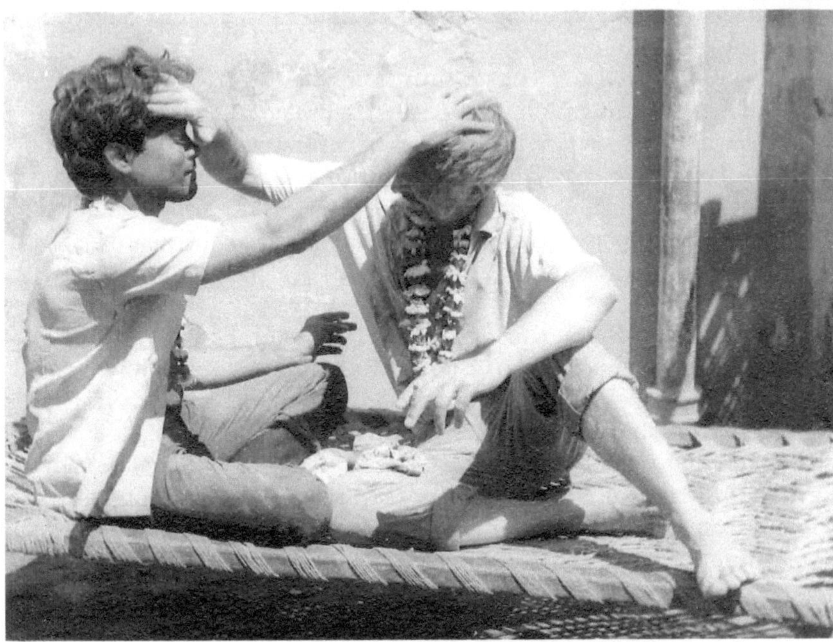

Figs. 2 and 3 Fritz Bennewitz in India in the early 1970s. Courtesy of Fritz-Bennewitz-Archiv, Leipzig.

financial support received from the GDR consulate, since his presence had been requested by the ITI centres of the GDR and India (Arbeitsbericht 20 Jan.–19 Feb. 1971). The West German critic Freimut Duve, however, in a review in the prestigious weekly *Die Zeit*, the only West German critical response to Bennewitz's work in India known to this author, had ridiculed the ideological worries of his country's diplomats and had called the production thoroughly bourgeois theatre for the Indian bourgeoisie.

The actor Uttara Baokar, who played the role of Polly, reminisced about the style and success of the production in her written response to the author's interview questions:

> Mr. Bennewitz in his production of *The Threepenny Opera* tried to project the theme of the play, which deals with corruption, bribery and prostitution of body and mind, with his unique design, which was humorous and stylized, making fun of bourgeois society, who uses these people for their own good.
>
> The crisp stylized movements, combining songs with rhythmic body movements, sharing dialogues directly with the audience and commenting on situations, brought out the required 'Brechtian Experience' of entertainment and social comment beautifully.
>
> The production was a great success for the Delhi theatre audience and for all the participants – especially the drama students – for understanding Brecht's method, his approach to theatre and his philosophy. The production received overwhelming reviews and reports in newspapers and magazines in Delhi and also wherever we performed. In Mumbai, Pune and Bangalore, people were amazed to go through this new theatrical experience.

In the letters written during his stay in Delhi, Bennewitz does not comment on the question of the production's success. However, his subsequent published and unpublished statements reveal a transition in his assessment. In an interview given in 1972, later published in English, likely in a publication of the GDR Ministry of Culture, Bennewitz says that the production received a very good and satisfying response. He compares his *Threepenny Opera* and Carl Weber's *Caucasian Chalk Circle* in terms that echo the Ministry's directive cited above:

> And there were wider implications involved, because in 1968 the school had scored a notable success with Brecht's *Caucasian Chalk*

> *Circle* – produced by a West German director – and it was only natural that our production would provoke a comparison. The press reacted with interesting comments and observations. One critic, for instance, wrote in connection with our premiere that despite the brilliance of the production [by Carl Weber], Brecht's message had been deliberately understated in the *Chalk Circle*. In our production, on the other hand, the substance and purpose of the play had been brought out in startling clarity and the barbed weapons of humour, irony, biting satire and ridicule employed to attack bourgeois society. In another review the comment was made that whereas the *Chalk Circle* represented a literal translation of Brecht's words, my production revealed the genuine spirit of Brechtian theatre, providing significant evidence of how well the ensemble had understood both the technical approach and the philosophy of Brecht ("Teaching and Learning").

In his article "Experiences with Brecht Abroad," published in the GDR's leading theatre journal *Theater der Zeit* in 1973, Bennewitz acknowledges the limitations imposed by his lack of knowledge of Hindustani but comments:

> The disadvantage of being unable to understand the language soon turned into an advantage. At first, I had to base my control of the exactness of the actions and attitudes on stage almost exclusively on the gestural material. As a consequence, this production was gesturally rich and, in the conscious use of existing traditions especially of the still very lively Indian folk theatre, it was also narratively precise. In this production we refrained from the usual adaptation into Indian conditions and rather used Victorian England as a means of double alienation. ("Erfahrungen" 42)

In the same article, he also praises the social and political effectiveness of the production:

> It was remarkable how quickly the actors understood how to take sides and thus avoid identification with the characters and instead create identification with the intention of the play, how through precision in the performances they had obtained an unusual freshness of improvisation. For me, the memory remains astonishing how they conducted almost every performance

> according to a specific plan of attack, how they gathered allies in the audience during the performance and, with the laughter of those allies backing them up, shot barbs against those concerned.
>
> Despite very forcible attempts, above all from the USA, to politicize theatre in the Third World in such a way that it abandons true progress for the sake of pseudo-experimental influences, the significance of Brecht is recognized precisely in these countries and by those who want to learn to use the theatre in their struggles for liberation. ("Erfahrungen" 42)

Later statements by Bennewitz reveal a change in his assessment of the production's success:

> The *Threepenny Opera* that I did in 1970 with students of the National School of Drama in New Delhi, and with which we toured in 1971 through Central and South India (along with four other plays from the classical and contemporary repertoire of the school), was significant for imparting methods and succeeded in raising curiosity about Brecht where he was hardly known. However, it did not make a lasting impact on the young Indian national theatre movement, because the production had been created from our European traditions and acting conventions. (Letter to Ingeborg Pietzsch, 10 August 1982)
>
> The production was not able to avoid imitating imported ways of translating behaviour into attitudes, and thus it remained similar to parallel Indian experiments that understood the conception and method of Brecht's theatre as a copy of models. ("Mit *Puntila*" 1)

It was this re-evaluation of the *Threepenny Opera* production that led Bennewitz to seek other, more appropriate ways to put on Brecht in India and to find one such way in his collaboration with Vijaya Mehta in his next Indian production, *The Caucasian Chalk Circle* in Mumbai in 1973.

Mumbai, 1973: Brecht, *The Caucasian Chalk Circle*

Bennewitz had already discussed the possibility of doing a Marathi adaptation of Brecht's *Caucasian Chalk Circle* with Maharashtra government officials and theatre people during a brief stay in Mumbai, while on his way back to Germany from the Philippines. The purpose of the discussion was to flesh out the project schedule for the renewed cultural exchange agreement in December 1971 (Arbeitsbericht 3–10 Dec. 1971). The idea for an adaptation became a concrete plan after his encounter with Vijaya Mehta in 1972. Their collaborative production of the *Chalk Circle* proved to be a pivotal moment in Bennewitz's engagement with Indian theatre.[7] He describes its genesis and context and evaluates its impact in the following article he published in *Theater der Zeit* in 1974.

An Indian *Chalk Circle*

Ajab Nyaya Vartulacha: The familiar story of *The Caucasian Chalk Circle* is hidden behind the foreign words of its title in the Marathi adaptation, *The Strange Judgment with the Circle*. Because *ajab* can also mean "beautiful" or "wonderful," the "strange judgment" is evidently beautiful as well.

"Strange" (in the sense of "remarkable") and "beautiful" also apply to the events and experiences of my second project under the aegis of the German Democratic Republic – India Cultural Activities Plan. In the spring of 1970 I put on Brecht's *Threepenny Opera* in Hindustani with the students of the National School of Drama in New Delhi. This production was an enduring success because of its well-educated student actors – even a year later on a tour through Bombay, Pune, Hyderabad, and Bangalore. It promoted interest in Brecht, and through the graduates of the school it has remained influential beyond the school itself as a means of communicating the method. Yet the results of this project are limited because they are largely based on *our* theatre tradition and *our* performance conventions.

My expanded and deepened knowledge of the Indian theatre in the years since then, my close contact with the people and improved grasp of their history and culture, and my work as a consultant on the Third World Committee of the International Theatre Institute (ITI) have strengthened my conviction that our experiences benefit theatre in India most when they are closely tied to the experiences of the Indian theatre.

During the First Asian Theatre Conference in Bombay in November 1972, I met the actor and director Vijaya Mehta, a woman seasoned and successful in Marathi theatre. An exchange of experiences and opinions

7 For an analysis of the production's evaluation by Bennewitz and of its critical reception, see Esleben, "From Didactic to Dialectic Intercultural Theater."

resulted in the mutually advantageous suggestion of co-direction. We were able to interest the Mumbai Marathi Sahitya Sangh as an organization to support and promote the initiative, and received encouragement from both of our governments for this international cooperation in the theatrical sphere, the first attempt of its kind.

Before describing the experiences arising from this project, a brief account is needed of the conditions under which the project (and Indian theatre in general) operate, though I cannot even begin to describe Indian theatre comprehensively. There is no unified or even national theatre milieu. There are language barriers (fifteen primary languages with far more than three hundred dialects, often with almost no similarities), still-unsettled religious conflicts, caste distinctions, separatist movements, natural catastrophes, demographic problems, and so on. There are professional actors, there are commercial theatres, and a number of theatre buildings, including new ones, in Delhi, Bombay, Madras, and Calcutta which belong to private societies and organizations and must be rented. There is also a minority of actors whose rates of pay by the evening are high not only by Indian standards. But there is no theatre as a cultural institution. The exceptions prove the rule: nobody can live from theatre performances – there are no contractual agreements or employment provisions, and rehearsals are unpaid and usually take place after work hours and on Sundays. The rate of pay per evening runs between five and forty Marks (if the play is a success, it runs on average five times per month); in the last weeks rehearsals run around twelve hours per day.

The following four categories (with indistinct boundaries) can be identified in the theatre sector:

(1) Commercial theatre, whose profit-oriented repertory fills the house and the cash register by means of popular comedy stars and occasional ensembles under contract;
(2) Professional theatre, whose repertory includes regional classic dramas with material from history and legends – predominantly farces imported from folk theatre (but also adaptations of plays by Shakespeare, Molière, and contemporary Anglo-Saxon drawing room comedies) in which the influence of the musical stage and a certain filmic attitude weaken the inherent vitality of the source material;
(3) Professional and amateur troupes which endeavour to preserve traditions, creating literary theatre mainly with contemporary Indian plays. In their increasing distance from folk theatre, they are starting to become receptive to the Theatre of the Absurd;

(4) Finally, a growing number of smaller progressive troupes which perform without remuneration and often by making personal financial sacrifices, which can rarely put on a production more than three to five times because of the high cost of renting a hall. Paradoxically, they put on progressive works of world literature (often including Brecht) in English in order to reach a minimal audience with purchasing power.

I haven't considered in this list folk theatre in its vital existence as a means of living in the villages in its various traditions and forms. Nor have I described the traditional dramas of legends; and I assume that the world-renowned accomplishments of Indian dance drama such as Kathakali from Kerala, for example, are familiar.

The theatre – understood as a complete ensemble of all the performing arts – is older, richer, more varied and potentially more alive in the Third World than elsewhere, and at the same time it is younger, less experienced, tentatively groping toward an understanding of itself, and learning about its identity and productivity. This contradiction expresses on the one hand the disrupted unity between existing and created history and on the other, an inadequately developed consciousness of history as such. I am simplifying and generalizing: in the inexhaustible richness of the performing arts of old Asian cultures, for example, history seems to be preserved in the traditional theatre as a story untouched by history. Amazement and admiration for the beauty and purity of such a presentation (particularly of stories from the great epics *Mahābhārata* and *Ramayana*) are tempered by the question whether this is mere persistence through the centuries without living development.

That question seems doubtful and almost irrelevant when one experiences the lively and passionate participation of the audience (not only) in the villages, or the penetration of the traditional Yatra (Bengal), Bhavai (Gujarat) or Tamasha (Maharashtra) theatrical styles by socially relevant themes. But the issue persists where the audiences witness legends rather than experience history.

It is no coincidence that the question of the current value of traditional theatre is connected with struggles for the solution of national and social issues. The theatrical work of Utpal Dutt in Calcutta demonstrates how this can be resolved. His People's Little Theatre has achieved influence and significance in the theatre of West Bengal through the translation and production of Brechtian plays, and through Brecht and the social theatre experience he has introduced the great historic and contemporary themes of independence and the anti-imperialist struggle for freedom into the Yatra folk theatre. (The experience of a Yatra performance of the history of anti-British rebellion in the time of Warren Hastings belongs among my greatest theatre impressions: there was an audience of 5000 in the open air). But this example is still an isolated one, and influence and exchanges across the borders of the Indian States have yet to be achieved.

This short account of the Indian theatre situation describes the reality, while the Bengali exception shows what is already possible. Our work in Bombay was a first step towards this possibility for Marathi theatre. Through Sahitya Sangh, the support of an organization was gained whose range of impact reaches the masses. Thus a Brecht play was seen on an Indian stage with a grass-roots base for the first time (outside of Bengal). Integration through assimilation was the premise of our work. The adaptation of the play evolved into a lively collective process involving all the participants in the production. It was not restricted to giving the characters Indian names and costumes, or considering customs and practices – an adaptation must integrate the play as a story into the history, theatre traditions, and performance conventions of the country.

This involves considering the specificities of the audience's historical associations and possibilities of comparison: in the history of Maharashtra there is no historic event comparable to the carpet weavers' uprising (at least not in the public consciousness). Because of non-dynamic, non-dialectical habits of thought, unpractised thinking about historical processes, and the habit of directly accepting events from history or legends as present events, the figure of the good robber Irakli would give rise to an unacceptable, misleading comparison with the terrorist practices of ultra-right and ultra-left groups. Compressed dialectic ideas in the play would be overlooked all too quickly.

The rich, varied traditions, and the forms and performance conventions of Marathi popular theatre offer a compelling advantage in the face of these difficulties. The highly differentiated traditions and forms of folk theatre – despite their wealth of differing means of expression – have the following in common: open undecorated form; direct contact between stage and audience; epic orientation and structure; unbroken unity of instruction and entertainment; the actors' highly developed art of free improvisation; and the direct existential understanding of the actors, for whom theatre is still more than just specializing through division of labour. Taken altogether, this offers varied and unique possibilities for translating the explanations and knowledge necessary for essential appreciation of the play into dramatic scenes; for clarifying compressed dialectic ideas with examples; and for bringing relevant current social and political material into the play.

The highly stylized movement art of the Dasavatar (a form of folk theatre which originally contained entertaining instruction about the ten incarnations of Vishnu) alienates the members of the feudal ruling class, who are more representatives of a class than individual portraits in the play. The story of the maid has been determined by the traditions of realistic dramatic art, deepened and enriched through Brecht's method of constructing characters and relationships, thereby understanding a character as the combination of his social relationships. The art of Tamasha, so close to the audience and open to improvisation, offers ideal possibilities of interpretation for the story of the judge. In the final scene of the judgment of the chalk circle, all the stylistic elements have come together to form a unity of dialectical contradictions. [...]

Traditions, forms, methods, and also talent are merely preconditions and opportunities for a compelling theatre experience. Credit for creating a performance out of them and with them – one that challenges the audience to judgmental activity, that enables insight, discovery, and assessment through enjoyment (so necessary in the theatre) – is due to the highly poetic arrangement and adaptation by C.T. Khanolkar, a leading playwright of the Marathi theatre; to the compositions of Bhaskar Chandavarkar, developed from folk songs; and to the mature production art of Vijaya Mehta, who directed the play with admirable energy and authority, and brought together actors of the most varied backgrounds to form a single ensemble. And not least it is due to the acting skills and vitality of the performers and musicians themselves. Choosing any individual from their large number is to do an injustice to the others, yet nonetheless I must name some individuals as representatives of all of them: Bhakti Barve as Hansi (Grusha), Suhas Bhalekar as Ajabdas (Azdak), Kusum Naik as the Queen (Natella Abashwili), Madhav Khadilkar as Sanadav (Simon), Suman Shirvatker, Bal Karve, Kamalakar Kulkarni, Janardan Parab, and young actors such as Ahamsuddin Momin and Ulhas Sawant.

Ajab Nyaya Vartulacha has become something more than just an important play for the Marathi stage. Its continuing success and enduring significance derive from the character of international cooperation of this kind, in which the partners integrate their experiences and knowledge to mutual advantage for a common mission, in respect and admiration for their respective traditions and each other's accomplishments.

(*Theater der Zeit* 29, 1974, pages 44–7; translation by Susan Thorne)

Fig. 4 Vijaya Mehta and Fritz Bennewitz working on the script for *Ajab Nyaya Vartulacha*, the Marathi production of Brecht's *Caucasian Chalk Circle* in Mumbai in 1973. Courtesy of Fritz-Bennewitz-Archiv, Leipzig.

The basic sketch of the *Chalk Circle* production provided in Bennewitz's article is given colour and expanded onto a wider canvas by the following passages from his letters expanding on his stay in Mumbai.[8]

> Mumbai, 7 October 1973
>
> Each time I return, it's a real effort to confront this India, the poverty, the misery, the indifference. And it's unbearable to the point of making you want to faint when you see poor people with missing limbs struggling along. I don't want to escape from such sights by crawling into a taxi. I have to expose myself to these realities in order to become hardened to them – as awful and lacking in compassion as this sounds.

8 Translations in this section are by Joerg Esleben and Katy Heady.

The drought of the last two years in parts of India and the floods in other parts have made food scarce and prices high – and the black market and powerful crooks make the scarce food even scarcer and the high prices even higher. Small groups of women demonstrate in the streets. The sight is both absurd and cruel: groups of maybe fifty demonstrators under the surveillance of more than two hundred policemen with lathis (bamboo sticks that resemble the rubber cudgels we are familiar with from our own history). Throughout the evening and night you push through crowds like we don't even see on the First of May, walking in cheerful processions, making music and noise and dancing for hours without interruption during the frequent festivals. Yesterday it was Dasara, a ten-day festival which reaches its climax on October 6th, when they celebrate Rama's triumphant victory over Ravana, metaphorically understood as victory of good over evil. Thousands assemble in front of a stage to witness the Ramlila, a very amateurish show hereabouts, in which parts of the *Ramayana* are sung and mimed, concluding with fireworks spewing out of a ten meter tall effigy of the demon Ravana until it goes up in flames and burns to ashes amid incredibly noisy cheering. The crowd is nearly beside itself when the good triumphs and evil falls, and people accept the somewhat awkward lay performers as the actual heroes (though their playing makes one miss very much the brilliance and craftsmanship that are so astonishing here in similar but well-rehearsed performances developed over many years). You never lose the nagging feeling that hunger is being appeased with circus spectacle here.

Of course need is discussed much more in the houses of people who, sitting at a reasonably well-supplied table, complain how long their servants had to wait in queues – in the streets and huts they complain less, and not only because they are more used to hardship, but because most of them do not experience something as having become scarcer which has always been scarce because it was unaffordable for them.

Mumbai, 9 October 1973

I often think of home, whenever the thoughts that I need for here and now allow this to slip in. And when I have time to think about it, like today when I'm at the hotel at nine-thirty already, then I also think about what that means for me and maybe generally what it means to be "at home." I'm at home here, too. I'm not a stranger in a foreign country. Life seeps under my skin and is exhaled as my very own, and it itches, because its wounds do not scab over with indifference quickly – or not at all, actually. It is as if I dissolved and reconstituted myself in a new way. I am even starting to experience local history and legend here like my very own memories. And yet I am an "other" and not at home, but at home I am an "other," too. Perhaps people there have gotten used to me in their indifference – and I to them. I am a devil, I know. Definitely sometimes and maybe all the time. The few actors whom I have worked with already (especially Grusha,[9] who is not called Grusha here) ask themselves and me why I have to go away again. Surely I have both in me: the desire for a home and the inability to ever be completely at home anywhere. The Jews have the myth of restless, unredeemed wandering (like the Flying Dutchman's) – mine is different, not restless, not unredeemed.

Mumbai, 14 October 1973

This afternoon, the Little Ballet Troupe[10] danced the *Ramayana* – as a puppet play. This is the first time I've seen art here, great art. At the same time this was a great delight for children, too. The stories from the great epics are as known and familiar here as *Struwwelpeter* and *Rumpelstiltskin* are among us.[11] A German author who also travelled through India a few years ago wants to tell those stories to our children in a book. They are worth it. In this case, the great epic of heroism and love was told through dance with a lot of fun. There is no "intimidation by the classics" – the stories never became classics because they remained alive by being passed on from mouth to mouth. Even poor children [...] are sung to sleep and awoken for the day with the stories of Rama and Sita, and

9 Bhakti Barve (1948–2001), whose character was named Hansi instead of Grusha in the production.

10 A dance drama company and training centre founded in Mumbai in 1952 which employs folk dance traditions in its productions. The Little Ballet Troupe moved to Gwalior in 1964 and then to Bhopal in 1984.

11 *Struwwelpeter* is a still popular nineteenth-century German children's book by Heinrich Hoffmann. *Rumpelstiltskin* is among the best known fairy tales collected and published by the Brothers Grimm.

the loyal brother Lakshman, and the demon king Ravana, and the good, strong Hanuman with his army of monkeys.

Yesterday, too, I spent half a day with art, but with far less profit than today. Professional theatre here often alternates between kitschy emulations of film (the argument being that it's what people like, but perhaps they'd prefer other things if they were exposed to them), farces and West End parlour adaptations. In the afternoon from four to five I saw a one-act farce with actors trained in Tamasha, who already act much more with the competent routine of the music hall rather than showing the natural wit of the village. They do a bit of a slapstick routine and are more entertainers than actors, closer to the Distel cabaret[12] than the Berliner Ensemble. Of course, we would benefit from a bit of their immediate contact with the audience – while they would benefit from a bit more substance; whether we can achieve that with the *Chalk Circle* is still quite in doubt. It would be a great opportunity for theatre here, a kind of model [...].

The abilities of the actors and their understanding of acting are almost as varied as the number of roles in the play. They all have the best of intentions, most of them show curiosity, but few of them are experienced. Add to that the differences in education etc. [...] I have organized the play and have handed it to Vijaya for the moment (a way of working that's not dissimilar to how directors at great theatres often work, who leave the production, i.e., rehearsals, to their assistants for a while and then return after some time and correct and fine-tune or reject everything). She rehearses the general thematic lines and arranges them into the Tamasha form, which works without sets and enables and requires the actor to improvise and be open to the audience. The difficulties consist in disciplining their acting, in wresting style from their habits, in giving the actors a sense of spatial relations, in short: in making art out of it all, which essentially means introducing the large and small WHY into their actions. The play could reveal entirely new perspectives and effects if the experiment of transposing it into this form of popular theatre succeeds. In the short time available and under the unusual conditions (which are normal here), I can't yet see it happening.

12 Distel (i.e., Thistle) is the name of a satirical political cabaret founded in East Berlin in 1953 and still thriving.

> Mumbai, 25 October 1973
>
> I was supposed to be at some theatre again this evening, but after nine hours of rehearsals I was too tired, even though rehearsals really are not strenuous for me, because Vijaya is an ideal collaborator – or rather, it is really I who am the collaborator. Today I had some of Part One and a few of the Azdak scenes shown to me. The first part is highly ceremonial, which is very fitting. I only have to put the story in order, organize the pivotal points, make the themes clear, iron out some kinks – revise the whole thing to give it sense and style. Azdak and Schauwa[13] are two exceptionally experienced Tamasha actors, whose talent for improvisation reveals whole new sides to the play. But because a large portion of the text has been completely altered, I do have to watch like a hawk to make sure that the Tamasha style's inherent tendency towards farce always finds its way back into the depth of the characters and situations. Everything is performed without sets, and the imagination of the actors and audience contributes crucially to constructing the play. Vijaya is a work horse: here, the director takes care of anything at all related to managing a production, including even the organization of rehearsals and copying new texts by hand – dramaturges, prompters, or stage managers are completely unknown here.

Mumbai, 9 November 1973

After reporting on a short trip to Goa and on his experience as guest of honour at a Theatre Day held at the Kala Academy, Bennewitz concludes his description of the event:

> With rare exceptions, theatre here is very amateurish, but sometimes there are extraordinary talents to be discovered. In general, there is no real direction yet, which is not so noticeable in the traditional popular theatre, where the improvising actor dominates and determines the play and the scene. But in dramatic theatre it is noticeable in the actors who have no direction, the irregular rhythm of play, the lack of narrative clarity – in short,

---

13 In *The Caucasian Chalk Circle*, the character Schauwa is a policeman and helper of the main character Azdak as judge. In the production, Azdak was named Ajabdas and played by Suhas Bhalekar (1930–2013), and Schauwa was named Shiva and played by Kamalakar Kulkarni.

everything that a director should be responsible, necessary, and useful for. Where there are attempts at directing, they consist in the use of red, blue, and green light and music as a melodramatic mattress. It would be too tedious to describe the stories presented in the scenes, even though this would be of more interest than just the names of the authors and the titles of the plays [...].

The audience is more interesting. They react very immediately to beautiful textual passages, charming musical phrases, and stories, not so much to a coherent narrative whole but rather to individual events in which there is a reckoning with someone, particularly when it is a good character who gives it to an evil one. It is the immediacy of judgment and the noisy approval with which children respond to the puppet theatre. It has something very nice and fresh about it, even if it is still completely undifferentiated and is not yet the dialectic joy at arriving at one's own judgment [...]. That also explains why the audience was not at all interested in the introductions to the individual scenes given by a girl, whom they constantly tried to chase off the stage by interrupting with premature applause, in order to see the next scene with unbelievable attentiveness. When they are interested in the scene, they hardly care about the art of acting – when the scene does not interest them, they only care about real talent, although their reaction is different in that case. In scenes that interest them they intervene immediately with their judgment, but if it is only an actor that holds their interest, while the scene does not mean much to them, they sit quietly like mice without intervening.

[...]

In Goa I received a heartfelt farewell and, as so often, the request to return and do a play with them. I am always too cowardly to disappoint them outright, and so I say that I will probably be back the next year. I don't say anything more because I know I will certainly not put on a play here again, after seeing the progress our work on the *Chalk Circle* is making and understanding that this kind of cooperation in a guiding, revising, and consulting role is the only possibility to participate with mutual benefits in work within a theatre tradition foreign to us.

Mumbai, 10 November 1973

I'll try and begin the difficult task of describing our work. I have already written about the general difficulties of mounting a production here. [...] For the show to take place at all, the actors have to be asked to quit their jobs for a while or at least to take unpaid leave, something the organizer of the production (who is comparable to the producer in the film industry) pays a top-up for. From then on there are rehearsals all day and often into the night. This is equally stressful for the actors and the director. Since most of the (good) actors, particularly those coming from popular theatre, are masters in the art of improvising (including the poetic text), there is no great need for spare time to learn their lines. Unfortunately, there is also no great need to take the time to do individual work on roles, because the art of acting here does not focus much on motivations, discovering situations, and linking motifs, but rather consists of natural talents acting insouciantly as if flying by the seat of their pants, or of the use of established traditional forms of expression (roughly comparable to the codified rules of Elizabethan theatre). Thus, a large part of rehearsals consists of almost military drills, interrupted only for lunch or an occasional tea. Nonetheless, the result is sometimes exciting.

The more I deal with the theatre of the Third World and particularly of India, the more convinced I am that someone who has not grown up with this culture, these traditions, this lifestyle, these habits, and these ways of thinking will not be able to produce a show for Indian theatre that will reach the masses. The best we can do is use our work here to inform them about our way of making theatre or to provide the actors with a course on methods (like I did in the National School of Drama). The resulting show may be good or even very good – but the question remains: good for whom or what? The so-called educated public can be reached with it, but only because they have imbibed European ways of thinking in the course of their education. These are precisely the people who are not very receptive to the messages of a play, because they are not very interested in thoughts that could change them or their status quo. An audience interested in stories has to be told the stories in its own way. The measure of how to do things must be drawn from the audience itself, taking into consideration two aspects: they must be done in the guise of the audience's own customs as well as with the necessary amount of innovation so that the customs do not turn into habituations that prevent new insights. This balance is not easy to achieve because audiences here are not yet used to the pleasure of making discoveries. They still react more to new effects (such as colourful light) than to new ways of thinking. The tendency towards mysticism and irrationalism and the unfamiliarity with the pleasure of using one's own reason demand a very careful and patient approach to the process of education.

[...]

The cultural agreement only states that a director from the GDR will produce a play from the GDR on an Indian stage, and that the GDR will pay travel costs and India will pay costs arising during the stay. There is not a word, not even a hint of a thought devoted to the question of what should take place where. Of course, that's where my experience here and in the international field generally is useful or even necessary, because otherwise it could not take place at all. So now it is taking place, next Friday to be exact. The highest law was that the play with its story, its content, and its intention must reach and interest the masses. Thus it was clear that this could only be achieved with an adaptation of the play, by means of which the play can be integrated and assimilated by the local theatre without being devoured by it, in order to have the catalytic effect of enriching the local theatre and offering it new possibilities.

In German theatre history, we do not have an unbroken tradition of popular theatre, one could even say none at all. [...] So Brecht does not simply continue popular traditions (which do not exist in that sense at all), but rather bases his way of thinking on a thoroughly grounded relationship to the people in the present and the past, and this universally and not limited to Europe. Thoroughly grounded here means: grounded in reasons, from the ground up, at the root. His theatre is popular theatre in the sense of theatre for the people – not in the state of "still being naïve," but rather of "already being naïve," for his naïveté is a high state of civilization which has sublated the old naïveté, in the Hegelian sense.[14] Thus it was easy to decide that for the integration of the play into the local theatre no consideration could be given to the

14 The reference is to the concept of the dialectic usually attributed to nineteenth-century German philosopher G.W.F. Hegel, in which the tension between a thesis and an antithesis is sublated (*aufgehoben*) into a higher synthesis.

tradition of Sanskrit drama (which surprisingly is not at all alive here, by the way), but only to the tradition of popular theatre.

Now, popular theatre here is infinitely varied in its forms and means of expression. In Maharashtra alone there are over forty forms still alive in the villages today; the best-known are Tamasha and Dasavatar. We decided on Tamasha, which is the most popular and most widespread of these forms, as our first and basic point of orientation. Literally translated, Tamasha means nothing more than simply "fun." As a form and dramaturgic structure, Tamasha, like all popular theatre, is not a rule-governed construction (with division into acts, exposition, rising and falling action etc.); it is not literary theatre at all, but rather a total actors' theatre extremely lacking in rules. To use a (not all that) modern term: it is Total Theatre,[15] meaning that it takes in all means of expression provided by acting, music, and dance. Usually they take an old story, mostly from the abundance of commonly known legends, or just familiar constellations of characters from these stories (distantly comparable to the serious and the comical pairs in operettas). Within this framework they then improvise freely, often with some critical spice like in our cabaret scenes, though the ridicule targets village affairs more than world events.

This critical horizon, albeit limited, has provided unduly ample space for vulgarities in Tamasha, which is why it is not attended and taken seriously by the "educated" classes. Of course, that does not necessarily speak against Tamasha, but says much about the Victorian prudishness of the educated, who do not discover the vitality expressed in the often obscene directness of Tamasha, just as they are not willing to accept the almost shocking erotic sculptures on many of their temples, especially in Khajuraho and Bhubaneswar and Konark, as an expression of a liberating worldly religion, and would like to disavow this great tradition in their art. However, vulgarity cheapens Tamasha much less than the constantly spreading influence of film taste, which in the cities is beginning to gravely weaken the refreshing originality

15 Total Theatre is a conception developed by French theatre artist Jean-Louis Barrault, who argued that all theatrical elements, including text, music, visuals, movement, voice, etc. should be regarded as equally important and explored for their theatrical potential.

of Tamasha. Add to that the loss of ideological orientation (though perhaps this has never existed in the sense I mean), by which the fun has degraded itself to mere entertainment, where once the unity of entertainment and enlightenment, which is perfected in Brechtian theatre, was surely present at least in a vague way but definitely as an ideal possibility. (This potential, however, is more marked in Dasavatar, [...] where moral values were passed on through the legends and thus the aspect of educating through entertainment became significant.)

The advantages of Tamasha – its entirely direct addressing of and communication with the audience, the creative freedom for the actors, the equal claims on the creative imagination of actors and audience alike, e.g., through the absence of sets – certainly outweigh the form's limitations. Of course, the wonderful freedom of the actor, his ability and obligation to improvise, have their dangers too, especially when a literary work like a Brecht play is put on the Tamasha stage: as I mentioned, a Tamasha actor improvises his lines. How does he handle the Brechtian text? He reads the play, or at least the scene at hand, very carefully, takes up the situation and the idea, and begins to paraphrase the literary text. At first it was not all that easy to keep the actor as close as possible to the Brechtian text, to discipline and guide him in his freedom to improvise, and to add to his tendency towards fun the desire to make fun the vehicle of wisdom. The results did and in part still do vary: the more talented actors, usually also meaning the more mature ones, understood the creative challenge posed by the Brechtian text and used free improvisation to produce the text in unusual freshness as their own, not at all as something merely re-produced or re-created in the poet's wake. The less talented actors or those with a slower grasp danced (and in some cases are still dancing) along the edge of the abyss of slapstick, and quite often they fall into that abyss – then you have to say with Brown from the *Threepenny Opera*: "only the iron fist can help here."

Let me first say some more about the adaptation. The point of departure was a literal or at least faithful translation of the Brechtian text [...], taking into consideration already that adaptation at first simply means transposing the play into Indian circumstances by using Indian names, landscapes, customs, and rituals that the audience can understand as pertaining to themselves. So the goose becomes a fish (the play is set in Konkan and the Western Ghats) and the Christian wedding becomes a Hindu ritual, and naturally the outward appearance is completely different. Those seem merely superficial changes to begin with (just as in the Middle Ages the Biblical story was painted in contemporary rather than historically and ethnographically accurate guise). The true process of integration takes place during rehearsals. There were difficulties posed by the play itself, which we had been aware of beforehand. For example, how would we make the uprising of the carpet weavers, which is so crucial for the plot, comprehensible for the audience here? Indian history does not know such uprisings, and comparisons with uprisings during the struggle for independence from British colonial rule do not provide the social context needed for the play. They are also not so alive in the consciousness of the masses, and generally you cannot count on any developed historical consciousness here.

Add to that problems like the one that became apparent only the day before yesterday: a character like Irakli is not comprehensible at all here. It is different with our own audiences: they have learned to experience stories as history. Here, history is understood as legend at best. We know comparable good robbers who give to the poor what they take from the rich, such as Robin Goodfellow, Schinderhannes, Stülpner Karl, and Schiller's Karl Moor.[16] There are similar stories here, but those who took from the rich with weapons and violence have disappeared from public consciousness due to the Gandhian theory of non-violence, and the Sadhus are more like saints who have brought about a kind of "redistribution of goods," so they are not relevant to an understanding of the character of Irakli either. However, the far more weighty problem is a very different one, and it made something clear to me that I knew theoretically but had never been forced to contemplate so deeply in practical terms: theatre always happens in a concrete here and now, and one has to take into consideration not only the specific receptive abilities of any given audience, but

16 Robin Goodfellow is the other name of the mischievous sprite Puck in Shakespeare's *A Midsummer Night's Dream*. The reference is puzzling here; Bennewitz may have meant the English folkloric outlaw hero Robin Hood. Schinderhannes and Karl Stülpner are legendary robbers from German history. Karl Moor is one of the main characters of Friedrich Schiller's play *The Robbers* (1782).

also the wider historical and political situation, in this case India's present one.

Now, there is a song in the Irakli scene which is then illustrated by Irakli entering with a weapon like an axe or a gun, and by the old woman telling us that the miracles she has encountered were the result of not very gentle force. The song goes: "When you go to the beloved neighbour, then go with well-sharpened axes / Not with emasculated Bible texts and chit-chat! / What good is all that sermon rubbish, look, miracles are worked by axes / And at times Azdak believes in miracles." This is all well and good, and above all correct, too. But what also has to be thought through well and correctly is what is said and how in which situation. At least two essential ideas must be preserved in the scene: when has a poor person ever received an abundance or sometimes (often, here in India) even just the minimum necessary to live on without a miracle? And the other idea is that Azdak asks the old woman to sit on the judge's chair, not in order for her to deliver judgments right then and there, but to make her, as Mother Grusinia, into a symbolic figure for the people. Through the image of Mother Grusinia he wants to say: "I, Azdak, have been placed on the judge's chair only by the circumstances of the general upheaval, and my reign of justice will be of only limited duration once those in power have returned to their positions. However, let us dream that the time will come when the common people sit on the chair in judgment and rule generally." So these ideas must be preserved.

Now, of course it is correct to think that there have been times when due to a lack of justice the people had to create justice for themselves by means of the axe (and to broaden the idea: for the good of the people, an armed uprising might be necessary). So far, so good. But firstly, India's main historical task today is not armed uprising, but the unification of all national powers for the preservation of national independence and for the construction of a stable democratic order, even in its bourgeois form, as the basis for a possible socialist revolution later. This present struggle is directed against neo-colonialism as well as against right-wing and left-wing extremists, who exist here in abundance. Secondly, an audience that is not yet used to thinking historically understands events on stage either as legend, which lies in the distant past or is not history at all, or as immediately related to the present (and that is how Tamasha brings them across). That means that here they have not yet learned to think in terms of historical processes, but only in terms of far distant pasts that are not related to the present or in terms of immediate undialectical parallels.

There is, right now (and for the very poor, always [...]), a noticeable shortage even of the basic necessities of life, and to many it must seem like a miracle if they receive these necessities. Recently, "help-your-selfers" and seemingly good robbers for the poor have appeared: the Shiv Sena, an utterly fascist organization almost directly comparable to the Nazis and the SA. They exploit unemployment and all other kinds of misery and dissatisfaction in order to drive the masses into the arms of reactionary forces. The Shiv Sena publicly boasts that they alone are able to prevent the communists from gaining supporters. They have occupied the shops and forced the small shop keepers to sell sugar and rice at low prices, which of course had to seem like a miracle to those who before had to buy expensive sugar and thus were not able to buy it at all, and it must have made the Shiv Sena appear like Irakli to them. (This despite the fact that the Shiv Sena prudently did not carry out or initiate any action against the bosses of the Black Market, because they number among their leaders, or against those who hold back goods in bulk so that the prices can rise.) Those are the right-wing extremists. Then there are the others on the left, who seek the salvation of the country in individual acts of terrorism: the Naxalites (groups influenced by Maoism and Anarchism), who make daily headlines because they are involved in murder (the Baader-Meinhof-Group[17] would fit in there) and because naturally they are welcome fodder for the reactionary press's endeavour to denounce the communist movement, since of course they claim to be the true communists and deceive the average Indians (or the ones who are not politically conscious, which means 559 of 560 million, at least as far as ideas about communists and communism are concerned). Thus, it could easily happen that dear Irakli is turned either into a Shiv Sena man or into a Naxalite – and neither option would accord with history, with Brecht's ideas, or with my own. So we try out solutions that preserve the kernel and the two main ideas and simultaneously avoid Irakli.

---

17 A radical group that emerged from the 1960s West German student movement, which founded the left-wing terrorist organization RAF (Red Army Faction) in the 1970s.

In addition to the difficulty of grasping historical situations and events for which there are no points of comparison in public memory or current consciousness, another difficuly is posed in the dialectical complexity of Brechtian sentences. That problem is easier to solve, though. For one thing, there is the possibility of commentary due to the form's openness to improvisation. Such commentary is immediately improvised in the scene, and poetic beauty is renounced for the sake of a more direct translation of the basic idea, because even the most beautiful poetry loses its poetic force if it is not understood. Take, for example, the wonderful scene between Azdak and Schauwa, where Azdak makes Schauwa understand that his days of servitude, during which Azdak kept him under the iron yoke of reason, are numbered, and that soon he will be able again to follow his baser instincts which have taught him to plant his boot in the faces of other people etc. The scene is beautiful, but even the most dialectically trained audience must be very attentive during the performance if they want to understand the beauty of the sentences and of the meaning. Only the more direct method can help here, and loss is gain if the thought is expressed in a simpler and certainly less dialectically rich way, but is understood in its essential meaning. By the way, [...] there are always common folk sitting in the auditorium during rehearsals here, so that the test of what is comprehensible and what is not can be done on the spot, and now and again they even make suggestions [...].

Those were a few thoughts about the adaptation of the play and the process of adapting it further as part of the collective work. I am sure you must be curious as to how this will look on stage and what my tasks are in the production. [...] My function consists of a combination of dramaturge, artistic advisor, commentator, organizer of the plot, guardian of the turning points, and mediator of acting methods. In practical terms, this looks as follows: to begin with, I discussed the play in detail with Vijaya, organized and arranged it with the actors, worked on the Simon-Grusha-scenes, and gave methodological examples in other scenes as to how a character builds his individuality through the social relations of the Brechtian *Gestus*. This was all done in a loose way to provide a flexible frame. Then Vijaya took on the detailed work, and after each manageable chunk we sat down together and discussed the necessary corrections of the scenes if the content was not understood, a character had not grasped the basic attitude of a scene, the arrangement had lost its narrative power and beauty, or if sentimentalities were presented instead of thoughts, judgments, and decisions.

I needed quite some time to accustom myself to the stylistic conditions of the Tamasha stage, to its expressive specificities and to the customary relations between characters; for example, how shame, embarrassment, anger, sadness, and joy are expressed. We, too, have certain grown forms of expression and conventions for these, but it is so much more pronounced here, where not only in dance theatre but also in daily life there is an infinite wealth of formulae, a unique language of hands, body, play with the sari, postures of the head, movements etc. etc. An additional factor is that although we take Tamasha as our point of departure and play within its basic premises, we also integrate elements from all forms of popular theatre, including the aforementioned Dasavatar.

Roughly speaking, the play contains two stories – the Grusha story and the Azdak story – and three stylistically distinct parts that are clearly set off from one another and simultaneously blend with each other. The first part is essentially determined by the world of the governor and the upper class, from which the Grusha story grows. The narrative nature of this story and its representative character types pose the greatest demand for stylization, so that the Dasavatar method is dominant here. The second part consists of the Grusha stories up until the child is taken away, and is essentially determined by the simplicity and beauty of the Grusha character. In the theatrical realization, this is the level with the lowest degree of stylization, where the realistic method in the spirit of epic theatre is dominant. This is where I have to intervene the most in terms of acting methods, because although Indian art has much richer epic traditions than ours in literature, dance, and popular theatre, the actors who have not grown up artistically in the popular theatre (like, for example, our Grusha, who is ideally cast in terms of appearance) have acquired to a surprising degree the very bad habits of a misinterpreted Stanislavskian method with its tendency towards the sentimental, and so they quickly become general and uninteresting. Finally, there is the third part with the story of the judge, which is predominantly determined by Azdak, until all three levels merge in the last scene of the judgment with the chalk circle. Due to the almost Shakespearean clowning qualities of the Azdak character, a comically heightened way of acting is dominant here, meaning almost a pure Tamasha style with the admixtures demanded by the scenes.

It is very surprising that the result is not a hodgepodge of means of expression and ways of acting, but rather an excitingly living combination of the most varied elements, precisely because they retain their unmistakable individual character. This is most likely because all these different elements have a common denominator: they all are ways of acting from the popular theatre. So their unity is not that of a stylistic uniformity, but instead the dialectic (ideal-democratic) unity of independent multiplicity. So far, the first part has my complete consent and almost my enthusiasm (we have not yet worked on the prelude – it will be an entirely new story, because nobody here can make sense of the original historic example of the conflict over collective farming). Unfortunately I am completely unable to describe the music [...] with its exciting rhythms and poetic finesse. Due to the tradition here of using music as an essential part of popular theatre and due to the dominant role of the lead singer and his co-singers it is possible to integrate the narrator and music into the play in very different ways than have been or would be possible for us at home.

The play begins with the usual ritual of Ganesh devotion. The music sets in, and in the background of the stage Ganesh (a dancer with elephant mask) and two female dancers enter behind a curtain carried before them. After this is over, the governor, his wife, the child, and the beggars and soldiers are introduced in a rhythmically danced pantomime as they are mentioned during the first song. This is a great initial pleasure to watch. After that, two soldiers come on stage and announce in a customary speaking ritual that we are in front of the governor's palace (remember, we have no sets!), and then the action begins. The beggars come out, and the noble child is carried past in a kind of sedan chair, accompanied by a dedicated song which is sung here in devotion to a newborn god. Often, by the way, an improvised sentence addresses the audience's knowledge of their legends and their immense love for their stories and heroes; for example: when Grusha has placed the child in front of the door and the woman has decided to take it in and is refuting all her husband's counter-arguments, she adds the sentence (referring to the *Ramayana*, the story of Rama and Sita) that Sita was also a foundling – of course she says it in more beautiful words than I can here.

I wanted to tell you something about hands, too. [...] Hands here have faces; I don't mean the inimitable beauty and grace in the movements of their hands [...], but rather the thousands of hands held out by the beggars. Remember one of my 1970 letters from India, where surely I described to you how a woman in Old Delhi who had given birth to a son followed the local tradition of going into the street with a plate of rice, and how the poor and the cripples reached out for it – despite the cruel misery, this is beautiful and more eloquent than a thousand tongues. In those letters I probably also wrote how I passed by hundreds who crouch immobile all day and reach out their arms with the open hands. Very rarely the arm is stretched out straight; the begging always consists of the imploring gesture in which the arm reaches diagonally upwards. If you imagine the further movement, you get the gesture of most extreme need, when a cry for help to the Madonna is not in itself sufficient anymore and Gretchen in *Faust* stretches her hands to heaven but cannot even touch the hem of the Madonna's robe. There is submission in the gesture from below to above. The whole human being becomes a HAND. I brought this into the *Chalk Circle* here as a theme with variations. First, there are the hands of the beggars, which stretch towards the governor and (if it is well done by the actors) really are deeply moving, these bunches of hands. Then the coins are tossed among them. Their fingers have been parched by the sun and are somewhat cramped by the imploring gesture that seeks to receive the coin in the palm. So these are not the dancing hands that are grasping at the end of long arms to the floor for the coins thrown among them. Finally, when the noble child is carried past, there are the blessing motions of the hands in the local ritual, with which they, in their ignorance, bless the one who will have their children whipped by soldiers just like they themselves have just been beaten and are beaten again even in the final movements of their blessing gesture. Then the noble couple arrives with their entourage. This entrance is also accompanied by rhythm instruments, just like the procession into the church, i.e., the temple, and back from the temple to the palace, all of it in those steps blending dance and pantomime. I find this exciting, and something similar occurs at the entrance of the Fat Prince, a genuine Dasavatar character. Then there are the rejecting gestures of the governor and of the lieutenant. All of this is accompanied by percussion instruments from the orchestra. The whole thereby acquires a breathtaking rhythmic structure and, by means of stylization, something of the beauty of miniatures. What at home we tried to achieve and maybe did achieve with masks – the delineation of the separate worlds, above and below – happens here through varying theatrical tempi and the use of various traditions of popular theatre.

[...]

I just happened to remember some funny difficulties with Indianization as well. There is the scene when Grusha, mortally ill, comes to her brother and sister-in-law in the mountains [...] and has to submit to her sister-in-law's interrogation.[18] The cowardly brother wants courageously to help her by at least interpreting his sister's situation in such a way to his wife that she cannot throw her out immediately. Now, Brecht sets this scene during a meal, and the text constantly makes reference to this. Well, it is not so crucial that here among the vegetarians, something other than meat goes cold, and that the sentence "she is a kind soul – but only after eating" does not work so well because the woman serves the man (even if she is wearing the pants, as we say) and only then eats in the kitchen. But I was wondering why the brother was not eating the whole time. The explanation: we eat with our hand here (the right one, since the left is used differently) and it is impossible that someone would touch someone else with the hand he has eaten with before he has washed it. Well, he cannot very well leave the stage to wash his hands before he rushes to the aid of his sister as she falls unconscious. I will see tomorrow how the problem has been solved, since neither can we cut out the meal nor the brother's taking of the child thrust into his arms by Grusha as she falls unconscious.

Of course, improvising lines is not the standard procedure, but only occurs in the Tamasha scenes, i.e., predominantly during those with Azdak, where most of the improvised "commentary" is needed, also because this third part (almost exclusively) contains the ideological problems and multiple possible references to present conditions. In the wedding scene I do not understand everything to do with the ritual, also because it is played in Konkan dialect. In many scenes I can often follow the text where it has

18 Grusha's brother (called Laxman in the production) was played by Bal Karve. Her sister-in-law was played by Meera Dabholkar.

remained the same or at least similar to Brecht's. The situations have all remained, and naturally the meaning and intention of the play, since having these reach the viewer by means of modifications is the very meaning and intention of our work. Sure, some beauty is lost (but other kinds of beauty won), some things are certainly simplified and sometimes coarsened – but that is a small price to pay for the potential greater gain of the play and its stories and message reaching the masses. Of course, the show value of the play is greater here (even without sets) than in our productions of it at home. For example, the play has an uninterrupted flow due to the fact that there is no set except for Azdak's chair and the gallows. It is thus equally possible and necessary that Azdak, right after he has been made judge, be lifted in his chair onto the soldiers' shoulders and carried around the stage to the next place of judgment, that the same circular run begins after the Ludovika scene, and that a lot of people who appear as onlookers in the yet unresolved Irakli-Mother-Grusinia scene join the procession and begin to dance to the song and the rhythm of the music.

Mumbai, 19 November 1973

I will receive a tape of the whole performance – but unfortunately that cannot give an adequate impression to others. Even the photos don't reflect anything of the uniqueness of the performance. I can say this because in that sense it is not my own production, even though it *is* mine. Its beauty lies in the combination of all elements. The first part, for example, is predominantly in the theatrical tradition of Dasavatar, a form of popular theatre about the ten incarnations of Brahma (or Vishnu or Shiva – I still don't know exactly to this day). The costumes are exquisitely colourful. The rhythm of movement of the ceremonial steps, though very simple in itself, raises the whole to a stylistically high level and produces even more of an alienation effect than the use of masks. Add to that the rhythm of the music and there is not a single dead moment in the whole performance; one element transitions into the next but is simultaneously set off from it. It is even more astonishing how the various traditional elements in the play differ from one another but blend into a new unity of multiplicity.

As I mentioned already, the play itself has three parts. The first is set at the court. It has the highest level of stylization with the most stylized characters (conceptualized as such already by Brecht), who have more representative features than individual biographies. This part is oriented towards Dasavatar. The second part, which mainly tells Grusha's story, is the most "human." It is dominated by the least heightened form of acting (I wish you could see this girl – she is world class!). The third part is determined by Ajabdas (Azdak), who is closest to the Shakespearean clown. This part is oriented towards Tamasha. In the last scene, all these elements meet and, in the scene of the chalk circle, form a wonderful unity of contradictions. For many reasons it is understandable that the art of improvisation is most pronounced in the third part, in order to make many things more comprehensible. The audience is not yet used to or experienced in transposing historical examples to the present situation, but must be provided with contemporary examples or at least clear parallels.

There are lots of great examples, like the issue of corruption, or when Ajabdas plays the Grand-Duke and the nephew of the Fat Prince asks him whether he is claiming that the nobles of the land did not fight in the war, and he answers: of course they fought – for profits (e.g., by not delivering horses they had been paid for). That's when Ajabdas gives an example from the latest war against Pakistan for the liberation of Bangladesh, where clothing and blankets for Bangladesh were collected in India and then sold on the streets of Bombay (even by public officials). Another example: when Ajabdas says that the money of the governess and her palace should be turned into a children's garden bearing his name, the actor adds that it should be built right next to the garden and palace of some Maharaja well-known in this city, in order to hint that it is time to contemplate using the palaces for the good of the people. The censor has shown up already and apparently objected to some expression in a song (Tamasha is sometimes not very delicate) – so yesterday the singers simply sang hmdada, hmdada at that spot in the lyrics, and the audience immediately understood that the censor had been there.

The prelude that was invented for the play here is a great pleasure for me. After prayers in the temple, the village assembles to discuss an important problem: water. During monsoon season, there are floods, and afterwards there is drought. Everyone consents to building a dam. On the left, there are the rich land-owning kulaks, on the right are the village poor. The dam is supposed to be built on the land of the kulaks, because it is more suitable. They protest, and there are counter-protests including questions like: who built your houses? who works your fields? There are caste problems, too, and so on and so on. The situation is very critical. It is salvaged when one of the kulaks is possessed by a god (which happens frequently in the villages, and the utterings of such a delusional person are accepted and carried out like oracles). He suggests performing a play to solve the problem. […] There are two things that get everyone's attention here (at least in the villages) – religion (meaning superstition) and theatre. So why doesn't the divinely obsessed one immediately provide an answer (favourable to the kulaks) as to where the dam should be built? The answer is dialectical: superstition is no longer so deeply lodged that it could be used to solve questions of class struggle. And the next level of the dialectic: though the obsessed kulak can suggest the play, he cannot determine how the poor peasant playing the judge will decide (since it is assumed that the whole is an improvised game). So, in his obsession he also cannot foresee that Ajabdas's judgment will be directed against him, since he is used to rulings according to the law books, which have always been written in favour of the kulaks. So he cannot anticipate that Ajabdas will pass a new kind of ruling that things should belong to those who have expended work and effort on them.

Of course, improvisation harbours dangers, too. If the actor does not have enough taste and if an audience insists on seeing the vulgar kind of Tamasha on stage, the play can easily be dragged down to a dubious level. That's why constant vigilance is necessary. Vijaya is like a hawk in that regard. Even on Sunday after the premiere she rehearsed one scene and parts of others because they were not performed precisely enough for her; and even after the brilliant performance yesterday she had some critical points to raise. So at midnight the whole cast had to come on stage for thirty to forty-five minutes to receive the critique, even though most of them have to travel home for more than an hour and transportation is hard to come by at that time. Most of them have to get up early again, as well, because their jobs are also so far from their dwellings. […]

Here are some nice ideas from the performance: since we play without sets and it is not so easy to tell that Ajabdas goes among the people with his judge's chair and the people thus do not have to come to court anymore, they carry him across the stage on the chair, with a sign attached to the backrest to which the audience reacts with great mirth: Touring Court. For the sentence "They say about

> me that I would go outside before announcing a judgment and smell a rosebush – such tricks are necessary today," Azdak improvised a lovely interpretation: "because the law has begun to stink."
>
> Well, I am happy because of the rich experience and the people around me, [...] but I am also sad that once again I have to leave people like these for others who do not want to understand me or whom I do not understand.
>
> Naturally, difficulties remain in the reception of the play and certainly as far as a deeper understanding on the part of all actors is concerned as well: the juxtaposition of GOOD and EVIL is still static like that between Rama and Ravana, not dynamic and dialectical, just like historical consciousness is static rather than dynamic and dialectical; there is no thinking and experiencing of historical processes. The children already are accustomed to regarding the existence of beggars and cripples as something that is just there, something one has to get used to because it has always been there and will always be there. To slightly modify a well-known saying for theatre habits here: what the Marathi doesn't know, he won't watch [...].

Contrary to this bonmot, *Ajab Nyaya Vartulacha* became a major success among Marathis and others, audiences as well as critics, after both the premiere in Mumbai on 16 November 1973 and a guest performance in New Delhi on 2 December 1973, as well as during the subsequent tour to the GDR and Switzerland in 1974 with guest performances at the Berliner Festtage theatre festival in East Berlin, the German National Theatre in Weimar, in several other East German cities, and in Zurich (Esleben, "From Didactic to Dialectic"). This tour was a milestone in the introduction of modern Indian theatre in Germany and laid the foundation for a series of guest productions by Vijaya Mehta in the GDR and later united Germany, initiated and co-organized by Bennewitz: she directed German productions of Visakhadatta's *Mudrārākshasa* in Weimar in 1976, Kālidāsa's *Śakuntalā* in Georg Forster's German translation in Leipzig in 1980, Girish Karnad's *Hayavadana* in Weimar in 1984, and finally Karnad's *Nāga-Mandala* for the Festival of India in Germany in 1992. A number of Indian theatre artists accompagnied Mehta to Germany as part of the production teams. Moreover, the test productions of *Mudrārākshasa* and *Śakuntalā* which Mehta directed in India in preparation for the German productions were instrumental in reviving and modernizing approaches to Sanskrit theatre there. This aspect of Bennewitz's contributions to Indian-German cultural relations, while not examined in detail in this

Fig. 5 Scene from *Ajab Nyaya Vartulacha* (Brecht's *Caucasian Chalk Circle*), dir. by Vijaya Mehta and Fritz Bennewitz, Mumbai, 1973 (with Azdak as judge in the chair labeled "Touring Court" in Marathi). Courtesy of Fritz-Bennewitz-Archiv, Leipzig.

book, needs to be kept in mind as crucial evidence for the equitableness and genuine spirit of exchange of his intercultural endeavours. It awaits its own scholarly documentation and analysis.[19]

In a 1982 letter written to East German theatre critic Ingeborg Pietzsch, Bennewitz takes stock of his international work to that point, and recounts the impact the *Chalk Circle* production had on his further engagement abroad in the 1970s as well as its relation to other Brecht productions in India:

> The experiences of this work provided the interest, courage, and invitation for an international series of experiments: we wanted

19 An article about Mehta's production of *Śakuntalā* in Leipzig is forthcoming in 2016; see Esleben, "*Śakuntalā* in the GDR."

Fig. 6 Fritz Bennewitz and Vijaya Mehta (front row) with members of the cast of *Ajab Nyaya Vartulacha*, dignitaries, and children from the GDR consulate, Mumbai, 1973. Courtesy of Fritz-Bennewitz-Archiv, Leipzig.

to test and experience, through the integration of Brecht plays (mainly *The Caucasian Chalk Circle, The Good Person of Sichuan,* and *Puntila*) into foreign national cultures, how the social intention of the plays is realized artistically and politically under differing historical, cultural, ethnic, and other conditions.

[…]

The Indian *Chalk Circle* project was followed by the New York experiment to test the significance and appropriation of Brecht for the social and cultural self-understanding of national and ethnic minorities in the USA.[20] A remarkable result of this work lay in the

20 Bennewitz is referring to his production of *The Caucasian Chalk Circle* at the La MaMa theatre in New York, which premiered in March 1977.

experience that the basic questions of the play were able to create a social organism from members of fourteen different minorities and were thus able to organize solidarities. At the same time, the play also fulfilled the function of the *Lehrstücke*[21] – to experience one's own social and historical existence and responsibility.

In the production of the *Chalk Circle* in Manila that followed,[22] the national question played a decisive role in the basic social theme of the play. Due to current events, we had decided on an adaptation into the history and pre-colonial cultural traditions of Muslim minorities on the southern islands of the Philippines. In this way, our work was capable of strengthening the consciousness that the region is part of the nation and that the culture of Muslim minorities is integrated into Philippino national culture, whose wealth lies in the unity of diversity.

This work has given us a renewed sense of learning from Brecht, due to the advantage that the plays are being alienated into an alien world, which makes them newly familiar to us since they offer up their epochal questions more clearly and emphatically. This is often also because the actors there (amateurs in the sense that they do not practice theatre as a profession and earn no money with it) have first-hand experience with social conflict, and because different historical circumstances come to and into the play: due to the experience of centuries-long double tutelage of the people by colonial and home-grown oppression, there is a lot of inexperience and insecurity in the departure towards doing and deciding for oneself, so that with all the newly-won freedoms they are also waiting for someone who will do it for them. That's why it was important to the actor playing Malik-Azdak in Manila that the audience should not burden him with false hopes and expectations: he wanted the line that he will not play the hero for anyone placed at the end of the chalk circle story, before the singer's epilogue; the audience should be left with the sense of responsibility of each for all and oneself. If he interpreted the role of Malik-Azdak as

---

21 Bertolt Brecht's short *Lehrstücke* (a term variously translated as learning-plays, teaching-plays, or didactic plays) were conceived as exercises for actors to explore and learn how to build roles and connect them to social attitudes.

22 Bennewitz directed the play there from October to December 1977. For a detailed analysis see John, "Fritz Bennewitz."

related to the "self-helpers in anarchic times" known from history and literature, he simultaneously played the new historical variation of this theme, its collective quality: the oppressed cannot delegate their liberation to anyone but themselves.

[...]

At the same time as the *Chalk Circle* adaptation of 1973, experiments with adapting Brecht were undertaken in Calcutta. While the Bombay project largely maintained the social and historical conflict situations in accordance with the original plot and story, the Bengali experiments departed very far from the original plots, without however breaching the basic conflict. These efforts made Brecht adaptations sprout like mushrooms in almost all states of India in the following years. Next to excellent results such as M.K. Raina's production of *The Mother* and *Chalk Circle* or Habib Tanvir's *Sichuan*,[23] there soon were tendencies that often left little more than the reference to a famous Brecht title. Among these was the *Threepenny Opera* in Pune,[24] which, though musically excellent and well performed, overemphasizes the musical entertainment value and thus leaves the social context, which is still so significant here, far behind.

The folkloristic and commercial appropriations of Brecht are attempts to push back his influence on the shaping and promotion of a contemporary Indian national theatre. This observation was one of the reasons why I decided to continue my work in India with the production of an adaptation of *Puntila*.

(Letter to Ingeborg Pietzsch, 10 August 1982)

New Delhi, 1979: *Brecht on Trial* and Brecht's *Mr. Puntila and his Man Matti*

After visiting India for several shorter stays in 1974/5 and 1978 and after his productions in New York and Manila, Bennewitz's next major work

23 Bennewitz's former NSD student M.K. Raina directed adaptations of *The Caucasian Chalk Circle* in Punjabi in 1976 and *The Mother* in Hindi in 1978. Habib Tanvir directed *Shaajapur ki Shantibai*, an adaptation of *The Good Person of Sichuan*, in 1978.

24 Jabbar Patel directed *Teen Paishacha Tamasha*, P.L. Deshpande's Marathi adaptation of the *Threepenny Opera*, in Pune in 1978. See Aparna Bhargava Dharwadker, *Theatres of Independence: Drama, Theory, and Urban Performance in India since 1947* (University of Iowa Press, 2005), pp. 378–87 for a detailed discussion and very different evaluation of this production.

in India took him back to the National School of Drama from October to December 1979, on the invitation of B.V. Karanth, then director of NSD. Here, Bennewitz worked on two projects. Following his recommendation to emphasize an experimental and training program rather than production of a single play, the students of the second and third years worked on *Brecht on Trial*, a collage of scenes from *The Caucasian Chalk Circle, The Threepenny Opera, The Good Person of Sichuan, The Life of Galileo, Mother Courage*, and *Arturo Ui*, in Hindi and Urdu. The collage was performed for the public on the NSD grounds from 9 to 14 November on four outdoor stages, connected by introductory commentary and framed by a program featuring Brecht through slide shows, an exhibition, and song recordings. Starting in early November, Bennewitz then directed the production of Brecht's *Mr. Puntila und his Man Matti* with the NSD Repertory Company, adapted by Anil Choudhury using Hindi and Urdu (as well as Punjabi and a number of other Indian languages and dialects for the minor roles) under the title *Chopra Kamaal – Naukar Jamaal*. The following selections from Bennewitz's correspondence begin with his reflections on two other performances he saw early in his stay, before moving into documentation of the works mentioned above.

New Delhi, 4 October 1979

I witnessed an event around the corner: a child (a boy of maybe 12, if that) narrated the *Ramayana* through song. How will I ever be able to describe this? He sang in the classical style with the mudras (hand gestures) of classical dance for nearly an hour and a half, and everything in childlike playfulness, not precocious, as in: show it to aunty, say your little poem, do your little dance, no, not like that at all. I learned much that is barely accessible to us anymore, and again (as on the street during Dasara) had the experience of the innocence of joy and joy of innocence. One should let such a child narrate *Faust* sometime! Nothing is drill, the most complicated ideas are incorporated only to the extent the child grasps them and wants to do them for his own enjoyment. We are screwed up and irredeemably spoiled in our adulthood (also in our civilizational one – but soon, here too, there will be a lost paradise); the only option remains hard to imagine: forward into childhood, into a different kind of naïveté.

New Delhi, 5 October 1979

Yesterday evening I saw a student production of Ibsen's *Ghosts*. European imitations here do not thrill me – too much of themselves remains left out. And we don't find out why they do Ibsen, what moves them in and about the play. Everything remains "nice" and really devoid of any opinion, and therefore devoid of protest (e.g., against living a lie, against hypocrisy, against self-deception etc.). From this, and positively from the child singing the *Ramayana*, my head is spinning with ideas, and I feel good because thoughts come to me about how I can help them reach themselves through Brecht.

New Delhi, 12 October 1979

Yesterday I had an early afternoon of despair and was already thinking I should depart, because the difficulties are enormous and larger than ten years ago. What generally can be considered progress – that the INDIAN National School of Drama is more oriented towards INDIAN culture than under Alkazi – is a disadvantage for FOREIGN WORKERS like me, since there is hardly any prior training for Brecht, at least no practical training. The adaptations of the last years (initiated by Vijaya Mehta and myself!) have gone to seed, and have been adapted away from Brecht, so that most often little more than his name is left. So, the generally lamentable practice of Brecht copies or of productions transplanted from the soil of European theatre traditions during the adaptation period had at least the advantage that the social base and background of the story, of the characters, and of their relations to one another and the world were imparted as a training program. Nowadays, the younger students only know of Brecht what the bad adaptations have retained of him, namely nothing ESSENTIAL.

Add to that the problem – also arising from the advantage of the school having become more INDIAN, including in the selection of students – that the percentage of students coming from folk theatre is larger, which also means that the language problem has become more pronounced: many of them understand only very limited English and also only very limited Hindi. Now, the work I do is very dependent on precise understanding, because in the first place it is TRAINING OF OPINIONS. And so yesterday this desperate situation came about, for which nobody can be faulted since it is no shame for an Indian student NOT TO SPEAK ENGLISH and since I can't be expected to speak enough Hindi right away to work in this language. Even if I could work in Hindi, I would still need interpreters for the many cases where students know their mother tongue, but not our working language to the same degree. So now you can imagine the result when a thought has to go through so many languages before it arrives at the recipient!! Basically, I have confirmed for myself what I have known since 1971, that in a foreign culture you can only collaborate. The late afternoon was more encouraging and I have to wait and see to what degree this was just a hitch or whether I am exaggerating the initial difficulties and over-interpreting them as absolute ones (BASICALLY I don't think so).

I have only been able to write this page because I probably fell victim to another linguistic misunderstanding: the adaptor of *Puntila*[25] finally arrived an hour late and we had barely begun our work when the students came with whom I wanted to inspect the playing space; so I asked the adaptor to sit tight in my room for about 10 minutes, to read my corrections, and to WAIT as I would be back RIGHT AWAY – and now he has disappeared and can't be found. He is supposed to be very good, with many successful adaptations and works of his own already, BUT he too knows only very limited English. When he does an adaptation, he has someone translate the Brecht text into his mother tongue. I had the same problem, by the way, with the great poet who "translated" and adapted the *Chalk Circle* into the Marathi folk theatre, and did a SPLENDID job; BUT there it was Vijaya Mehta who was in charge of TRANSMISSION, and we specifically met in Berlin for the sole purpose of checking the not yet adapted translation against the original by means of re-translation from Marathi into English and German.[26] Oh well, we will see – it's not all just easy fun, but I have to manage it. But this I know, too: I recklessly promised to do this a year ago DESPITE KNOWING BETTER FROM EXPERIENCE!

Now I have to go and look for the adaptor, or else I don't know where I will find the time. I got him – and now, as predicted, he is gone again to look for someone who can re-translate his text

25 This was Anil Choudhury.

26 This stands in interesting contrast to Vijaya Mehta's recollection of the process of translation. In an interview with the author, Mehta recounted that during their preparatory work together on the script in Berlin, no Marathi translation had yet been done. According to her, Bennewitz had the German original and she had an English translation, and they worked through every nuance of the script; then she tape recorded a rough Marathi translation and brought this to C.T. Khanolkar, who transformed it into a very different text, such that Mehta and Khanolkar went through seven drafts.

from his mother tongue to English in order for me to check the adaptation.

New Delhi, 23 October 1979

Let me delve back into some work-related problems, e.g., of translation; yesterday we sat for a long time over Brecht's use and meaning of the word "freundlich" as THE human attitude. The problem begins in English already with "kind" or "friendly," and in Hindi there is only the noun "friend" and no adjective or adverb derived from it. But how fruitfully derived from this difficulty was our dialogue about attitudes and behaviour, about the discovery of different ways of experiencing and relating to reality through the different use of the similar word, or its non-usage. This is what makes the work enjoyable because it means a constantly new learning process for me.

[...]

Today we worked on *Arturo Ui*. It is astonishing what results the transposition (in this case I don't mean: translation) into other traditions of thought, association, and acting yields. Fundamentally, my training program is to show that there is no BRECHT STYLE, that the style is inherent to the play and dependent on conditions of location and time (and of course on individual imprint – but that only in the very last place). This also shows that there are no limits to the choice of means (except that the means must be mastered) when you start from the conviction that the means have to serve the imparting of mean-ing. So, with *Ui* we had started from clowning and allowed ourselves to think of and try all kinds of things – and suddenly there was the question whether you can treat Ui, who stands for HITLER, and the riff-raff around him so comically. These were the same arguments that Brecht had to respond to. So this was a good occasion to deal with these questions and answers and to bring in our history, too; and so the clowning was essentially confirmed but simultaneously questioned, and all of a sudden it became richer as the imagination went in search of discovery of the background.

First we had a red carpet in the scene at the Mammoth Hotel (Scene 10). Today the thought of blood entered the clowning. The actor playing Ui[27] masters multiple dance forms, and yesterday

27 This was Anil Kapoor, now a major Bollywood star.

for fun we tried out dance forms from the local legends about deities in his speech on belief, in order to express in a parodying manner that he is building up a religion of personality cult and is making the move towards self-elevation and self-worship. So today we discovered the dance elements of Kathakali, which goes more in the direction of Japanese Kabuki,[28] where more expressive elements of demon incarnation can be found. Since, apart from the rich mudras (hand gestures), these dances are also marked by extraordinarily complicated and rhythmic rapid steps, we hit on the idea to use a white carpet which during the danced 'conversion' speech becomes bloodied by Ui's footprints. Almost every spontaneous idea can be transformed into meaning; for example, when Roma,[29] in a scene where they squat on the floor, suddenly has Ui on his shoulders, he becomes, in Christian terms, Christophorus carrying the little Jesus through the raging floods (there are equivalent legends here) and the sacred is parodied, with Ui hanging up there like an ape (I am reminded of a painting by Otto Dix, where the little Hitler with his moustache is carried around on some animal.)[30]

New Delhi, 28 October 1979

After lunch we continued the training rehearsals with a blocking/explanation rehearsal of the final scene from *Ui* and then the difficult *Galileo* scene with the Little Monk, a scene of which we (including me, whose trust in what is humanly possible has grown with the years) thought that we would have to take it out of the program, because the boy playing the Little Monk[31] did not seem to grasp anything and because the scene seems to be far, far removed from local acting traditions. The content is not easy to

28 Kabuki is a classical Japanese form of dance-theatre that shares an emphasis on stylization and elaborate make-up with Kathakali.

29 Played by Saleq Khan.

30 Otto Dix (1891–1969) was an important German painter with ties to the movements of Dada and *Neue Sachlichkeit*. He was known particularly for his critical, often brutal, depiction of the realities of the First World War, the Weimar Republic, and the rise to power of the National Socialists. The painting Bennewitz likely means is Dix's *The Seven Deadly Sins* (1933), in which a diminutive Hitler representing Envy sits astride a bent hag representing Greed.

31 Played by Vijay Dalvi.

grasp, and without identifying with the intent, without worries for his peasants on the stony fields of the Campagna region of Italy, and without knowledge of their lives, this can't be done. I know how dissatisfied I myself remained back when I directed the play in the Berliner Ensemble. But yesterday he showed that he just needed time. After the re-translation we had to do two new translations, and Hindi is a foreign language for the boy. He does know about stony and drought-ridden fields here, and about bent backs and women who have been exhausted and made sexless by regularly occurring births. The result is astonishing, also due to the logical clarity with which he delivers his arguments to Galileo. I remember working in Torino,[32] where there was a similar problem, not specifically with the Little Monk, but generally with the actors not trusting that they could demand logic from their language and that they themselves could express themselves logically, also and especially because their acting habits were more based in emotional and temperamental expression. They were finally astonished when I remained tenacious enough in my conviction and expectation that for them, just like in any other language, communication with one another takes place through argumentation. Besides, they have the advantage of not delivering the argument in cold blood. So we had a result that not only let us breathe a sigh of relief but was also consistent, beautiful, and altogether remarkable.

New Delhi, 4 November 1979

I had read myself further into *Puntila* and then out again and wanted to rest a bit, when the thought came to me how relevant to the present the Brecht plays are made through adaptation. For example, the scenes from *Mother Courage* can contribute to an education of historical and patriotic consciousness because they are not about war in general, but rather about JUST and UNJUST war. When [...] the soldiers in the British army are at the same time Indian peasants who want to slaughter the oxen and cows of other Indian peasants; when the son of the Indian peasants does not show the way to the British soldiers; when

32 Bennewitz directed an Italian adaptation of *The Life of Galileo* at the Teatro Stabile in Torino, Italy, in 1972.

mute Kattrin drums her fellow citizens awake; when the Indian mother sits by the body of her daughter killed by British bullets fired from British guns by Indian soldiers (can you imagine in what complexity one could teach Brecht here if one can think across from that to his play *The Mother* and the song "But when he went to the wall," where the wall is erected and he is shot by people just like himself ...); when this same mother wants to get back into business and calls after the passing regiment, "take me with you" so that she can continue her dealings, and it is a British regiment, then one has several lightbulbs going off and the examples for the usefulness of adaptation and for the effectiveness of Brecht in these countries multiply.

Think of how I was able to use the *Chalk Circle* in Manila for the illumination of the national question, how Brecht here is useful in the education towards PATRIOTISM ..., how I can prove in *The Good Person of Sichuan* that the deep humanism and richness of the individual characters is revealed when, following Brecht's teaching, they are understood as social characters, including but not only through the example of the young and the old prostitute [...], or how the *Threepenny Opera* takes on the new task of creating a parody of commercial Hindi film to unmask the social basis on which it is made, and so on and so on.

By the way, [...] I found out that the actor playing Macheath,[33] who seemed so bad, with his stiff and manneristic way of speaking, is actually a very successful film actor, and precisely not in the unspeakably clichéd mass products of Hindi cinema, but in his home state of Assam; that means, he is just having difficulties in the foreign language, Hindi, which really is very far removed from his mother tongue and is written in a different script.

New Delhi, November 1979

I am facing the by now familiar but – since this is not a single play – more complicated difficulties of beginnings: adaptation, too, is fundamentally TRANSLATION of a play even if finally it is TRANSPOSITION into the foreign in order to become the (alienated) familiar there. So then it becomes apparent whether the language has *Gestus*, i.e., how it provokes the body and its attitudes

33 This was Pranjal Saikia.

and behaviours or not, how much or how little of the poetry of Brecht's images and examples it has grasped. And so we are held up, sometimes for half an hour or more for half a sentence or even just for the right word, with only four and a half weeks for the whole thing.

New Delhi, 10 November 1979

At first, I didn't have that opening-night feeling at all, maybe because it was a training program more than a production; but then the feeling came after all. I always notice by how I feel with those up on stage, the joy I feel when they are good, the sadness I share with them when stage fright affects their voices, and this time the disappointment and anger I experienced when a scene slipped far below its potential because two actors became strutting peacocks when and because there was an audience. This was the case with the gang in the *Threepenny Opera* yesterday. However, the *Ui* scene in turn was tops and had EXTRAORDINARY acting from everyone in it, most of all the actor playing Ui, who would have reaped astonishment and stormy applause by the most discerning audiences in any high-level production in a big city. He reaped them here too, considering that the norm here is a bare three-time clapping motion or none at all, not as a sign of disfavour, but just because applause isn't customary. But after the *Ui* scene there was loud, spontaneous, long-lasting applause.

After that, it was very tough for the *Galileo* scene, of course, especially since unlike the previous scene, this one can't work with clown face, perverted Indian classical dance, or the fantastically effective blood brother scene with murderers' hands and the music from *Love Story*.[34] The *Galileo* scene relies so much on understood and understandable speech, on the actor grasping the sense and imparting it to the audience – and now to play this OUTDOORS with traffic noise from just over the wall and something like children's choir songs being broadcast by loudspeaker across the street. Though this was nothing yet compared to the acoustic coverage of the whole area later during the *Chalk Circle* scene, where an unending election speech was carried

34 Bennewitz is referring to the soundtrack of the Hollywood film *Love Story* (1970) based on Erich Segal's romance novel of the same title, directed by Arthur Hiller.

from the gathering site to the entire neighbourhood via loudspeaker. I regretted then that the speech had not been held an hour earlier, because that of course would have been terrifically provocative fun if we could have countered by also broadcasting by loudspeaker Ui's closing speech from the flat roof of the two-story building into a wider area than just our outdoor stages, especially since that speech comes with the taped sounds of fireworks and bomb blasts as a background.

Anyhow, during the *Galileo* scene I was very happy about the Little Monk with the difficult long lines about his Campagna peasants and with the difficulties he had had so far a) to grasp the sense in the first place and b) when he had grasped it beautifully and from his own experiences, to recreate it from one rehearsal to the next. Well, that Little Monk was very good, which makes me happy for his sake as well, while the usually excellent Galileo[35] was not so very good – everything came out with precision and depth, well-grasped and with exact *Gestus*, but in large parts like in a silent film, because apparently stage fright had clamped down on his voice. The *Sichuan* scene with the pilot in the park with Shen Te and the two prostitutes was better than it had been during any rehearsal, where it often had been quite good already. What was especially nice was that social connections and poetical situations received constant resonance from numerous audience members, who were sitting cross-legged on laid out carpets and had to stretch to look over the heads of those in front of them, since the stages were not build high above their heads.

So we took great and beautiful satisfaction with us into the intermission, during which people went to have tea or Campa Cola[36] and look at an exhibition put up with remarkable love and care by the students in the previous sleepless nights. Then came the *Threepenny Opera* wedding scene and my disappointment and anger about it, and I could say nothing to them afterwards except: REHEARSAL tomorrow afternoon 5:15 pm! But the *Chalk Circle* scene was beautiful – and again, what a beautiful and good audience: they still follow the fable and react with APPLAUSE to the judgments of Azdak. I admire both audience and actors for

35 Played by Mahesh Vashishta.

36 A popular Indian brand of soft drink.

listening and playing against loudly broadcast election speeches as if nothing disruptive at all was happening. And then the *Mother Courage* scene – of course, the play alone gets under your skin emotionally, but when Mother Courage[37] took up her two-wheeled ox cart (she has to get between the shafts, which makes much more of an impression than if she takes a rope over her shoulder) and pulled the cart through the audience with bent back but also with dogged energy (which moves us, because we KNOW her efforts are in vain) and called out to the far-off singing British soldiers "take me with you," rhythmic applause erupted, such as I have never heard in India. Still – and perhaps unfairly – my disappointment about the derailing, tasteless, non-artistic behaviour of the two actors seeking laughs and applause, which poisoned the *Threepenny Opera* scene, reduced my happiness by a measure. Then the audience members came in droves to congratulate, and it was nice to see that they were still deeply impressed but not swept away by little emotionalities. The *Mother Courage* scene, I think, was a great demonstration of the narrative power and clarity and the emotional depth of Brecht's plays.

New Delhi, 12 November 1979

I told you earlier about the woman who played the title role in Brecht's *Mother* last year who is now active in a street theatre group.[38] She picked me up right after my rehearsal to see one of theirs. [...] It is a play about the terrible increase (or increase in exposure) of dowry murders. The group consists mostly of women and girls and three or four boys/men, and they have created an improvised play about this topic, which lasts 45 minutes and which I watched with the same pleasure I felt when I observed what it means to have a collective interest in a cause that you promote with a passion, but for which you don't earn a paisa[39] and for which you cannot spend a paisa, for which you commit all your spare time after work. THIS IS NO LONGER POSSIBLE AMONG US. Really? Perhaps really so.

---

37 Played by Sarabjit Kaur.

38 This was Maya Krishna Rao, who co-founded the group Theatre Union in 1979; the play Bennewitz discusses is *Om Swaha*.

39 Very small unit of Indian currency, there being 100 paisas to one rupee.

Now that it will end tomorrow, it is just beginning to be fun. The word has spread and spectators come streaming, along with judgments such as about the *Ui* scene: "that's out of this world …" and so on. It truly is a great success, comparable only to very rare events. But this has its disadvantages, too: at the moment, I would not know anymore how I could do these plays at home.

New Delhi, 15 November 1979

Yesterday morning, it was touch and go whether I would drop out of the work on *Puntila*, because the moving appeal of the lead actor in tears – "you MUST help me" – had turned into a tough fight for prestige for him, and he began to launch it. Re-casting of a role had never happened in the NSD Repertory Company, and after the director of the school he is the company's leader; the Repertory Company has a highly developed self-confidence, since they are the only standing ensemble in all of India and thus a kind of national theatre, so they are quick to think "there is nothing above and beyond us" (although hardly any of them watch any other theatre, like our Berliners). The first shock was the Brecht evening by the student actors, which most of the Repertory Company members had seen, and some of them several times, and this had thrown them off balance a bit. And now, ten days later, I spring the re-casting of the two lead roles on them, because I had made this the condition for my further work on the play. Now I have to say hats off to that actor, given everything that was at stake for him internally, externally, and in terms of prestige: he resigned of his own accord, and I returned to work in the afternoon. It is an extraordinary pleasure and entertainment now with Matti and especially Puntila – but hard work, because fewer than four weeks remain before the preview show on December 10th.

New Delhi, 21 November 1979

I wanted to use this letter to think about the question of where the gracefulness of Indian hands and their movements comes from. It has to do with the fact that they are used to eating with their hand and have learned to speak with their hands, and that their clothes are pieces of fabric: shawls and stolas are worn differently over the arm, and the wrapped garment makes for a different posture. If I could only bring back a film at least, even just of the scene with the women of Kurgela (Haryana) telling their stories – so much beauty, grace, directness, so much richness in simplicity – I will have a hard time to readjust artistically to conditions back home. And the nice thing is, I can now bring it out of them myself. That is also a new experience – in 1973, it was mostly Vijaya, and I was the ideologue, arranger, controller, and corrector of the production. Now I am capable of being closer to and deeper within the action.

New Delhi, 23 November 1979

The rehearsals today were a joy, especially in the second part of the afternoon after I had to use the early afternoon to tell the most established, unrivalled (but still not arrogant) artists of Hindi-speaking theatre in the most emphatic manner that these prefabricated sentences are from the prehistory of any conception of theatre, and that observing, listening, thinking are not forbidden attitudes on stage. This made them quite upset, so I had to cheer them up again, which was not so difficult since I do not do it as pedagogical advance payment but only when they really improve – and then they were even excellent.

We stopped rehearsing half an hour early because over at the school a children's troupe from Karnataka (one of the union states, with Bangalore as capital, where the director of the school hails from) gave a Yakshagana performance for children of all ages. Well, that was quite something – my God, what culture, beauty, rhythm, style, and all – where does that leave us with the poverty of our arrogance? And this from children! Yakshagana is the form that is related in stories, style, mask, and movements to Kathakali from neighbouring Kerala. While Kathakali is the highly refined classical form, Yakshagana is the folk version and is still rich and graceful, and at the same time sufficiently vigorous.

New Delhi, 27 November 1979

Yesterday there was an annoying rehearsal, by way of exception. The props guy is a phlegmatic person. He has not been specifically appointed for props, but is one of the actors, and not one of the best among the otherwise nearly consistently good ones. Certainly, there are mitigating circumstances, e.g., that it costs money to get an old car tire, let alone an entire wheel, because there are no scrap yards – rather, everything used is reused again and turned into cash [...]. So there are no props or not the right ones, e.g., an unstable table (built by carpenters who are excellent craftsmen but have little or no training in practical stage set design) on which Puntila has to do his drunken walk, and the costumes!! – well-meant and delivered with the comment "that's what they wear in this region" – I believe it and I won't contradict it, but I know and have seen that they also wear other things. These designs brought fabrics with patterns, diamond squares, and ornaments onto the stage, so that the eye is forced constantly to stare at them and is drawn away from the faces. [...]

When I am irritated by something (more than by someone) I always have the feeling that my voice gets a terribly sharp edge. Of course, I prefer myself when the sharpness has worn off, which happens quickly, and then I become accessible again and we deliberate on what can be changed. The irritation, though, has understandable causes, I think (which is not identical with EXCUSABLE reasons): the costumes are also designed by one of the actresses, and I am not a costume designer; it's easy for me to say what DOESN'T work and for what reasons, but that doesn't mean I know what works and is better. Add to that the constraint of knowing that I see and judge based on differently evolved/ grown taste. You see, it is not all that easy.

And in a complicated and yet simple way, the true causes lie deeper: in the fundamental CONCEPTION OF THEATRE, which here is basically NATURALISTIC (which is astonishing given both their folk theatre and classical theatre – although there the costumes also are just fabrics wrapped in multiple ways around the body, with fantastical head gear and in COLOURS, COLOURS, COLOURS, or the simple cotton cloths of the poor, also in COLOURS, COLOURS, COLOURS or natural tone). In their training and understanding (and it is even obvious in their eyes) no inner or outer bridge has been built between what they see and do in folk theatre and the "modern" theatre. And this with Brecht, where the characters need CONTOUR and the clothes BIOGRAPHY. Not that they should be Brechtian grey here, I am not an ignorant idiot, but in bright colours as well there has to be harmony, contrast, narration, sense. Because of the enjoyable work climate and because a presentable result has to be put on stage in an extremely short time, I tend to forget that all this is a COMPLETELY NEW EXPERIENCE for them, just as it was a new experience for our actors to move in the *Mudrārākshasa* according to the laws in Bharata's *Natya Shastra* [...].

I am not writing this to complain, but to inscribe it into my own understanding, so that I won't demand too much beyond what is possible. I noticed it yesterday, as a scene was rehearsed and a contradiction within it discovered, when Puntila-Chopra had suddenly grasped something fundamental and passed it on to the others, overjoyed, with red ears, warm heart and inflamed mind. It was just at the point when the controversial costume question was being debated and thought through. This raised the question of the difference between a SOCIAL character and a LOCAL one. In other words, they were still oriented towards showing a landowner from PUNJAB and poor women from HARYANA, rather than a LANDOWNER from Punjab and POOR WOMEN from Haryana. That, of course, is a great joy, to trigger and witness such discoveries and how they then react to them spontaneously. Still, it means having five weeks [...] to impart through the production of a lengthy play a new, unfamiliar conception of theatre which does not simply consist of learning new, unfamiliar step combinations, but must reach their own deep understanding. But it is fun – and what is then achieved, REMAINS.

New Delhi, 8 December 1979

I was picked up and taken to a street play on the lawn of a girls' college around the corner. How simple, inexpensive, effective, and swiftly created theatre can be! Eight people and no props and just one costume: a pundit (not a bandit, though they are sometimes portrayed as such, but a Hindu priest and here a religious political leader, say like from the Christian Social Union in Bavaria)[40] in a saffron-coloured kurta with the Ram-Ram shawl and the prayer beads around his neck. The play is called *Juloos*,[41] which translates as *Procession* in the sense of demonstration, and comes from the ever heated political scene in Calcutta. It very effectively sets a simple topic into action, tempo, sense, and relations and attacks local customs such as the one to hold a demonstration for any bullsh..., to use it to blow off steam, and to essentially DO or EFFECT NOTHING.

[...]

40 The CSU (Christian Social Union) is a political party with Catholic roots in the southern German state of Bavaria. It was one of the most conservative parties in former West Germany and continues to be so in contemporary German politics.

41 Written by the Bengali playwright and director Badal Sircar (1925–2011).

Yesterday after rehearsal, Pankaj Kapur, the actor playing Puntila-Chopra, asked me what I had planned for that evening. I said I had an interview right then, to which he said "oh, I wanted to invite you to the Sakuntalam Theatre because my wife[42] has a Kathak dance recital there tonight." I said "too bad, and Kathak of all things" (because our Leipzig production of *Śakuntalā*[43] will be Kathak based), "well, I'll try." I did try, even though the performance was supposed to begin at 6:30 already. Romesh took me in his car to the theatre on the large grounds of the Indian Trade Fair [...]. There was an enormous crowd in front of the theatre even though it was already 7:20. I daringly pushed my way to the front and told the police guards that I was Professor Bennewitz from the GDR and had been invited by the dancer, and the title and foreign name and German-ness made a big impression, and I was let in without any proof whether I am really me. Inside, I stood among the equally dense crowd and was told "just wait a moment," and fortunately for me the performance had not started yet – not so fortunately for the artist, who had to wait for over an hour with tense nerves for her performance while some so-called VIPs such as a minister or half minister or quarter minister at best held endless speeches.

And then the performance began, and it was yet another miracle for me. I had seen a bit of Kathak style in Vijaya's *Śakuntalā* production,[44] but only yesterday did I fully grasp why Vijaya decided to not use Kutiyattam (which I would say is stronger and more strict, more masculine) as in *Mudrārākshasa*, but rather Kathak, which is softer, more flowing and feminine and therefore corresponds better to the different kind of poetry of *Śakuntalā*. But even if we don't expect German actresses (and a few actors too) to move in perfect Kathak style – even the basic gracefulness of the entire body while simply standing there!! Well, and then the woman was young and more beautiful than beautiful, because her beauty was humanly expressive. She also did something that was both extraordinary

42 Neelima Azeem, a Kathak dancer and film and television actress.

43 Vijaya Mehta and Bennewitz produced a German version of the classical Sanskrit drama *Śakuntalā* in Leipzig in 1980.

44 Vijaya Mehta had directed a pilot production of *Śakuntalā* in Marathi prior to the German production.

and unavoidable: she interrupted her performance twice – once, because directly in front of her in the first row [...] two old, fat guys thinking themselves VIPs were chatting loudly, and she asked them politely to not do it so noisily because it very much disrupted her concentration on the dance.

And indeed it was apparent [...], how unbelievably difficult it is and what concentration is needed to dance in the most rapid tempo and to a highly complicated and variable rhythm and beat, with the feet moving to a different beat than the hands and arms and neck muscles, all of that in perfect balance and harmony, then suddenly to stand or kneel in absolutely unstrained repose like a flowing sculpture, all while making everything appear playfully easy and fun. So there was the one interruption, and then – imagine! – while she was dancing one of those complicated dances and making it seem effortless, they handed out soft drink bottles to the VIPs in the first two rows – and these people took them, too! So she had to stop a second time, and still she remained polite. She danced another story, but people came and went and there were obviously too many in the audience who had no idea why they had come to the theatre. This was too much for her and she – again very politely but also firmly – broke off her recital. I could understand it and I also admired her for her attitude: she did not do it due to offended vanity but rather due to (this does exist) respect for the art that she served in dancing. I thanked her backstage.

New Delhi, 10 December 1979

At 9 am yesterday morning everyone was assembled in the Yoga Hall and I had to go on the carpet on the dais. The speeches were short, which I took as a nice honour because it meant that any distance between them and me had been lifted, and because they showed naturally and with great warmth that I was not a foreigner among them. This was beautiful, even if a beautiful sadness, because at least at the time we have our sentimentalities or even truly deep emotions. But of course we know that it was foremost and almost exclusively the work that connected us with its excitingly beautiful experiences, and not some melodramatic feelings of love and bonds of friendship. At the same time, we know about our/my basic infidelity, meaning the fact that this emotional experience repeats itself in other parts of the world if the work and living conditions and the conditions for learning and making an impact are similar [...]. Well, if it is true that it is always a new experience, then the infidelity in the melodramatic sense is not what counts, but rather, encouragingly, what counts is that my energies and capacities have not diminished. This was at the heart of my decision in favour of the project in America after the accident,[45] because I wanted to know whether creatively [...], in the sense of being able to both give and learn, I had lost anything. I had not – it has rather been a gain. This has repeatedly become apparent, and now, too, immediately after the production, in the deep effect my work has had on people, despite or perhaps because of the deep crises filled with threats and mean words around the middle of each respective project. Because such critical situations arise on account of work, not due to problems in the human relations beyond work, they are not crises but rather interruptions of what would otherwise be all too beautifully harmonious. So, back to yesterday morning: it was so nice because outside of the usual protocol, which has its normal expressions and slogans [...] – there was a large painted banner at the entrance to the hall: "Dear Fritz – Please Come Back Soon!" Well, that was joyously thrilling. And the director wanted my promise that *hamare dost* – our dear friend – Fritz *jaunga jera* – has to come back every year.

New Delhi, 11 December 1979

Because you won't believe me, I will say it cautiously: this is (perhaps) surely one of the best, most beautiful, most right, most important, and most effective productions that I have ever directed – and not because audiences can exaggerate and especially here, so I write their words down uncommented: "tremendous," "the right play for India in the right moment," "beyond words." Anyhow, I am happy, but also sad, because I belong in our country, after all, where I have learned the fundamentals of what I know and can do – did I actually learn it there? That's not the question right now. The issue at hand is that NOBODY from the embassy is interested in it, and the argument of the

45 Bennewitz was involved in a severe automobile accident in 1976 that left him with life-threatening injuries and the loss of his right eye, as a result of which he subsequently wore glasses with the right lens darkly tinted.

Fig. 7 Scene from *Chopra Kamaal – Naukar Jamaal* (Brecht's *Mister Puntila and his Man Matti*), dir. by Fritz Bennewitz in Hindi at the National School of Drama, New Delhi, 1979 (starring Pankaj Kapur, lying front left). Courtesy of Fritz-Bennewitz-Archiv, Leipzig.

ambassador was just: "I didn't come to the Brecht evening, so I guess I have to come to this." Do you know what the students and actors say and ask? "Where are your people?" "How many seats or rows should we reserve for them?" Do you know how I have to lie then? And do you know what I would hear if I would even cautiously question this publicly? I do know … and that only makes it worse. But then, how interested are they, the GDR, in the country and the people to whom they represent us? And how interested are they in what we have worked out together? The West German camp (their embassy and the Goethe Institute, which here is the Max Mueller Bhavan) were present with a big delegation – even if perhaps it was just with the curiosity of competitors.

Letter to Ingeborg Pietzsch, 10 August 1982

This was no longer just the introduction of a hitherto unperformed Brecht play into Hindi theatre, but also and more importantly the attempt to create an unmistakably "Indian" play with characters grown here, while remarkably holding the changes to the original to a minimum. The worrisome experiences with the flood of adaptations have called attention to a problem and a danger: often, they take the easy way out into ethnic authenticity, rather than seeking out what is socially representative. Among the joyful discoveries for the actors was the ability to reveal the social character within the local, or, as one of them said: "I began by creating a landlord from PUNJAB and learned during rehearsals that I have to represent a LANDLORD from Punjab." The gain from this work at the end of 1979 was the discovery of a great realistic comedy integrated into Indian culture instead of a naturalistic ethnic spectacle.

During the integration processes, special care has to be given to the balance between acknowledgment of grown traditions and cautiously vigorous encouragement to conscious change. It is not at all surprising that in the semi-rural and rural areas people react to the plays with much more immediate judgment than in the urban theatres with predominantly petit bourgeois to middle class audiences (where the entrance fee is often triple the daily wage of a road worker). The difference between the spontaneous reaction despite an apparent lack of education and the de facto firmer ideas about tradition among the lower classes (if we do not perform in front of a politically educated and struggle-hardened audience) can be explained from a very real contradiction: Roti (comparable to the herring in *Puntila*) as daily food is the beginning of a naïve experience of dialectics. The intellectuals have a harder time with Brecht, because the knowledge and acknowledgment of the method has still not replaced the question of Brecht style.

[...]

With the experiments and experiences throughout the 1970s we had understood in our work that the alienation-induced amazement about the fact that things do not have to remain as they are must be preceded by an invitation to identification. It was the decade of integration through adaptation.

2 The Early 1980s – Firsts, Lows, and Highs

Kolkata, 1980: Brecht, *The Life of Galileo*

Bennewitz began the 1980s phase of his work in India with an important milestone, his first production in the theatre hub Kolkata. After plans fell through to adapt *The Good Person of Sichuan* with Vijaya Mehta in Mumbai due to lack of funding and delays in signing the cultural work plan for 1980 (see Arbeitsbericht 16 Sept. 1980–1 Jan. 1981), Bennewitz instead accepted the invitation from Kolkata to direct a Bengali adaptation of Brecht's *Life of Galileo* under the title *Galileor jeeban*. There was immense public excitement about this production even before it got underway; in fact, it had been deliberately conceived to make Bengali theatre history. *Galileor jeeban* was the inaugural production of the newly founded Calcutta Repertory Theatre (CRT), formed by the leaders of six of the prominent theatre groups of Kolkata – Rudraprasad Sengupta (Nandikar), Bibhash Chakraborty (Theatre Workshop), Arun Mukherjee (Chetana), Jochhan Dastidar (Charbak), Nilkantha Sengupta (Theatre Commune), and Dwijen Banerjee (Sudrak), along with the dramatist and Bengali adaptor of *Galileor jeeban*, Mohit Chattopadhyaya. They had brought this project into being in order to overcome what was perceived as the flagging, disorganized, and amateurish state of the leftist group theatre that had emerged from the Indian People's Theatre Association (IPTA) of the earlier twentieth century, and to establish a basis for a progressive, professional theatre of high aesthetic quality, political relevance, and cultural-political clout (Lahiri; Bennewitz, Letter to Ingeborg Pietzsch).

The inaugural production was therefore invested with high expectations and significance, and Brecht's *Life of Galileo* was likely chosen both for the cachet of Brecht as a dramatist in West Bengal and for the canonical status and topical nature of the play in the intensifying nuclear arms race of the later Cold War. Moreover, the production needed the prestige of star power. Bennewitz as director fit the bill because by this point he had acquired a reputation throughout India for his Brecht productions in Delhi and Mumbai and for his role as a mediator of Brechtian ideas and acting methods. In 1973, he had come to Kolkata and given public lectures on Brecht and theatre in the GDR which met with considerable resonance (Bandyopadhyay). His acceptance of the invitation to his first directing work in Kolkata was therefore a major public relations success for the new CRT.

An even greater PR coup, however, was to get Sombhu Mitra (1915–97) to come out of retirement – he had been retired since 1971 – and accept the lead role of Galileo. Mitra was one of the most celebrated and popular actors the Bengali theatre had ever seen, and his decision to come back to the stage caused a sensation, including a mad rush for tickets. The actor-directors of the CRT's six founding groups, prominent theatre personalities in their own right, worked as assistant directors and took on various other roles in the production, as did a number of members of their groups and other prominent members of the Kolkata theatre scene. Jochhan Dastidar was in charge of set design, Rudraprasad Sengupta played the Cardinal Inquisitor, and Bibhash Chakravarty played Sagredo. Sona Adhikary designed the costumes for the production, and Tapas Sen was in charge of lighting. Dwijen Banerjee took on the role of the mature Andrea, Ashok Mukherjee played Cardinal Barberini, and, intriguingly, Galileo's daughter Virginia was played by the lead actor's daughter Saonli Mitra. Thus, it seemed that in every sense the stars had aligned to guarantee the success of the CRT's first venture.

However, from the start the production was surrounded by controversy. Not only was the theatre group Bohurupee, which Mitra had helped establish and had led until breaking with it and retiring, conspicuously absent from the list of groups that founded the CRT, but they also launched their own Bengali production of Brecht's *Life of Galileo* under the direction of Kumar Roy at the same time as *Galileor jeeban*. While it might be difficult to reconstruct whether this was done independently or as a deliberate response to CRT's plans, it seems quite unlikely to be a mere coincidence. Mitra's decision to make his comeback under the auspices of other groups is very likely to have incited enmity among the members of Bohurupee and may well have fuelled desires to engage in a direct rivalry with the CRT.

This was far from the only controversy plaguing *Galileor jeeban*. This chapter section will conclude with an account of how the critical reception of the production was overshadowed by a ban the CRT pronounced on two theatre critics, a ban that helped the production make theatre history in quite a different way than the intended one. Furthermore (and for our purposes here more importantly), as the following passages from Bennewitz's letters will show and explain from his perspective, conflict gradually entered into the very heart of the production, namely into the working relation between Bennewitz and Mitra, after an auspicious beginning of mutual admiration. The first two passages compare and contrast the plans for the Kolkata production and for Bennewitz's production immediately thereafter of *The Life of Galileo* with PETA in the Philippines (begun in October 1980). The subsequent passages trace in detail the work on *Galileor jeeban* and the developing conflict between Bennewitz and Mitra.[1]

Letter to Ingeborg Pietzsch, 10 August 1982

I had to leave the decision to my friends in Calcutta and Manila as to which play by Brecht they saw as most useful for their needs and intentions – independently from each other they decided on *The Life of Galileo* for what are fundamentally identical reasons: "The play shows the dawning of a new age and attempts to revise some prejudices about the dawning of a new age" (Brecht) – it reflects historical, social, and individual conflicts in our epoch – no village in today's world is so remote that it would be distanced and detached from the fears and hopes that threaten and strengthen mankind; nobody can escape the responsibility that history assigns to him. The play had been understood as both warning and encouragement in equal measure.

Kolkata, 22 September 1980

I have some exciting conceptual and transpositional ideas for the Manila *Galileo*, but I simply cannot consider using them here with a major personality [Mitra] as the central character, because the casting of a play sets the standard for its overall interpretation. In Manila, the actor playing Galileo is only in his mid-thirties, and those around him are mostly young boys and girls; this

1 Translations in this section are by Joerg Esleben and Susan Thorne.

tempts and forces one to experiment. But when you have a more mature and rich actor-personality in his mid-sixties (although giving an impression of being in his mid-fifties both mentally and physically) this calls for – even requires – a more traditional narration and style, even if here these are derived more from the sparser richness of the first American version by Laughton[2] than from the more opulent spaces and costumes of homegrown Brechtian clarity and rigour. That is not just a question of available means – the decision for restriction should never be based on poverty, but rather on one's conception, which one has to deduce from traditions and capabilities, e.g., from the elements and the fundamental attitude of local folk theatre and its more direct relation between stage and audience.

Kolkata, 24 September 1980

Yesterday, I met with Sombhu Mitra and Sengupta at ten to check the translation and think and talk about the role and its situations. The intensive weighing of sentences, which costs time and yielded only half the first scene in one morning, also saves time, because by listening and watching (since an actor translates with his eyes, with gestures and intonations – and it will be a boon for the younger actors to work with such a master as partner) I can see and hear how I will have to guide him and the play, what unique aspects it will yield and what, in order to make it comprehensible, will take more effort.

Kolkata, 25 September 1980

We travelled two miles to another one of those houses marked by smog and decay, where on a covered balcony I met the fifty or more people wanting to take part in the *Galileo* adventure. For two hours I talked with them and got to know them. We could not yet get into the planned orientation and blocking rehearsal for the first three scenes, because the new translation of the play was not yet ready to be distributed. So we continued the patient effort of checking and re-translating the translation some of them had already done. In this process, no stone (i.e., word) of the built house (the translated sentence) remains unturned. But it is

2 The English-American actor Charles Laughton (1899–1962) worked closely with Brecht on an English version of *The Life of Galileo* and played the lead role in the Los Angeles premiere of that version in 1947.

not even me this time who causes the prolongation of the effort, since hardly any corrections are necessary due to the exacting testing for precision in the re-translation. Rather, the extraordinary effort of creating what is essentially a second, new translation arises from the fundamental advantage that Sombhu Mitra forms the sentences in the language of action of an actor with rich experience and with the law-like, law-giving instinct of a great talent – of course, also not without an overbearing attention to detail, which leaves no sentence untouched and which is as much pedantic as it expresses playfulness (which so easily forgets the ticking of the clock). I was astonished that those who had first translated the play, which is neither easy nor short, were not offended but instead displayed a friendly patience.

This went on until 1 pm. Then I was brought back to my abode with the saffron-robed monks,[3] and around 2 pm a young woman came who had been asked to design the costumes and who had actually heard of the play before. There is no set designer because the only person who usually does this for them is off somewhere working on a film, but at least they brought me some people who build furniture and such, and I am now supposed to tell and show them what the set and props should look like. Everything must be able to fit into any space, because the venues have to be rented and our arrangements are contingent on which one is available when. There is no need to worry about the number of shows that can be sold – when Sombhu Mitra's participation is announced, the first 50 000 tickets (i.e., the first fifty shows) are sold out the same day. I keep having to tell myself that opening night is on October 23rd. Of course, the time loss due to the re-translation has its advantage, too, at least for the lead actor, since he can translate himself into the play and thus enter it in a more practical manner. The stage-set-explanation session went past four o'clock, at which point the translators arrived again, along with the copyists, who immediately take down the translation corrections and duplicate the script by hand. So there were 15 people in my cloistered abode until ten o'clock at night. And today they are coming at nine in the morning for the whole day, because the entire play MUST be ready by evening, and yesterday we had completed all of four of the thirteen scenes to

3 Bennewitz was staying in a guesthouse of the monastic Ramakrishna Mission.

our satisfaction. Tomorrow, on September 26th, I am starting with rehearsals of scenes. That makes four weeks minus a day until opening night. But the days are long, after all!

Kolkata, 27 September 1980

Yesterday rehearsals started in the old, decayed villa two or more miles from here [...]. On the first floor there is a hall with chandeliers on the ceiling, which go out more often than they give light, and therefore we always have candles ready when it becomes dark around 5:30 after daylight ceases to come in, so that we can continue working even if we only sense each other in the candle light. As was to be expected, I enjoy the work and it brings new discoveries; I am dealing with a broad range of individuals, from the highly talented and experienced through the very intelligent to lovably willing amateurs, with whom it will have to be somewhat of a drill. Yesterday I was already able to clarify and block four scenes, and to get a sense of where it might lead, and with what difficulties and potentially beautiful results. Fundamentally, the healthier vitality of expression in life and on stage here, if it can be brought to logic and clarity and differentiation, has the advantage of immediacy over all our interpretations at home.

Kolkata, 29 September 1980

Here in Calcutta, the British colonial legacy is visible everywhere, including in the greater poverty and misery: the problems of the subcontinent are focused here as in a magnifying glass. This probably also accounts for the greater intellectual volatility of life here, the greater cultural vivacity. Because Calcutta has been marked more visibly during colonial times and bears its wounds more conspicuously, it therefore also has the more pronounced consciousness of protest against oppression. The intellectual revolutionary movements start from here, the fractionism of the leftist parties is fanned out most widely here. Besides, the city is situated in the state that is closest to the Chinese border (not counting the direct neighbours to China in the Himalaya like Assam, Sikkim, Nagaland, Tripura etc.), so it was easier for Mao's bible[4] to

4 The *Little Red Book* (*Quotations from Chairman Mao Tse-Tung*) published by the leader of the Chinese Revolution in the 1960s.

cross the border. Marx and Lenin are ever present around every corner in some bookstore, and no fewer than four communist parties claim the sign of the hammer and sickle with a star.

This political, ideological climate, even in so many shades of difference and complexity, enters into the work here very differently, of course, because it has created a wider consciousness than in the greater naïveté of Bombay theatre makers or in the Delhi theatre scene isolated from any masses. That naturally makes scenes like the fifth in the Collegium Romanum interesting, because in the throng of monks and scholars waiting for Clavius and his pronouncement,[5] for whom every minute spent looking through the telescope means too much recognition already for Galileo's discovery, the different factions of divergent interests and opinions, whose only common denominator is their shared reactionary nature, come into sharper focus. So then work, of course, holds ever new joys when you see how sensitively the play reacts to different political, social, and cultural conditions, when you manage to sensitize the play and also the people doing it. With all its exhausting strain, this really is a thoroughly pleasurable profession.

Kolkata, 30 September 1980

We had a brilliant third scene between Galileo and Sagredo yesterday. Sombhu Mitra really is internationally first class and his partners have to watch out that they keep up, while at the same time they also profit immensely from this chance and challenge to work with him. It's too bad that it is so expensive and such an effort to import a production from here to Germany, because this one would provide a good counter-illustration to what was lamented and criticized at the last Brecht Dialogue in 1978,[6] namely that our Brecht productions have become anaemic. If, as seems to be the case, I succeed here in imposing the discipline of clarity of situation and logic of argumentation, then everything will be alive with a strong, rich vitality, and

5 In this scene in the Collegium Romanum, the scientific centre of the Vatican, the chief astronomer Clavius examines and eventually confirms Galileo's discoveries while a group of cardinals mock and insult Galileo.

6 The Brecht Dialogue 1978 was held in East Berlin under the title "Art and Politics."

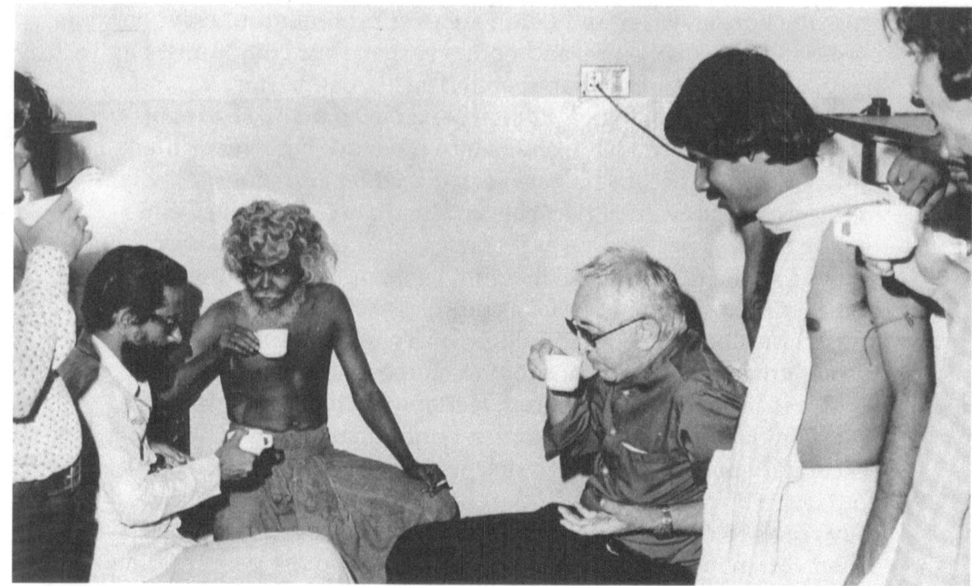

Fig. 8 Fritz Bennewitz with members of the Calcutta Repertory Theatre, Kolkata, 1980. Courtesy of Fritz-Bennewitz-Archiv, Leipzig.

the Galileo character will once again have those qualities which Brecht admired in Charles Laughton: the union of naïveté and high intelligence.

By the way, in an astonishing manner, this partially has to do with the philosophical and storied soil that people here grow up in. This is less of a contradiction than one might think to my observation and experience in 1973 that the Brechtian dialectic had to be translated into a morally rigid emotional system, where GOOD and EVIL oppose one another instead of existing one within the other – less of a contradiction, because that view has to do with the later interpretation of the stories and stems primarily from the later of the two epics, the *Ramayana*. Those who have confronted the philosophy and the sources of the stories more consciously live with the advantage that they have not grown up with the unbridgeable Christian dualism of heaven and earth, God and the devil, where there is no bond or exchange between both poles, but rather with the gods here, who are both good and evil at the same time. The most striking image for dialectics is the three-headed Shiva in the cave temples of Elephanta near Bombay, representing the god of threefold unity as creator-preserver-destroyer. I would have liked to use that for *Faust* in 1975 to represent the image and conception of the Earth Spirit,[7] because there is nothing that could define his nature better and more precisely. But it is all perhaps not as simple as that.

Anyhow: because Mitra is building the character of Galileo in the childlike naïveté of his Indian experience, he is building it full of Brechtian contradictions and is revealing a joyous vivacity of the character. Of course, what brought joy in the morning brought difficulties in the evening, because there are some who cannot keep up, and this is not just a question of acting quality, but the story then becomes thin or false or reduced in dimension.

Kolkata, 2 October 1980

The competition (aka the Goethe Institute of the FRG), who are always trailing me here [...], did not rest until they also had persuaded a prominent director from their country to come here. They sent Hansgünther Heyme, then artistic director at the Cologne theatre and now in Stuttgart, here to Calcutta. He created a very lavish production of Sophocles' *Antigone*, with a psychologically convoluted conception. Not only did his state pay him a fortune in Indian and West German currencies (despite his already high salary at home), but the Goethe Institute also tossed around large sums to finance the infrastructure for his venture and to PAY the actors, something that those I work with cannot even dream of. Of course, the result was predictable: some elitist intellectual circles felt wedded to Europe and the whole huge effort bypassed INDIAN theatre completely, without the slightest point of contact. I have that satisfaction and it will remain, if I even needed anything beyond the fun I have with my work: what we do here goes into the heart of people and the marrow of the country.

---

7 In Goethe's *Faust I*, the Earth Spirit is summoned by Faust in his endeavour to unravel the secrets of nature, but Faust is unable to endure its presence. Bennewitz directed his second production of both parts of *Faust* at the Deutsches Nationaltheater in Weimar in 1975.

Kolkata, 5 October 1980

On Friday we drove straight from the morning rehearsal to Jadavpur University in the deep south of Calcutta, where the Department of Comparative Literature was hosting a university-wide seminar. The seminar room was full to the point of overflowing into the hallway. Because I had not been so very happy with my performance at the Presidency College last Tuesday, I had prepared for this one with a few notes at least, in order not to let my free improvisation run away from the topic too fast and too far. And in that way it actually turned into a brilliant event. I spoke about my experiences with adaptation and cooperation, and this turned into an interesting dialogue about problems of tradition – about progressive and reactionary searches for identity, when traditional theatre is carried over into contemporary struggles and the search for roots to ground continuity, in contrast to the departure from the present into mythical depths of the past, which then is no longer understood as a historical and social space but rather as an ahistorical place of the soul. Such a flight from history is precisely the astonishingly generously supported program of Jerzy Grotowski's *Theatre of Sources* (for which UNESCO supplies funds and for which paradoxically even the Polish government provided a village near Wroclaw). Peter Brook's African experiment *Ik* also belongs to this category.[8] Certainly, these are all articulations of civilizational discontent with imperialistic society, which drives these people (probably with subjective honesty) to the forms and expressions of primitive cultures (something that existed in similar and better ways in visual art from the beginning of the twentieth century into the 1920s, though more vigorously and successfully in the discovery of primitive art). But the UNESCO (i.e., the representatives of the Western countries claiming leadership, above all the USA) is letting the cat out of the bag when it lauds and supports Grotowski's *Theatre of Sources* for exploring the shared rootedness in myth of African and Asian folk theatre and Western avant-garde theatre – at that point it objectively becomes cultural neo-colonialism, because the vigorous forms of African and Asian folk theatre

8 Jerzy Grotowski (1933–99) and Peter Brook (b. 1925) are among the most prominent exponents of intercultural theatre. In 1975, Brook directed *The Ik*, a play about this East African ethnic group based on the controversial study *The Mountain People* by Colin Turnbull.

Fig. 9 Fritz Bennewitz lecturing, perhaps Kolkata, 1980. Courtesy of Fritz-Bennewitz-Archiv, Leipzig.

are thereby robbed of their social and historical roots. I have written all of this down quickly and hastily and in no detail, and certainly all of it is not as one-dimensional as it reads – I just lingered on it because it directly relates to my work at least since the Indian *Chalk Circle* and the international experiments derived from it, and because the event at Jadavpur University was confirming proof that my work is the counter-program to Grotowski and Brook.

Kolkata, 11 October 1980

The advantage of being able to choose actors from six troupes for a production faces the limitation that six different acting cultures come together, since there are no specific and shared training institutes and acting is learned on the job. And another phenomenon has become clear to me since yesterday: even with a great actor there are peculiar difficulties, especially when the legend knows he is a legend – this has nothing to do with star vanity or arrogance, but rather with the fact that the great ones retreat into themselves, not having worked in an ensemble for a long time, even though the likes of Sombhu Mitra are for all intents and purposes the founding fathers and patrons of the group theatre movement. So their talent does not lose its astonishing qualities, but as mentioned earlier it retreats towards and into itself, and they view the character more from inside than as social individual. Thus the psychological motives in exploring the Galileo character might outweigh the social ones, and then it can even happen in some scenes that lesser actors are (at least temporarily) better in terms of the play itself, because they are more clear, more contoured than he, who easily wanders into naturalistic colouration.

I can hardly believe myself that I have worked through the WHOLE play in fourteen full days of rehearsals; nevertheless, a lot of work remains in terms of fine-tuning, e.g., to bring all actors onto a near similar level, to approximate the different acting cultures even if they cannot be entirely levelled out, etc. It will HAVE TO BE an excellent model production, both in their and my interest: they are beginning a new chapter that does not have only friends in the city, Sombhu Mitra is making his first stage appearance in a long time, and I have to prove my name in Calcutta, too, and also counter Stuttgart's Heyme and the financially strong front of the Max Mueller Bhavan that backed him (though in terms of mass appeal his inconceivably elitist theatre was quite a flop).

Kolkata, 12 October 1980

With the good progress in the work its difficulty is becoming more apparent: the actors ranging from very to moderately talented are becoming better, good and even very good – the great actor is getting worse: acting here, too, is a question of time, not the time one has, no, I mean, a question of history, of the time one lives in and has formed one's self in; because that formation is complete, one can only repeat oneself, and that means to deplete and exhaust oneself. It is as with humankind: if there is only simple reproduction, humankind simply marks time and dies of itself (do we know whether it is better to die of oneself or through oneself?).

He is beginning to "colour" the character and thereby is blurring the character's outline – the naturalistic school is coming through, with impressionist dots and lines, the willing renunciation of CONTOUR, which then also looks like the renunciation of decision. And what was well and good for Chekhov or Strindberg or Gerhart Hauptmann or lesser lights illuminating life – the same applied to Brecht makes Brecht worse because there are no longer situations, no more contradictions – and if there are, they are flattened and resolved, where the "BOTH" and the "AND" are not opposed in harsh and astounding ways, but have been blended into a sauce which, like in bad cuisine, does not even create a new taste from two or more ingredients, but no taste at all.

For now, all hope has not yet floated down the Ganges, because I am beginning (with the carefulness that is demanded by his age and achievements and the care that a raw egg needs if it isn't to break) to make him uncertain by praising and encouraging the growth all around him and sparing him any comments (including laudatory ones). Moreover, it makes him unsure when his partner has suddenly become sure and good, so that yesterday he fairly lost his bearing in the scene with the Little Monk, where he lost his lines, intentions, and any kind of recognizable acting. He feared the levelling of the differences, though he never formulated it in an arrogant way – it certainly is not arrogance, it is holding on to what was good and even best YESTERYEAR. Not that we do it better today – no way, worse rather, much worse, that's not the issue – the issue is: providing different insights into the world differently, and this may then – all told – be better, because it can tell the audience more about the world than admiration of the ability to change into and pretend to be another person – who in the end is just another variation of ever the same means (though with good actors this is not so easily noticed since they have a wealth of means at their disposal), i.e., it is ever the same person just with different noses and not with new and different opinions. I do not mean to censure and bemoan it (why not?) – but it is good to be forced to think once again, including about the fact that it is not always a boon for a director to have the great actors fall into his hands (or to fall into theirs). With the younger good ones and even the less good ones it is better to do school(ing) work: they are still curious.

Kolkata, 25 October 1980

Well, work has wandered into a thick fog of crisis, which was not entirely unpredictable: if I had thought about it more thoroughly beforehand, I could have known and foreseen it. Could the crisis have been avoided? The date for the premiere [...] was a fantasy date in any case (*Galileo* can't be done in that time frame, not even when rehearsing ten hours a day, if it is not to remain superficial). Then it was supposed to have been a full pre-performance, a test and a final look for me, so that I could say where one just needs to let it grow, where it needs to be polished or roughened, or where more work or even (seemingly less likely or necessary) re-casting was needed. But it became the first run-through of the play at all. That, too, one could have predicted given the circumstances under which theatre has to take place here. No troupe owns a theatre space, which needs to be rented for rehearsals, too, along with the technical equipment. You have to leave the stage by 1:30 or 2 pm at the latest because the evening performance needs to be set up. Building and assembling sets in our sense is new and more difficult, though carried out with accurate craftsmanship [...]. Costume design and tailoring are liable to give you a stroke: if costumes do not come from the local historical and mythical stock, the kind of non-taste that is presented even after most detailed negotiations is ghastly – without an easily conjured up parallel – and at the same time touching in its helplessness, ignorance, and inexperience. So then I have to be the final arbiter about cut and colour and buttons. [...]

This is just an imprecise description of all the obstacles and roadblocks in the way of creating a production of such dimensions, even if infrastructure and execution are held to very modest limits due to lack of expertise and budget – the troupe had gone into vast debt because not only did the state government not honour its written promise to provide for my subsistence costs, but worse: after promising and assuring that they would bear the costs of the production, they did not even respond to multiple written inquiries, requests, and urgent reminders. So no copper and fabrics woven specifically for the production in prescribed colours, like at the Berliner Ensemble. If it were only such obstacles we would still be much further along, because a lot that is lacking can be substituted for by more enthusiasm. But even the greatest enthusiasm cannot make up for the power cuts.

In the rehearsal space we could still manage with candles and feeling our way around the room, but when the time comes for final dress rehearsals, there is no alternative for lack of electricity, and catastrophic power cuts have forced us to interrupt and then cancel two of them.

But all of these are just contextual reasons, not the actual crisis. So, we had the first run-through on the evening of October 23rd, for the first time with lights, costumes, and make-up; many things did not work for many reasons, but it was astonishing and admirable what did work against the odds: there were delicacies, surprises, growth spurts in individual actors as well as scenes, making the great potential of the production visible. The immediate vitality and unfeigned artistry of people here, coupled with the nearly digested and appropriated understanding and capacity for discipline through the imparting of ideas, produced the most gorgeous results, e.g., in scenes three, four, five, and six, so that people happening to watch the rehearsal applauded spontaneously. So then why the crisis? As mentioned above, it could have been foreseen. The assumed and wished for advantage of casting Sombhu Mitra in the title role – who undoubtedly is his own living legend in the history of Bengali theatre, with proven and lasting artistic achievements, especially in Ibsen roles – this advantage DOOMS the production.

And now I have to see whether I can describe the multiply interwoven reasons in a comprehensible manner; I might mix up the relative importance of some and forget some others. As I mentioned, the mere announcement of Sombhu Mitra's reappearance on stage makes for fifty sold-out shows a few hours later. But this also means that he knows it, and since it is a comeback after about eight years of very few appearances, with attendant gossip that he might not last health-wise, he must have a success. He is sixty-six years old, at which point a missed chance cannot be redeemed, and it would be difficult for him to live out his days with a verdict like "he should not have gone back on stage." Though, if he acts Galileo as he is able to and perhaps/certainly wants to, he might have a great success among his tens of thousands of fans – but it would not be the Galileo of the play, and the audience might not even notice this, but I know it and the younger generation of theatre makers, whose project this is, know and fear it. His acting abilities are of the highest order and rightfully mesmerized audiences, just like Asta Nielsen and Greta Garbo mesmerized their audiences in their time.[9] But this art of portraiture is of yesterday and yesteryear, and even though I wish these abilities on all younger actors, they alone are not sufficient nowadays to tell stories and represent human beings in the theatre, least of all in Brecht's plays.

To illustrate with an example, though not in sufficient extent and depth for the problem: if someone can play an old man (Galileo in the last scene) with all the tricks of the highest art of mimicry and representation, this may have mesmerized the audience a decade ago and may still mesmerize them today, but it is not even HALF the truth if the old man does not play the TRAITOR to his cause and the encounters and conflicts he lives with because of this. What remains, after the initial impressiveness of the ability to mimic to the point of complete believability, are boredom and disappointment, because the old man has nothing to say and to show except that he is old. Then even the impressiveness of the means wears off and revelations or insights do not take place. And this is the difference from Wolfgang Heinz,[10] who was even ten years older when he played Galileo: the great, famous, experienced actor also brought with him all his artistry and experience honed on Gorki and Chekhov, and yet he came to this Brechtian role with the knowledge and willingness that he needed to let himself be questioned, that he would experience and have to deliver something entirely new. It was this attitude of knowing that what he had known and been able to do up to now was not enough, this great curiosity about himself in the new, never experienced task which allowed him to discover so much that was new in himself and in the role, so that the old actor could set an example for young actors with his experiences.

That great curiosity, that capacity to call oneself into question is lacking in the great man here, who is not so great after all. How was this discernible? In the first scene it might still have been the excitement, but it wasn't, because I have seen this going on for

---

9 Nielsen (1881–1972) was a Danish stage and film star, the Swedish Garbo (1905–90) a star of Hollywood's silver screen.

10 Bennewitz directed *The Life of Galileo* with Wolfgang Heinz in the lead role at the Berliner Ensemble in 1971.

days, much to my dissatisfaction: he fidgets, smiles, and moves trippingly through the first scene (and has wonderful partners in the gem of a boy, Mrs. Sarti and Priuli – only Ludovico is weak), because he plays the YOUNG (forty-six-year-old) Galileo instead of the one who feels the power and desire for conquest, knowing that a new age is beginning. But then, in the third scene, where again he began by fidgeting naturalistically, Sagredo[11] grew so immensely into the situation after the first few lines that, in his surprise, Mitra could not but accept the challenge and let himself be drawn out of himself and into the debate, where the issue was not atmosphere and the sounding out of the soul but rather the nature and consequences of the discovery. There, he really was great, and also in scene four, where the philosopher and mathematician had grown so precisely into their characters and the situation in the process of rehearsing that he, too, had to accept this kind of theatre and was GOOD at it. I won't count the eighth scene because we have a still newly re-cast Andrea in it, but nonetheless it did start in the seventh scene with the Little Monk (who is also excellent!) and became more and more obvious in scene ten with Vanni, after the inquisition and very clearly in scene thirteen, the final scene, that the problem lies not just in a different (though admittedly great) older kind of acting art but, and that is what makes it fateful and a crisis: it is also a matter of a different CONCEPTION in terms of understanding and above all intention. He is not willing to expose the character, so to speak. He wants to JUSTIFY the recantation and is not prepared to acknowledge Galileo's guilt, failure, and crime.

Sombhu Mitra is obviously not willing or able to see the contradiction that Galileo first leads the sciences into social struggles and then withdraws and sows the seed for science and scientists to become asocial. But that is the HEART of the play. And so the suspicion rears its head that he is bringing in his own biography: in the 1950s he led theatre in Calcutta into the struggles of the time, and yet he never fully participated in them (from the start, there was the bourgeois pure artist, even if totally honest, obsessed, and therefore great within his limits), and then – disappointed – he withdrew from the movement and left his

11 Played by Bibhash Chakravarty.

own troupe in the lurch when the class struggles pushed into the theatre more immediately. That was HIS recantation: first he led the theatre into the struggle, and when the struggles intervened in the art he withdrew from them; and now he does not see himself as a traitor but as the betrayed one, and he is obviously projecting this into Galileo. So now we've got ourselves into a fine mess.

I have told him in all friendliness and so gently that it was just comprehensible without injuring his (very large) vanity, where I see the fundamental dangers of his interpretation. He was taken aback but obviously not ready to let it enter his understanding; he used misunderstandings and, which was terrible, the inadequacy of his partners as excuses. Yesterday he came to rehearsals and, most disconcertingly, did not go on stage but had himself doubled by a stand-in to look at his partners from the auditorium, in order, as he claimed, to find out how he needs to relate to them (which is nonsense, of course, since nobody can play their role without their partner). And now he expects my Bengali assistant directors to drill his partners of the final scenes and, in his words, bring them to a level that enables him to play his role. Basically, it is the tragedy of the great aging artist who encounters a new generation of actors who do not master the finesse of his skills, who make different theatre differently, and who care for the effect of the play rather than the effect of their personality within the play.

In the interest of the disappointed people who had hoped for a good start for their very new endeavour with the production and his participation, I have avoided a scandal and will not say anything disruptive or destructive in public and to the press, radio, and TV, although I know the limits to which I can allow myself to compromise in the interpretation of the central character of the play. They know my objections and demands and hope that they can bring it to a good end with him in about eight to fourteen days. Otherwise, I have left them with the alternative decision to have the excellent Sagredo take over Galileo and someone else the role of Sagredo. All of that is of course the stuff of a potentially great uproar in Calcutta when I'm gone – but I have to stand up for a cause and for my conviction of what is truth.

The premiere of *Galileor jeeban* took place on 18 November, nearly three weeks after Bennewitz left Kolkata for the Philippines on 26 October. True to his promise to himself, he did not go public with his misgivings about Mitra's interpretation of Galileo, whose participation led to the desired popular success of the production. It was reported that people queued for up to 36 hours to get tickets, which sold out within hours of the box offices opening. This seems to some extent to have been the result of a deliberate marketing ploy by the CRT: in his interview with the author, Samik Bandyopadhyay recounts that their strategy was to announce dates for the show in batches of about five, with no indication whether and when any further performances would take place, contributing to the mad rush for tickets. The theatre-going public thus responded enthusiastically; in one review, a "middle-aged housewife" is quoted describing the audience as unusually mesmerized for raucous Kolkata standards ("Brecht in Bengali").

The response of the theatre critics was more mixed, with Mitra's performance and the production's relation to Brecht being the two major and overlapping areas of contention. While many reviewers were highly laudatory of Mitra and the rest of the cast, Niren Bhanja in his review for the *Hindustan Standard* intuitively came closest to Bennewitz's position. He wondered: "how Sri Mitra's portrayal of 'Galileo,' as he did, was approved by the East German director is an enigma to this critic." Bhanja explained this doubt with the following assessment: "In this role he failed altogether to deliver the goods. [...] His acting was anything but Brechtian. With his sing-song modulations and mannerism (which he ritually observes in all his stage performances) he let us forget 'Galileo.' [...] In Sri Mitra's portrayal of Galileo, we saw Galileo in Sri Mitra and not Sri Mitra as Galileo." Even the laudatory reviews could be inadvertently revealing in this regard. In his review for *Capital*, Sankar Ray praised Mitra's performance and saw a definite line of continuity to the present from Mitra's earlier melodramatic heroic roles such as the Quit India activist Dasu, the blacksmith in the film *Beyallish*: "My chagrin against the British raj would not have been intensified that much had the character of Dasu Kamar not been acted so powerfully. The long curve from that role up to the portrayal of Galileo is not just my imagination but a deductive result of some cause-effect continuum." This emphatic truth claim is borne out by Samik Bandyopadhyay, who in his interview with the author recounts that the general impression was indeed that Mitra acted Galileo like any of his hero roles, and who quotes one intellectual as making the ironic comment that having missed out on seeing the great Bengali heroic actors of the early twentieth century, he had finally seen one now in this production.

For *Indian Express*, Urmimala Lahiri saw the production as a success due to its "refreshing approach towards Brecht" free from "'alien' techniques." She observes, "The CRT production adapts Brecht retaining the familiar stage medium of Bengali: the forms and manner of acting is never a serious departure from the Bengali context. The success of *Life of Galileo* is that it is no theoretical interpretation of Brecht as most other 'adaptations' are, but it is a realistic transcreation of Brecht." Samir Dasgupta in his review for *Amrita Bazar Patrika* even saw Mitra's portrayal as perfectly corresponding to Brecht's theories and intentions, and the reviewer for *India Today* claimed that "Mitra [...] lives up every bit to the high hopes that Bennewitz had bestowed on him before leaving Calcutta. Ultimately, as Bennewitz explained, Brecht implied that it was not enough to create: one must be accountable for one's creation." Bennewitz himself, meanwhile, would surely have taken such positive judgments as ironic confirmation of his conviction that Mitra's performance led to a failure of the attempt to bring out the historical, political, and social relevance of Brecht's play and of the lead role in the current Bengali and global context.

The critical discussion of the content of the production, however, was overshadowed by a massive controversy over efforts on the part of the CRT to prevent two prominent Kolkata theatre critics, Samik Bandyopadhyay and Dharani Ghosh, from seeing it. The sequence of events, motivations, and interpretation of this ban are complex and were subject to intense disagreement at the time. The following account is based primarily on Anil Grover's overview of the case published in April 1981. What is certain is that as a first in Bengali and likely Indian theatre history, "the first few shows had tickets with the legend, 'Probeshanumoti Natya Kendrer Dwara Shangrakhito' (Permission to enter Controlled by CRT) printed on the face of the tickets" (Grover 7). Later the line was changed to "'Jaara Baangla Theatrer birodhi taara aashben na,' i.e., those who are the enemies of Bengali Theatre do not come" (Grover 8). Leaders of the CRT made declarations in public and internally that the two critics would not be admitted because they were not friends of the CRT. When Tapas Sen, the lighting designer for the show, tried to give two tickets from a contingent reserved for friends to Bandyopadhyay, he was reprimanded by the CRT leaders; he publicly protested and resigned after the first show. There were even provisions made to station a CRT member at the entrance to the theatre to ensure that Bandyopadhyay and Ghosh would not be allowed in. These events led to and were fueled by an intense debate in the media, with claims about the violation of freedom of the press and of expression pitched against the CRT's defense of their right to the private decision as to who would be allowed into their shows.

The key question is: what motivated this historic attempt at controlling the critical response to a theatrical production? According to Anil Grover, insiders claimed that it was Sombhu Mitra who instigated the ban (6). He cites Ghosh as surmising that Mitra targeted him because of Ghosh's acerbic assessments of Mitra's performances in the past, but also that the CRT generally feared negative reviews from him due to the wide circulation of his paper *The Statesman*. Ghosh also speculated that the reasons for banning Bandyopadhyay had to be of a different nature since Bandyopadhyay had been fairly kind in his reviews of Mitra (Grover 8). This begs the question of what those reasons may have been. Looking back thirty years later, Bandyopadhyay, in his interview with the author, sees the cause as determined by the political-historical context of leftist theatre in Kolkata. His argument goes as follows: when the Left Front came into power in West Bengal in 1977, the left-leaning theatre groups felt they should be rewarded for their part in the struggle, and the new government did indeed do a lot for these groups institutionally and financially. The activist thrust of the left theatre was thereby blunted into complacency. Some groups, however, challenged this complacency in the late 1970s by rejecting the proscenium theatre in favour of more open settings and forms and a critical dialogue with the audience. Several Brecht plays were being done in such non-proscenium settings and forms (e.g., in productions by Badal Sircar). Some critics including Bandyopadhyay were taking a strong stance that the left theatre needed to go along more decisively with this development. This put him into conflict with the groups represented in the CRT, who viewed his critique as an attack on their style of proscenium theatre; in his view it was for this reason that he was marked as a detractor and, as a consequence, banned from the CRT's epoch-making inaugural production.

This rather plausible explanation brings the story back full circle to the conflict between Bennewitz and Mitra over the interpretation of Galileo, which at the core was a fundamental disagreement over the political meaning and efficacy of the role and the play. This conflict was by no means limited to the director and lead actor: the members of the CRT certainly also had their problems with Mitra's interpretation. Bandyopadhyay claims that his recent discussions with some of the CRT's leaders show that they now feel that Bennewitz was in a losing position because of Mitra's status and ego, to which they acquiesced. (Through his own research, Bandyopadhyay has confirmed that Mitra even insisted that on the advertisements for the show, his name should be printed in the largest font, Bennewitz's in the second largest, and Brecht's in the third largest.) However, in spite of what the success of the first shows may suggest, the conflicts had not ended with the director's early departure. Bennewitz recounted the end of the endeavour in a 1983 interview:

> Since Mitra's interpretation led to contradiction, conflict, and criticism within the CRT, he left the production – for health reasons – after about 25 performances. The new association of the CRT was not stable enough internally to follow my suggestion to re-work the production from among their own ranks and on their own steam. Particularist interests, anarchical attitudes, and an orthodox dogmatism were allowed to set back a significant historical initiative from the avantgarde to a place even further back than the beginning.
> (Pietzsch, "Theatererfahrungen" 46)

New Delhi, 1981: Shakespeare, *A Midsummer Night's Dream*

A year after the disappointment of the Kolkata *Galileo,* Bennewitz returned to India to a more familiar setting, the National School of Drama, to work with students in the final year. He had been asked to produce his first Indian Shakespeare play there. Thus, after having become an important mediator of Brecht, Bennewitz began to participate in another, far older process of integration of a Western canonical dramatist into Indian culture.[12] In over three centuries, this process has taken on many forms, directions, and political functions.[13] After having been introduced in India by travelling troupes and served as source of entertainment during the eighteenth century, Shakespeare became a key ideological instrument of British colonization in the early nineteenth century.

---

12 A valuable source of information and analysis regarding these processes is the 2005 anthology *India's Shakespeare: Translation, Interpretation, and Performance* edited by Poonam Trivedi and Dennis Bartholomeusz. However, it is telling that Bennewitz's significant contribution is ignored in this book. For example, in her survey article "Translation and Performance of Shakespeare in Kannada" (106–19), Vijaya Guttal does not mention Bennewitz or include his productions at Ninasam and Rangayana in her list of productions.

13 The following overview is based on Poonam Trivedi's "Introduction" and her article "'Folk Shakespeare'" in *India's Shakespeare.*

At the same time, the plays were freely adapted and blended with indigenous performance traditions, particularly by the Parsi theatre. Following a period in which Indian theatre turned away from the key author of the colonizer in the wake of the budding nationalist movement in the early twentieth century, there was a rehabilitation of Shakespeare as his work took on new significance after Indian independence. The two dominant strands in staging his plays were a universalist one that translated the texts into Indian languages but not Indian performance traditions or philosophical structures, and an indigenizing one that did the latter, most importantly transposing Shakespeare plays into Indian folk theatre forms. It is particularly this last strand that has played a key role in enlisting Shakespeare in Indian searches for identity in the theatre and in posing critical questions about colonial history, the postcolonial present, and domestic Indian social and political realities.

Bennewitz entered this field of tension with his own cultural baggage regarding Shakespeare. The latter's plays had held a key role since the eighteenth century in German literature and theatre as well, inspiring dramatic revolutions from Lessing and Goethe to Brecht and Heiner Müller. After the Second World War, they also became a key cultural-political battle ground between East and West Germany, with each state subsidizing their production along with productions of German classics in efforts to gain cultural capital in support of their ideological positions. Bennewitz, like many of his fellow German theatre artists, held Shakespeare in the highest regard, and expressed this both in his frequent production of the Bard's plays and in his active role in the East German Shakespeare Society. He was therefore very much inclined towards extending the integration of his Brechtian directorial approach in India to the production of Shakespeare plays.

For his first endeavour in this regard, the NSD had accepted his recommendation to produce *A Midsummer Night's Dream* "because its cast in general is close to [the] age and experience of students, its plot, story, characters, conflicts, and world of ideas and emotions can easier be adapted than any other play" by the Bard (Bennewitz, "An Interview with the Director"). Before he could begin to focus on the task of adapting the play in a Hindi translation by J.N. Kaushal, Bennewitz had to deal with a traumatic event at the school: a student, whom he had had a conversation with just the previous day, committed suicide by hanging himself on the set of the *Cherry Orchard* production being mounted at that time. In a long letter, Bennewitz recounts meeting and trying to console the student's family and being present at the funeral by fire, an experience which brought home for him differences in European and Indian conceptions of death (New Delhi, 29 Oct. 1981). His role in this situation made a mark on the cast members: Hema Sahay, who played Titania in *A Midsummer Night's Dream*, later wrote that the students were depressed due to the death of their classmate as well as production problems with the *Cherry Orchard*, and that Bennewitz consoled them and met their emotional needs in an astonishing manner for the short span of acquaintance ("The Interpretation"). He also demonstrated his willingness to meet them and their working and living conditions at eye level by opting to share one of the NSD student dorm rooms with four of them rather than to stay in a relatively luxurious hotel.

To Sahay's article we also owe some valuable insights into Bennewitz's ways of motivating the student actors. He exhorted them to work hard at staying close to their characters and finding out their situations, conflicts, and contradictions. Sahay credits him with creating a friendly, cooperative atmosphere and teaching the students to cherish their role, to listen to each other on stage, to focus on the content and argument of their text, and to let gestures and actions develop from that meaning. She also recounts some tricks he used when their energy and motivation were flagging: on one occasion, he gave them a day off from rehearsals to do something pleasurable and unrelated to the play; on another, he had them rehearse with a cup of tea in hand to eliminate histrionics and get back to the meaning of the dialogue.

The entire style of the production was based on this primary focus on the training of fundamental acting skills. Bennewitz decided on a stage set of such simplicity that it was remarked upon by all commentators at the time and thirty years later by former NSD students and present-day faculty members Suresh Bhardwaj and Tripurari Sharma in interviews with the author. The entire stage was covered with a plain mattress, was surrounded by benches on three sides, and had a variable backdrop of "four curtains of four different hues to change the atmosphere in different scenes" (Sahay, "The Interpretation"). The costumes were equally plain and mostly kept in white. Bennewitz justified this simple design of the production with reference to the plainness of the stage in both Elizabethan and Indian folk theatre, where actors were and are compelled to appeal effectively to the audience's imagination to create a world ("An Interview with the director"; Sahay, "The Interpretation"). He felt that this aspect was of particular importance in a training exercise such as this production, and that it allowed the student actors to experience and focus on the fundamental historical dimensions of

Fig. 10 Caricature of Bennewitz from the program notes for the production of Shakespeare's *A Midsummer Night's Dream* in Hindi at the National School of Drama, New Delhi, 1981. Courtesy of Fritz-Bennewitz-Archiv, Leipzig.

the play rather than on an illusory recreation of a particular historical epoch ("An Interview with the director"). As some of the following passages from Bennewitz's letters about the production make clear, the latter aim was motivated both by his perception of the Indian students' distance from the European Renaissance and his desire to help them make the play more deeply and radically their own.

New Delhi, 2 November 1981

This morning I was finally able to ring in and think about the *Midsummer Night's Dream* with the students. As usual, I feel a timorous excitement over whether and how I will get a handle on the project – I am quite happy about this recurrence of excitement. And despite or precisely because of my having grown into this place as a home I have to alienate the situation for myself and imagine I were sitting (not me) in front of our German students and wanted to begin working on a play from the Indian past with them. Shakespeare is the highest of peaks, and people here do not live close to the summit (despite the astonishingly high level of knowledge the students do have about European history and the nature of the Renaissance). Talking to curious eyes makes it easy for the tongue to speak from the heart, though. We checked the translation by means of reverse translation until the early evening, and later [...] a student will come to check newly translated passages. The constant discovery of the unknown in what seemed to be thoroughly known and familiar makes the work here so satisfying. How many things had I not read in the *Midsummer Night's Dream* so far! I hope I can continue well on this path.

New Delhi, 4 November 1981

I begin each day here with joy and with nightmares and waking-mares as well, because not many more than two handfuls of days remain for the *Midsummer Night's Dream*, and it is more difficult than Brecht. The translation sends the play into a completely different rhythm. Hindustani is a foreign language for most of them, and the writing is different from theirs, too, so during the first reading they stumble uncomprehendingly and awkwardly through the lines. If I then let them tell the same story in their mother tongue, right away it has sense and wit and grace. However, I can't (though why not?!) let each play their role in their mother tongue – which surely would have its own beauty, but there is a but: they would not understand each other if one speaks in Marathi, the next in Punjabi, Bengali, Kannada, Telugu, Gujarati, Malayalam, Kashmiri, etc. Moreover, due to the long-lasting lack of direction of the school, the current crop of students suffers from lack of experience, for example, and particularly in everything that can be learned and trained through Brecht.

So then time is needed to talk about the world, about the inner and outer human spaces into which Shakespeare opens windows so wide as to make us terrified about ourselves.

New Delhi, 6 November 1981

Fundamentally, work here is and remains a joy, because I am historical to the people here, meaning: for the first time they find out something about themselves in the work process, and if and where it goes well, they fully experience themselves (I can hear it late in the night still, when my roommates think I am asleep, how they marvel about the miracle that is happening with them). That makes being here worth it, because it does not remain limited to the twenty five students in third year but can be multiplied through them tenfold, a hundredfold, a thousandfold when they go back home and with their newly discovered selves sensitize others to ideas and creativity in the south, north, east, west and in the middle of the subcontinent. Truly, this is in no way comparable to artistic achievements that the queen of Denmark applauds in her private theatre box. Of course, this here is nothing for the headlines, but emotionally it is a tree planted a thousand times over. The work here is certainly more difficult, though less noticeably difficult because it rewards me with the satisfaction I have just described.

[...]

It is not just the constant need for vigilance in order not to let anything get past you in the one foreign language coming from the other foreign language(s); it is also the fact that what I do is so new for them that there is a great oscillation of widely dispersed amplitudes in what I live, feel, despair about, and am joyful about here. Often I think for many hours that it can and will never succeed, and I hold the diminutive thought in my diminutive brain that I might only do a scene training and not a whole play. But then again and again there is the experience of what it means to them to find themselves through me. There may well be traditional plays here for which you just send the actors on stage and tell them "do it," and work is then actually just the organisation of the scene, and the results are appropriate. When the play is from beyond the traditions they have mastered, they add lots of spice to the dish, meaning, then the ingredients become key: gorgeous

> costumes, an expansive stage set, clever manipulation of light, music in the background of all dialogues if possible. I am only exaggerating a little, at least judging by the current state of the school and the experiences of the students. How the standard has slipped since Alkazi's time! And these bad habits, more than the good traditions, have slipped under the students' skin almost as a second nature, so that they begin with surrogate acting, because they are used to and expected to jump onto the stage and start with the result, and they are subjected to the worst abuse if they do not have a result or at least a surrogate result available. Do you know how much energy is needed every day and every hour to tear away this armour of bad habits around them? But then, do you also know what a great, deep joy it is to see their hearts and minds shine from their faces and their gestures when they have found themselves in the beauty of simplicity?!
>
> [...]

Bennewitz concludes his description of classical Indian dance performances by one French dancer and several Indian ones with some general thoughts:

> [With the Indian dancers], everything participates in the dance that has been experienced and practiced since childhood (and has nothing at all to do with dance yet): how one sits, eats, greets one another, what stories one hears, under what skies one walks, etc., and then the five thousand years of culture before that. [...] They should NOT leave the world to us with our occidental ARROGANCE (I am not talking about socialism, which should rule the world because otherwise mankind won't survive). And nobody should come here and dress in the local garb of life here [...].
>
> [...] I know this so well because over the years here I have experienced myself and what I am doing so clearly, and each time anew and more clearly: what I am and do here is a path to my own identity, to my difference to here, NOT to copying but rather to understanding the OTHER and to the discovery of shared humanity, which precisely lies in how we differ from each other.
>
> Yesterday I almost committed the thoughtless act of suggesting an exchange for experts in technical disciplines

between the school here and our acting school, e.g., that someone comes here to teach them pantomime – I know now that this does not work, and if humankind and the respective cultures are to thrive, then precisely something like that is to be avoided. Methods and ideological concepts can be imparted through exchange, because they are an impulse to think about what is one's own in an alienated way, but techniques, means, forms are goods grown in local soil fertilized by history.[14] Today I understood again what I can and should do: make them known to themselves. I can bring them to an understanding of the *Midsummer Night's Dream,* I can make them offers for recognizing, discovering, and using the plots and structures of plays, I can help them understand WHAT they can do with the play – but I must help them so that THEY find and fill in the HOW, that they bring their daily and historical life into the play. I have to remember this for the "Third World" seminar that I am supposed to lead in May,[15] with people from our place who – certainly with good intentions and the best enthusiasm – want to teach them our ways instead of offering what is ours as something to be used through a completely different HOW. I'll have to think about this more clearly.

New Delhi, 16 November 1981

I am feeling quite dissatisfied with myself because the effect my work is still having here in every encounter no longer justifies the amount of time spent. If I compare it to the theatre-historical event of the *Chalk Circle* adaptation in 1973 and the things I got underway in the following years with the Sanskrit plays produced in the GDR or the *Puntila* adaptation and the Brecht program with the students in 1979, what I do now is NOT

14 Bennewitz felt so strongly about this that he later included a recommendation *not* to send such experts with similar arguments in his official work report to the GDR Ministry of Culture, in the context of discussing possible exchanges between NSD and the Ernst Busch Theatre Academy in East Berlin. (Arbeitsbericht 25 Aug. 1982–13 Jan. 1983)

15 The GDR national ITI centre hosted a seminar held by the Third World Committee of the ITI in May 1982, which was dedicated to examining the significance of Brecht's work and method for the discovery and fostering of national and cultural identities by theatre in the Third World (Bennewitz, "Theatererfahrungen" 42).

CRUCIAL, it CHANGES nothing, it does not inspire anything NEW. I could have known that before coming here (if there is any excuse, it was originally supposed to be for the daredevil plan to bring *Faust* into the Indian historical and intellectual universe).

New Delhi, 19 November 1981

Despite the great fun at work it is certainly a bit inhumane what the dear boys and girls have to and want to accomplish. Always bear in mind, if it is even possible to imagine, that among them there are those who cannot READ Hindi (which I can, very haltingly, but still) – they have their lines read out by someone and then write them down by sound in their own script. And since the translation is not good (one certainly does not expect Shakespearean poetry, but there should be a whiff of richness, or at least a sentence structure that enables ACTING instead of TALKING), every day and with every gain they make in sounding out and mastering their role, the text is checked and changed in order to find the best possible approximation to the original intent.

It is not just a question of translating into another language but also into a different world of imagery, relations, historical attitudes; the European Renaissance with its discovery and promotion of the individual did not take place in the non-European world. This has nothing at all to do with being behind or having missed out on history. The individual in his greatness and terribleness (historically speaking) has not entered into consciousness here to the same extent, as a basis for identity. Individualism exists here, yes, but in a different way, and it has entered experiences and consciousness differently through a distinct, non-collective form of deity worship; individualism as egoism is a modern influence from outside.

One also has to consider their acting experiences and habits. On the one hand there is acting where the chest is pumped full of air [...] – I don't mean this as ridicule, particularly considering how theatre resonates in the audience. In Ujjain [...] there were more than 10 000 people at the show;[16] nuances and shades of differentiation do not make it there, and it is an audience that

16 The third-year students traveled to Ujjain for a guest performance of another production (a play from Parsi theatre) during Bennewitz's stay.

talks back and cries and encourages and warns the hero, like we had and hopefully still have it among children when they play along with the protagonist in the puppet theatre. On the other hand and as with us formerly, there is the bad habit of following what one has not understood or misunderstood of Stanislavski, which leads to the shallow weak-chestedness of sentimental non-representation.

However, once I have gotten through straight into their hearts, then it has a beauty that is not possible to create among us (I am not blaming us – we also don't have their velvety brown skin), it has the beauty of passion, of passionate emotions coursing through nerves and veins guided and controlled by reason and making everything well-rounded.

New Delhi, 24 November 1981

This is the most beautiful, or at least one of the most beautiful productions I have done out in the wide world (and if I leave aside the *Faust* that is still very dear to me, I should say, that I have done ANYWHERE). And that within 3 (three!) weeks plus two days. However the show will be when it encounters an audience for the first time on Saturday: I/we HAVE SEEN IT. I am overjoyed about what I was able to draw from the core of every single one of them and from the whole. And in addition we had musicians with us for the first time today, who improvise WONDERFUL things SPONTANEOUSLY right when called upon, which gives the undecorated scene (being played on a big mat) the splendour and meaning of three worlds. Oh, that I can NEVER bring something like that home! [...] And that it does not stay alive, because the students will be dispersed to all corners of India by the first half of next year already. Of course, that means that they also take it with them to all corners of India, and in their three years here they have not experienced what they learned and experienced of the world in these few weeks. That's why it is good that I was here: the result takes back the intermittently recurring doubts that despite all my experience by now, I never know beforehand whether the result will be and remain good and useful. HERE and NOW I do know it. And I am glad that I am allowed to experience so much meaning in my life.

The reviewers of the production for the *Times of India* and for the *Hindustan Times* echoed Bennewitz's sentiments in the preceding passage.

Both praised the performance of the cast, and the former even felt that Bennewitz had "brought about a complete metamorphosis in the final year students of the National School of Drama" (Chander, "Excellent production"; Nagpal, "Poor Theatre at its best"). The reviewers also responded to the political dimensions of Bennewitz's interpretation. They both highlighted the critique of male domination that the production suggested, particularly through its portrayal of the differential responses by male and female characters to the night's events. Kavita Nagpal also picked up on Bennewitz's interpretation of the Mechanicals, and Nick Bottom in particular, as visionary critics of feudal power: "*A Midsummer Night's Dream* in Bennewitz' hands became an uproarious play of dreams dodging reality with a view to overcome it." Bennewitz reported that he had never before been so able to understand and make understandable the Mechanics, which he surmised might be due to the rural and folk background of many of the students (New Delhi, 24 November 1981); he also commented on the irony that Bottom, in whom Bennewitz had discovered a revolutionary dreamer, was played by a millionaire's son[17] (New Delhi, 26 November 1981). This political interpretation had concrete effects on the production. When Bennewitz was asked why he eliminated the play's concluding scene that suggests everything was a dream, he responded:

> We didn't add a new dimension to the play – editing is also discovering and stressing what had been brought to light from the play's own body by our own aspirations. Maybe Shakespeare had to add the Fairies' blessings to the house since the play was performed for a noble's wedding party and it is a quite unabashed attitude on such an occasion to tell the Duke that Bottom's dreams and visions will overcome a day not far away ("An Interview with the director").

Despite some adverse conditions and occasional self-doubts about his ability to still have an impact, Bennewitz clearly experienced his first Indian Shakespeare production as a highlight of this phase of his work in the subcontinent, both in terms of the resulting artistic and political qualities and of the pedagogical depth he felt he had achieved. His feelings would be very different concerning his next Indian production.

---

17 This was Ashok Banthia.

Bangalore, 1982: Brecht, *Mr. Puntila and his Man Matti*

Bennewitz's next work in India was another debut – his first of many productions in the southern state Karnataka and in its language Kannada. On behalf of the Karnataka branch of the India-GDR Friendship Association, he was invited to direct Brecht's *Mr. Puntila and his Man Matti* by film maker and theatre enthusiast T.S. Ranga, who had founded the Prayoga Theatre Group in Bangalore. The project was originally meant to bring together theatre artists from numerous progressive groups, similar to the Kolkata *Galileo*, but was eventually taken over entirely by Ranga and Prayoga (Arbeitsbericht 25 Aug. 1982–13 Jan. 1983). Bennewitz worked on the production from late August to late September 1982, with the premiere at the Rabindra Kalakshetra Theatre falling on the 28 September. The three main roles were played by the actors Sundar Raj, Suresh Shetty, and Poornima Vyasulu. Bennewitz's assistant director was his former NSD student Raghunandana, a native speaker of Kannada. Despite this support, language emerged as a major problem challenging the work, though not at all in the form of any insurmountable linguistic barrier between director and cast. Rather, as the following passages by Bennewitz explain in detail, it was the Kannada translation of the play under the title *Donku Desai Naukara Shahi* by the well-known dramatist Chandrasekhar Kambar (b. 1937) that undermined his intentions for the production.

> Bangalore, 30 August 1982
>
> There have been translation problems throughout the years; I have described and explained them recently for the *Midsummer Night's Dream*, and in 1977 I wrote from Manila after checking the translation that translating is not primarily a question of language (also of "speaking," since often an originally gestic text turns into just talk), but of social knowledge and taking sides.
>
> Dr. Kambar here is an expert in his native language Kannada [...] and its dialects, and he is also at home in the folk theatre with his plays, though from what I hear about these they are very schematic and distinguish themselves from *Ohnesorg*[18] farces only by the more earthy sound of the words: the same triangle

18 Reference to the Ohnsorg-Theater in Hamburg, famous for its farces and Low German (Plattdeutsch) dialect comedies.

in multiple variations – the villainous land owner, his beautiful daughter, and the maltreated peasant labourer, with love glances back and forth between upper-class beloved and lower-class lover – and in the end they get each other. As a consequence, and in all seriousness, this dear adaptor wanted to end *Puntila* with Matti and Puntila's daughter going off to a happy life with each other – "and if they have not died, they are still procreating today." The reason, of course, is that folk theatre is optimistic – and the reason for that reason: without dialectic, knowledge of life remains outside of life. Thus, the solution usually remains biological in melodramatic tragedy, when the peasant labourer is killed by the land owner but the land owner's daughter bears a child by the labourer: life goes on, and in the body of the woman the classes are reconciled. To approach Brecht with such an attitude is murder by conviction (or rather: by lack of conviction).

I have nothing against and am all for changes that are necessary to transpose the play into Indian customs, but the problem there is primacy of ethnic authenticity over social truth. And if at least it was genuine care and will for authenticity! The ethnic itself is seen only in its surface and not in a historical and social manner. In the region where the play is supposed to be situated, EVERYONE (thus goes the argument) eats *roti* (the poor-people food, standing for the herring in Puntila) and that's that – no further thought is given to the fact that some eat it with chicken, others only with chilli peppers. And every line is read as an isolated text instead of within the coordinates of a situation, as a sequence and contrast of motives in a network of actions; the well-rounded rich individuality of Brecht characters is translated down into stereotypes. And it is not lack of ability that is the cause [...] but the conviction or wanting to be convinced about the unchangeability of the world that has thus been created once and for all. Brecht's humour with a deeper meaning becomes a biological joke, and the Brechtian tenderness in roughness is lost altogether.

The intention and task have been completely misunderstood. What I meant and wanted (and the entire justification for my being here) is the consequence-rich experiment of mutually suffusing folk theatre and Brecht, integrating and leaving them both changed. Here, the translation and adaptation pull the Brecht play down into the folk theatre, which is no longer even itself but merely its run-down, sloppy entertainment value, with which surrogate history is imparted through surrogate stories. We laughed, and there was something in it for the soul – and in the end the world remains as it is. The audience for these plays is not the people in and from the villages – it's the petit bourgeois of the cities, for whom in the West the cheap romance novels are written. In Bombay we entered and historically explored the ESSENCE of folk theatre – and we had ONE YEAR for the script. Here I am supposed to deal with the script DURING rehearsals in FOUR WEEKS. Really, I should not allow myself to do it. But whom do I abandon if I leave?

Bangalore, 1 September 1982

Last night, doubt and despair raised their heads for about an hour. Here, they are used to reading a play again and again for a week or even longer, and then blocking it on stage for the remaining half of the time or less. To discover it gropingly, text in hand, by trying out arrangements is as alien to them as telling stories through blocking. Not so hard to understand, when one knows and understands the conventions of theatre that they are used to. Folk theatre in urban theatrical practice is no longer that which has grown in the village, but formal habits that have been taken from there and that often still function when the original reason and spirit have been driven from them or have become lost due to socially one-dimensional relations. Although it voices criticism, this is not true criticism of the times and of the system, but at best satirical barbs against the state, village, family, without burdening wit and sharpness with the intention of and belief in change. The framework of relations among social classes and strata (which hardly is a framework but individual crates and castes, hermetically closed off from one another) remains unquestioned and is seen as not changeable. When theatre that has grown from such social structures is passed down, it often takes the form of RITUAL and the RITUALISTIC – and ritual is a functional form, either grown or sometimes introduced, to shore up and promote new, not as yet fully viable orders. But what served the purpose of fortification can also lead to ossification.

Back to the beginning of the thought. If one knows that folk theatre has passed down its rituals, which are easy to take over because they can be learned by heart and practiced like dance steps, and when therefore finding one's way around the story and on stage is no problem, then the rehearsal routine practiced here is in itself rational. The text is hardly read for its meaning – they read words, hardly ever sentences, and, what they do not notice: with assumed voice – often a third lower, but at least a half-tone beneath their normal speech level, forming the character out of the probably unrecognized and unconscious experience of the other tone. This, too, is understandable, because in the folk theatre and more precisely in the classical, e.g., Kathakali, thinking in oppositions without bridge and exchange between black and white has led to firmly marked and fixed characters, among whom black stands for demon, red for king, and green or blue for the lover. So, when the play has entered into the subconscious through reading and re-reading, it all too easily goes to the feet, because the movements and encounters on stage are KNOWN since they have been handed down as RITUAL (I am only describing the worst case and not what I have also seen: great acting that takes tradition into itself and is open to the laws of the time and to change in motion, and that creates new things from what has been handed down).

Bangalore, 2 September 1982

For long passages of the play, we have now reached the third translation. We put a poet to work on it, who brought us the first pages of changes to the rehearsals, and with him came a new problem: [...] unlike at home, dialects here play a large role in the theatre, they ground the play in native soil. Language also means grown customs, clothes, and habits; language is the decisive determinant for ethnic authenticity. Now, the problem was that the dialect into which the play had been translated for us knows no social distinctions in speech.

[...]

It became doubly (and glaringly) clear what had already been known and disturbing to us: translating is a question of class (not always the class one belongs to – intellectuals are no class at all – but the class one is inclined towards). The translator had constantly withheld the social *Gestus* of the characters and situations from us and had thus translated the play down to a trite and vulgar level.

[...]

Now the offer of a different dialect from a region that has been shaken and stirred by other historical and social forces has come into the play, a dialect that shows a different social *Gestus* of the characters in language, as well. It is also a dialect that, unlike the first, has different words for "farmer" and "hired hands."

The problem also plays a role in the political situation of the state and has led to civil-war-like riots and fights not only in newspapers and the parliament but also in the street – in place of the better-known and historically more effective slogan "Proletarians of all countries unite!"[19] there is this one: "Kannada speakers of the country unite!" – the language question in place of the class question.

Bangalore, 3 September 1982

I'll come back to an example from the translation problems. The first translator may have been pleased (due to his stance or lack thereof) that the dialect he chose allowed him to constantly make "farmers" out of "hired hands" (i.e., peasant labourers), so the reach of his thinking and of his will did not extend down to where the class exists close to the possibility of revolutionary thoughts. The dialect in its historically and socially limited vocabulary is not amenable to the translation – the English "hired hands" is at least unambiguous. A "farmer" is more liable to remain close to his land and soil, his role as provider, or whatever – he will not so easily become a class, part of the exploited, liable to strike, etc.

And there is also this: in order to drive the play from narrow ethnic confines, it also has to explode the boundaries of region and let itself be brought into the entire country and into history. The next step would be to carry history across borders in the story, as in the narrative of Brandy-Emma about the old peasant Atthi, to whom she has brought fish and butter from the (good) land owner's wife but who will not take anything from those people; that's where the story goes over into the October Revolution and the concentration camps, where the inmates ate grass. That is exactly the kind of story at issue here: it cannot be narrated and thus an important point of reference in the play cannot be provided, if the play is not allowed to leave the Thuringian forest[20] (just as a comparison) or

19 Famous quote from *The Communist Manifesto* published by Karl Marx and Friedrich Engels in 1848.

20 Bennewitz evokes the central German region Thuringia (where Weimar is located) and its famous forest as example of folksy regionalism.

is supposed to be adapted and played according to the sentence "we don't eat that here." Of course there haven't been revolutions and concentration camps here in the south of the subcontinent, and the October Revolution is too far away, also geographically, for the local Brandy-Emma to have it in her trove of experiences – BUT what she CAN have and what can be known by others is that someone from her village took part in the struggles for liberation and independence and can tell about a similar fate. That's how a wider historical horizon can come into the play.

Bangalore, 5 September 1982

The actors are fundamentally different than I know them from elsewhere in India and around the world. They are also amateurs, but amateurs who have grown up with successful entertainment and through that – cheaply manufacturable – success have become fixated in their ideas about acting, also because they have never been challenged by a play that demands such dialectically complex situations and characters as a Brecht play. To make a long story short, the actor playing Puntila,[21] who held the promise of good work and discovery in his build and in the good impressions I had from talking with him and from some unaffected readings of scenes – this actor cannot cope with the demands of basic acting. When he takes the stage, he brings with him that unbearable unnaturalness, the cliché of a character (if even that), completely leaving out his own person and personality. So now he is a victim of confusion. If he DOES nothing but just reads or plays the sense of the sentence in the text in a given situation, he is good, rich, vital, full of charm and wit – and whenever I tell him so to encourage him, but at other times refuse to allow him to bark out the "character" without a trace of thinking, he is always in confusion: "when I am boring and uninteresting and do not act at all" he says, "the director thinks I am good, and if I am good and do act, the director thinks I am bad."

This all is written down so easily but is a huge problem and not easily explained in two sentences. What clashes here are two completely mutually exclusive conceptions of theatre, and more fundamentally, different ideas about the world and the possibilities of intervening thinking. And since actors cannot and ought

21 This was Sundar Raj.

not to be forced (because in the end they have to be responsible for their acting and cannot interrupt the play and tell the audience "excuse this nonsense that I am playing – but the director wanted it this way"), I throw them into not just an artistic but an existential conflict. And just think: in the way he understands and plays theatre, he has been successful for three decades already, has experienced himself through and by acting. Normal behaviour on stage that is different from the daily life and behaviour of the actor only through the situations offered by the dramatist and the peculiarities he gives to his characters – this denies such an actor the experience of acting. Add to that what might be the deeper reason: theatre here is played spontaneously and can be done like that if the situations do not need to be more life-like and the characters any closer to reality than those in an operetta. They have never heard, learned, or experienced here that rehearsing is a journey of adventure into the UNKNOWN and requires the attitude of the researcher much more than the routine of the garden gnome producer. I have to stress again that I am NOT talking about the fantastic spontaneous talents of folk theatre, but about an art of acting that has long been degraded from this folk theatre and about actors who have grown up in the urban lower middle class and live in a city that has 137 cinemas but only one theatre building for all dramatic activities taking place in the city.

I have just told the actor playing Puntila – and this is good and very nice here, that this can be said in all friendship and respect for one another and met with good understanding – he ought to consider whether he wants to continue having the thumb screws of what he is utterly unused to put on him (which means, whether he wants to joyfully participate in the risk of experiencing his own creative freedom) or whether it is so remote from his inner habit or even conviction about theatre that continuing would just mean production of unhappiness for him.

Bangalore, 7 September 1982

From rehearsals I always go back into the original text, known by heart, and then I understand Brecht's wit and sharp mind and his tenderness better, when I have to mediate it through a foreign language into yet another completely different language. But it is probably always a satisfying joy to let others discover new things and themselves anew through one's own discovering.

Fig. 11 Bennewitz with the cast of his production of *Donku Desai Naukara Shahi* (Brecht's *Mister Puntila and his Man Matti*) in Kannada, Bangalore, 1982. Courtesy of Fritz-Bennewitz-Archiv, Leipzig.

Bangalore, 29 September 1982

The miracle did not take place. The run-through three days ago in the rehearsal room provided a glimpse of what may have been possible, and it was joyfully there with dialectical wit and charm and elegance that has its feet on the ground. What had been learned was a guiding presence in the joyful playing of the responsibility-free fun of such a rehearsal. When the burden of responsibility entered in the form of fear in front of the audience, the joy became short of breath, and since what had been learned had not yet become experience, this new learning and the freedom for new fun were left behind. The escape into comedic clichés still brought loud pleasure to enough audience members, but an agonizing experience to their victims on stage: story and characters dried out, shrivelled into roughness, and those who played knew it while they played.

Bennewitz's account suggests that even though the translation problems were eventually overcome to some extent, combined with the extremely short time frame for the production and with incompatibility between director and cast, they led to what he perceived as a disastrous failure. A newspaper report from the time, quoting both sides, shows that this incompatibility seems to have been a mutual impression:

> Bennewitz repeatedly emphasised the great importance of the actor's individuality, his freedom in the making of a successful play. Describing his crew as 'highly intelligent and competent' he said because of the kind of work they have been used to, they tended to wait for instructions. His duty was to rid them of this diffidence and put confidence in them.
>
> Thus the intensity of the actor's involvement decides the fate of the play. Acting, Bennewitz seemed to imply, requires commitment, to the play's meaning and to its relevance. It therefore becomes more than a profession.
>
> Ms. Poornima, speaking for the players, said the most difficult obstacle in their way was the director's method of functioning itself. They were totally unused to being left to 'provide the leverage' themselves, to suggest and make moves without prior direction. ("Brecht not the monopoly")

Both sides here hint rather politely at the same acting problems, though clearly with different interpretations as to who was responsible for them. Still, as Bennewitz made clear in a letter written a year later, the translation problems were the real key to the failure and were instructive beyond this particular production, in terms of "integration of a play not into a foreign language as such, but into particular, historically conditioned dialects" (Bhopal, 27 August 1983). Despite his attempt to derive a lesson from this failure, it very much grated on Bennewitz, who many years later referred to the production as "the terrible *Puntila*, the greatest flop of my life" (Mysore, 13 March 1991).

New Delhi, 1982: Brecht, *The Caucasian Chalk Circle*

From Bangalore, Bennewitz went directly to the NSD in New Delhi to work with the students there on *The Caucasian Chalk Circle*, thus retreating from the disappointing first work experience in Karnataka to familiar territory in terms of place, language, and play. Nevertheless, this stay also included a new challenge, because Bennewitz transposed his prior experiments with directing Brecht for children in the USA and the Philippines to India for the first time. In addition to a version of the *Chalk Circle* for adults in a Hindi translation by R.G. Bajaj under the title *Insaaf ka Ghera*, he worked on a parallel production of the play for children. This was done with an entirely different cast and in a different translation than the version for adults. Because Bennewitz also taught a seminar on Brecht's *Messingkauf Dialogues* for directing students and gave numerous interviews, his days were very busy indeed.

> New Delhi, 14 October 1982
>
> Tomorrow around 10 o'clock a Miss Geeta Lal of the *Financial Times* will come for an interview. I am not much in the mood for interviews. We'll see, maybe it won't be the same old questions again. Then there might be students knocking at my door wanting private advice for their roles. Or Mr. Werner Kuhn from the guest room opposite, with whom today I chatted away an hour about *Hamlet* and Shakespeare generally. He is a pleasant person from Switzerland, who made theatre with Eugenio Barba in Denmark, then had his own Danish troupe, participated in group theatre in Paris and with Grotowski in Poland, and has studied Kathakali in Kerala and Noh and Kabuki in Japan.[22] Really, he represents the conception of theatre that I attack because it not only has sneaked away out of history but has also taken the human being along with it out of history into mythical spaces. I take it easy and do not open the battle – there are so many rooms in God's house, and in the wide landscape of theatre each one can find a place. If for once I am left alone tomorrow morning, I'll continue my reporting in the letter, e.g., about the founding of the Brecht Club at the New Delhi University.

> New Delhi, 21 October 1982
>
> I'll say it again: when the students have grasped it and themselves, it has something richly vigorous. Of course, I'll not deceive myself – what we are doing here is normal acting training towards normal behaviour on stage, and has nothing of what the

22 Eugenio Barba (b. 1936) was a disciple of Jerzy Grotowski and has in turn become a major figure of intercultural theatre. He founded the Odin Teatret and the International School of Theatre Anthropology in Denmark. Noh is a highly codified form of classical Japanese musical drama. For Kabuki, see p. 68 n. 28.

experiments had and were meant to be – explorations, observations on how a play reacts under other historical, cultural, and ethnic conditions. For that, the students are also too far removed from the roots here – sometimes I have to lead and seduce them into Indian behaviour and Indian attitudes.

Aside from this perceived need to lead the students back to their own roots, Bennewitz also saw another, more concrete lack of leadership at NSD. He wrote of a severe conflict between acting students and directing students as to who had the right to translate the *Chalk Circle* for the children's version, and he attributed such conflicts to the weak direction of the school in general (New Delhi, 18 and 19 October 1982). Nevertheless, the work on both versions progressed well and, as he explains in the following passages, satisfied Bennewitz to a high degree despite the absence of the experimental excitement of the early years.

New Delhi, 15 November 1982

Yesterday morning we gave two performances of the *Chalk Circle* for children here in the school. In the first were the children from our embassy and in the second there was Amal with her three beautiful children. [...] Well, all very well brought up kids (not just specifically Amal's) from the upper middle class, who in contrast to kids from the street are quite reserved. Sure, they also have the big eyes and bite their lips, but they never become loud like for example in Manila, where the enthusiasm sometimes overpowered the actors' speech. Anyhow, in the middle of the play, before the river scene, we ask which child from the audience wants to play Michel – normally we get dozens, yesterday it was Amal's eight-year-old, and the six-year-old sat on Amal's lap and was terribly anxious about what was happening with his brother. He could not stand the soldiers that led his brother away. [...] And the playing in front of and with the children was again a great pleasure – that was one of my happiest ideas back then in New York, which by now delights tens of thousands of kids in the USA, the Philippines, and now Delhi (invitations to come to the schools after the break in December come pouring in). Those are the kind of tender shoots I have planted in the world and that have now become forests. And to think that if I wanted to do this at home the Brecht heirs would prevent it and I would have to apply for it with the schools a year in advance. Still, I'll enjoy coming home.

Fig. 12 Fritz Bennewitz during rehearsal, India, 1980s. Courtesy of Fritz-Bennewitz-Archiv, Leipzig.

New Delhi, 21 November 1982

The first performance suffered (quite) a bit from the excitement that everyone wanted to do their best, and this can easily make a performance slow, because everyone also thinks they have to show and give EVERYTHING they have learned and understood. Reception was friendly, but no sign yet of an EVENT. And of course during the break and afterwards, there were the comments from the Mandi House intellectuals (Mandi House is a well-known building, a former palace of a Maharaja, but today refers to a roundabout with fountains, where the "Mandi House intellectuals" sit and spend their unemployed or lazy evenings, talk about the art scene, and feed the gossip mill). Their comments: "that is not Brecht" – "where is alienation, and it isn't Brecht style at all" – "how is this Brecht, such strong emotional participation in the audience and even on stage no coldly distanced report but passionate playing," etc. It is telling how for decades already the harmful idea is regenerated and reproduced by intellectuals who are themselves alienated, that Brecht's is a fundamentally anti-human conception which puts the human being into the coldness of mathematical construction and mechanical relational structures – this stupidity cannot be eradicated.

But then came the second day with the second performance [...] and the actors had the necessary control over the play and themselves, so that the audience was taken by storm and the applause during scenes would not end. We went into the night happy and thankful, thinking that this now could not be topped, because we could hardly be better than on this evening. So the miracle was possible again – and had begun with disappointment [...]. The next performance was like a run that only occurs once in many Olympic or Asiatic Games, and there was unprecedented cheering during it and clapping through the entire final song, and when the actors came on stage, there was rhythmic clapping, nearly unheard of in Indian theatre. The audience came on stage and behind the stage, and many who had understood knew it and said it, that with this production a new level of Brecht interpretation, of dialectical theatre, of the art of acting had been reached. Of course there is exaggeration in the joy (I mean not just mine, but among those who voiced it) but also this: the production split the audience much more, and more definitively, than any preceding Brecht production including the *Chalk Circle*, which had always ended on a reconciliatory note because the stress lay on the Grusha scenes, and the Azdak part was more Tamasha and fun due to the overemphasis on the entertaining elements of folk theatre. Here, we had succeeded for the first time in India to descend into the complex dialectics of the play especially in the Azdak character and story, so that its social, historical, and political weight determined the production.

Thus, in Bennewitz's view both the children's and the adults' version of the *Chalk Circle* produced satisfying and innovative results. After the low points of the Kolkata *Galileo* and the Bangalore *Puntila*, these two productions represented more successful "firsts" for him – introducing Indian children to Brecht and opening a new interpretation of the *Chalk Circle* for Indian adults – and concluded the early 1980s phase of his work in India on a high note.

3 The Mid-1980s – Brecht and the Bard in Bhopal

Bhopal, 1983: Brecht, *The Caucasian Chalk Circle*

In the mid-1980s, the centre of Bennewitz's theatre activity in India shifted to Bhopal. B.V. Karanth had founded the Rangmandal ensemble housed in Bhopal's Bharat Bhavan cultural centre in 1981, with the aim of starting a sustained movement based on blending folk and modern theatre. Bennewitz was invited there several times over the next few years, was touched deeply by his encounter with the ensemble and the place, and gained important stimulation for his work and thought. His first project with Rangmandal was once again to test the adaptability of Brecht's *Caucasian Chalk Circle* in yet another regional, linguistic, and theatrical context. He directed the play with the assistance of his former NSD student Atul Tiwari. It was translated by Madan Soni into Bundeli (or Bundelkhandi), a regional dialect of Hindi spoken by the lower-class characters in the play, while the nobility and members of the bureaucracy spoke varying shades of Urdu. Once again, however, there were problems with the translation whose painstaking rectification during rehearsals caused time delays in the already tight schedule and some amount of tension in the production team. But these tensions also led to very productive thinking about problems of translation, register, and ideology in the theatre. The music composed by Karanth played a central role in the production and also gave Bennewitz ample food for thought. So did his encounter with this particular cast, in which the Nacha actor Dwarika Prasad, who would become an important point of reference for Bennewitz,[1] finally played both Azdak and the narrator-singer, while the role of Grusha was played by Vibha Mishra.

Bhopal, 18 August 1983

Yesterday morning we had the actors improvise a prologue story with the village conflicts between zamindaar (big land owner) and peasant labourers. A law passed by the government orders land distribution to the labourers and land consolidation at the same time. The village is called to assembly, and there are only seconds between joyful hope for their own land as protection against starvation, and horrified despair, because the law has strings attached: it demands distribution and allows for re-allotment, so that on balance it means gains for the land owner. Through re-allotment, he can take good pieces of land on the edges or within his large fields, and can get rid of new or poor land on stony ground. The letter of the law is thus fulfilled, since it says nothing about the quality of land to be exchanged and distributed. Disappointment and despair unleash aggression, which can easily be brought under control, because the zamindaar has brought along his "private army," who are able to literally show the villagers their limits, driving them behind barriers.

But the situation is no longer simply masterable with clubs and guns, the protest of the peasants threatens to get out of hand. In order to at least gain some time through stalling and deception, the land owner's steward calls back the thugs, promises new thinking and discussion of all suggestions, and tells a traditional story similar to the chalk circle, where however the struggle over the child ends according to the biological right of the mother. Then, knowing the law on the side of the land owners, he suggests a play in lieu of further quarrelling, but the villagers are not dumb and insist that one of them should play the judge. That's the rough outline of the prologue, the result of a conversation the other night.

This was narrated by one of the actors with beautiful clarity and demonstrative gestures, and I like to use something like that

1 It has proven somewhat difficult to find biographical information on Prasad. A German review of the production reported that he was from the third generation of a family of artists of the Chhattisgarhi folk theatre form of Nacha, that he was brought to Delhi where he trained and performed in Sanskrit theatre as well as plays by Molière and Brecht, and that his performance in the *Chalk Circle* was world class (Pflaum).

right away to let the others observe how rich their utterances are when they know what they want to say, and when they want it to be understood. In fact, they are far richer and more precise in body language than we, in whose daily lives the word has made itself independent from the body. Then it is always astonishing again that even those who in conversation and when reporting their ideas can do it so richly and clearly and comprehensibly, cannot do it on stage, do not use it, do not consider it acting.

So, the story was told, the possible positions of the classes in the village towards one another were understood, the arguments had been stated, and we started into improvisation. If one weren't to look more closely, one would quickly arrive at the judgment that here people who had been locked up are released into freedom, and now they throw out everything that would otherwise have been hemmed in by the cell walls; above all, everyone and everything is going at once, and when there is conflict, then it is even more jumbled and one is louder than the next, and there are many, many words and much gesticulating (not the beautiful clear gestures described earlier). Still, this is good for sorting, because there are still enough good ones and enough offers that allow me to glimpse the kernel of the intention. Of course, it begins with setting a milieu, since something has to happen, something has to be "done," meaning: they play village life. This has the advantage that it allows me to easily read the level of imagination each of them has at their disposal. Two of them played an elephant, with another sitting atop as the Maharaja who himself is bringing the news of the land distribution to the village (it probably had to be the Maharaja because it is so much fun to play an elephant), and with their love of mass movement they play three different climaxes of the conflict – once one climax has calmed down, the next springs up, because then they can use their vocal cords so expressively and because then the clubs of the private army can spring into action.

Still, there is enough to see in the chaos to organize something from it: how one of the armed thugs encircles the peasants, not alone of course, but others improvise to follow his intention; how the steward takes aside the land owner and whispers something in his ear, then placates the peasants with his deceptive plan. Of course, one has to have a trained eye to see the key points of the story and the wealth of narrative offers, because everyone is always active at the same time, gesticulating, and what takes place is more punk than jazz – "I have to make my instrument heard and therefore be louder than my neighbour's flute," so only percussion instruments are played. But the sorting is a lot of fun, because the chaos is not made from nothing, it is made from multiple somethings that somewhere connect with their experiences, and I am here to teach them how they can learn to use their experiences.

I just had the thought that today in rehearsal I will suggest to them that we don't leave the story-telling and the suggestion of the play to the steward alone, but let him tell his story which puts the letter of the law on his side, and let the suggestion for the play come from the peasants.

Bhopal, 20 August 1983

Since their theatre is oriented towards music and mobility, they soon come up with rich offers of movement. And for the interpretation of the play I should not set my expectations too high, that an entirely new play will emerge – the shared social reality is not so fundamentally different culturally and ethnically that it would not bring similar results as elsewhere in India with the same play previously. Besides, it is much too early to think about and judge this – it will only reveal itself in the Azdak story.

[...]

Two actors from Habib Tanvir's troupe[2] are now here at Rangmandal, and one of them is playing the Dairy Farmer. THAT IS IT! I just say one or two words of explanation about the situation in a way that connects it to his life experience, and then the character is fully there at the blocking rehearsal already. And this is not emotional identification like back in the days with that actress who closed her "body eyes" and opened her transcendental ones and let the character slip over her like a dress (that's what the character was then like, too); no, with this boy the instincts have social experience and understanding. So I was thinking that if there were a whole ensemble of such people (as I had hoped for to some extent here),

2 Habib Tanvir (1923–2009) founded the group Naya Theatre in 1959 and increasingly relied on Chhattisgarhi folk theatre artists for his productions. The two actors Bennewitz mentions were Dwarika Prasad and Amar Singh.

then the Brecht plays – no, not all of them, *Arturo Ui* likely not, but I'd be interested in *Galileo* – could be broken open to their innards. And maybe one could even deliver alienation and all that, without loss of vitality, because so much has entered into their spontaneous playing reaction to the world, including epic playing, which distances in its content and form, i.e., it alienates, so that alienation as means and method is known and mastered. So then work with them could be focused on extending theatrical communication through alienation towards the question "to what ends?" Towards opening their world into thinking that intervenes.

Then there is their oft-described experience of dialectics, because this experience is seated on the floor, with the bum on the earth, and this metaphorically and literally: sitting on the earth is touching the ground differently than on a chair or couch or when sleeping in a bed – they don't sleep in beds in the huts, and they don't sit on the floor only for meditation.

And there is also the playing without vanity. The other day, during conversation after a concert, which really was not a "concert," someone said about the singer – and "singer" also doesn't capture it – about the woman who sang: "she is the most un-glamorous I ever have seen" – that is the right word: "un-glamorous." And with this actor (my God, how used up, burned out, and dried up words are, how far they have strayed from life, when one wants to use them for here AND there: what does the word "actor" say here?) – anyhow, for this player, playing is just as much an expression of life as other daily activities, only heightened by the fact that this particular expression of life in its foundation is COMMUNICATION. And then comes his partner, who is doubtlessly a talented (another one of our concepts, "talent") actress – here the word is accurate, because it is far below the word "player" used above, and "act" does not just mean that it is public and for others but also includes self-presentation.[3] She, with her three years of training, has a hard time just knocking on the door of the real world translated into theatre; there is the middle-class background, sitting like sludge and syrup in her skin and being, expressed in clichés (not even

3 Bennewitz plays here on the components of the German word for "actor": "Schauspieler" – literally "show player."

primarily acting clichés, but worse: clichés of life) calculated for effect and not for effecting something. It is too bad, because it is not even very intentional, it has become her nature, because from the very get-go she cannot live and grasp her own life and that of society as BEING, and so her work becomes stereotypical.

[...]

I now have fourteen years of experience with life here already. I am also finding my way around the language faster than even last year. And for the first time I am working out series of movements independently. How come? It is a genuine question, because I would be hard-pressed to describe by example how I am leading the production from Indian culture into Indian culture. This can't be demonstrated with reference to individual gestures alone or a series of steps, a sequence of movements. I also cannot describe in detail my increased capability to find and organize Indian and Asian forms of expression from folk and classical theatre from the content of the play or rather, to help the content. A lot of it is finding and expressing myself in the habits of life here, forgetting for a while that and how one can eat with knife and fork instead of one's hand, wrapping and tying the lungi around my body not because it is exotic, but because it is useful in the house, always being curious about the history and stories of the country, and no longer thinking about taking off my shoes at the door and walking barefoot in the house. I will not become an Indian, but my knowledge becomes eye, ear, hand, and mouth, and that's why it actually is quite easy for me to express myself in my work from the local to the local here, even though this is still alienated habit, because it is not unconscious, situated in the subconscious, but rather acquired, assumed habit, which then expresses itself outwardly through the contact with my OTHER unconscious.

I am also discovering something new in my work here and now: that I organize contents from RHYTHM, and because I know this rhythm I can improvise it through many forms of expression with great ease – not, of course, at the height of musical Indian improvisation, but rather from the freedom of the fun in playing, which, since it is rhythmic, stays within the discipline given by rhythm, and of course also in that which is my very own brought with me from our culture: discipline of mind, of thought.

Bhopal, 27 August 1983

Bennewitz describes his experience of a performance by a male classical Indian singer:

> I will try to describe the indescribable. Everything the singer did has names, I mean: the stylistic particularities of his singing or the school to which he belongs – his style is supposed to be the rarest form of classical Indian singing. If I repeat words I have found before, this only places him into my basic experience of Indian music and not where he properly belongs: beyond it. He sings Kandinsky images, woven carpet patterns, sends tones into space and on their way, where they describe curves, run around the corner, found cities – that's it: he sings SPATIALLY; that's why his singing is not just audible but visible; and sometimes [...] he closes his eyes and there is a very thin tone in the room, which we do not see nor know where it is coming from, not even where it is, and then we discover that tone is in him and he is in the tone, it is all around him like a universe. That's how I felt in front of the Buddha in Sanchi, that he can lift off the ground, not in order to drift away, but surrounded by the universe, which is concentrated into such small dimensions that he floats as in a diaphanous sphere, and the sphere floats where? in what? in emptiness? And he sings himself out from such interiority, without having to struggle or smash something, and he sends the tones (which vary in set intervals – of 4, or 7? – in infinite combinations and sequences) back on their way, sometimes like electrons, like silk threads, sometimes like thinnest wire, like a laser beam, sometimes like a present from both hands towards a listener, who becomes a fellow singer and can catch the present in tones. In his singing – that's how I feel with this strange way of singing along – there is nothing from and in this world and in other worlds that cannot become tone; music is thus experienced as revealed secret and – I always come back to my fundamental experience [...] with Buddha, although this singing and many things I relate the experience to have nothing at all to do with Buddhism – it is not an open secret in the sense of the Book of John and certainly not in the sense of Walpurgis nights, dark, and in rain-dripping forests, but lucid,

diaphanous, thus truly REVEALED, which does not mean that it could be recorded by science.

But even when it floats in such a universe-sphere, it sits with crossed legs on the ground; the feeling and experience of singing along, or rather, singing oneself probably also stems from the fact that we, too, sit on the ground with crossed legs and certainly receive currents that have been sent through the air and combined with the multiple energies in and under the soil (you know the sensibility that reacts to subterranean things – secret without mysticism – just as in the mystic Master Jakob Böhme and his crystal ball there is little mysticism, but rather insight into humans). But again there is difference here: the singer is right among us, next to us, inside us, and not so completely opposite, both externally and internally, as in a European concert. Each one is connected to him directly from within themselves, and yet not excluded from their neighbour's experience. And if the human voice can be compared to instruments at all, then all instruments were in his voice, even those that have not been invented yet. And there is tenderness that goes towards the inaudible (and also the unheard-of) next to a power in tone, that I immediately had a sensual concept of Durga (Kali), goddess of prime energy – and so translucent, humanly friendly in principle, then suddenly a sequence of tones that tears open the earth downward into what is threatening, where the asuras or demons dwell (to say 'devils' would make it too diminutive, we have familiarized ourselves with devils too much in expressions like the 'poor devil').

Bhopal, 3 September 1983

Yesterday we rehearsed for the first time Grusha's[4] parting from the child, before she lays it on the doorstep of the friendly farmer's wife with the milk. We talked about the situation and I made clear the conflict that she has no choice: she has no more money for milk and she is exhausted, and she wanted nothing other than bring the child to safety; the lonely hut in the forest is far enough from the city, and there is also her beloved, who might come back from the war, and what if he didn't find her then?

4 Played by Vibha Mishra.

Those are all good reasons, and now we start trying it out, and suddenly, when the actress is supposed to lay the child (a doll) on the doorstep, she starts crying and runs off stage to Atul, the assistant, in other words to an Indian instead of to me first, because she knows her feelings will be understood by her fellow countryman. What had happened? "I cannot give the child away." Strange and almost beautiful, actually (though fortunately actors are normally more hardened, ours at least, or else every Othello might run away from the stage before the murder, or actually commit it) – in a way it was nice because it offered such a good occasion to talk and think about how little our feelings help if they cannot give milk – not that they shouldn't be there, they are also present in Brecht's character – that's why Grusha's soliloquy is so long, and she has to convince herself, because the little feet on her back during the long flight from the soldiers have not only made her back hurt, but have also awakened her affection due to the care invested and the shared hardship.

Of course, there is still the problem – perhaps only as the flipside of the quick, genuine, but fairly easy tears – that the sentimental wave overcoming the actress does not have enough emotional power to help her imagination translate her own experience into the stage events appropriately. So then the action of placing the child on the doorstep, which Grusha does precisely because of the emotion overcoming her, because of her claim to her own happiness with her own children (which by the way is expressed by Brecht in great tenderness and human warmth, when Grusha does not say "... and what, if **I** don't find him?" but rather "... and what, if **HE** doesn't find me?") but struggling AGAINST emotion, this action slips into cuteness, into cliché, and either denounces the actress's preceding tears or simply means that she has not learned the art of acting yet, which she can't be blamed for. But it is also that elsewhere they bake and eat bread differently – the reaction to the world is different here, more emotional, more sentimental than with us, where philosophy and interests have been placed between skin and world.

Bhopal, 4 September 1983

The boy we had given the role of Azdak had too much trouble with that confounded guy and generally with himself on stage, because he belongs to those cases I have described for whom

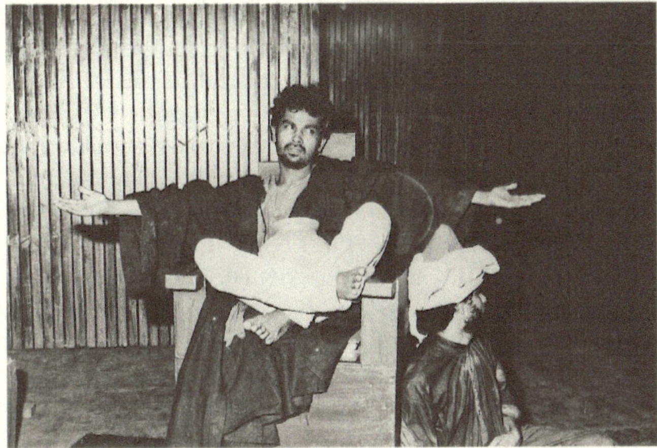

Fig. 13 Dwarika Prasad as Azdak in Fritz Bennewitz's production *Insaaf ka Ghera* (Brecht's *Caucasian Chalk Circle*) in Bundeli, Bhopal, 1983. Courtesy of Fritz-Bennewitz-Archiv, Leipzig.

thinking seems to get in the way of playing, which is not at all lack of intelligence, but rather an understanding of theatre that varies pre-formed characters in known situations only in name and costume. Its effect on the audience lies in their joy to meet old acquaintances – I don't mean it all that ironically: people need a place where the world remains the same in a cheery way. So, with his understanding and agreement, we cast him differently, keeping him as understudy for Azdak, and have been rehearsing since last night with one of the two actors from Habib Tanvir's troupe, who thus far had been and will remain the main singer in the play (just like Ernst Busch[5] played both for Brecht: the singer and Azdak). And that's where something remarkable takes place, that coming to an understanding about the situation and character are sufficient, and a hint here and there for deeper

5 Ernst Busch (1900–80) was a prominent communist actor and singer who worked with Brecht both in the 1920s and again in post-WWII East Berlin after returning from exile and imprisonment. In addition to his role as Azdak, he starred in Brecht's *Threepenny Opera* and *The Life of Galileo* and was well known for his interpretations of Brecht songs.

understanding that something is happening on stage. Of course, this is no different with all talented actors elsewhere, and theatre should actually only begin from that precondition. I am also exaggerating it a bit, because this great talent makes clear the difference to most of the others, who have to be painstakingly taught the basic patterns of seeing and hearing. And still there is more, which does not show itself, yet right with the first walk across the stage: already when he is reading, every sentence receives the background of his experience, I don't mean the kind of experience reached through analysis, but the kind that has become bones, blood, and flesh, certainly that one in great measure, or is it what Brecht talks about when he lets someone describe a photo of Busch as Azdak and explains the describable richness thus: yes, well, there are 40 years of experience with class struggle sitting in the judge's chair. Well, I do not want to raise the actor here into Busch's realm, and it is not a question of experience with class struggle in the Spanish civil war and so on – I am just curious what new aspects the local actor will take from the character.

He brings me back to the topic of the folk(-theatre), which I also wanted to write about on the occasion of Bhaskar's thoughts about his music in *Hayavadana*.[6] Haven't I written and talked about it before, when I spoke of Chérif Khaznadar's (very meritorious) Festival des arts traditionelles in Rennes?[7] He brings people from the most remote corners of the world to Rennes and now to Paris, who then make their music there and dance their dances, and there is no other place where one can see and hear this endless variety, the never-heard tones, the never-seen steps that still take place in those corners of the earth, untouched by civilization, as they may already have taken place a thousand years ago; or they come from less remote corners, where there are still people who can sing, play, and dance traditional forms, but where these

6 The reference here is to plans for the production of Girish Karnad's *Hayavadana* directed by Vijaya Mehta in Weimar in 1984, for which Bhaskar Chandavarkar composed the music.

7 Chérif Khaznadar is a theatre director, writer and now Chair of the Advisory Board of the Al Ain Center for Music in Abu Dhabi. At the time of this letter he was the artistic director of the Maison de la culture de Rennes (1974–86), and the Théâtre de la ville de Rennes (1980–3).

forms are already threatened by impoverishment and extinction. This is what can be seen and heard in Rennes and Paris (I'll say again: with much merit), and it is very significant for an experience and knowledge and understanding of the world, although all those performances – taken away from their place and the people for whom and with whom they usually happen – are not free from the whiff of the zoo and the Zirkus Hagenbeck in Hamburg, which around the turn of the century "exhibited" members of African tribes.

Now, there are (also meritorious) endeavours to preserve for mankind what has made it mankind in the experiencing of the self through singing, music-making, dancing, and that is good and necessary and deserving, like the restoration of old bridges and castles; but there are purists among them who want to leave things untouched and to make what has been touched untouched again, and they count folk [...] only as FOLK if it is free from the "taint" of any contact with (whatever kind of) history or if it can be cleansed of such contact. This may sound like a laudable eagerness to keep old cultural goods clean from contamination, degeneration, and deformation, and like the necessary pains to work against pollution by commercialization – but because it remains within the system and does not acknowledge a new historical conception of the people and of folk, the pernicious aspects of this trend become clear as well, since cultural expression, i.e., singing and dancing, cannot be sent into preserves that can be kept clear of technological and historical progress. And so the preservational impulse to hold on to what has been passed down can easily be replaced by the demand to stay at the hand loom – the purest argument to maintain markets and spheres of influence and dependency. This is neo-colonialism in the mask of the friend of culture (and there are so many pure-hearted fools among the friends of culture, who are as serious as the Greens[8] are about protecting the environment, and do not know whose business they are furthering). The choice has become difficult.

8 The reference is to the West German Green Party, which had just gained its first representation in the Bundestag, the national parliament, earlier in 1983.

Back to the people and the folk song – the other day after rehearsal, as heavy rain was coming down and we sat at the open door and sang away time (me hardly singing, but glad to be listening), there was an old watchman of the compound who was asked and also sang. His song had depth and simplicity, and yet, as I was told on the walk home, it was an old Hindi film song (we would call it a schmaltzy song), but in the singing of this old man, where his life sounds along in the tones, it had become a folk song. And then I understood Bhaskar's simple sentence (which is not so simple after all): folk music is what the people make and sing as music – of course, a certain definition of "the people" must be understood along with this. I also remember a drive into the countryside two weeks ago, where a cow herd was sitting beneath his umbrella woven from leaves not with a pan flute, but with a transistor radio.

Bhopal, 9 September 1983

We will have to go through the trouble of making Brecht's conception of the world and the theatre understandable, so that through this consciousness – like a medium and catalyst – life experience as organism of the basic chord brings the upper and lower tones of the CONSCIOUSLY plucked strings into resonance. I need to return here to the photo of Busch as Azdak and Brecht's commentary: "yes, well, there are 40 years of experience with class struggle sitting ALONG WITH HIM in the judge's chair." I think I left out the "along with him" when I last cited this, and yet this makes all the difference in the final analysis: the 40 years of experience with class struggle do not fully explain Busch's Azdak; the local Azdak's unalienated connection to life is not yet the character.

[...]

It is not easily explained why the day before yesterday the miracle man playing Azdak had such a deep low, and then the next day, yesterday, a high close to the limit of expectations, in which through him an interpretative accent of the production here becomes interesting. There is the scene where Azdak does two things: because he has not managed to escape at the last minute, he convinces the soldiers that they should place the candidate for judge on the chair for a mock trial, and he offers to take on the role of the Grand Duke, the arch enemy of the Fat

Prince, in order to accomplish two things in this role: open the eyes of the soldiers as to who has started the war, who earns what through the war, and how much of that is at their own expense; and thereby to achieve the other aim, to save his skin. And in that passage, where he risks the courage to accuse the Fat Prince in a revealing manner, the representation through this actor gains the anger of rebellion, i.e., a truly affected person, someone who has the wounds of exploitation, deception, and betrayal bleeding on his own body, who has sublimated these experiences into his consciousness so that they can become enlightenment.

What I mean is that in the net of contradictions of the character, the attitude "I will not be the hero for anyone, and especially not a martyr" is countered – possibly and necessarily – by the idea that history cannot be made without risking one's neck, either, and that this is doubly necessary in a world in which people quickly resort to the short-circuit action of pouring gasoline over each other and setting one another on fire, but where the knowledge of experience does not as easily become an existentially risky argument. The miracle man has now obviously understood the play and himself within the play, and my sharp reaction to his detour into cliché and half-dimensionality seems to have hit the right sensors. Though, when I think about the possible reason for the low, it falls back on me: the day before, I had encouraged him to think of Azdak as related to the Sutradhar in their own playing tradition, a character akin to Vice[9] from pre-Shakespearean traditions and to the Shakespearean clown. I had forgotten to say that "related" does not mean "identical." "Sutra" means string, and "dhar" denotes the one holding the string, in other words he who holds the play together and maintains the connection to the audience, making him also the commentator of the play. All this, I said to the miracle man, Azdak is as well, but I should have said: Azdak is related to this tradition. That explains better why the actor left the richness of experience and the existence of his person to pursue a representational code and manner of playing which has been ritualized over centuries.

The direct address to the audience, that we are not all that used to and not at all in the Azdak character, is not only possible

9 Vice was a stock character in medieval morality plays, personifying the temptations by evil. Over time, the role became a comic one and developed forms of direct audience address.

here but even necessary and advantageous, because the core of the play that promotes understanding and Brecht's innovation in the plot lies in the Azdak story and can be brought more immediately to the audience in direct interaction. And as opinion coming from the actors, it is already commentary. Thereby, the miracle man becomes the law giver of the production in his interpretation of Azdak. The phrase "in his interpretation" is not very accurate here; interpretation is mostly calculated reality-strategy (to use a fashionable catchphrase from current GDR theatre studies) – here, interpretation is more of a reflex, thus immediate reflection of reality, though guided by the impulse from my experience and opinion, and since it has been reflected through experience (which also is opinion), it is commented and therefore also revealed reality. And it is alienated in its own way in the sense that it is not uncritical identification, but identification that lies in the conscious presence of the actor's person within the character, and it is intentional and yet again not intentional, because I don't want to call intention what is the playing-law of theatre here. This is where the creative provocation of theatre here by the Brecht play occurs, although that is also not accurate, as the experience of many years shows: the play is not yet the creative provocation of traditional folk theatre, but the method and the capability to use it, not in general, but under conditions here; thus, simply and clearly, that which we have known since the first year of Communist Party School: the practical APPLICATION of the method – and practice is always defined concretely.

I have always generalized about actors here that they are ahead of us in terms of vitality, directness in dealing with reality and theatre, and reality in theatre. Through the miracle man, vitality and directness can be defined more precisely as unalienated relationship with reality, side-taking behaviour in reality primarily due to two experiences: one is having been born at the bottom and having grown up with the bum on the ground instead of a chair; the other is heathenism in the sense of basic rebelliousness. In the family and in the village, he has gone through theatre that lives from the carefree handling of gods and heroes and easily makes them into clowns. So there has been no intimidation through ideology (which is generally more foreign here than in European ideological history – the law of the devil, repentance, and mercy is absent). There is a being at home in ritual and ritualistic acts, through which life is organized and directed – of course, it is thus also kept away from explanation, since what has been formalized has become so much reflex that it has been taken off any list of things that can be questioned.

In this sense, a performance here is NAÏVE – which does not at all mean primitive or simplistic, but rather entirely non-intellectual; it is also naïve in the unity with an audience who potentially come from the same space of experience, which can be touched by and with consciousness through the Brecht play and a way of playing inspired by his method.

When I spoke above of a postulated, imagined audience, I wanted to mark the difference between the reactions the performance (different from the usual fare) will receive from the expected intellectual, middle-class audience in Bharat Bhavan and from the audience encountered in the semi-rural and rural areas, where theatre is a kind of life encounter anyhow.

Bhopal, 23 September 1983

Yesterday I didn't come back home from rehearsals until quarter past one in the morning. And what we would call the first main rehearsal had not been all that lively. The music has not been composed to the end yet, there is a good stretch still missing on the admittedly long musical road of this play. The singers only know parts of it securely, so the play does not take off, because the music has to carry it essentially. In addition, it is all in original folk tone – (too) little modulated – it sounds good when it is securely in the head, but the habit of forgetting about the lyrics and their meaning in the joy of singing makes the performance slow. Even if the music has been composed from and for the word, so that it can become a story and address for the audience, the structures of Indian song and singing have entered into this good intention, among other places in the repetitions, which turn the sung sentence around in a circle at least three times.

There it is again: thinking and living in circles, cyclically – "kal," after all, means "tomorrow" and "yesterday." And despite this great narrative tradition with and through song [...] – the circle is a return of the line to itself, and the line is not even a line sent out from a beginning into infinity, existing in a space that – because of the infinite goal – also becomes infinite in extension, but the line as circle is endless because the beginning and end can be set arbitrarily an infinite number of times, thus space is circumscribed finiteness, which does not end due only to the reason that the circle is the movement of the line.

Let me leave philosophy and enter the other, hopefully breakable vicious cycle where a different kind of circular movement takes place in the form of a return of the line to itself: the still not learned though often demanded repetition of the creative process, or in simpler words, thinking while speaking so that it can become playing. If they were all Muslims (but only two of them are) and had all gone through the Quran schools, where the words of the prophet are beaten into the subconscious (and while learning the *suras*[10] the – often still little – children move their upper bodies back and forth, so that it is woven into the body as with a loom, otherwise it just needs to be put into the head. It does not need to be understood to be followed, because what has been learned through thinking can be questioned and therefore subjected to criticism) [...] I would find it easier to explain that what they had already understood [...] and played excellently can languish in the mechanical repetition of words the next day, like prayer wheels (but that is among the Tibetan Buddhists). Brainless lack of energy – and then I think it is just understandable fatigue and find out – for the umpteenth time! – that moderate criticism based on insight and clemency changes nothing; and so I have to (how absurd: deliberately and pointedly) fall back into the terrible behaviour of former years at home, and sharpen my voice, become loud, and berate them to the point of destroying their dignity – and that works (those are the terrible wonders left over from the history of oppression) and brings them back to reason. I leave aside the miracle man and his like here – with them, not everything has the same lustre every day, but everything is motivation, impulse, thought-about and acted-upon text; the terrible method is only necessary where art has not been inborn as a basis of life.

Bhopal, 24 September 1983

Where the play has been woven into the music, which it has except for a few centimetres where the threads are bare and the

10 The suras are the chapters or sections of the Quran.

knots not yet tied, it has – also due to my tenacious insistence on the narrative aspect of the singing – this origin from music, and as a play and performance has something of Indian singing and music-making [...]; it is so thoroughly rhythm in steps, gestures, words, and still just music in its own medium, not because the scenes are sung or danced. That is the most visible consequence of my work, that within discipline and through motivation they find their way to the great freedom of their expressions of life in playing, in the marriage of precision and original simplicity – actually, just like classical Indian music: the most unlimited freedom through unconditional submission to the acknowledged basic law of the chosen raga and rasa.[11]

Bhopal, 27 September 1983

I found the singers doing their "Quran exercises" and discussed with Karanth how we could bring the music more prominently into the play before the first public performance in the evening, because even with greater security among the singers and with more energy to come into the narrative character of the music, which means making the word and its sense prominent in the singing, in the second and third part there is still too much of a hammock between the scenes in which the music sways and does not push the play forward.

There is the song by Azdak-Ajabdas, when he comes to the soldiers in the court and thinks they have hanged the judge. He thinks now something has erupted like his grandfather experienced for three days forty years ago and about which he left him a song. So now he wants to sing this song for them, so that they understand that a new age has begun. In that song, composition and performance are the ideal example of what I had envisioned for the part of the narrator in the production. The miracle man has it in his power to lift the people out of their seats or to make them fearful: "is he allowed to sing and say this here?" He starts to address the audience from the first line of the song, which here starts thus: "well, talk! why don't you say what's going on! talk" – and that

11 Raga and rasa are fundamental concepts of Indian performing arts. Roughly speaking, ragas are melodic modes and rasas refer to an aesthetic form of experience modulated by basic emotional moods.

with such a sly aggressiveness, "don't be cowards," "say it" – and then he sings the line and reaches with a long gesture towards the singers, drawing them in, and when they sing this "bolo, bolo re," he points to them and looks into the audience, saying with his eyes: "see, listen, they have the courage and say it, and I will say even more in a second" – and in between he keeps encouraging the singers to join in and say their opinion, to repeat what he sings [...] – yes, that is exactly how I had envisioned it, and how it cannot take place consistently now, because for that the texts had come too late for composing and learning due to the translation fiasco. But perhaps we can at least still come close. First of all, yesterday morning I moved the musicians and singers out of their corner and closer to the audience onto a platform, and this afternoon we'll rehearse further direct interventions in the scene by them.

Bhopal, 28 September 1983

The show yesterday was a good present, in front of a full house and very engaged interest. It confirmed in a new way the experience in Delhi with *The Caucasian Chalk Circle* last year: compared to the first adaptations of the play in the early 1970s, where Grusha's story moved people and along with the judgment of the chalk circle was the main attraction of the play, now in the 1980s it is the Azdak story almost from the start, but at the latest from the second scene on, when he comes to the soldiers accusing himself. I don't think that it is only due to the open way of playing with the audience, because the finest nuances are drawn not just from the direct audience address. Perhaps the reason lies in the fact that references to present issues come more directly from the play; there surely is also increasing interest in our historical and social life, because that has become so precarious due to the general threat to our existence, and because it is questioned more in the daily confusion or non-realization of justice. Last year in Delhi it could not have been caused by a weaker Grusha making the interest in the story more pronounced, and here in Bhopal, Grusha has grown excellently in the last few days and hours (of course, somewhat due to total exhaustion, which cannot cover up anything on stage anymore with false acting, and so it was nice to see that so much had been basically understood and worked or liberated into the subconscious that the character came to meet the height of expectation – through fatigue), so there was enough engagement and observing insight and judgment – nevertheless, what the audience was truly affected by and intervened in was the Azdak story, even though the miracle man had a totally exhausted voice and could not quite take the lustre of the last rehearsals with him into the show; so it can be confirmed that it is the Brechtian situation, Brecht's text, whose present relevance is brought out by the play, which can also be seen in the fact that the attention does not waver when Grusha's story, formerly regarded as the main story, is over on stage. We changed it around dramaturgically here, and before the final song end with Azdak's "I put down the judge's robe, it has become too hot for me – I will be nobody's hero." Then there is an alert curiosity about why Azdak is remaining behind. How the miracle man plays it! He sits beneath the gallows, looks at Grusha, the child, and Simon leaving, holding the wine jug in his hand, and when he is alone, he drinks the last sip [...], turns over the empty vessel, and touches it for a tender farewell, because the wine was his friend in difficult times. He carefully puts it down, looks up at the gallows, walks to the front, looks at the audience and smiles, takes off the robe, throws it over the judge's chair, takes the banda (a cloth that is also worn as a belt sash) and wraps it around his neck, smiles his "I won't be your hero" into the audience, and goes away, refusing with all friendliness the expectation that he might stay and solve the problems.

New Delhi, 6 October 1983

An incident at the performance of the *Chalk Circle* in Bhopal on September 30th is worth reporting: in the Ludovika scene during the sentence "... and he put his hand on my left breast ...," a girl some twenty years old stood up and, loudly protesting, demanded that the show be stopped, shouting that she had come to the temple for devotions, not to a whorehouse, and asking what kind of audience this was who did not get up and protest against the dirt and trash they were being offered up here. She was then escorted outside by Karanth and Ashok Vajpeyi [...] and Grusha, who was not in that scene, because the audience was becoming agitated towards the girl, and she kept yelling that she wanted to speak to Brecht and to Bennewitz – well, both were not there. And when Vibha – the Grusha there – told her that she should calm down and come back to the hall and finish watching the show, and then they could discuss it calmly, the protester said she did not need to see the rest of it because she was already watching it for the fourth time. She had brought along another girl and two boys who protested along with her, but supplied just the chorus to her song – and then it became clear that the protest had been pre-planned, especially since it came out that she is the daughter of a party boss of the BJP,[12] the reactionary Hindu-chauvinist organization, which obviously has quite a following in Bhopal. [...] The next day, the incident was reported with a headline in the newspaper, and now they say that that party wants to use this as a pretext for an inquiry and complaint against Bharat Bhavan in the state parliament. Of course, the incident and the press reports have attracted more audience members now, and according to the eye witnesses both the show itself and the reactions of the audience to the play have gained considerably.

As this last passage shows, Bennewitz's first Bhopal production was embedded in social and political tensions to a higher degree than in the sheltered environment of the NSD. This was true from the most personal to the most global level. In one letter, Bennewitz discusses the case of a female member of the ensemble who had been murdered by her brother some time ago, apparently in part because he resented her being an actress (Bhopal, 20 August 1983). In terms of regional politics, he reports on mass demonstrations (due to a rise in food prices) that led to the imposition of emergency law and affected the dress rehearsals and performances indirectly (Bhopal, 24–8 September 1983). And on a global level, Bennewitz saw the production as closely related to the newly intensified Cold War and nuclear arms race of the period. He therefore highlighted in one interview what he called "Brecht's militant anti-war component of the play" (Gupta), and elaborated on this idea in another:

> In this play the war as a backdrop plays an important part. But for the war, the mother (Queen) would not have deserted her child and the maid (ayah) would not have taken care of him and would not have been separated from her lover. Because of war the mask from mother's face drops and the maid's humanity awakens. The war precisely does this. I see the play as an anti-war play. (Abhinav)

Two indicators for the success of the production are its wide dissemination within India and its longevity. It was performed at the NSD in

12 The Bharatiya Janata Party, founded in 1980 on a platform of Hindu nationalism.

New Delhi for seven days in November 1984 as part of the Days of GDR Culture in India. Bennewitz was present in Delhi at the time and voiced his pleasure at meeting the ensemble again. He reported that Rangmandal was taking the production to Bangalore, after having toured with it in several other Indian states and all over Madhya Pradesh, including a performance for tribals in Bastar where an audience of over 6000, including 3000 women, took a lively interest (New Delhi, 20 November 1984). And still in 1991, a review praises the quality of the revived production in a performance that year in Lucknow (Kumar). Bennewitz regarded the production as his best Indian *Chalk Circle* yet and as the culmination of his previous experiments with the play and of his other work in India (Gupta).

New Delhi, 1983: Shakespeare, *Othello* and Brecht, *The Life of Galileo*

From the *Chalk Circle* production in Bhopal Bennewitz went straight to the NSD in Delhi, where he stayed from late September to early December 1983. There he worked on productions of Shakespeare's *Othello* with the Repertory Company and of Brecht's *The Life of Galileo* with third-year students. After the exciting Bhopal debut, this Delhi stay threatened to turn into quite a disappointment for several reasons. Bennewitz had conceived the *Othello* production in the hope of being able to test how the Repertory actors he had trained in Brechtian acting during the production of *Puntila* (particularly Pankaj Kapur and K.K. Raina) would apply this training to a Shakespeare play. But these actors had all left Delhi, most of them for Mumbai (Interview Kolkata 1988). He held himself indirectly responsible for this exodus of the most talented actors, arguing that by casting them in the *Puntila* production, he had provoked the mediocre but more powerful members of the Rep to push them out. As a consequence, he perceived a sharp decline in acting quality in the Rep (New Delhi, 11 Oct 1983). In his early letters from this stay, he decried the lack of leadership in the school and of discipline among Rep actors as well as students. In particular, he describes a controversy over the casting of Desdemona. He wanted to cast his former student Hema Sahay (incidentally the daughter of the play's translator), but this was successfully opposed by the troupe's leader and some of its senior female members. This conflict prompted him to adopt a more distanced and impersonal attitude than usual towards the production and his stay at the school generally (New Delhi, 4 Oct. 1983).

Nevertheless, Bennewitz immersed himself in his work on the two productions with his usual energy. This was likely due to what he perceived as the potential political relevance of both plays, despite his disappointment over the thwarting of his original plans for *Othello* and over the arduous task of making even the most fundamental premises of *Galileo* comprehensible to the students. He frequently stressed the importance of Brecht's play for understanding the root causes and consequences of the contemporary global threat of the Cold War nuclear arms race and what he called "the global encircling strategy of the USA" (New Delhi, 6 Nov. 1983, 161). In one letter excerpt included below, he even blames himself for not having insisted on *Galileo* for the Rep production despite the political urgency. However, as we shall see, he also developed an interpretation of *Othello* that was political in its own way and resonated as such with reviewers and colleagues.

This Delhi sojourn was also important for Bennewitz in providing several encounters with different kinds of performances which increased his stock of experiences and prompted reflections. He visited Varanasi and witnessed the Ramlila at Ramnagar, which he described in exhaustive detail in letter passages not included here. Three other encounters are reflected in some of the following passages which contain reflections on a certain kind of political theatre, on ritual, and on the meeting of Kathakali and Goethe's *Faust*.

New Delhi, 3 October 1983

I am not quite sure yet how much fun I will have working on *Othello* with the Repertory Company. There is just not the same curiosity justifying the effort as with the *Puntila* adaptation, where programmatically here in the capital a counter-example was created against the loss of content in the Brecht adaptations in the country, an example for total integration into Indian culture by way of making no compromise whatsoever in the social dimension. Also, with that production Brecht was added to the repertoire of the company. And simultaneously, the scenes from six Brecht plays under the title *Brecht on Trial* here in the school delivered convincing proof against the intellectual nonsense of the Brecht style and of the dogmatization of his method through formalization.

New Delhi, 13 October 1983

I don't know how I should comment on the following: this morning, I read in the events listings in the newspaper that this evening at 5:30 pm, around the corner from here, there would be an event held by the All-India GDR Friendship Association (INFGA) on the occasion of the 34th anniversary of the GDR in the presence of the ambassador. I cancelled the evening meeting with the students and went to where I belong. The great hall was full to capacity. The President of INFGA delivered the welcome, and then someone spoke who apparently had formerly been in the diplomatic service, and then someone else who was a leading member in the cadre of the Communist Party of India, and then another one and another one – and it was moving and thought-provoking, even if and because one knew what was being talked about, and because it was like one of the speakers said: "What do I have to say about the GDR and the historical hour and its consequences?" Such speeches never fail to touch on the experience of fascism and on the consequences of the war, but soon they land in the misery of our own time, the threatened annihilation of mankind – and then it is about problems here, and in the problems here the inseparability of the danger and of peace efforts becomes clear. It is remarkable how the speeches, though full of pathos, have high rationality, find convincing words from passion, and do not talk things to death. I was and am very affected, because it became very clear to me that I had made a mistake that should not have been allowed to occur. In this endangered world I would have had the duty to be RUTHLESS in pushing through *Galileo* against all resistance, even with the prospect of going through a period of suffering due to the non-comprehension, unwillingness, and incapacity of some or even many. By giving away the play I betrayed my reasons for suggesting it: not to leave out the slightest chance of creating new supporters for reason and responsibility.

New Delhi, 18 October 1983

In the evening a troupe from Andhra Pradesh was here in the school – there was a meeting here of street troupes and other theatres who had joined in an organization to promote a revolutionary democratic culture, and today's players came from these circles. They performed old songs and dances that they give new lyrics and meanings to, and a dance play about something that has actually happened and is often still occurring [...]: there are tribal communities who have lived in the forests for millennia and enjoy customary rights there, but now traders have invaded who first dupe the tribals with cheap goods and alcohol and then later come back as money lenders to give loans to those who have become poor due to buying from them; later again, the traders/ money lenders, who have already become rich on the tribals' backs, return to collect the money and the interest, but since there is no money to collect, they buy the tribals' claims to the land and have them sign with thumb prints. They had stained the thumbs with blue ink, and for the last tribal, they ran out of ink; but the thumb print had to go on the document, so they used a drop of blood from a cut in the thumb – hm, what play do we know this from!?

I should report the whole thing more sympathetically, because it was all thought and done really well. But then came the heavy touch: the whole time, the leader of the troupe had already sung, danced, and talked about taking song and dance from the people to give back to the people, and the word "revolutionary" occurred three times in every two sentences, and "radical youth" as well, who are supposed to go to the villages. As the exploitation became worse in that dance play, and the state intervened with its police force, a young agitator came to the village and told them that they must organize, and then out came the red flags (not like our official little paper flags to wave at parades), clenched fists, and guns, and in between the troupe leader always inserted his songs of freedom, saying that the American and Russian imperialists should get what they deserve. Well, that's not my ideological cup of tea. It's too bad that once again the "leftists" do so much damage with what they make young people full of good will do, who dance and sing their lives with such conviction.

New Delhi, 22 October 1983

Yesterday, the Sangeet Natak Akademi organized a lecture-cum-demonstration in preparation for a Kathakali performance today "based on Goethe's dramatic poem *Dr. Faust*, script by Prof. Aymanam Krishna Kaimal and performance by Mankompu Sivasankara Pilla and party."[13] The auditorium in the IIC

13 For a detailed discussion of this production, see John, "Goethe's *Faust*." This letter also serves as a corrective and supplement to the discussion on Bennewitz's Mumbai *Faust* in John, *Bennewitz*, p. 211.

(India International Centre) was packed to the point of people sitting in the aisles, either reflecting curiosity about Kathakali (which apparently cannot be seen more often in Delhi than in Weimar) or even about Goethe's *Faust* or both. [...] If in the end it had gotten under my skin more I would try harder to describe it.

The thing that remains astonishing and admirable is the unlimited control over the body, the guiding of every muscle by the will, the freedom through the greatest discipline, as a result of hardly exceedable 'non-freedom' in the most rigorous training for ten years and beyond. From earliest childhood, the exercises begin before dawn, and hours are spent just practicing the raising of an eyebrow or the rolling of an eye. Everything thinkable is also sayable – just not with words but rather – again astonishingly – with a codified body language that has a limited vocabulary. And everything individual is erased, since the masks, too, are codified language. It brought all this back before my eyes and into my mind, since it has been forgotten in "modern" theatre, where – as is shown during the *Othello* experience with its slow and cumbersome work – acting, instead of inward to outward, works from the outside to the inside, and consequently nothing comes from inside but a strained face from a strained soul. It should not be like throwing out all your inner garbage – even though such chaotic purging can have its liberating effects, but those are more therapeutic and not related to acting. No, acting has to find the way into a form that is eager to impart meanings and capable of doing so. So it certainly is not Kathakali, but it is on the way to Kathakali, which after all has coded its highly stylized means of expression out of imitative, descriptive, symbolic everyday gestures.

Then came fat Mr. Nair,[14] or rather he did not arrive just then, he had been there all along and had called on slides and Kathakali dancers and musicians to illustrate his lecture, which was a good general introduction to Kathakali. Then he added introductory words about tonight's presentation, and I am not sure that I am still as curious after that introduction as I was beforehand, but that is just stupidity and arrogance on my part, for I know well and have experienced what rubbish we say about Kālidāsa if we have

14 This may have either been D. Appukuttan Nair (1924–94) or M.K.K. Nair (1930–87), both enthusiasts and scholars of Kathakali.

to give an introduction about him back home. So, first has to come the astonishment and admiration that *Faust* takes place here, in Kathakali and not based on Marlowe or the popular Faust book, but derived (however derivatively) from Goethe's play. I wonder whether the Goethe Institute/Max Mueller Bhavan doesn't have a hand in the conception; after all, they also wanted to do Goethe's *Faust* with Vijaya in Bombay during the Goethe anniversary year – whereupon I leapt and was left hanging in mid-air, because the most numb of all skulls ever sent into cultural diplomatic service by the GDR, that dim-witted cultural attaché Schwarzbach, did not waste a thought on it, did not stir a finger, and made no connections to Germanists at universities here to make that experiment of *Faust* in India happen. Now, someone will surely do it, because that is the experience here: whatever innovation is introduced, it is copied and varied by the dozen – that's how it was after the Bombay *Chalk Circle* ten years ago.

How the spirit of something like this might look, I can gather from the fat man's introduction yesterday. It's not such a disaster that the fat man made Goethe the minister of finance of the Weimar Republic[15] (who knows what we make out of Indian poets) and what he has to say about *Faust*. I just react in such a know-it-all fashion because I happen to know all this better, but how many at home know it better, and how many things from here do we know worse? Anyhow, he said that Faust wants more and more knowledge and power, and beforehand there was this quarrel with the devil in heaven, where God believes and knows that Faust is good, and the devil knows that he is a licentious villain and always consorts with women and bad people, so that in the end he would belong to the devil. Well, go ahead, says the Almighty, and in order for it to be more dramatic than in Goethe's version with its philosophy, which has prevented the success of the play with audiences, Kathakali is the way to finally bring it to the people, though with some liberties with Goethe's text. That, the fat man said, is what made the play famous beyond its borders and why Goethe with *Faust* belongs at the very top

15 The Weimar Republic is the name given to Germany during its first phase as a democracy between 1918 and 1933. Goethe, by contrast, lived and held political posts in the Duchy of Saxe-Weimar-Eisenach from the 1770s to the 1830s.

with Homer and Dante and Shakespeare and Kālidāsa – because Faust sees reason at the end and repents of the things he has done wrong, and therefore the Almighty can say to the devil, "you see, that's why I take him back into my arms."

Well, then there was a taste from the performance: Faust woos Gretchen. It was a good Kathakali demonstration, but it may just as well have been Moritz woos Maxi, or Romeo woos Juliet, though the dancer was too old for that, but that is fine in Kathakali, where they get better with the passing years due to the longer training, as long as age has not crept into lesser mobility of the facial features. I am indulging in mockery and arrogance here, so I slap myself for it and go now to rehearse scene eight of *Galileo* and will later tonight see the Kathakali *Faust*.

New Delhi, 22 October 1983

There are things worth thinking and talking about from yesterday, when the Kathakali version of "*Dr. Faust* based on Goethe's dramatic poem" took place, apparently eagerly awaited with curiosity at least by intellectuals. We were sitting in the already cool Delhi evening, a full moon at our backs, on the lawn of the IIC. The stage was a raised platform with trees behind reaching into the black night sky, against which the opulent costumes, masks, and crown/helmet/halo-like head dresses of the traditional Kathakali dancers stood out. There was minimal space for the great play and theme – to the left was just enough space for the chanda and maddalam drummers, centre front was the oil lamp that is the only source of light in traditional Kathakali performance spaces; here there were spot lights added. (The sparse light is probably also a reason for the white, beard-like frame around the faces, which not only gives contour to the green, yellow, red face but may also be meant as a light reflector.) The only prop was a stool that could be used as a seat or as the stand for an imagined book.

Now came the performance, which had about as much to do with Goethe's *Faust* as my life does with Rama and Sita. Everything took place in the traditional costumes and masks, which only distinguish between GOOD and EVIL, within the multiple differences between head dresses, colours, scarves with tassels representing garlands and flowers, and then in the make-up: God has a yellow face, the archangels blue ones, Faust is green, Margarete flesh-coloured, and the devils Mephisto and Lucifer (who had been introduced to presumably heighten the dramatic tension) had red faces with very artistic beards and black decorations. The bad guys had bulbous white noses and are the only ones who can make noises (inarticulate ones, of course, meaning noises that spread terror). It all was a delight to behold, including the artful pantomime with its codified language of muscles moved at will, so that an arrested shiver of the cheek muscle or of an eyebrow can send emotions deep under the skin.

At first the lawn had been packed, was still fairly full up to the break, but only a few interested souls remained to the end, and among them some for the following reason: the Kathakali dancers have spent hours getting their costumes, masks, and make-up on, and ten years of gruelling discipline of learning and training, just to be able to begin with Kathakali, so it simply is a question of respect that one remains to the end and leaves the lawn only after the dancers have left.

Other than that, there is nothing much worth reporting – boredom on an evening that was too long, basically for a simple reason grounded in variations on the theme of "content and medium": the dance language of Kathakali, which in its present form dates back two hundred to three hundred years, has its origins in pre-Christian times and has evolved with certain story motifs and plays that had created this medium for their expression, just like other materials, stories, reasons and intentions have created other means and forms, which then have effects back on the content. Thus, nowhere, including in this case, can a grown or handed-down form take in every kind of content with impunity – one is destroyed by the other, in this case Goethe's *Faust* (or any other *Faust* except perhaps the one from the popular book). No, actually each side is destroyed, as could be seen yesterday: the play was no longer a story (not even the one that had been pressed from the Goethe play), and the exciting beauty of Kathakali became depleted of energy and beauty due to the foreign unmastered material. All too soon there was repetition of gestures. If the form, the medium does not take up the challenge offered by the material, the other story, which after all is not just *another* story, but comes from other history, then both go to the dogs. That challenge is exactly what I am taking up with Brecht and folk theatre (though far, far less complicated than attempts at integration in Kathakali): MUTUAL INTERFUSION.

New Delhi, 27 October 1983

In the evening, Rati Bartholomew and Anuradha Kapur (two teachers from the school) took me with them to Delhi University, where the Sangeet Natak Akademi was hosting a troupe from Kerala. It was quite worth describing, and not just because of the exercises in martial arts – though I always half-close my eyes when watching demonstrations where they stab, hit, and throw with knifes, swords, and razor-sharp rolled steel against each other. The show began with a ritual that is still alive among the low-castes in Kerala, in which dancers in masks are possessed by the god to the rousing rhythms of the drums, and then for the villagers and for themselves they ARE the god, to whom they offer thanks and requests in the fullest belief (this is not so remote from the Catholic ritual of communion, where bread and wine ARE flesh and blood of Christ and not just a representation).

It starts with the chosen one sitting on a stool, his feet and legs start twitching as the immense head dress is tied on him, and the helpers must hurry because the twitching moves from the legs to the body, and the process of becoming possessed does not wait for the mask to be finished. Then he stamps, turns around in circles, doing who-knows-what, because the process of becoming indwelt and possessed also takes its psychological time, perhaps in a kind of self-hypnosis. (When I listen to the drums I can understand that they can drive one from oneself – again compared to us: at a Rolling Stones concert and sometimes just in disco dancing, people get so beside themselves that they truly don't know who they are, which of course does not mean that they knew who they were beforehand.) But before this process in which they drive themselves out of themselves and let the god in, they look into a hand mirror as the head dress is put on during the initial twitching, and once the mask in the image of the god is done they recognize the god in the mirror and begin to be that god from that moment on.

It has its own fascination to be present at such a ritual and event, although it – denouncing itself – is a performance in front of people who were not raised in and with this ritual, so it no longer is a ritual but the performance of a ritual and has thus become alien more than alienated, if one becomes too aware of the audience and oneself. It is like descending into the earliest history of mankind and participating at least by seeing and by being moved by the rhythm of the drums, where history is not yet history and yet already history, because it already represents the social existence of people. What I mean, and what I have been reminded of very immediately by yesterday evening's performance, is what I saw in the 10 000-year-old cave drawings in Bhimbetka[16] and now experience similarly: the hunting magic, turning oneself into the animal in order to make the fear of it manageable. And is it then too far-fetched to think that our carnival custom of wearing costumes comes out of the desire to be something other than what we are? So H. going to the ball in the costume of Carmen[17] really believes she has Carmen's charm and seductive power, whose costume she has only borrowed, but whose being she believes to be her own being in the costume. I don't know if H. ever went to the ball as Carmen – I am just using it as example that we, following Brecht's advice of alienation, bring what is alien so close to us as if it were akin to our senses. Thus the alien becomes something comprehended as close to us, and what is close (our joy in dressing in costume) is alienated and becomes clearer in a deeper sense, as something from the beginning of time, as originally and causally present and always repeated as a means to power: the power to defeat one's fear, the power to charm and influence others.

New Delhi, 31 October 1983

Yesterday morning I explained the tenth scene of *Galileo*, we read it and blocked it on stage. It's the scene when Galileo wants to present his book to the Grand Duke, when Rector Gaffone does not greet him anymore, while the iron maker Vanni, who stands and falls with men like Galileo, offers to take him out of the country, the Cardinal Inquisitor greets him not without respect, and the court can no longer withstand the wishes of the Inquisition, which wants to interrogate the great scholar in Rome. I had fun analyzing the scene and letting them look into history and see how Brecht builds situations and weaves a play like a precious carpet, and what joy of discovery and recognition this yields.

There was great attention and the joyful affect of insight among those who had read or heard a bit of Marx; big astonished eyes

---

16 The Stone Age cave paintings in Bhimbetka, Madhya Pradesh, are a UNESCO World Heritage Site. Some of them are thought to be up to 30 000 years old.

17 The reference here is to the gypsy title character of Georges Bizet's opera *Carmen*, which premiered in Paris in 1875.

among those who have not experienced anything of the world and had up to now never experienced the world like that. I look into those eyes and see not a trace of contact with our history and thinking (but also nothing of their own life world among some – interest in the world and in human beings does not arise spontaneously, and even less so a way of thinking and experiencing that orders the world and integrates us into the recognition of our duties and tasks [...]). Well, if I look into this empty nothingness, which is NOT the nothing of absence of interest(s), my God, I could think: it's all for nothing and every day is a waste of intellectual effort, but no, when I see in their eyes that they want to know ....

But how to even begin with the basic building blocks of explaining and providing insight into the world, when even the factual knowledge about history needed to understand the field of tension between humans and the consequences for us today, when the European Renaissance is remote from them in terms of knowledge and as cultural experience (just as Akbar and Ashoka and the Ajanta cave paintings are remote for us)?[18] This cannot be a reproach, just a realization that I could have had beforehand, because I knew that here and in the present state of the school no comparison is possible. If it were possible, it could just be a comparison with PETA and their *Galileo*, which they tackled at a similarly young age but with a different understanding about the world and different goals for the world through playing theatre, and, of course, more points of contact with European history. The Philippines became Catholic with the Spaniards long ago. So, here in Delhi in the school, we would have needed the realization that two or three scenes could bring more comprehended and comprehensible results, though on the other hand only the knowledge of the ENTIRE play and its exploration can bring insights into the world as process, and into the many and multicausal contradictions in it and in human beings. Still, it cannot and will not become a full-fledged production of *Galileo*.

---

18 Jalal-ud-Din Muhammad Akbar (1542–1605) was the third Mughal emperor of India and renowned for his political achievements, cultural patronage, and religious tolerance. Ashoka (ca. 304–232 BC) was an Indian emperor of the Maurya dynasty who embraced Buddhism and was instrumental in its spread as a world religion. The Ajanta caves in Maharashtra are a UNESCO World Heritage Site containing famous rock-cut monuments, sculptures and paintings which depict scenes from Buddhist mythology.

New Delhi, 2 November 1983

What happened at work yesterday? Nothing unpleasant with *Othello*, nothing remarkable either. It was a normal process with normal progress and the familiar difficulties of a conception of theatre that leaves out human beings and opinions when it ingests and spews out words without sense. There was a weariness in *Galileo* and it did not really get off the ground. There are difficulties there now that I cannot simply sweep aside mentally, because I myself have loaded them onto my back when I was under no obligation to do this work. If not a word was said or known about the work and the author before I arrived, I should not be surprised that not everyone knows what a model of the solar system is, and that there was one with the earth at the centre and then one that banished earth from the centre, and I should not marvel that they do not know that this had social and historical consequences because class and power interests were touched by it. I should be even less surprised when volumes of Karl Marx's *Capital* lie on the table as props, brought by the students from the costume department, where the props are kept, while in the library of the school the books of Marx are NOT to be found. I have to teach them that, too, and can hardly dare to tell people at home about this, because the (understandable) reaction would be: "how can you do that play at all, then?!" But a start must be made in inspiring the right thinking and not just thinking in general – and that, at least, I do.

I cram my days full of work, first and foremost because all the work is steering towards a good result. When I leave the house in the morning to go across to the Rabindra Bhavan,[19] the day is really already over, I do not notice during work how the hours pass, because I need constant, alert attention, even if I am feeling more at home in Hindi every day.

Sometimes I ask myself about what will have to be and will be [...] when I won't be able to work and have an effect through my work anymore. But is that the question? There are the other circles – Weimar and Dresden and certainly also Leipzig. But all that is not the question. The wide world – even if I traverse it in

19 Rabindra Bhavan is a building near the NSD and seat of the Sahitya Akademi, the national Indian academy of letters. Bennewitz was using rehearsal space there.

a fairly narrow circle – and the breadth of thought in the other life here is different and makes for a different life. I am afraid of the narrow thoughts of many narrow-minded people at home. And there is the more fundamental task of slowly withdrawing from life – I am not talking and thinking about death, but moving from the experience of having a quiet effect on the world to being less needed. I have been highly indulged by life. I have led a communist life and a privileged one through deep contact with the world. I did not call all that much attention to myself in the world, in order to be able to have an effect on it from within it. That has to do with the fact that I don't go to a fancy hotel here, I am reluctant to demand things, and I am also tired of interviews. I don't want to come to my work and to those I work with from outside, and this integrates me into life here and gives meaning to my work, so that even this year, where it is under very difficult conditions, I am not casting my seeds onto stony ground.

New Delhi, 6 November 1983

With the following passage, Bennewitz concludes some reflections that seem to justify (self-)censoring reportage about inner conflicts in India and the Philippines in order to focus on the role of these countries in resisting US imperialism:

Internal politics need to be subordinate when it is a question of the survival of mankind. I know that. Those are the coordinates within which I have to see my work, and that's why *Galileo* is more important than *The Mother* can be now. It would be worth inviting an audience even to just a reading of *Galileo*. Since the play not only expresses a warning of the global holocaust but also radically grasps the reasons that lead to the catastrophe at their roots, it does not just provide a warning of the consequences but also deeper insight into the causes, which lie in social systems. So there are not just references to US imperialism but also to the questioning of orders that need to be questioned but are not allowed to be questioned now. It all sounds so complicated but is really very simple. And that is the reason (and not just because we need a diversion from the shock-value news in our papers) why we need reporting from countries outside of Europe about the global encircling strategy of the USA, and

> why the reports need to concentrate on the growing consciousness and protest in those countries, rather than news about earthquakes or cyclones or snakebites or calves with two heads. That's when I understand the position of my work in public. It is not underground work, but absolutely not work in the foreground that is suitable for headlines like a victory by a swimmer or a concert at the Gewandhaus.[20]

New Delhi, 11 November 1983

Bennewitz concludes his discussion of the case of the student playing Andrea Sarti, Jitendra Shastri, who is overly intense in his identification with the role, to the point of pathology:

> What affects me is how [...] the program of instincts enters here with the Third Theatre[21] and, with the kind of national emotional character that [...] leaves no protective layer between the self and the world, finds a mass of predisposed victims. The slogans from the circles of the unemployed and indolent Mandi House intellectuals demanding a theatre of biological reflexes, freedom of instincts, and death to reason and "intellectual" theatre are entering the school. We know from our own history and from the history of mass murder that intellectualism was shouted down and defamed and mocked when intelligence and reason were the actual targets for denunciation. There are articles, written by writers who have not digested information and read without understanding, about work experiences with Peter

---

20 The Gewandhaus is a famous concert hall in Leipzig, Germany and home to the prestigious Leipzig Gewandhaus Orchestra.

21 Bennewitz does not make explicit whether he is referring to Eugenio Barba's or Badal Sircar's concept of "Third Theatre" here. Barba began formulating his conception of a theatre different from both commercial and avant-garde forms in 1976. The concept is related to his theatre anthropology and to his method of theatrical barter and focuses on the creation of autonomous meaning independent of cultural constraints (see Barba, "The Legacy"). Sircar developed his conception in the early to mid 1970s and published his book *The Third Theatre* in 1978. He sought with his group Satabdi to combine elements from urban and rural styles and to thus overcome what he perceived as the staleness and limitations of narrative proscenium theatre. The context here and later references by Bennewitz make it likely that he is referring to Barba's conception.

Brook in the African experiment *Ik*, and there are simplistic anti-reactions to primitive descriptions of a Stanislavskian method lacking training or a true discovery of acting. There is the magic phrase "creative opening" – "something is happening within me" – and above all there is the world that is not understood and is hard to see through, the refused experience of the self in this society, the thousand barriers of tradition, superstition, and the evil of personality deformation by the world of consumer goods and consumption, the growing distance between human beings and their products, and the general lack of insight into processes.

How extremely important this makes Brecht: to make the invisible visible. Of course, the escapism is understandable, even though it is deadly because it is without effect, this way out of the pressures of non-recognition, of not being acknowledged, of not being active and needed, out of the daily frustration into the self-deception of seeming self-recognition when there is a diffuse creative opening. Sure, it is not all that simple and not grasped or understandable with the categories of left vs. right, up vs. down, true vs. false. We, too, have degraded Brecht to a mathematical equation without unknown variables. The old way remains the newest, leading through Shakespeare to Brecht into the world.

New Delhi, 16 November 1983

Here is something worth thinking about: you remember my shock and astonishment in America about the main phrase of communication for actors: "what do you want me to do and how?" Yesterday, an actor here asked: "Sir, may I move my hands at that point?" Imagine him asking that! That's how they were taught, that's how they have been placed on stage – where and how should independent thinking and decision-making enter the profession, and responsibility? I do not alienate the situation enough: it is not so long ago that we did not know any better. It is the director's own insecurity that lets him put the actors in such a straight jacket and lead them on a tight leash. My first director's notebooks prescribed even the movements of the small finger. Moreover, their traditional theatre and the *Natya Shastra* have fixed rules that can be learned and followed. But there is a difference there: in Kathak and Kathakali and in the rule book of the *Natya Shastra*, there are rules that are ingrained by training for years, so that then even within the force of prescription performing becomes free steps and free speech.

New Delhi, 20 November 1983

The set designer is talented but unreliable and lazy [...], and they draw up neither set designs nor detailed construction plans here. They just go to the workshop and tell the carpenter or metal worker what should be done and how, and then they do it, and often very well, because craftspeople here still carry out their craft as an art and not as a business. They work with love for the products coming from their own hands. Capitalism will destroy that, too. When I think about the terrible world and that I work on a play that shows how it began to develop into today's terror, I also think of many contradictions, e.g., how can it be pleasurable to discover how terrible the world is and what it has brought about between human beings. For this is what happens in work like mine: the deeper the insight into the truth of such a world, the more pleasurably satisfying that insight becomes, which of course does not mean taking pleasure in what is terrible and bad, but in discovery. But the next contradiction follows: what consequences does this have? What do I do with my anger about the world? What does it achieve? Is the work I do here to help others reach this experience of anger already the answer to those questions? From the work on *Galileo* I can report similarly pleasurable experiences, even if there the pleasure is easier to define: for the students the play is also a medium, because unexpectedly, after six trouble-makers had been asked to leave, the others had the experience of having effects. This is a retrospective justification for my decision – which of course is not a source of pleasure and goes against the very experience of Galileo. He does not do his experiments to find out THAT he is right but WHETHER.

New Delhi, 23 November 1983

My Hindi is still cumbersome and not fluid in daily life, but at work it flows freely and well-comprehended into my ear, and not just for fun little things like the two lines of the soldier song I translated myself. It goes into very fine detail, e.g., when Emilia, in that absurd situation with Othello nearly putting his own doom into her mouth, swears to him on her own life that there is no more faithful woman in all the world than Desdemona, and he hears it echo in his own depths, that what Emilia says could be true. He goes away from Emilia and says to himself quietly: "tis strange" – and something was not right in the *Gestus* of the actor, and I thought and thought and listened and listened, and I heard that the Hindi word has just two short vowels, which of course cannot carry the meaning and atmosphere of this moment, this meeting of someone else's report and his own deep inner experience. The word is "ajab" (which you know from the title of the Marathi *Chalk Circle* adaptation: *Ajab Nyaya Vartulacha*, the "strange judgment with the circle," and also from the name of the Azdak character: Ajabdas). And so I thought and said, my God, don't you have that other form, which sounds softer and carries the breath longer, and I said it and it was right, with a long "i" at the end (Ajeeb). Or there was the time in *Galileo* when a logical contrast did not have enough force, and I heard that the problem was that they had a word for "because" in the translation that has several sharp "i"s – "isliye" – instead of the stronger, more gestural "kyon-ki."

Of course in previous years I was finished faster with productions because I was not able to enter into the language, which is one reason, but not the only one. Here and now I can and have to work hours on a single word or expression, because there is the ingrained bad habit of playing just with the vocal chords, and the vocal chords are connected only to themselves and the words and sentences learned by heart and then no longer thought through; they are not connected to the cornea, the heart muscle, and the grey cells.

New Delhi, 25 November 1983

Of course the set and before that the conception for *Othello* came from the Weimar production in 1974; the stage has the four towers with spot lights and the platform in between and the curtain that is swayed by wind and tears open, and casts harsh light on the end at the beginning. Yet the same is not the same, it is different, very different not only through different actors, but through a world that has evolved differently. Would I have read and produced the play as so politically charged already in 1974? And yet it is exactly this that brings out the love story more deeply. Again something has been written into a vision that would not give enough material for an image to even the liveliest imagination. Besides, I have grown older, which counts and pays in experience; in some respects I am also more behind things, meaning, I have experiences and expectations from life behind me whose facts, beauty, and necessity thereby become more precious to grasp. Also, I am less distracted here in my – admittedly more difficult, but perhaps therefore more beautiful – work.

[...]

It was in Kerala, where I watched some show as guest of the government, and there were delegates from a lawyers' congress sitting next to me. We made conversation and I remember a sentence one of them said without contradiction by the others, namely that they would never watch *Othello* (I don't remember how we got to *Othello* in 1973), because there are dead people on stage and even a murder. That has to do with a long historical tradition: in Sanskrit theatre, death on stage is taboo. You know this from *Mudrārākshasa*, that the worst cruelties, the least among which is sending out the poison girls, play a significant role in the intrigues of state, but all of that is only reported, nothing is physically shown on stage. Of course, times have changed and with them the things possible on stage have changed. I only mention it because that, too, can play a role (among others) when what has been alienated might appear estranging. And we don't know to what extent the questions WHY and HOW things come to such bad ends are embedded in public consciousness and interest. Just think how quickly the questions WHY and HOW Buchenwald became possible can slip from our consciousness and interest. And here we are trying to create this kind of consciousness in the first place. That's where the advantage of the merciless light towers and the raised platform with their definite boundaries comes in: that the actor cannot hide behind or in anything, that he is put on the witness stand. With that, the story and – as my assistant Atul, for whom the platform and towers at first were foreign, said yesterday – human beings and their relations and actions appear as under a magnifying glass.

New Delhi, 29 November 1983

Once again, what hardships of the most desperate kind have been endured with *Galileo*, which have been definitely worth it!

> The most beautiful and important argument came from the Indian students: this work and this production are a great encouragement for us, to be able to do such a difficult and important play with just fifteen actors, props that can be made anywhere, the simplest costumes and without make-up and glitter, and to do it ANYWHERE. That is one of the important points I have been demonstrating here since the *Midsummer Night's Dream* experiment, that the most challenging play can be played on planks laid across barrels, when the WHY, WHEREFORE, and WHAT of the play have been grasped. Essentially, I learned it from them. I remember how it started in Bombay (no, please, don't remind me of the set weighing tons that Alkazi had made for me for the 1970 *Threepenny Opera*), where I wanted to convince Vijaya to at least use gates for the *Chalk Circle*, then renounced them with difficulty and wanted to push through at least two columns to hint at castle and church – and with how much patient insistence she convinced me that in such theatre we do not need anything besides the actor, and that sometimes we can even leave props to the imagination. The usefulness of this material restraint for the actors' purposes promotes our shared purposes. As I have repeatedly written in the letters: everything is new for them, and most often through it they are new to themselves. And the book that records what happens in this process remains unwritten.

Bennewitz would likely have enjoyed the irony of including this last sentence in a book documenting the process of his cross-cultural work in India. This process seems to have yielded relatively successful results once again during this Delhi stay despite Bennewitz's own misgivings. While this evaluation of success has to rely exclusively on his own words for the student production of *The Life of Galileo*, we have some external evidence to consider in the case of the Rep's *Othello*. Three extant reviews of the production are all thoroughly positive, all stressing the effectiveness of the simple stage set to present the characters of the play in an unusual perspective (Bajeli; Chander, "Simplicity"; Sinha). Romesh Chander explicitly addressed the political nature of this perspective, commenting that "Bennewitz has the Company highlight not so much the characters but the 'monstrous world' around them" ("Simplicity"). This interpretation is supported by interviews the author conducted in 2012 with three faculty members of NSD, who all had either been involved in the production or had seen it. Kirti Jain argues that the play became far more political than in the earlier NSD production directed by Ebrahim Alkazi, because "the racial part was much more highlighted, Othello's insecurity as an outsider was much more highlighted." Tripurari Sharma agrees that Bennewitz stressed Othello's status as an outsider and argues that he did not sentimentalize the character's pain and suffering. She recalls that Bennewitz designed the play in very geometrical lines and patterns to frame the characters in their social positioning and dynamics. B.S. Patil, who played Rodrigo in the production, argues that Bennewitz highlighted the critique of materialism already present in Shakespeare's text. He also recalls that the production made Shakespeare communicable even to rural audiences during the subsequent tour of *Othello*. Overall, then, the stay seems to have yielded some fruitful results despite the problems and misgivings Bennewitz reported. This positive summary, however, is somewhat tempered by a comment from Bennewitz in a 1988 interview typescript, in which he agrees with the interviewer's negative assessment of a later guest performance of the *Othello* production, arguing that by then it had gone "off track and after one year out of the director's control" (Interview Kolkata, 1988). This sentiment is echoed in one of the letters below from his stay at the NSD the following year.

New Delhi, 1984/5: Shakespeare, *Hamlet* and Sophocles/Brecht, *Antigone*

Bennewitz came back to NSD a year later and stayed from early November 1984 to early January 1985. The initial plan had been to produce Shakespeare's *Twelfth Night* with the students in the third year. On the recommendation of NSD director Mohan Maharishi, who warned Bennewitz that the students of that class were neither talented nor disciplined enough for this task, he decided to do only a scene-based seminar with them, including some work on Sophocles's *Antigone*. However, when he agreed to Maharishi's request to also produce Shakespeare's *Hamlet* with the students in second year, those in third year revolted and were pacified with the promise to accomplish a full production of *Antigone*. Bennewitz had hoped to use Brecht's adaptation of Friedrich Hölderlin's German translation of the drama, but he had to wait until well into his stay for the hastily prepared Hindi translation of this German version, and that translation then turned out to be incomprehensible. So he finally reverted to another available Hindi version of the Sophocles text. The resulting production seems not to have been performed publicly but rather only internally for members of the NSD, again in part due to the fact that among the third-year students, the discipline problems of the previous year continued and hampered the production further. As some of the following passages show, the story was very different for the second-year group and their performance of *Hamlet*, which additionally profited from the first guest visit to NSD by Franz Havemann, a set designer from the German National Theatre and close colleague of Bennewitz, who contributed to the set and lighting design for the production.

Bennewitz's Delhi sojourn that year was framed by two important sets of events in the recent history of India: the assassination of Prime Minister Indira Gandhi by two of her Sikh bodyguards on 31 October 1984 with the subsequent retaliation pogroms against Sikhs and eventual election of her son Rajiv Gandhi, and during Bennewitz's stay the poison gas disaster in Bhopal.[22] He commented extensively on these events, having close personal links to both. He had personally met Indira Gandhi, who had moreover been instrumental in fostering the ties between India and the GDR that enabled Bennewitz's work. The Bhopal disaster, whose full horror only gradually became apparent during the latter part of December, was even more poignant since he had close working ties to the place and was heading there immediately after finishing his work in Delhi.

New Delhi, 20 November 1984

Explaining the world is fun, as is this ever-new climbing around in plays that seemed done and known and yet always offer new views down into their depths and through them onto the world when they are touched in new ways. And every excursion into a situation, a relationship, an event, a character ends in the conception of the human being, who is always worth it. I see again and again that Brecht was a very tender man; his truths are heartfelt, full of hope and trust in humans, especially where they live through murder. The reason for this touching one so closely here is probably due to the recent spate of killings, which, however, is no longer so easily put down to religious fanaticism. How many Hindu families gave their Sikh brothers protection and shelter in their houses when the mob – youthful gangs, easily organized under the mantle of

---

22 During the night from 2 to 3 December 1984, a chemical plant managed by the Indian subsidiary of the American Union Carbide Corporation accidentally released poisonous gas over Bhopal that killed thousands of the city's residents and injured hundreds of thousands more. The incident is considered one of the worst industrial disasters in history.

public pain – burned and killed. It is becoming clear again and again: a different world must come. Basically ours. But, oh, what mankind still has to go through until then. People, cars, and houses set on fire may not remain the worst, if the murder of conviction, opinion, conscience, and judgment by the commercialized and commercializing media continues unabated.

New Delhi, 23 November 1984

I think it was foolish to commit so quickly to working in both class years, not because of doubling the work but because of halving the time available to do it. Maybe I'm also just tired of students for a while, because yesterday the effectiveness and meaning of my work with troupes like Rangmandal in Bhopal was confirmed; they have the play running for a year and longer and tour with it through the country, and besides, they want to do theatre. Since there is so little professional theatre in the country, the personal motivation for the students in the school is FILM, and you can see that in their faces in the last few years. Under Alkazi the educational background of the students was decisive for their acceptance into the school, and they were exposed to hard discipline and well thought out training with excellent teaching. With Karanth came a new quality because he brought in students from far afield in Assam and the interior of Karnataka, which brought faces and attitudes of Indian life and thought into the school. Of course, Karanth himself was more of a practicing artist than a director and organizer. Now that he has gone, the school under the rhino B.M. Shah has neither program nor face and certainly no theatre, including in the expectations of the students for their careers after graduation, and so film and television have put their stamp on the faces and the attitudes towards learning.

New Delhi, 25 November 1984

The work IS a joy, because – as a necessary precondition – discipline has improved very much compared to the chaos and anarchy of last year, and because there is always enough curiosity to also formulate questions and opinions. (This leads to the tea break becoming long, also because we have to go to the tea stall on the corner, since the delivery of tea to the rehearsal room has yet to be organized again). Work is also better because far-reaching questions are more likely to be broached, like yesterday about the general difficulty that materialist dialectics have in entering into the grown conceptual structures here and changing opinions and attitudes. The contradiction within this contradiction is this: since dialectics are not an invented law, but a discovered one (and can therefore be an instruction for actions appropriate to reality), they are naïvely grasped, used, and confirmed at the bottom of society, where life is unalienated, while conscious actions express themselves in moulded patterns, e.g., in not questioning the world outside or in the home – it is the habitual, moulded attitude of ACCEPTANCE (always useful for the rulers, and facilitating survival for the ruled), i.e., the present existence is accepted within the given conditions.

New Delhi, 4 December 1984

Yesterday's nine-to-nine working day was well spent, particularly with the second year students, whose curiosity picks on me like on a ripe fruit and who have new questions for every answer: Does the king love the queen? When did their affair start? Aren't we all Hamlets? And the unavoidable question, posed by a student from Calcutta: "we wanted to learn from Hamlet how to rebel against society, so what social relevance and consequences does the play have today?" This, by the way, led to an interesting discussion about dangerous tendencies in commercial Hindi film, which increasingly turns to social questions – also as a selling point, of course – and finds ample material about social injustice for the script. Then they shoot Michael-Kohlhaas-stories[23] from that material (of course superficially cheap and plucking on the heartstrings) about the self-helper in an unjust world, which ultimately and in short-circuit fashion leads to the justification of individual terror. These are questions whose answers I cannot simply pull from Santa's bag, because the answers unavoidably lead deeper into the play and into life and the world and become a further occasion for my own pleasure in new discoveries. If only there wouldn't be so damn little time, and if only it wasn't supposed to have a public performance as its conclusion, but naturally they want to show what they can do and what they have learned.

23 *Michael Kohlhaas* is a novella by German author Heinrich von Kleist (1777–1811), in which the horse trader Kohlhaas, after being denied juridical redress of an injustice committed against him, takes justice into his own hands and, in doing so, resorts to acts of terror.

New Delhi, 5 December 1984

Of course, it would be and is interesting to find out how Hamlet as character and play can be read into history and the soul here. It seems as if he is a very Indian figure, if the interpretation as ditherer were even slightly correct – but is in fact an entirely un-Indian figure, if the possibility in the play is of the angry young man who strikes all about him in his knowledge of and disgust with the world, because the fundamental attitude here that has become nature through the tradition of centuries is ACCEPTANCE, non-revolt. So it is not a lack of understanding if the recognition that the world is out of joint is not formulated as a disaster that needs to be averted, but instead as "if the world is like that, out of joint, then that must be accepted." This is not a conscious, purposeful conception, not a learned ideology, but an acquired reaction, a reflex-like response – which of course can be broken by insight and ideology, but that means offering the stomach a dish it does not know, and then the stomach reacts like a vegetarian to beef [...]. However, all this takes time and cannot be done as a quick fix, because in addition most of them still read the text as words and not as meaning, let alone as opinion. Does that sound like a reproach? No, it is a thought intended to identify reasons. Theatre here comes from other traditions, and between these traditions and today lies the fateful influence of a misunderstood Stanislavski, through whom they are being taught (as the *Othello* experience last year showed) to suck in the world so that it can be found again in the soul; but it then often goes down the wrong pipe and lands in the stomach and guts, and then it is excreted the wrong way. By the way, the *Othello*, which gave me such birthing pains and which then became a show – in a few performances at least – appropriate to the play and to realities here, is reported to have gotten out of control so badly after leaving my hands that only unbearable melodrama remained.

New Delhi, 7 December 1984

It is always newly astonishing how, when the knot has been untied, when the bud has opened, the pathway from the head into the feet is shorter here than at home [...]. It probably has something to do with their more immediate connection – living and playing – to the world. They have less trouble extricating themselves from ideological slings and inhibitions. Philosophy, too, is more a matter of the gut than the head. Life in general is more unconstrained, which certainly is a question of a different culture and mentality, but not fundamentally. Rather, much more fundamentally, culture and mentality are a question of class. From the lower middle class on up the differences are blended together, and hardly any outward signs remain for differentiation – only the brown skin, because it can't be washed off. It always comes back to the question what world culture can, should, must, and will look like – the crossing of borders by consumer goods erases the beauty of differences, and what has grown and been handed down by tradition will soon only survive in preserves – is that ideological, cultural nostalgia?

New Delhi, 9 December 1984

For the past two to three years, increasingly I have had to persuade myself of the SENSE of what I am doing and can do here. [...] My impact in the country stems from my achievements in the 1970s, which have become a matter of history and are the reason why I am invited to non-theatrical organizations such as schools, colleges, universities either as chief guest or for a lecture, seminar, or discussion, and why I appear in interviews and reviews in theatre journals. They have become an historical variable in the positive sense of past achievements continuing to have an impact, i.e., the impact of my current work is limited and really only exists through the pioneering work of the 1970s. That is also the reason why I don't go into my days with the same "wake up my heart and sing" kind of joy, especially since with the time pressure under which the work takes place, it cannot be oriented towards a result and towards experimentation in a way that could bring it publicity beyond the small radius of the school. Otherwise I could have entered new territory with the Brecht version of *Antigone*, or I could have given an impulse with my Shakespeare interpretation at least in the wider inner circle of experts. There is not just the factor of limited time but also the fact that it is teaching matter rather than evidence for the public when I have to do a difficult play, the discovery of its relevance in a different culture and in a world shared by all, with second year students for whom it is news that hearing and seeing are basic prerequisites for the art of acting. This is not a complaint or reproach, just sober knowledge about the limited pleasure with which I can expect to continue working here. Besides, my work here is nearing the critical fifteen year mark [...]. What will be my new circle of activity?

New Delhi, 17 December 1984

Bennewitz reports from a theatre festival organized by the Sangeet Natak Akademi:

The irrelevances of the previous days became a nuisance on Sunday afternoon with the performance of the Calcutta Living Theatre.[24] The whole thing would be excusable if it had some naïvité, but it lays claim to "creativity" and is exhibitionistic in the worn-out ritual of the actors showing the audience their relaxation exercises for ten minutes before the play begins. It claims ambitiously to portray "our society as woman sees and suffers it," and that turns into political and aesthetic shallowness, so that after the performance I know no more and no better than before, or than the man in the street, who experiences it before he finds out about it from the newspaper and television: that women are still oppressed and exploited in myriad ways, and that the declarations of equality by men are still hypocritical (even in our socialist world now and then and often very much so). All this is presented in variations with at times beautiful contortions of the body, but it is ideologically lightweight and a falsification by simplification, as if it were men who oppress women rather than society through men. Oh, well.

Afterwards, there was an hour's break until the next performance, and that was THE event of these days, to which "winners" of regional competitions have come, often from far away – it was a Tamil adaptation of *Antigone*, and as I am just reading from the header of the invitation letter that you forwarded to me, it was conceived and excitingly directed by an assistant professor of the Tamil University of Thanjavur with a troupe from Madurai (Nija Nataka Iyakkam). Now the time is too short to report this almost historical event, to my knowledge and in my impression and judgment the most successful adaptation of a play from classical antiquity into the national and local culture here.

24 The Living Theatre was a group for politically activist theatre founded by Probir Guha (b. 1945) in 1977 in Khardah, an industrial suburb of Kolkata, and renamed Alternative Living Theatre in 1991.

New Delhi, 1 January 1985

> Miracles continue to take place here, and this is another one, which rightfully demands the question: is it just because it is the most recent birth, the one conceived last? The *Chalk Circle* in Bhopal, the *Macbeth*, the *Galileo*, and the *Chalk Circle* in Manila, and the *Midsummer Night's Dream* and *Puntila* here now have a brother in *Hamlet* who at least resembles them. Aside from some rhythm problems in the final scene, the dress rehearsal yesterday was an EVENT of a kind that makes me wish the superstition connected to such good dress rehearsals to the devil. I saw the performance yesterday, and that is enough – that's how I think this morning, and am not sure whether I will think the same way tonight if the child does not appear in front of the audience as beautifully as it was conceived and born. The boy who plays Hamlet,[25] and who cost me so much effort to maintain the faith, is proving himself to be a rare talent, and this second year in general is such a fortunately talented and composed group as it only occurs once in a generation.

In the event, the premiere of *Hamlet* did not live up to the potential of the brilliant dress rehearsal. Bennewitz writes that the performance was so weak that he left already after the first half, though the NSD director came to the hotel after the show to tell him that it got much better in the second half (New Delhi, 2 Jan. 1985). His next report is of a brilliant second public performance, much to the chagrin of the jealous third-year students, who even cancelled an in-house performance of *Antigone* without notifying him (New Delhi, 3 Jan. 1985). The final letters from Delhi report very enthusiastic responses to the production from audiences, critics, and his GDR diplomat friends, the Fischers (New Delhi, 4 and 5 Jan. 1985). Kavita Nagpal in the *Hindustan Times* of 7 January 1985 called the production convincing and wrote of the second-year students that "Director Fritz Bennewitz of the GDR charged yet another group with particles of his vehement commitment." By then, Bennewitz had already moved on to Bhopal and his work there under the cloud (nearly literally and certainly figuratively) of the gas disaster.

25 This was Piyush Mishra.

Fig. 14 Bennewitz with the cast in front of the stage set (designed by Franz Havemann and clearly inspired by Pieter Bruegel and Hieronymus Bosch) for the production of Shakespeare's *Hamlet* in Hindi at the National School of Drama, New Delhi, 1984–5. Courtesy of Fritz-Bennewitz-Archiv, Leipzig.

Bhopal, 1985: Shakespeare, *A Midsummer Night's Dream*

Bennewitz stayed in Bhopal from 5 January to 10 February 1985 to work with the Rangmandal troupe at the Bharat Bhavan on a production of Shakespeare's *A Midsummer Night's Dream* in a Hindi translation by Raghuvir Sahay under the title *Bagaro Basanta Hai.* His assistant director was Atul Tiwari. This sojourn in Bhopal was deeply marked by the recent gas disaster. However, the following passages show that Bennewitz was also touched by his renewed relationship with his two "miracle men," the folk actors Dwarika Prasad and Amar Singh, as well as by his intensive engagement with Shakespeare's text. Both encounters led to profound interpretations and reflections, including on Bennewitz's own cross-cultural role and methods.

Bhopal, 6 January 1985

It is strange to land and drive into this city, where the sky is blue today and the lake still, and yet mass death took place here only a month and a few days ago.

Bhopal, 7 January 1985

I don't know how to explain and describe it: after I had arrived in the city yesterday and moved into the guest house of the Bharat Bhavan, I just had to go out alone into the old city and through the lanes, where the long rows of closed store fronts are not a result of it being Sunday, which usually does not close any stores anyway; it was like walking through a cemetery in order to honour the dead who are murder victims in a war in the midst of seeming peace – the class war of profit-hungry multinationals, who use the people of the Third World as lab animals [...].

[...]

I don't know whether I read it into the faces from my own emotions or whether it isn't really inscribed in their fear which will remain for the rest of their lives and which has marked them.

I am also writing the letter to put off dealing with the *Midsummer Night's Dream*, though that's not true at all; rather, I have to force myself into my encounter with the text, and I am finding an entry point where the play is cruel – which it also is. So, for now the encounter with the play is an obligation and task, not yet a pleasure.

But then there is also this: yesterday in the street one of the Rangmandal troupe saw me from far off and ran down the street into my arms with tears of joy that I am here, saying that I have to come to his house for dinner today; and just now he was here together with others he had met along the way. Something like that can and must be an entry point into the highly difficult work.

Even such strange, quite absurd thoughts as the following push forward to prevent me from immediately occupying myself with the *Midsummer Night's Dream*: I can remember the dreams of last night with their changing images as if they were true experiences, including the dream of a moment where a cloud laid itself across me like suffocating cotton wool, with choking arms and a laughing face – not at all an absurd image, but what is absurd is that since waking up I have had difficulties swallowing, which can either be attributed to the change in weather with the slightly cold night in Bhopal – even though I have a comforter here, but no heating for room and water as in the hotel in Delhi – or to the fact that an all too strong imagination can have temporary physical effects.

[...]

How quickly it happens: last night I was still dreaming of *Hamlet*, and now I have already made the transition to Bhopal – no, not yet to this city, the cloud is everywhere – to Rangmandal and to the entry into the *Midsummer Night's Dream*. In the encounter with the people of Rangmandal, who awaited me on the lawn and carried me on their shoulders down and into the Bharat Bhavan, the joy they expressed in that manner is the measure for my responsibility to give that joy back to them through newly experiencing themselves in their work.

Bhopal, 8 January 1985

Bennewitz concludes the description of a play he saw at a theatre festival of the state Madhya Pradesh:

Lakshman and Sita came onto the middle platform, and the light went out. Even Rama could not help, but at least he was on the side of the exploited and not of the rich. It was at the borderline down towards the unbearable, even though there was applause in between and laughter when there were lines about current events. Again it is hard to comprehend (but then again not that hard) that something like that can occur among a people who are naturally gifted for the performing arts, where one is moved to tears when folk theatre takes place. But that is the point: this was not folk theatre; rather, the class problem shines through here: this "theatre" is far removed from the people already, in the middle between classes, where even good will degenerates through the striving for higher things, which takes away spontaneity and the joy of playing as a life form. And just as their own attitude to life is an imitation of those above rather than a continuation from below, in other words a clichéd conduct of life, by the same token their gestures, gait, and tone of voice are also copied from clichés that have been coined by film. This is a form of cultural murder, too.

Now I have to travel far back in the letter and in my thoughts in order to find my way in both, which were interrupted yesterday. There was this thought that led straight into the *Midsummer Night's Dream*, in continuation of a sentence by Marx. I wanted to say that the laboriousness of all emancipation is also due to the fact that those to be emancipated themselves only grasp the historical task of their emancipation slowly, and rarely spontaneously. They prevent or retard the ending of their oppression because ideology and long habituation (the reason for Brecht's alienation) make them shore it up through acceptance and adaptation. What manifests itself in the *Midsummer Night's Dream* as a problem between the sexes must be made recognizable as a general problem of ALL emancipation. Of course, it also has its specific weight as a problem between the sexes here in this male-dominated society, which historically has been perpetuated by class since the replacement of matriarchy by patriarchy, as can be read in Engels' *The Origin of the Family, Private Property, and the State.*

And that's how the play begins, too, when Theseus drags Hippolyta home as war booty and the wedding announced for four days hence is the festival of her final submission, celebrated with pomp and games. On this occasion the Mechanicals perform their play of true love and fidelity, which the assembled society cannot and does not want to understand. Without transposing the play here in name and word – just as *Hamlet* was not transposed and yet became Indian – it remains local in gesture and costume. Thus in the opening scene Theseus with his war and hunting party triumphantly brings back Hippolyta in golden chains, she as a wild beauty or beautiful savage as can be found among the members of nomad tribes in the mountains here or in Rajasthan, with a gorgeous costume and heavy jewellery, and along with her come captured women like Helen of Troy.[26] Pitted against the costumes of the tribals/gypsies/Rajasthanis are the

26 In Greek mythology, Helen was the daughter of the supreme god Zeus and the human queen Leda. Her legendary beauty caused the Trojan prince Paris to abduct her from Sparta to Troy and thus to bring about the Trojan War.

imagery and costumes of the Mughals,[27] which also provides nice musical opportunities for the world of the court, with Pakistani ghazals etc. Even before the first word is uttered about the announcement of the wedding, the cups are raised among Theseus's hunting party, who are thirsty for both wine and blood after war and hunt, and in anticipation of the marital subjugation – and the blood of the wedding night is the blood of subjugation – and music and song accompany the drinking. So then the end in Act V can be imagined, when the wedding night is only hours away and the wild beauty and beautiful savage has been tamed, both through subjugation and conformity, a consequence of her own decision (and guilt?). Her conformity is visible in the splendour of the Mughal costume and the golden jewellery around her arms and neck, made from the chains by which she was led in. The motifs of subjugation and of conformity permeate the whole play.

Bhopal, 10 January 1985

Bennewitz concludes a lengthy interpretation of *A Midsummer Night's Dream*:

However awkwardly I have described it, it should be clear enough what I want to say: how in a world and society like this one, where nomadic tribes coexist along with growing and excessive capitalism as well as with existing socialism, there are not only aesthetic offers for the eye. Rather, the side-by-side presence of centuries and the orders proper to them sound out the human content of the stories more sensitively by making the human being historical, which is at the same time more representative and more individual.

I also wanted to say that Lysander's and Hermia's actions are not just typical for relations between the sexes but also a matter of historical imprint; after the duke leaves with the threat to Hermia that she must give up either her love or her life, Lysander runs away from Hermia and throws himself into the cushions in despair and thinks and bemoans HIS suffering – "Ay ME," not

27 The Mughals were the Muslim rulers of India, whose power was at its height in the sixteenth and seventeenth centuries. In other letters Bennewitz reports that he used miniature paintings from the Mughal era as well as the famous Ajanta cave paintings and murals from Shekkavati in Rajasthan as inspiration for the imagery of the production (Bhopal, 12 and 17 Jan. 1985).

"Ay US" – and it is the girl that props him back up and embraces him as lover, sister, and mother: "... If then true lovers have been ever cross'd, / It stands as an edict in destiny: / Then let us teach our trial patience."

I must write again and again how blessed my life is for being allowed to spend it in the (strenuous) pleasure of dwelling at the deepest foundations and reasons of life through Shakespeare and through what is heard and wrested from him in the alienation through a world that is seemingly alien to him. Can you understand now that I CANNOT work in Stuttgart or Amsterdam?! I am looking forward to coming home, because I cannot choose the world that has put its imprint on me and is my given homeland, but nevertheless I remain foreign in it, because for fifteen years now I have been living among humanity in ever newly exciting ways.

For example, how should I describe to you the afternoon hour on the rock at the shore of the lake (with the city opposite in the most still calm yesterday, the unstirred lake giving the most peaceful image, yet the cloud above it remains), when I [...] watch the work and life of the fishermen and have a conversation with a local who works as a mechanic in a workshop around the corner on the lakeshore; he has two children, a 5-year-old boy and 2-year-old girl, and the third child is due to arrive in three months, and he is not free from worry even though he and his family were not immediately threatened by the gas. Of course, it was quite a stuttering conversation, though with enough Hindi courage to enable communication.

Bhopal, 11 January 1985

As I have described in previous years, beauty is also a question of class; this, by the way, does not just concern the dignity engraved by hard work in the old faces and bodies, but the beauty of young faces and bodies is also more remarkable and more individually varied than in the fashionable uniform of the middle classes. Capitalism has also destroyed this diversity of humankind – it does not need such diversity because it needs consumers with mass tastes so that consumer goods can be mass produced in great enough numbers to assure profits.

Well, back to the actors playing the Mechanicals, who not only bring with them faces inscribed by life (differently than in the National School of Drama, where the unholy motivation of film has marked a lot of the faces), but through their imagination and observation and experience of life below they also bring in behaviour and reactions that mark their uniqueness within the commonality of all; therefore they do not adorn anything in Shakespeare but rather discover things in and through him and free them from within themselves. It is related realities that resonate together here, and with that the wealth of non-invented and acquired individual stories from the physically engrained knowledge of such people.

I just remembered in how shamelessly insolent and arrogant a manner the Mechanicals were used (and even more shameless, how much applause this received) in the production of the Deutsches Theater in order to denounce amateurish vanities there, which is not just a cause for shame but also evidence of lost innocence. So in itself it is more than just honesty, because in another way it would be shamelessness or at least evidence of lost capability to represent, where we don't have any actors (hardly any – Brecht had some in the beginning, and some workers' theatres still have them occasionally) who bring it with them. Our representation and exhibition and our flight from the human being into the put-on or made-up mask are likely also the involuntary (or is it so honest that it is voluntary?) admission that in theatre we have lost the innocence of class identity, that we do not have among us class biographies grown through centuries. For without basic identification there is no alienation and thus no insight possible. There are different kinds of "appeal" that are necessary in the art of acting, which anyone who is somewhat of an actor possesses to varying degrees and in various areas; then we say: he or she just has it. One could also call it charisma. I mean something more, and something more fundamentally historical and social, and that is class identity, which is also why I always stress that the goal and content of our self-education are to make our senses historical and social, so that they can react spontaneously to reality, which is and needs art; in other words, so that we can react sensually and thus arrive at effectiveness and discovery.

[...]

This is also closely related to the discovery I have made in the history of folk theatre here, and that can be repeated where such theatre still functions socially and has not been brought into the cities as exhibition: the art of improvisation is not primarily due to the general absence of written texts, but rather to the first-hand life experience of the actors, and the fact that actors and audience members literally are on the same level. The actor entering through the audience and addressing them directly also is connected with the fact that they live on the same level.

Bhopal, 12 January 1985

In the evening, I went to the last show of the ongoing drama festival, performed by a local troupe. Beforehand, they always read out the cast list over loudspeakers, and sometimes also some biographical notes by the director. The one yesterday told us in this way that his enormous abilities were inherited from his father. I hope I am not formulating it so cynically because the adaptation of Orwell's *Animal Farm* was as gut-wrenchingly reactionary as Orwell's book is anti-socialist; I cannot help reacting reflexively when on stage pigs take over power and address each other with "comrade." My assistant Atul said that now he had experienced how badly those sitting in our and his plays must feel if our ideology is indigestible to them. Since we were invited guests we had to wait until the intermission to leave.

Bhopal, 15 January 1985

Bennewitz concludes the description of a memorial event held in honour of the recently deceased Urdu poet Faiz Ahmad Faiz (1911–84):

The best part of the beautiful experience of having so many people of all ages brought together to celebrate the living memory of an important poet was that his work was read out by other poets, which showed that sense and sensuality condition and promote each other, or one could say content and form, but those words are too dry in relation to the phenomenon of language. Once this has been grasped fundamentally it is comprehensible in all languages. What I want to say is that it is not so surprising that even in a foreign language which I only know imperfectly for communication I can grasp its body and spirit, and that precisely because it is not my own language I have a finer ear for its unique beauties in the mutually dependent identity of sound and meaning. Of course, this is hardly if at all possible to convey in a letter, for how can I reach your ear if I write how differently "dil" sounds than "Herz" (heart), with the soft sound of the "d" – in Hindi there are eight different sounds for "d" and "t" and "dh" and "th," and those differentiated again by variations in position of the tongue – and with the "i" that is neither short nor long and thus does not sound sharp, especially with the soft final sound of the "l"; or if I juxtapose our word "Liebe" (love) to the word "prem," with a long "e." Of course I am prone to injustice towards our words, because the freshness of discovery lies with the other words – the miracle of alienation.

Bhopal, 23 January 1985

The experiment this morning of letting the play run through in its current rough state has shown how much work still remains to be done, after I had already thought that one or two miracle men and a couple of unspoiled actors could make it. Deep drilling and removing of bad habits are necessary here, too. As theoretical and practical experiments by intellectual enthusiasts showed years ago, it is not as simple as putting folk theatre actors into urban theatre and just seeing it rise like Phoenix from the ashes; that has as little chance of success as the "use" of stylistic elements from traditional theatre. In reality those are hard processes of integration, as I have named and described them already during the first experiment in 1973 with the *Chalk Circle* adaptation in Bombay: mutual interpenetration of play and medium, which is not – as I may have labelled it in one of the letters this year – simply an osmotic process, not a biological or mechanical one, but rather one that organizes a new organism. That is probably also the reason for my historical impact in the country, whereby performances of the Bombay *Chalk Circle,* the Delhi *Puntila,* the Bhopal *Chalk Circle,* and apparently now also the Delhi *Hamlet* as before the Delhi *Midsummer Night's Dream* are remembered as "landmarks," due to their uniquely Indian qualities. That has to do to a limited extent with my abilities and experiences, but more with the METHOD as a collective and historical experience and capability.

Bhopal, 31 January 1985

So work here had come up against some bad turbulence – which is an inappropriate metaphor since it could suggest that there are turbulent events involved, which is not actually so. It should rather be described as normal occurrence, of which no work and nobody's work is free. And yet, when it stalls it always seems unique and suggests that efforts were in vain and hope is lost.

Yet it must always be remembered again that Shakespeare is not normally the stuff for learning to read – though, why not? If the biographies of people reading it are those of adults, then reading in such a book is practice of life and discovery – why shouldn't it be difficult if it goes down into the depths of both, Shakespeare's play and those that play it?

Admittedly, though, I am often out of patience more quickly than is useful or the situation merits, and too soon let go of the knowledge that it is a new world and new challenge, and that my expectations of them and of myself are a high bar to clear; I should know better that it won't be cleared on the first attempt or the second, but that even a third attempt in vain does not have to mean disqualification. Despite all this better knowledge, despair remains and leads to doubt, when again and again the descent into bad habits recurs, the worst of which are brainless words, prefabricated delivery of text and steps, cliché and mannerisms. Even with the miracle man of 1983 I feared, not entirely unjustifiedly, loss of experience, diminishing contact with the ground, and breaking away from his origins and heritage, because after a year and a half, he had changed outwardly, too, with a film-fashionable haircut and fashionable clothes. These words exaggerate the problem, but the problem remains and also needs to be thought about in his terms: "my son should have the opportunity for an education and not have to wait until he is thirty to be able to read and write." That means a double breaking away from one's own past: a necessary overcoming of barriers to education and development, and a farewell to a humanity made ill by civilization.

Or, to pose the question in less grandiose words: with the distance of years and traversed paths away from one's origin, do the values and abilities nurtured and grown in this origin fade away, does the spontaneous reaction to the world suffer, does one's blood become more watery? So it is the Antaeus[28] question: his power grows from the ground – if Hercules can separate him from that ground, he can defeat him. The problem remains, even if the next day's rehearsal brought back the old lustre and richness to the play after the hours of despair. And there is also

---

28 In Greek mythology, the giant Antaeus was the son of the sea god Poseidon and earth goddess Gaia, and was undefeatable in combat as long as he could touch the earth, his mother's element.

another problem that is based on known and tested experience [...]: it is not enough to suddenly place the actor cultivated in unalienated soil into a play grown in and from a different culture, so that he can look differently and deeper into the play – the play must also do something with the man (as in the 1973 integration of the *Chalk Circle* into Marathi folk theatre: the play and the medium must mutually interpenetrate).

So the image is back again and makes sense: I must have or acquire the energy, patience, and ability to descend into the mine shafts of their biographies and clear away the waste in order to reach the ore, and even then it is still raw material.[29] Gains can hardly be made IMMEDIATELY. It is always about introducing them to themselves, which is not a look into the mirror or a walk through an exhibition, but hard and often painful work, because often they have to cut into their own flesh. What makes me suitable for this above any specific qualifications is my fundamental foreignness, non-localness, which with the precondition of my curiosity and my respect for their culture and their historical, social, ethnic, and individual biographies sees more through alienation than they (can) see in their habituation. Of course that is just a precondition, but a necessary one for my impact here which has ripened through knowledge, ability, achievement, steadfastness, and continuity, such that most of my productions here have become signposts and had an impact in the landscape of theatre, and that my name (as that of someone who now is not such a foreigner anymore) along with two others – Alkazi and Habib Tanvir – is known and named in the context of such markers and impacts. I must remember this and tell myself as encouragement and as a reminder of my responsibility, when now and again during these years and in desperate and doubtful situations (which also occur at home, and are essentially worse there because they are less dependent on cultural differences) I seem not to know what the sense and impact of my work here are if it is not always NEW and a NOVEL EXPERIMENT.

29 Bennewitz frequently used this mining metaphor for his work with actors. It is rooted in his biographical experience of working as a coal miner when he was a prisoner of war. In another letter (Bhopal, 19 Jan. 1985), he makes this link explicit when he concludes a long discussion of the Mechanicals with a comparison of their use of a lamp with his experience during a mine disaster.

Appropriate to the position he had established in Indian theatre, Bennewitz returned to the subcontinent many times over the next one and a half years. From September to November 1985, he worked with students at the NSD in Delhi on Brecht's *Man equals Man* in Hindi. He was joined by set designer Franz Havemann as well as by Professor Heinz Hellmich from the Theatre Academy Ernst Busch in East Berlin, who was sent as a result of a newly established exchange agreement between the two theatre schools. Bennewitz then returned to Bhopal from January to February 1986 for a production of Shakespeare's *King Lear* in standard Hindi and the Khariboli dialect. During this time he also visited various cities for guest performances of his Rangmandal productions of *Caucasian Chalk Circle* and *A Midsummer Night's Dream*, and he went to Mumbai as a keynote invitee at an international seminar on East-West relations in the theatre. The following excerpt from his work report on this event contains interesting reflections on his status in India and comparisons of his work with that of prominent Western exponents of intercultural theatre.

> Since the seminar had been planned as a workshop with practical aspects [...], I had accepted the invitation under the condition that Rangmandal would also be invited for a guest performance of *Insaaf Ka Ghera*. Sponsors of the East-West Encounters series (of which this seminar was the fifth event already) were the NCPA (National Centre for the Performing Arts) and the Max-Mueller-Bhavan (the Indian branch of the West German Goethe Institute); co-sponsors included the Alliance Française, the British Council, the House of Soviet Culture, and the Indian Council for Cultural Relations. Participants included leading Indian theatre practitioners (among others Vijaya Mehta, P.L. Deshpande, Girish Karnad, Habib Tanvir, K.N. Panikkar, Vijay Tendulkar, B.V. Karanth) and personalities of international theatre who were able to contribute experience and opinions regarding the topic of so-called East-West relations and practical cooperation (among others Eugenio Barba, Jean-Claude Carrière as closest collaborator of Peter Brook, Lamberto Lambertini, Manuel Lutgenhorst).
>
> The three foci of the seminar were Eugenio Barba's conception of the so-called Third Theatre and its demonstration by members of the Odin Teatret, Jean-Claude Carrière's report about the creation of the "script" and production of *Mahābhārata* with Peter Brook in France, and the description and principles of my

experiences of many years with the integration of Brecht plays in foreign national cultures, in conjunction with discussion about the very successful performance of *Insaaf Ka Ghera* at the Tata Theatre on the previous evening. The three participants mentioned had each been given an entire morning of the seminar, in accordance with the assumed significance of their conceptions and impact.

Barba's presence (the organizers had borne the significant cost of inviting the entire ensemble of the Odin Teatret from Denmark) and the time allotted to his events should be seen as an expression of the organized continuity of his influence, which has exerted itself since the initiation of the UNESCO project "Theatre of Sources." This project rested on Grotowski's influence on Western European and North American avant-garde theatre with the proclaimed identity with traditional theatre in Asia and Africa due to supposed identical origins in myth and ritual (it is telling that Latin American theatre had been excluded from the project and left entirely to the sphere of influence of Barba). In previous reports and publications I have described Barba's conception of the so-called Third Theatre, a term he coined in 1977 during the Bergamo workshop in the context of the "Theatre of Sources" project, as counter to the historically defined program of the theatre of the Third World. With this conception, Barba understands and promotes world culture as cosmopolitan, in contrast to the dialectical relationship of the national and the international which serves as basis, content, and goal of our cooperative experiments.

Due to their high degree of craftsmanship, their creative obsession, and their richness of imagination, the performances of the Odin Teatret are quite admirable events and do find great resonance with alienated intellectuals due to their immaculate perfection AND their seeming ideological abstinence. On the other hand, they remain without any influence on the national theatre movements, except perhaps in the sense that they promote the process of alienation of disoriented intellectuals from the people (not only in the theatre), where theatre is better understood and made in the context of the general historical situation. [...]

Barba's explanations and practical demonstrations understand the theme and practice of the so-called East-West encounter of cultures not as a process of integration but as blending by means of imitation (e.g., a European dancer learning Kathakali or the dances of Bali). The most extreme consequence is Richard

Schechner's conviction (and desired goal) that one day soon we can choose among cultures like we do now with cuisines: let's go for Chinese today. Carrière reported on the attempt to transpose Indian culture from the depth of legend and myth into his own European culture. This elicited very mixed reactions among our Indian colleagues, giving rise to two strains of thought for me: on the one hand, there is unjustified expectation and criticism that Peter Brook's *Mahābhārata* is not sufficiently Indian, which it cannot and does not want to be if it is a reaction to a nationally moulded inheritance of humanity under different historical and cultural conditions. On the other hand, the question arises: to what extent does the attempt at transposition, by bringing characters into contact with a different value system (not with a different history, but with a historically different class situation), damage these characters (e.g., Draupadi) so that the epic is damaged at its moral core. A related question is whether, fundamentally, the cause of these problems does not lie in an ahistorical concept of culture. This aspect of so-called East-West relations corresponds to thoughts about the experiments we have conducted with the productions of *Mudrārākshasa*, *Śakuntalā*, and *Hayavadana* in Weimar and Leipzig and want to continue.

My statements on the topic took up a central position during the seminar, given the principles of internationalist cultural politics, the long continuity of the process and its proven impact, and also given the general familiarity with my work in India and South East Asia since 1970 as well as the fortuitous performance of *Insaaf Ka Ghera* the previous evening. My report and the discussion took on the character of a reckoning about what has been achieved and what remains to be done. The example of the history of integration of the *Caucasian Chalk Circle* [...] allows one to discern the beginning, course, and temporary finish line of a historical experiment that has had a decisive influence on the development of contemporary Indian theatre in the 1970s and 80s [...]. The Bhopal version of the *Chalk Circle* appears to be the culmination of the fifteen-year series of experiments and a challenge to achieve a new quality [...] in testing the applicability of Brecht's method as a theatre conception and in experiencing the capacity of Indian theatre to integrate Shakespeare. This says nothing about the continuing significant value of Brecht's plays for Indian theatre; even less does it represent the claim that the methods and principles of integrating his plays

> have been successfully established everywhere [...]. When I say that the series of experiments has come to a certain close, I mean that integration has promoted, by its offer of identification through adaptation, the recognition of conditions as they are – what is necessary now is to cautiously promote the encouragement of impatience with conditions as they are [...]. The discussions of the Indian directors and authors have shown consciousness of the problem and given my thoughts above an orientation towards the future.
>
> (Arbeitsbericht 18 Sept 1985 – 24 March 1986)

From Bhopal Bennewitz went to Sri Lanka from February to March 1986 for lectures in Colombo and Kandy about Shakespeare, Brecht, and his own international theatre experiences. From October to November of that year, Bennewitz experienced his first stay at the Ninasam institute in Heggodu, Karnataka, where he worked with the institute's students on a Kannada adaptation of Brecht's *Caucasian Chalk Circle*. This stay established his link to a place and institution that would become immensely significant for him in the following years.[30] But first, he returned twice to another equally important locus, Bhopal's Bharat Bhavan.

Bhopal, 1987: Shakespeare, *The Taming of the Shrew*

Bennewitz's fourth production with Rangmandal was an adaptation of Shakespeare's *The Taming of the Shrew*, translated by Madan Soni into Bundeli, a dialect of Hindi, under the title *To Sana Purusa Na Mo Sama Nari*. The production, which premiered on 18 September 1987, featured music composed by B.V. Karanth and a set designed by Franz Havemann. Particularly in terms of media attention, it was linked to and overshadowed by the spectacular Mishra-Karanth case. The previous year, actress Vibha Mishra had suffered life-threatening burns while Karanth was at her house, feeding into rumours about an affair between the two gone wrong. Karanth had been implicated in injuring Mishra, had spent time in jail, and was still being prosecuted at the time (the court case was finally withdrawn after seven years).[31] When

30 See the character sketch of and interview with Bennewitz by Ninasam founder K.V. Subbanna in Part II of this book (pp. 259–65), which was produced in the context of this first encounter.

31 For a detailed account of the incident and its aftermath from Karanth's perspective, see his autobiography *Here, I Cannot Stay; There, I Cannot Go*, pp. 278–301.

Bennewitz arrived in August 1987, Mishra had only recently recovered, and her leading role as Katherina in *The Taming of the Shrew* marked her comeback on stage. This case charged the atmosphere around the production with heady theatre gossip, political wrangling, and uncertainty about Karanth's future.

Bhopal, 12 August 1987

Nothing runs completely without problems. The Bundeli translator was only able to begin his work on August 1st because the Hindi translation was not done – and it is not altogether clear why the latter had to be done in the first place. Probably because they were hoping to boost their prestige by winning over a prominent novelist for the translation, who reneged, however, so that it had to be passed on to the next lower celebrity, who in his turn passed it on to a student. That student has now translated word for word without bothering terribly much about the sense of the words and their meanings in the context here. So a short sentence will forecast long work ahead: we have sent our ensemble home this afternoon and Atul and I are sitting over the correction of the Hindi version, which comes close to our translating everything new, with me helping out by glancing at the English commentary of the Shakespeare text.

Bhopal, 13 August 1987

Yesterday, from the afternoon until after 10 pm, we got as far as the end of the second act in the correction of the Hindi translation. During this morning's rehearsal we will go through the Bundeli text of the Sly scene with the ensemble. This evening, the first act will come back from the Bundeli translator, and then we have to begin checking that version – the final version will then emerge in the rehearsal process.

[...]

It is an interesting question how far and why and with what consequences the decision for a translation is a political decision in a situation where unique national problems of identity arise, e.g., the so-called Sikh "identity," or the problem of regional "personalities," the self-assertion and persecution of minorities, what is the guiding majority, and so forth.

[...]

Yesterday it was not yet hot at noon time, and so we went outside under the tree with a view over the (half dried-out) lake towards Bhopal, from where the poisonous cloud came. Because the Bundeli translation of the prologue has not come back yet from copying, we started to just talk about the play, meaning we had a few people tell us, after having read the unspeakably bad Hindi translation and having listened to us talk about the text, what they knew and thought about the play and their role and its relations to other roles. That turned into a great pleasure of sharing conversation and opinions, and of the discovery [...] with what liveliness and with how much sense and relation to their own life and experience they each told about their part and the whole, so that I just had to look and listen in order to know how I can direct the play from out of them and towards them. That, too, is what I (we) mean by INTEGRATION in contrast to INDIANIZATION.

It is also astonishing how in the relaxed, cheerful conversation dimensions of the play are revealed that are rarely attributed to plays like *The Taming of the Shrew*, which belong so fully to the theatre. But Shakespeare is always Shakespeare, after all, and the purest fun has deep foundations – just think through the prologue with the nobleman who, for his own entertainment in his uneventful and inactive life, has a drunken beggar dressed in his silk clothes, in order to take perverse pleasure in the identity confusions of the poor man – but when the poor man does not do him the favour of being all that confused about his identity, could the nobleman's prank not get out of control and turn against him? So then, of course, from the interpretative ideas immediately scenic ideas come tumbling – if I could only describe it more clearly and in more detail, you would easily understand why I think that the more difficult work here is also the easier.

Bhopal, 2 September 1987

Dwarika Prasad, the (Azdak/Bottom/fool in *Lear*) miracle man, through whom I wanted to and certainly still will experience the character Petrucchio in a new way, once again is providing new food for thought about a number of interesting phenomena. Well, Shakespeare's Renaissance characters are not the daily bread of theatre here, and ways and means have to be sought and tried that will help to establish relations to the actors' own daily individual and social experiences (I am bracketing out historical experiences here, because HISTORY is not a component of experience here – what we see and read in them historically is individual biography).

I too hastily had imagined that Prasad would have no problem taking on the character spontaneously and naïvely and without fear of its historically and geographically remote foreignness, i.e., that he would grasp the character on his own ground, which is his origin, his unalienated breath of life. I had forgotten or underestimated that by now he has accumulated new layers from living in another environment and with other ways – urban ways with their (supposed?) upward social mobility through educational opportunities and material amenities, and with their deforming influences of media-controlled ideology, the alienation from class and soil, getting sucked into levelling petty bourgeois concerns. These consequences of bourgeois and imperialist causes and influences erase all specific cultural identity in individuals and groups. So, Prasad's senses already read and see a (foreign) play and its characters with the virus (or even cancer cells?) of newly internalized values, with respect to which he does not realize, in the first encounter with the foreign play, how far they range below his native values accumulated through experience. He does not realize this quickly, because it seems to be a generalizable terrible truth that new (non-) values are held in higher esteem than those one has brought with one, and that the behaviour of the new (anonymous) community (which only has in "common" that it is a mass without identity, though with the advantage of the great number and the intimidating pressure that majorities always exert) oppresses and represses the values of the old community which has been left behind (but which as a tribal community had shared everything in common).

Let me return to the practical application of these ideas: Prasad approached the character of Petrucchio with an urban pseudo-elegance obviously gleaned from film clichés, mixed in with his Sutradhar experience from folk theatre, which, however, degenerates in this mixture. His origins were only (but then immediately) visible where the character appears in coarsely comical situations, such as his first appearance and the ensuing scene with Grumio, or in Act III, when he comes to the wedding on his sick old nag in gypsy-colourful attire. In such moments, his artistic biography unlocks the expected pleasure from the play and the role, because the situation does not allow the character to succumb to clichés. I am certain he can be brought back to his cultural self-confidence. I/we have come up with a helpful approach already, and that is to remind him of his

> Pandavani stories [...], where there are episodes with one of the five Pandavani brothers, Bhima, who is similar to the character of Petrucchio.[32] After all, our actors also cannot evoke such a character from out of themselves and their present. What helps them is history, their knowledge about figures like Francis Drake, the adventurer of the Elizabethan age. Whether they then can play the character with the vitality of such figures is another question altogether.

The remaining letters from this stay report ups and downs in the quality of the production, with the latter due in part to quarrels among the members of the ensemble, but conclude with a very enthusiastic assessment of a dress rehearsal. The process thus seems to have mirrored the plot of the play itself. According to a report from a press conference held to promote the production, Bennewitz argued that the play "is aimed at harmony between the sexes based on mutual respect and love which can only be attained by [a] permanent endeavour to gain and retain each one's own character and role in [the] creative dependence of both parts" (Manmohan). Given the high drama and gossip of the Mishra-Karanth case surrounding the production, this interpretation was quite poignant.

From Bhopal, Bennewitz went on to Sri Lanka, where he worked on productions of Shakespeare's *A Midsummer Night's Dream* and of Brecht's *Threepenny Opera* (in Sinhala under the title *Andi Rale Nadagame*) from September to November 1987. Afterwards, it was straight on to Kolkata, where he had been invited by Utpal Dutt and his wife Sova Sen to work on his first full Indian production of Brecht's *Mother Courage*, which Dutt had adapted into the historical context of the 1857 Indian uprising. Such a collaboration of Bennewitz with Dutt, Sova Sen, and their People's Little Theatre had been envisaged for years. However, Bennewitz reports that the Indian Council for Cultural Relations (ICCR) and the Bengali government, contrary to expectations, did not financially support the production, due to cuts to cultural programming (Arbeitsbericht 6 Aug – 30 Dec 1987). Nonetheless, Bennewitz stayed in Kolkata from November to December, housed privately by Dutt and Sen, and the plan was now to hold a production-oriented seminar

32 Pandavani is a narrative ballad form of the central Indian state of Chhattisgarh. The stories are based on incidents from the epic *Mahābhārata*.

on *Mother Courage* aimed at a public premiere in February 1989 in conjunction with Brecht's ninetieth birthday (ibid.). However, this work seems never to have been completed, the reasons for which remain unknown despite efforts by critic and theatre historian Samik Bandyopadhyay to find out (Interview Bandyopadhyay).

Bennewitz instead returned to complete his second full production in Kolkata the next year, working with the theatre group Padatik from September to November 1988. The leader of the group, Shyamanand Jalan, had invited him to direct Padatik's first Shakespeare play. They produced a Hindi translation of *King Lear* by Akshay Upadhay which presented Bennewitz with the oft-encountered problem of a translation where the newly rendered text lacks "the qualities of what we call a 'gesture language' which motivates the actor to act rather than to recite" (Interview *Jugantar* 1988). Reviewer Abhijit Gupta seems to have agreed with Bennewitz, writing about the Fool's lines that the "oblique idiom of the original was rendered distressingly bland." His review took a generally negative view of the production, arguing that the acting was too filmy and that "Jalan and Bennewitz have given us nothing new by means of interpretation." Overall, in contrast to the considerable excitement with which the production had been anticipated, its critical reception remained rather lukewarm.

In August 1989, Bennewitz returned to Bhopal for his fifth and last production with Rangmandal, Brecht's *Threepenny Opera* in a Hindi translation by Atul Tiwari under the title *Paisa Phenk – Tamasha Dhek*, with music composed by B.V. Karanth. The production premiered on 13 September 1989, and Bennewitz left five days later, closing the Bhopal chapter of his Indian endeavours and moving on to Heggodu for his second production at Ninasam. Neither he nor anyone else could have anticipated that during the remainder of his stay in India, beginning only a few weeks later, momentous events back home would ring in the end of another, far larger part of his life and career. As many passages in the next chapter will show, the opening of the Berlin Wall and subsequent end of the GDR deeply affected Bennewitz, shaking or even shattering his faith in the possibility of a just, socialist future society, and these events also affected his attitude towards his work in India.

4 The Late 1980s and Early 1990s – Gaining a Village, Losing a Country

Heggodu, 1989: Brecht, *The Good Person of Sichuan*

After leaving Bhopal and spending a brief intermezzo in Mumbai, Bennewitz came straight to Heggodu to work on a production of Brecht's *The Good Person of Sichuan* (in a Kannada translation by the Ninasam founder K.V. Subbanna) with Ninasam's Tirugata ensemble from September to the end of October 1989. The letters from this stay reflect two radically different experiences. Bennewitz commented with a mixture of disgusted anger and doubtful self-questioning on the momentous events at home – the exodus of thousands of GDR citizens via Hungary and the West German embassies in Poland and Czechoslovakia, the growing protest movement in the GDR which culminated in the Monday demonstrations in Leipzig, the dismissal of Erich Honecker as head of government, and the rise to power of reformers within the ruling party and government. He condemned those who were advocating the end of socialism and leaving for the capitalist lifestyle of West Germany, but he also asked himself probing questions why the socialist system had not been more successful in winning the hearts and minds of the people, and whether he and others faithful to the communist ideal had been too smug and uncritical in their privileged positions and too accepting of the status quo. In contrast to this inner turmoil, Bennewitz experienced life and work in Heggodu as a haven of calm, simplicity, and friendly human contact. This extreme contrast clearly cemented the deep connection he developed to Ninasam and to what he would henceforth affectionately refer to as "my village." His thoughts about his work with the actors of Tirugata, documented in a few passages here, also reflect these positive feelings.

Heggodu, 29 September 1989

It is past nine in the evening. We've had nice rehearsals with ever freshly astonishing phenomena: these past few days, the actor playing Wang had cramped up, i.e., he had landed on the road of clichés again, where words come from the vocal chords independent of any connection with the brain, and there is no real sense and even less liveliness in them. The three Gods had been infected by the virus, as had the girl playing Shen Te,[1] so we seemingly called it a day and suggested that they should just report about their characters in the third person and demonstrate how they would play the events if they had to become the characters. You and anyone at home can hardly imagine what happened then; it was gestic, epic theatre of the highest quality, as Brecht might have dreamed it: it had precision, lightness, rhythm, relation to partners, wit, charm, everything that makes for good theatre. They were in their element – disciplined improvisation. This comes from folk theatre, it is the Indian art of acting in its inner essence. When we, at their request, let them play it in the first person again afterwards, it was like dry bread or stale rice, a foreign conception of theatre, imported nonsense of a misunderstood Stanislavski of identification. Akshara, my collaborator (and former student and current director of the ensemble) probably said it best: "the character hangs heavy on them" – that is exactly it, and difficult to translate as succinctly; roughly, it means: the identification with the character hangs on them like lead and prevents them from freely playing, which is why they fall into the error of playing theatre.

In the evening, we went through the second rehearsal of the first scene in the tobacco shop in such a way that that scene could have its premiere the day after tomorrow. And once again they were astonished how I cope with the very foreign language – they think it is the language, but it is this: when I manage to motivate them in the right way and to put them in touch with themselves, their gestural expressiveness is so precise and rich that I can identify every sentence (and especially every forgotten one).

Kannada is a Dravidian (South Indian) language and not at all related to the languages of Aryan origin in the north, so that I cannot do anything much with my accumulated Hindi even among the two or three of them who understand it. So we have

1 Wang was played by Siddaraja Kalyanakar, the three Gods by Prakash Garud, Ganesh Prasad, and Gopal Rao Manvi, and Shen Te was played by Rajini Kerekai.

to work mainly through English again. It is a strange thing with my identity: the other day while eating at the long wooden tables, some of them asked me whether I really was a German – two of them swore that I looked exactly like their grandfathers. (Another thing I have to get used to: no longer belonging to the generation of fathers but now of grandfathers.)

Heggodu, 2 October 1989

I have to correct my report from the rehearsal the other day about the difference between having them play the scene in the third person and the relapse when they played it in the first person again. The observation is correct that it was also a relapse into a conception of theatre that is not at all their own – but the reasons are not as simple as I had described them. It has to do with language. When I asked them what they think are the causes for the difference, they said: "in the third person it is our own words," which does not merely refer to the difference between their own (and thus definitely understood) utterances and a literary text learned by heart, but "own words" also means: in our own language. Now, of course their common language is Kannada. But what I had not been fully conscious of is that there are hundreds of dialects in Kannada, and some are as different from each other and as mutually unintelligible as Bavarian and northern low German. So they have to reach a shared Kannada in which they can express as much of themselves as in the dialect they grew up with and in, and that process takes time.

Heggodu, 21 October 1989

I just came back from the first run-through, and it was such that neither can I go to sleep right away, nor can I put it down on paper easily. Perhaps I will think of the right word for it tomorrow; then I also can't be accused of exaggerating from the immediacy of the joy, astonishment, gratefulness, and happiness – however one might call all that beyond such words. The word "art" does not grasp it – and I am rather timid in using it – although what is happening here deserves the name a hundred times more than in theatre at home, where the word is traded with great claims. But at home (at least in theatre) often the human value has been sweated out of the word "art" in all the exertion of extricating this value by jumping and shouting. Here in the village, more than in the city and even among my beloved Bhopal troupe (where quite a few still have it), every

> sentence, every gesture is a human event. There is truth and genuineness of thoughts and emotions, and such a richness of *Gestus* from the Indian bodies that Brecht would have moved his theatre down here onto the subcontinent. I was able to remember the word "beauty," so that I came out of bed again to write it down.
>
> Heggodu, 26 October 1989
>
> The artistic event of the performance this evening is remarkable, but its human value counts for more. There was genuineness, truth, and modesty without histrionics and fake voices. And there was the actors' own joy, not just due to their gratefulness about my joy, but rather because they had a new experience with themselves of complete freedom, perhaps for the first time.

Ninasam and its actors clearly made a large impact on Bennewitz. The reverse was also true, as is demonstrated by an interview conducted by the author at Ninasam in March 2012 with Rajini Garud (née Kerekai), who played the title role of Shen Te in the production of *The Good Person of Sichuan*, and her husband Prakash Garud, who played the First God. This interview deserves a somewhat detailed summary because it reveals interesting aspects of Bennewitz's attitudes and methods at the time. Both actors stressed his importance for their understanding of theatre and their careers. Rajini said that she learned all about movement, gestures, dialogue delivery, rhythm, timing, space, and other aspects of acting from him. Interestingly, she recalled that Bennewitz worked more with other actors than with her and she learned by observing these interactions. Prakash confirmed that he noticed this method of working less with actors in the main roles than with the others as a general characteristic. Both were of the opinion that Bennewitz did not put undue pressure on actors, but got things done through his sheer presence, active nature, and human concern, though he could get angry like a child at times. They agreed that at the time, they sometimes found his behaviour as a director strange. Prakash recalled that the actors were often mystified that if they played a role with much energy and concentration, Bennewitz would reject their effort, but when they played it lightly and relaxed, he would be satisfied. He stopped a dress rehearsal and left the theatre in an apparent rage, but accepted what they thought was the same kind of performance as fine the next day.

The two actors also stressed Bennewitz's concern for the Indian and local context of the production. Rajini said that he insisted on the incorporation of specifically Indian gestures and postures, and Prakash recalled that Bennewitz justified the very simple but dynamic set by saying that he would do the production in accordance with the Indian context and economic conditions and hence without undue strain on the budget. Of course, this attitude could also move Bennewitz to depart from Indian theatre traditions. In contrast to Prakash's expectation that (as usual in the Indian theatre) the Gods would be lavishly costumed and decorated, Bennewitz had them arriving in all simplicity on a bicycle. The two actors recalled that Bennewitz had some differences with B.V. Karanth about the latter's music for the production, which consisted of a mix of various Indian styles, and that as a consequence Karanth changed the music somewhat.

Finally, it is worth mentioning that the two interviewees felt that Bennewitz had a special ability to mediate Brecht, both to the actors and audience. They recalled that in his directing he did not dwell on aspects of Brechtian theory such as alienation, but taught them to the actors through the way he helped them shape their characters and situations, leading in turn to a Brechtian production that the rural audiences of the Tirugata ensemble could fully understand and profit from.

Bennewitz left Heggodu on 28 October 1989 and spent the remaining two weeks of this stay in India in Mumbai and New Delhi before flying home on 11 November, only a few hours after the tumultous events of early November had led to the opening of the Berlin Wall by the GDR authorities. In his work report from this stay, written in Weimar on 12 – 13 November 1989, he reports that his Indian partners were guarded in their responses to the events and that they expressed the hope that the events would not negatively affect cultural relations between the GDR and India or lead to the abandonment of socialist positions (Arbeitsbericht 5 Aug. – 11 Nov. 1989). His immediate personal reactions to these events and those that followed in the few weeks he spent at home in Weimar before leaving for his next long stay in India are not known to the author, but they undoubtedly had a profoundly negative impact on his outlook and feelings about his identity as a German and as a communist.

New Delhi, 1989/90: Volker Braun, *Great Peace* and Shakespeare, *Twelfth Night*

Bennewitz was already back in India by mid-December 1989, in order to direct the NSD Repertory Company in a production of *Great Peace,* a play by the prominent GDR poet and dramatist Volker Braun in a Hindi translation by Ram Gopal Bajaj under the title *Mahashanti,* and to train NSD students in the third year through a Hindi production of Shakespeare's *Twelfth Night*.

Braun had written *Great Peace* in 1976, and it was first performed in April 1979 at the Berliner Ensemble in a production directed by Manfred Wekwerth and Joachim Tenschert. Bennewitz had then directed a production of it in Leipzig in September 1979. The production of this play had been agreed upon in the summer of 1988 as part of the Indo-GDR cultural work plan and originally projected to premiere on 8 Dec 1989 as part of the Days of GDR Culture in India and celebrations of the GDR's fortieth anniversary (Arbeitsbericht 11 Sept. 1988–6 Feb. 1989). The choice of play turned out to be poignant in several respects. This was Bennewitz's only production of a contemporary German play in India; indeed, after twenty years of working there, it was his first complete Indian production of a drama by an author other than Brecht or Shakespeare.

Great Peace also happens to be a play that can be read as highly critical of the political situation in the GDR. While it is set during a historically documented successful peasant uprising in ancient China, its theme of revolutionary processes ossifying into new hierarchies and new relations of exploitation, and its confrontation of utopian ideals and political reality could be (and likely often were) applied to conditions in the GDR. In fact, the Stasi (*Staatssicherheit*, the GDR secret police) were very worried about the play's critical potential. Files re-discovered in 2000 suggest that the Stasi, as part of an eight-year campaign (from 1975 to 1983) to manipulate Braun and neutralize him as a critic of the regime, enlisted director Manfred Wekwerth to produce a politically palatable version of *Great Peace*, a charge Wekwerth has vehemently denied (Kulick). In any case, it is clear that Braun and *Great Peace* were eyed with great suspicion by the authorities. In light of this, the choice or at least approval of the play by the GDR Ministry of Culture for the official event in India is surprising and could be interpreted as a symptom of slow political liberalization in the GDR in the wake of Mikhail Gorbachev's policies in the Soviet Union.

Of course, the production was given additional poignancy by the recent events of November 1989 and evolving upheaval in the GDR, which in significant part were the culmination of protests against the very political stagnation and new forms of oppression represented in *Great Peace*, protests in which Volker Braun initially played a prominent role. While chronology rules out the possibility that these events were considered in choosing the text, the coincidence of the historical moment and the production of this particular play is astounding. As we will see,

Bennewitz, too, read the drama with new eyes, as he did conditions in the GDR, the role of the communist party, and his own positions.

New Delhi, 27 December 1989

It is past seven in the evening, and I have just returned from work. It is a great pleasure to enter a play in this way (and with such an ensemble), and to get to the bottom of *Great Peace* through three languages, moving from the German original via checking the (bad) English text into the Hindi translation. Can you imagine how one can get to know a play and impart it that way? But: there are barely five weeks left for it.

[...]

Work is (still) a joy, the days pass very quickly, and people are friendly. The news from the world outside is less friendly. I hear almost nothing about home. I do my work, and do it with pleasure and as well as I can (and I can do it quite well here). I am less receptive to world politics, which I rather look through as through a window. Instead, I have a keener eye for the life I traverse daily on my way from the Ranjit Hotel across the Bengali Market to Rabindra Bhavan. I see those who have no shoes in the cold and no roof over their heads in the cold nights spent wrapped in torn blankets – and I myself am poorer in spirit than years ago, when our state was still a beacon of hope for the world, when it was easy for me to think that the world has no alternative to socialism. That certainly is still the case, but when will it come, and which socialism? If only I could do without my work here, I would gladly spend my/our life in the warmth of the Rembrandtweg house, and leave the world to those that still have their future ahead of them.

New Delhi, 1 January 1990

Last night I dreamt of Volker Braun, and someone sat next to him and told me that he had a very simple solution for the stage set, and idiot dream me replied that we already have our set in the works. If only I had let the guy finish because the set design is in very inexperienced hands; in addition, the stage where the show will take place is available for only four days for technical set-up, blocking rehearsal, run-through, and dress rehearsals, since the Repertory Company itself only has a small studio theatre and a beautiful open air stage that we cannot use in January/February. Sure, I can draw sketches, but we would need someone who can translate them, above all into technical drawings for the carpenter and the other craftspeople. So, even in my dreams I still have to learn to listen.

New Delhi, 3 January 1990

Late yesterday evening there was a documentary film on television about Safdar Hashmi, a pioneer of the Indian street theatre movement who was shot dead a year ago. He was not yet in his mid-forties, and a member of the Communist Party. It was a moving film and nearly brought me to tears – also because of the insurmountable shame that has been heaped on our party[2] by its own leaders (how terrible even that word sounds) through arrogance, mediocrity, and betrayal of principles and people. And we tolerated it knowingly. This is a betrayal, too, of people like Hashmi, who are shot dead for their ideals here. My shame and sadness are so great that I take in even news like this morning's about the tearing down of the Berlin Wall without much emotion. And with respect to the new optimism emanating from the events that began in Leipzig, which – according to the news here today on the occasion of Vaclav Havel's[3] visit in Berlin – make the GDR the centre of the democratic movement, for me this optimism is overshadowed by the fact that this process was not initiated by and from among the party, but rather against it, and rightfully so!

New Delhi, 10 January 1990

How perverse the world has become, that it can be good luck to be so old and not have anything ahead of you. But the world was hardly different before – only we perceived it differently. I am not at all interested in Honecker, Stoph, Sindermann, Tisch, Mielke, etc.[4] – I have never been interested in them – they were not the

---

2 The SED (Socialist Unity Party), the communist ruling party of the GDR, of which Bennewitz was a member since 1948.

3 Vaclav Havel (1936–2011) was a renowned Czech playwright who was critical of the communist regime in Czechoslovakia and became the country's last president (1989–92) and the first president of the newly formed Czech Republic (1993–2003).

4 These were all leading members of the GDR government. Erich Honecker (1912–94) headed the government as General Secretary of the communist party from 1971 to 1989 and as head of state since 1976. Willi Stoph (1914–99) was head of state from 1973 to 1976 and Chairman of the Council of Ministers before and after that. Horst Sindermann (1915–90), Harry Tisch (1927–95) and Erich Mielke (1907–2000) occupied leading posts in the state apparatus, party, and secret police.

IDEA, not the personifications of our dream of a just world. I am not even surprised how they have betrayed that dream – I am just sad, also because I do not know whether and how I should take part in the historical change, and whether I even want to. This has nothing to do with the party. As long as it expresses even a hint of the ideals of a possible socialist future for humankind, I will remain a member. What I don't have the energy for anymore is to live on the barricades, as long as my work here makes sense – and even there I am not entirely sure whether it makes sense and has meaning, or whether I impute that meaning to it. It's just that here, every day I live closer to the truth and reality of actual problems of humankind, which include the lack of a roof over every head and of rice in every hand. Of course, even here I don't leave the house with a song on my lips, and some days I wish it were a free Sunday with no invitations. It is more the satisfaction of doing my duty and being needed in my way – which is not in order to create works that will move the world and posterity. It is the satisfaction of not yet being superfluous, and at the same time having my own pleasure of discovering a play like *Great Peace*, which up to now I had hardly understood at all, or of once again looking into Shakespeare's innards. And that's what I don't know, whether it is the same moving astonishment and pleasure if one only reads for oneself, or whether it only hits one because one is allowed to impart it to others.

New Delhi, 15 January 1990

I don't know what everyday life is like at home (I have not received any newspapers from the embassy), and what I hear in the television news every now and then is not encouraging, and sometimes disgusting, like two days ago, when the crowd (or is it a mob already?) tore at the GDR flag to rip out the national emblem. There was a girl or young woman among them with her face distorted by such anger and hatred that I don't know where it will lead if THAT is the street under whose pressure the government changes its decisions from one day to the next. [...] And always the shouting about German unity.

The reasonable ones have apparently become or been made silent. Yesterday I had a conversation here where the following question was derived from our situation and related to the world: are we fighting for freedom and democracy or for the choice between ten different brands of toothpaste? In the hope of the world, there is fear, too. What have (we) the communists done, that communism is not only met by disappointment and distrust, but hatred? You are closer to it all and it might concern you much more immediately than me here. It would be better to report about joyous things. But the thought just will not go away that I did not question my belief that a more just world can be built by us in the GDR, that I also parroted the sentence about the "wisdom of the people" (which Brecht did as well) and did not believe Schiller, who expressed a different view in the *Song of the Bell*[5] and was called petty bourgeois by us. I have become so bitter as to say that the wisdom of the people is its greed for consumption. The peaceful revolution that began in the streets of Leipzig was started by intellectuals, and their historically astute manifestos were written by Volker Braun and Christa Wolf[6] – and what do they say and do now? Let me finish with that topic for now.

Here, my working days are packed full. [...] But even then: what use are the deepest insights into the world and into human beings, when my belief and therefore also my interest in humankind have diminished so much? (And what is humanity? I see it where it has no roof over its head and no bread in hand, and as a community of solidarity it only appears dimly to my eyes; whatever happens in Europe and influences the world – the centre of humanity is to be found in the problems of Asia, Africa, and Latin America.) It's not a good attitude – but I have no other at my disposal at the moment.

New Delhi, 1 February 1990

The only path that remains open is the ACTIVE self-dissolution of the party (the future has not yet arrived for a communist party). My opinion about that is in the letter of January 10th; if I have something to add, then it is this: even if I constantly had my problems of identification with our people during the twenty years of

5 In his poem *Song of the Bell*, Friedrich Schiller (1759–1805) expressed misgivings about the threat to public order brought on by the French Revolution and its violent mob excesses.

6 Like Braun, Christa Wolf (1929–2011) is an important author in contemporary German literature. Both lived and worked in the GDR, became increasingly critical of the regime and the stagnant political atmosphere there, and joined the protest movement in 1989, but supported fundamental reforms to the GDR's socialist political system instead of unification with West Germany.

my emigration into my work here, I had none with the people who overcame fascism, who died in or survived Buchenwald.[7] Hope for a world of peace and justice created by us – therein lay my identification with the state as an historical movement, not as an institution. [...] My grief is that at first, half a year ago, it was only LOSS of identification with this state, but now it has become worse with what has remained from the initial candle-light marches: my RENUNCIATION of this identity, and that is an emptiness like an open wound. I am fortunate to have my work here, in which I have my global identity. My home consists exclusively (though with all my heart) of Rembrandtweg 6 and the burial spot beneath the maple tree. I am lucky that in barely twelve months I can legally retire in our country, but I have to repeat that I still don't know how I will experience myself without the work here.

[...]

Great Peace will have its first preview show the day after tomorrow already. [...] It brings me such happiness (though limited to the here and now of the event) about what has come together here with a handful of world-class actors (and it is deeply satisfying that they all are former students of mine – and every day there is a letter or an embrace from a former student: I have helped shape three generations already over the twenty years). What is happening at home is certainly the necessary foundation for history that needs to occur for the future of humanity. I am too old to feel any happiness that might arise from that.

New Delhi, 13 February 1990

First about the show, and just briefly, because it remains indescribable anyhow and I unfortunately have used up all applicable vocabulary in past years to still be believable with the old words. If a high point for the twentieth anniversary of my contributing and receiving in India were thinkable and to be wished for, it would have been yesterday evening. Yes, the words are spent, but if I had to choose only half a dozen productions that would be

7 The Nazi concentration camp Buchenwald (near Weimar) held a large number of communist prisoners. Their suffering as well as their role in resistance and the eventual liberation of the camp were key components in the antifascist pillar of GDR ideology.

worth remembering, this one would be among them. It was not just a loudly applauded (in India!) performance by a brilliant ensemble, among which most of the actors in Weimar could only have functioned as extras – more than that, this play, which admittedly is not easy and even difficult for audiences untrained in dialectics, fully reached the audience, so that there was applause within scenes and, unusually, at the end. Some are of the opinion that *Mahashanti* (*Great Peace*) is probably the most significant and relevant play on Indian stages of at least the last ten years. In the problems it poses and in its performance it was received as an INDIAN play in the global context. After it ended, I was called up on stage by the audience and the directors of the NSD and REP and was celebrated on the same occasion with a speech for my twentieth anniversary.

New Delhi, 14 February 1990

I am saddened by the plight of those who are or are becoming unemployed, by the growing estrangement (which was already bad and hostile enough in our country – and yet, in principle there was still more mutual solidarity than in Western competitive society) through newly arising envy in the coming waves of consumption, by the decline of art, which will withdraw into itself – if new deprivations will not give an impulse to new social reflection. Today, there is a big interview with me in the leading *Times of India* – and when I read it, I think that our "artists at home" would laugh that out here in the world we talk about social engagement and responsibility and yet, or precisely because of that, also about art.

New Delhi, 16 February 1990

Before I leave the house to go to rehearsals for *Twelfth Night*, a word about yesterday evening. The performances become better and better every day, but yesterday there was a special little event. During the show, I had to go to the toilet and had to cross the foyer, where a small exhibition with photos from the show is displayed. I was passing it just as one of the guards explained the plot and the individual events of the play to two families (and here the word "workers' families" is still accurate) with such enthusiastic involvement that something like that drowns out all applause by an intellectual audience. When he noticed me listening, he interrupted his explanations to tell me how impressed he was by the play (in Hindi, of course, since for one thing he doesn't speak English, and for another all workers and employees here think that I understand everything in Hindi anyway, which naturally is an exaggeration).

[...]

One thing is being confirmed anew with every performance of *Great Peace*: no play in the last ten years has affected minds and discussions so much, even if it remains limited to circles interested in history and the present, and is not being discussed in the markets.

New Delhi, 18 February 1990

Yesterday evening marked a wistful farewell from *Great Peace* (for me – the show remains on the playbill), and what a show it was! And what an audience! Now the word has spread and the first reviews are talking of a "memorable" event and are saying that it has been a long time since the Repertory Company was this good. The play keeps many of those who have seen it talking for days afterwards. There is talk (also in connection with my work here over twenty years) that Braun surpasses Brecht; they don't mean that he is the greater poet and dramatist, but that he is more timely. If I were asked to choose the five most important productions from among the roughly 150 I have done, this one would be among them. Bhaskar Chandavarkar, who composed the music [...], also thinks that my twenty years in India could not have been celebrated better and more meaningfully than with this play and this production. I am glad about it and hope that this is not a final farewell to India. Not yet.

Kavita Nagpal's review of *Great Peace* provides one piece of evidence confirming Bennewitz's report about the positive critical reaction to the production when she argues that it "was the best work of his in ten years (after Brecht's *Puntila and his Man Matti*, NSD Rep Co *Mahashanti* is also one of the finest efforts by the company itself in many years)." Both Nagpal and Romesh Chander in his positive review also echo what Bennewitz writes about Braun being seen as timely, but they do so in a much more concrete fashion: both stress the relevance of *Great Peace* to the systemic problems and current challenges of the communist regimes in the Soviet Union and Eastern Europe.

It is interesting, then, that despite his many reflections about events at home and their consequences, Bennewitz nowhere makes an explicit link between these developments and the play,[8] neither in the letters nor in his director's note for the production program, where he interprets the play as follows:

> Three levels: tradition – Utopia – reality – within that relation of tensions the play moves on and at the end the tensions are not resolved.
>
> […]
>
> Volker Braun tells the story of a revolution from its starting point – the impossibility of the oppressed to live under the given conditions and the incapability of the rulers to maintain their regime – up to the end, when the new order already grows stiff again and the next historical revolution is in the coming.
>
> A piece of mankind's history unfolds in a story which follows quite precise, real events in old China – but in a way to make intelligible regularities of social development and to provoke the spectator's associative thinking.
>
> It is a global theme with a storyline from Asian history which finds the Indian context inherent in the play. ("Director's Note" on *Mahashanti*, 199)

This rather abstract conception was carried through in the production itself, at least in its visual style, as a viewing of the existing video of a performance in the Fritz Bennewitz Archive confirms. Nothing in its set, costumes, props or acting styles suggests any link to concrete contemporary events. Nonetheless, the link was clearly made by the reviewers, but even the following comment from Chander about the music underscores the abstract nature of the production: "Bhaskar Chandavarkar's music helps to underline the inner contradictions. What is more, at places it offers a comment on what is being enacted on the stage. The music, like the theme of the play, has no nationality or classification: it is universal." The abstractness also led to some less positive reactions even from connoisseurs closely connected to Bennewitz. In interviews conducted by the author, Kirti Jain, who was the acting director of the NSD at the time of the production, said that she did not enjoy the production and that Braun's play did not make an impact on her, and the NSD director at the time of the interview and long-time colleague of

8 The closest he gets to such a link is when he refers to Braun as "in the forefront of the anti-Stalinism movement in the GDR" in an interview published in *The Times of India* on 14 Feb. 1990.

Bennewitz, Anuradha Kapur, argued that despite the excellent acting, the production was difficult and not entirely successful.

Heggodu, 1990: Shakespeare, *A Midsummer Night's Dream*

After finishing his work on *Great Peace* and *Twelfth Night* in Delhi and spending a few days in Mumbai, Bennewitz went on to Heggodu. Here, he worked with Ninasam's Tirugata ensemble on a production of Shakespeare's *A Midsummer Night's Dream* in Kannada from early March to early April 1990.

Heggodu, 13 March 1990

After Bennewitz has given a detailed account of his average day at Ninasam, he writes:

> I have described my day in such detail to you, and the goings-on around it with people who live with equanimity and with the same regularity as the hours of the clock, the orbit of the moon, and the rising and setting of the sun, not to paint an idyllic picture – life here is too hard and real for that – but to show how everything here, including the most modest meal at the long wooden tables, is itself a rhythm within the rhythm of nature. This explains why the events at home and in the wider world seem absurd to me, but whether we want it to be so or not, and whatever our attitude towards it, these events are their own reality determining the course of world affairs, even if they are so contrary to the rhythm of nature. The world cannot move back(wards) into the village, but perhaps it could become more aware of its own nature, though we won't live to see that. In my dreams of realizable social justice, born from the (too narrow and one-sided) knowledge about the law of surplus value[9] and about the reasons for exploitation, I had no longer taken seriously the stories from the Bible and had wanted to refuse to acknowledge that man fundamentally is Cain, who kills his brother. I suppose Marx, too, believed his dream that it would take changing conditions for human behaviour to change. If you look at it closely, Marx was more Christian than Christianity: he believed that humans are good and that it was only conditions that made them bad. I know, I know, neither was he

9 Surplus value is a key concept of Karl Marx's critique of capitalist political economy.

nor is the issue that simple – but I still have trouble NOT believing that humans are basically NOT good. However, if I look into my mind and heart unsentimentally, I think all this no longer interests me. But I encounter it in my work again and again, and that's when I have a hard time to see humans as innately bad. Perhaps my lack of distrust is just another kind of laziness or disinterest.

Heggodu, 16 March 1990

The day before yesterday was very interesting. Our Ninasam students performed their Sanskrit play at a theatre festival in a village some thirty kilometres away. We drove with a small lorry over roads which are dusty in the rainless season, through a few villages to a dammed reservoir lake, where we took the ferry to the other side and a packed bus to our destination village. We had our dinner on banana leaves in long rows on the floor of the village temple and spent the few remaining hours of the night on straw mats, distributed among a few brick huts, before washing with water drawn from the well.

The performance took place with difficulties – there was a power cut throughout, so they brought in a generator, which produced just enough electricity to light the "dressing room" in a temporary tent – because putting on the make-up for the traditional masks alone takes about three hours – and to power one spotlight onto the stage, which was open to the outside because when an event like this happens, the peasants come from far and wide from the surrounding villages. This time, because of the power cut, few had come, but usually they come with ox carts and often travel two to three hours, and then back in the night. This would have posed a problem with the Ninasam play, which is only one hour long [...] – four hours of travel for a performance of less than an hour and a half. Well, we waited to see whether the light would come back on, but nothing came except from the intermittently working generator – so we began after 10 pm, and because it was the final performance of the week-long theatre festival, there was also a "function," i.e., speeches were given. Once again, I was invited as chief guest, and then there was another honoured guest one rung below, and two or three others also gave speeches (I kept mine short, because I know how the actors feel backstage, waiting for their entry). Around 11 pm the play could begin, and the acting students performed it with verve and great discipline. It was past midnight when we went back to the temple in front of the banana leaf plates and then onto our mats. At six in the morning we got up, took the bus back to the ferry, and drove back to Heggodu on the dusty roads. So in the afternoon, everyone was rather exhausted, and I let them and myself out of rehearsals after two hours, because we can rehearse this morning and afternoon. During their studies they have no Sundays off, which does not bother them – it is a different and always friendly way of relating to the world and to each other.

Heggodu, 21 March 1990

So now the "Helmut Kohl" screamers have managed to get 193 of the 400 seats in parliament, which will be called People's Chamber (Volkskammer) only for a few more months (if the powers around us allow it), and Mr. de Maizière foresees, and likely is happy, that we will buy Christmas presents in West German Deutschmarks.[10] We'll take it with equanimity, because it is what it is and nothing else will help us, and we will manage. I myself am at a loss for words anyway, even if the outcome had been better: I was away in exile when the candles were carried through the streets, and I did not contribute to cleaning up what needed to be cleaned up. I have a hard time grasping, too, that now 40 years of ALSO great historical achievements are supposed to be thrown on the garbage heap. But I also don't feel like commenting or making predictions.

Heggodu, 25 March 1990

At our age and in these times, we have to learn to live with farewells. Tomorrow in a week it is farewell to the village (to which I can always come back – though the "always" has a potential "not" attached for many reasons, including my age, even if work and life here do not allow me to conceive of or feel it at all). Were I to write you a word about work here, it would be about something I might find words for, but which is hard if not impossible to conceive of for

10 On 18 March 1990, the last elections were held in the GDR. A coalition of pro-unification parties led by the Christian Democratic Union (CDU), the GDR branch of the conservative party of West German chancellor Helmut Kohl, won the elections and made CDU politician Lothar de Maizière prime minister. The new parliament ratified the adoption of the West German Deutschmark on 1 July 1990 and German unification on 3 October 1990.

Fig. 15 Bennewitz in "his village," Heggodu, with Ninasam founder K.V. Subbanna, 1990s. Courtesy of Fritz-Bennewitz-Archiv, Leipzig.

anyone who is not experiencing it: the fact that each day, from the first moment to the last "see you tomorrow" after work, is filled with friendliness and joy. Perhaps I experienced something like it nearly 35 years ago in Meiningen, and in better Weimar times, and here and there in Leipzig, too – but it was something different then, because I myself was young and had energies from within which contributed to the pleasure of working. Here, at 64 years of age, I am experiencing the renewal of these energies – to the point of imagining that they are inexhaustible – coming from the people I work with.

I should not be surprised or disgruntled if ever I were asked to "pay the bill" (in whatever currency) for all this happiness through twenty years already now (and at home it also was there for many years, and sometimes even during the last twenty, in Weimar or Leipzig). Of course, there often were hours and situations (as the letters from past years show) when I asked myself [...] what and why in the world I was doing all this work all over the world – but that is only natural and does not take anything away from the foundations of my happy existence and from my gratitude to all that made it possible for me. Perhaps I even have a certain talent for it. It's just, I am not capable [...] of dealing with the world as it is and will become there in Germany. The world there lives at the expense of the world in which I live here. That's why I am not interested in taking even one step across the former German-German border [...], and my world there remains Rembrandtweg 6.

Heggodu, 31 March 1990

It was a difficult birth here, too, on the day of the show and even the day before: the colleague playing Bottom[11] had seized up [...], and out came only words learned by heart, and the more I tried to pry him open the more uptight I made him, so that I did it once again like in Delhi recently – I let the rehearsals be and sent them away, saying "we'll see tonight"; if it works out, we'll be happy, if it remains as it is, our efforts were in vain. There's always the nagging thought that perhaps I did not overcome the language barrier clearly enough, because my Kannada is not at all sufficient to reach them in their own words – I have to do it via English. But these doubts are not all that well founded, since I have reached actors across twelve languages including this one. That's because by gift and practice I have an ear that can hear in any language after a few days where the word is coming from: just from the vocal chords or from deeper depths.

So, it was a sad afternoon, but with experiences again that pale in description and could hardly happen elsewhere. When I left them to themselves in the morning, there was a great sadness, and I avoided them (and did not feel all that good about it). Then, one of them (precisely the one who had had and to whom I had given such a hard time) came to me around 6 pm and brought me coffee [...]. He came together with a boy from the village school who plays one of the Pucks, bringing coffee and cookies, and asked quietly whether I would come to the performance. Of course, I went over to the theatre at 6:30 (the show was supposed to start at 7, provided there was electricity) and was friendly but strict and had them start playing the first scene and then the second – and I realized that they played from out

11 This was Shi Nagendraprabhu.

of their happiness that I had come and had not abandoned them, so that I might well have shed some tears of gratitude and joy.

It was an evening that made every minute with them here in the village worth it. Sometimes I think it has to do with my autumn (really, late autumn at 64), I mean: harvest time, time of ripening, because here I don't have to fight my way through actors' arrogance and expectations of spectacular action, but rather everything happens for human reasons. So I repeat: it also makes up for the lack of pleasure in my last productions at home and for the correspondingly lackluster results. [...]

[...]

Oh, this is what I wanted to inscribe in my joy about the performance: they are all HUMAN BEINGS on stage, and that is what they want to be. Perhaps I am old-fashioned, but then the world here is too. The joy of the audience as of the actors is genuine – can you understand that I have nothing more to do or to say in theatre at home among "us"? And I am not unhappy about it.

New Delhi, 1990: Shakespeare, *The Tempest*

True to his proclamation above that he had "nothing more to do or to say in theatre at home," Bennewitz began his next extensive working stay in India after only a few months in Germany with a production of Shakespeare's *The Tempest* in a Hindi translation by Amitabh Srivastava with the repertory company of the Shri Ram Centre for Performing Arts in New Delhi, where he worked from late October to late December 1990. Once again, B.V. Karanth supplied the music for the production, with song lyrics written by Subodh Lal, a set designed by Jayant Deshmukh, and lights by Girdhari Lal. The production met with a rather indifferent response from the critics and even from Bennewitz himself, though it is interesting to note that in his interpretation of the play, he seemed to have been influenced by recent postcolonial readings; a journalist interviewing him for a preview of the production quotes him as saying that "even 400 years ago, 'Shakespeare was already writing about the history of colonialism!'" (Kazmi). In contrast to this specific historical reference, his words about Caliban in his director's note for the production program are more general:

> Caliban. His urge for freedom. The prerequisite of Prospero's freedom provokes the want for freedom of those oppressed by him.

> The human vision of a community worthy of human beings will remain within the limits of the given condition of history and man. The solution of that antagonism Shakespeare hasn't projected into a foreseeable future. Caliban remains to be freed. Whereby and by whom? ("Director's Note" on *The Tempest*, New Delhi 1990)

This interpretation seems more directed towards developments in Germany and the fate of communism again, though not in a direct or explicit manner. In any case, Bennewitz's writings from this stay are as interesting for his reflections about those developments and his attitude towards them, especially in the context of his pivotal encounter with the director of the New Delhi Goethe Institute described below, as for his descriptions of the production and his musings on Shakespeare.

> New Delhi, 2 December 1990
>
> I think it is the first Sunday of Advent. I have an easier time remembering that than the fact that there are elections at home. The time will come when I think about the contradiction that I am moved by my contact with history in my everyday life here, by my work on *The Tempest*, where I let myself be moved by power and powerlessness, by the good and bad uses of power and its non-utilization – but that I am INDIFFERENT about having resigned from our very own history there, which determines our life for the next day and for the coming years we will still live through; I am choosing the word "resign" in conscious parallel to my resignation from the party. Even after the finance scandal,[12] I have nothing against the party – it was more of an excuse to end a bond that no ties made firm enough or necessary for me anymore. This is the truth, even if not a good truth. If throughout the years of "our great youth" (Volker Braun) the reasons for belonging to the party, for finding myself within it, were a NEED and DECLARATION OF BELIEF with CONVICTION and the WILL to effect something in and through the party, then there would be at least two logical conclusions: the first is that when, as a result of my experiencing the world here, I felt displeasure with and alienation from the party, I should not have used my extraordinary condition of being

12 The reference is to a series of controversies involving the assets and financial mismanagement of the Party of Democratic Socialism (PDS), the successor of the GDR ruling SED party, which led to a wave of resignations by party members.

outside (geographically and work-wise) to remain on the outside and yet belong to the party, without doubts and without resistance to the mess it created, which, as we now know, was and remains a crime. The second conclusion, arising from my original motivation to belong to the party in order to further a cause, is that this motivation would be even better and cleaner today, because no other political force than the left can represent human value and dignity in a situation where even with the – seemingly – best of all democratic constitutions human beings remain reduced to their market value. I know this – and yet I have resigned. The time will come when I will have to answer this question more precisely for myself. That's not a thought that wants to take back the resignation, which is appropriate for me and my personality structure; the thought is not good, but it is true. I won't dwell further on it now – but it seems to belong among the farewells that we have to cope with in the late years of our lives. The farewells are also retreats.

New Delhi, 3 December 1990

As I work on *The Tempest* here, I get frightened and enthusiastic about how deeply Shakespeare has looked inside human beings and the world, and I try to lead the actors to the edge of these heights and abysses and to let something of this echo from within them. That is what I am good at. I can't think of anything else. And then I read in *Theater der Zeit* about a performance at a Dutch theatre festival that it traced the psychology of the characters, but did not take them apart, because nothing fits together anymore in the world and in human beings. There is probably some truth in that, and painting (e.g., Picasso) and music have done it. Why should theatre not do it? Yet, I CANNOT do it, which has nothing to do with not WANTING to do it. So it is probably time to think about stepping down. The thing that still gives my work legitimation is my ability to open up the actors to themselves – which also is simply good acting training. Realistic understanding and representation of human beings is still the foundation for whatever different conceptions and means of theatre are developed from or in opposition to it. Yet, one has to be wary of passing off the only way one knows as the only valid way.

By the way, the kind of thinking in cycles (cyclical movements that return to themselves and thus have no beginning and end) here in Asia and India, as opposed to our Enlightenment structures of a rising line or at least spiral, is easily transposed into one's own life. Perhaps the closing of circles is what we mean when we say: "that is a well-rounded life" – to have returned to oneself, and the circle is also the sign of harmony.

New Delhi, 4 December 1990

Work on *The Tempest* is in a deep crisis, and in the comedic scenes of all things, which, if I did them with people coming from folk theatre like the core of the Bhopal troupe, would be a pleasure. Here I am dealing with terrible, hardly eradicable theatre clichés. Today I was exhausted, morally, mentally, and even physically. If this mood will ever become permanent, I will have an easier time to readjust to home. But I might get it under control again, after all. And they could be so good, if only they understood that they need to take nothing and nobody with them into the play other than themselves – the rest, Shakespeare has taken care of.

New Delhi, 6 December 1990

I started yesterday with a company meeting to make them conscious of the crisis that our work is in, and also to make it clear that I have never given up on a production, but that I would also not be willing to deliver results below my and their potential. Afterwards, we had a run-through of the first act, and there (once again!) was the miracle. [...] It was not just that the acting was at a high level, so that the colleagues who are not in the first act sat there as excited and moved as if they were watching a crime thriller – something happened (again) that makes me wish I had the drive and talent to describe it: when the actors are liberated (sometimes I really think I must have something of the witch-doctor in me [...]) [...] and they come into contact with the play in a way that they can also connect to their historical/cultural subconscious. It becomes an interpretation that one might be able to anticipate in thought, but which cannot be manufactured by artistic "means" (because then it would be artificial).

The colonial past of India is present in them not just as historical knowledge (which they often don't even have all that much of) but also as inherited injury. This makes Prospero such a rich and contradictory character, and I can only capture it imperfectly by saying that he has the arrogance of the colonial ruler, and in the beginning of Act Five he has an apocalyptic destructive power like the god Shiva before his famous dance,[13] in which he smashes the world underfoot. Only then does it become comprehensible what an achievement it is to give up power and to practice forgiveness instead of revenge. But above all it is there in Caliban. The vulnerability and sensitivity to inflicted pain of the now oppressed former "owner" of the island cannot be accessed through intellectual approaches to acting.

New Delhi, 8 December 1990

Bennewitz reports about his meeting with the director of the Goethe Institute / Max Mueller Bhavan in New Delhi:[14]

I think he has not been in India all that long. With much respect, he spoke about what he had learned of my accomplishments in the country, and about the reportedly extraordinary quality of my last production (Volker Braun's *Great Peace*). Because we did not have all that much time, I asked him three questions. As I could have known, the first question, about what to do with the Indian production for the "Festival of India in Germany,"[15] did not fall under his responsibility. This is exclusively the purview of the Indian side and of the Haus der Kulturen der Welt, Berlin.[16] Fine, that's checked off.

My second question, since he himself had begun talking about the extent and effects of my work, was how and with what support it might continue (I cautiously bracketed out the financial kind and was for now just talking of support in spirit). In response, he began again with my work and said that the FRG[17] (when the GDR still existed) had done next to nothing in the field

13 The Hindu god Shiva is often depicted as the cosmic dancer Shiva Nataraja, whose dance destroys the universe in preparation for new creation.

14 Presumably, this was Dr Klaus Ferkinghoff.

15 The reference is to the production of Girish Karnad's *Nāga-Mandala*, which Vijaya Mehta directed in collaboration with Bennewitz in Leipzig in February 1992.

16 The Haus der Kulturen der Welt in Berlin is Germany's national cultural centre dedicated to the meeting of diverse cultures and the presentation of arts from around the world.

17 The Federal Republic of Germany, i.e., West Germany before reunification. Bennewitz's use of the abbreviation (in German: BRD for Bundesrepublik Deutschland) is somewhat polemical, since its use was controversial at times in West Germany, there being a perception among conservative circles that it was used in the German Democratic Republic to balance the common use of DDR (for Deutsche Demokratische Republik).

of theatre in India for the last few years, and that he was planning to pay more attention to it. For the "Festival of Germany in India" in 1993/94 he wants to not only bring a German theatre troupe to India, but also to have German directors produce German plays with Indian troupes in the five centres where the Goethe Institute has branch offices in India. Those are all fine perspectives, of course – I turned the conversation back to my own interests and revealed that the Repertory Company had made me an offer to do *Faust* with them. I asked him what the Goethe Institute/Max Mueller Bhavan's position was in that regard. So he went into a grand sweep of an explanation about the structures of the various institutes and organizations of foreign cultural policy, and above all of the Goethe Institute, stressing again how independent they are, e.g., from the German embassy, which would only interfere in case they did something politically irresponsible, but that they have no decision-making powers nor even the right of selection with regard to persons involved in projects. He said they could only make suggestions to the central office in Munich which activities in the country would be good and useful, and the central office then makes the decisions about budget and persons involved. In plain speak, this means that the Max Mueller Bhavan will suggest the link with NSD and the REP (and thus in turn will harvest the fruits of my labours here). NSD will suggest a play, which the Max Mueller Bhavan will then pass on to Munich, where the decision about the person to direct it will be made.

I returned to the question of *Faust*, which is nearly inextricably linked to my person, and explained that in no way was I making a claim for myself and this production to be included in the plans of the central office. He responded courteously that of course *Faust* would be a highlight for the "Festival of Germany in India," and since they had no authority to decide about who the director should be, he suggested that I should apply to the central office in Munich to direct the play. I don't know whether he was conscious of the implications – I would rather assume he wasn't, but I should be more realistic and know that this was not done naïvely, but is rather an agreed-upon policy, and that he escaped the embarrassment of taking responsibility for it to my face – after having stressed my merits – by means of the bureaucratic procedure of arguing that it was the exclusive resort of the central office. I remained completely composed, because it just made fully clear to me what I had already known. Why should foreign cultural policy be any different than the domestic one, where everything that is reminiscent of the achievements of the GDR is targeted for being taken out of public memory?

My third question, since he himself had brought up the *Great Peace*, was about the excellent video that exists of the production. I suggested that a screening of the video followed by discussion be included in the public program of the Max Mueller Bhavan. He replied that that did not belong in the program of the Max Mueller Bhavan, but why couldn't a small circle meet at his house and watch the video. I am not sure whether I should regret that my schedule makes this impossible while I'm in Delhi. I just found it suspect that it was not supposed to belong in the program of the institution which is in charge of representing and making known German culture – and Volker Braun remains one of the most significant German poets (or does he have too much GDR identity for them?!). I'll write more on this later.

[...]

Let me return to the conversation in the Max-Mueller-Bhavan, or actually, let me not. I am out, and feel liberated about it. I am glad it is so. The German state is of no concern to me – and I need not be their concern. It would not be good if it were otherwise. I have represented the GDR for twenty years; whatever state it had become – I was always proud to represent what it originally was supposed to aim for. Without this state, I could not have done the things I did, which have made an impact and become history here. My works were contributions towards establishing contact between what is proper and unique to here with what is international and proper to humankind. The cultural foreign policy of the FRG is something different: to propagate Germany as a country whose "great democracy" should be emulated. Shakespeare is of no interest in that – how did the ambassador put it: "that just reminds them of the British, and they integrate Shakespeare in imperialist and colonialist ways."

Now I do have something else to mention from the conversation yesterday, after all: as a rule, the usual activities of the Goethe Institute in the area of theatre here were such that they supported (financed) a troupe when it put on a German play, including Brecht in the 1970s. (In my letters from the 1980s, there must be a report from Calcutta where the FRG held a large-scale Brecht seminar with troupes from all over the country – and 80% were students of mine. That's where Dr. Erken, then chief dramaturge in Stuttgart or Cologne, said that one shouldn't deny or lessen the merits of Bennewitz, but that one needs to keep in mind that in the country Bennewitz comes from, Brecht's entire oeuvre is not allowed to be made public, claiming that Brecht's diaries were not published in the GDR, and more such nonsense.) This past January or February, when I was directing *Great Peace*, a former student of mine and now himself a prominent director came to me and asked for suggestions for a German play, because he had an offer from the Max Mueller Bhavan to produce one, but all of his suggestions were rejected, either because they were by a Swiss author (Dürrenmatt!!) or an Austrian (Bernhard!).[18] However, since there is no contemporary author from the Federal Republic (except for Krötz, who has been done) who could be integrated internationally, I suggested Heiner Müller's *The Mission*.[19] As I found out from Dr. Ferkinhoff [*sic*] now, this suggestion has been accepted, and Heiner Müller was even invited to participate in an advisory role, which he at first accepted but then declined – yes, Heiner Müller, because two years ago the West had oriented the entire Documenta in Kassel towards him, also in order to extract him from the GDR. So I had initiated something, and it was taken over shamelessly and declared as their own initiative. All this is not yet the final word about whether I will stop working in India – but it is an expression of my discomfort about transferring my work into the other Germany, which is supposed to be my country but cannot be. That's why I said earlier in the letter that the visit was a liberation.

New Delhi, 20 December 1990

My inner retreat from political participation into what at best is mere interest is increasing, and I will repeat that it does not

---

18 The Swiss Friedrich Dürrenmatt (1921–90) and the Austrian Thomas Bernhard (1931–89) belong among the most important authors and most frequently performed dramatists of twentieth-century literature in German.

19 Heiner Müller (1929–95), who worked in the GDR and later in unified Germany, is often held to be the most important twentieth-century dramatist in German after Brecht. His play *The Mission: Memories of a Revolution* is an experimental dramatic collage on the theme of revolutionary action.

even frighten me that this does not frighten me; Christa Wolf's sentence that "the grandchildren will fight it out better" marks the long distance between me and the grandchildren, leaving the struggle to them and their parents. The loss and withdrawal of my GDR identity is and will remain painful, and nothing fills the empty place. Rather, I am experiencing something else: one cannot be a citizen of the world if one is not a citizen of a more narrowly defined (historical, political, social, cultural) home. That's why this region, which you – and I myself – have often called my other or even true home, is not a second or third one, now that there is no first home with which I identify historically, socially, and culturally. More and more, I am comprehending the difficulties of the fate of the exile, for whom the countries of refuge can never become home. It is the emptiness of statelessness.

New Delhi, 24 December 1990

The evening's performance was beautiful, despite being the dreaded second one. Apparently, the production has been crafted well enough to allow for growth from within itself. There is a second reason why performances here often and easily become better – the actors are not vain and oversensitive, not even if I interrupt a run-through or even a dress rehearsal and have them start over because they are not themselves. I tried that once in Weimar, with unforgettable negative consequences. What I mean is that actors here allow me to plunge to their depths, often with the most difficult effort and sometimes with self-doubts, even if it is painful. They know that I am doing it because I have faith that there are depths to be plunged. Actors in Germany think that their talent makes this unnecessary, and they are insulted in their "creativity."

From Delhi, Bennewitz went to Bhopal to conduct a workshop, whence he sent the following elegiac note:

Bhopal, 4 January 1991

What I would most like to do would be to fly back home – but I have to go through (with) it to the end and stick it out. There are symptoms of dissolution everywhere, and the great warmth and friendliness of people do not make up for the fact that the work no longer has the meaning it had in the glorious 1970s, when

> there was a sense of departure in the Third World; even in the 1980s, the work was pleasurable and profitable. It is strange but also good that at 65 – the legal age to retire – I will be done here as well. There continue to be invitations – but the experience of not having a state and an idea to back me anymore finds me indifferent, listless, and declining them.

Despite this resigned tone, Bennewitz was far from ceasing his activities in India. After the workshop and guest performances of his Bhopal *Caucasian Chalk Circle* in Delhi, Lucknow, and Shimla, Bennewitz went back to Lucknow from mid-January to late February 1991 on the invitation of Professor Raj Bisaria, the founder of the Bhartendu Academy of Dramatic Arts. There, he worked with the repertory company of the Academy on a production of Brecht's *Life of Galileo* in a Hindi translation by V.K. Sharma.

After a brief interlude in Mumbai, Bennewitz then spent most of March 1991 in Mysore at the Rangayana theatre institute founded by B.V. Karanth in 1989 with support from the state government of Karnataka and housed in the Kalamandira cultural centre. Here, Bennewitz directed the Rangayana repertory troupe in a collage of scenes from Shakespeare's *Hamlet, King Lear,* and *Midsummer Night's Dream* in Kannada, entitled *Shakespearege Namaskara.* This stay, though not represented here in writings by Bennewitz, was significant for opening up for him yet another institutional base for his work in India, his second in Karnataka after Ninasam in Heggodu.

Bennewitz made a very strong impression at Rangayana. In interviews with the author, two actors Bennewitz worked with there, Pramila Bengre and Prashanth Hiremath, both stress his importance for their own development and for Indian theatre, as does Raghunandana, his former student, assistant director for *Shakespearege Namaskara* and several other productions, and now a prominent director himself. As at Ninasam, Bennewitz was and is held in high esteem as a guru at Rangayana. His photograph hangs in prominent spots in both places. It is therefore only fitting that his next long sojourn in India was spent entirely at these two institutions, beginning with work on a production of Shakespeare's *Twelfth Night* in Kannada (title: *Habbadi Hanneradeneya Raatri*) with Ninasam's Tirugata troupe from late September to late October 1991. It was during this stay that Bennewitz learned that he was to receive the 1991 Sangeet Natak Akademi Prize for Directing.

Figs. 16 and 17 Bennewitz during rehearsals for *Shakespearege Namaskara*, a collage of scenes from Shakespeare plays in Kannada, Mysore, 1991. Courtesy of Fritz-Bennewitz-Archiv, Leipzig.

Fig. 18 Group portrait with three gurus: Indian theatre personalities and former associates of Bennewitz under his portrait and those of K.V. Subbanna and B.V. Karanth at the office of Ninasam, Heggodu, 2012. Back row from left to right: Venkatraman Aithal, K.G. Krishnamurthy, M.K. Raina. Front row: Nataraj Honnavalli, Rustom Bharucha, Prakash Garud. Photograph by Joerg Esleben.

Heggodu, 1991: Shakespeare, *Twelfth Night*

Heggodu, 6 October 1991

I stopped keeping a work journal long ago, including in my letters – nothing by me and from my work here needs to be preserved. I say that without sadness, because I understand more and more how true the statement is that I once gave to an interviewer in order to express my lack of eloquence and comfort with interviews and to hint that he would do better to watch me work and then write and describe what he thinks he sees [...]: "My medium is the moment." And no one has better expressed what can be said about the moment than Shakespeare, and nowhere better than in *Twelfth Night*: "Look you, sir, such a one I was this present," which has been excellently translated by Schlegel as: "Seht, Herr, so sah ich in diesem Augenblick aus." He takes the smallest thinkable unit of time – the momentary look of the eye (Augen-Blick) – and already frames it with a verb in the past tense – "that's how I LOOKED in this moment." What can be preserved from this? It is completely different with those who write, paint, compose, etc., whose works you can have at the disposal of your eyes, ears, and hands whenever you want. And because nothing can be preserved from what I do and from my – enormously happy – experience, nothing that would even come close to representing it, I also don't WANT anything to be preserved. [...]

I am curious to find out what will happen with my production of *Don Carlos*, or rather, right now and right here I am not at all curious about it (and thus happy that I have done so much preliminary work on my conception and on the stage set with Panzer that I can begin with it in January),[20] because there is no inner temptation to think about it. When I start listening to the *Carlos* tape from time to time, I stop it again after just a few seconds. In THIS culture and nature opera is so foreign an art that its music – which moves me very much at home, where I can hear it ten times over without getting tired of it – does not reach me at all here. Opera is so exclusively a European art and music that here only those who have seen or heard it in Europe at some point might know what it actually is.

Heggodu, 9 October 1991

Working conditions here are as good as the human atmosphere and the rhythm of life in the village. The number of highly talented actors is far above average, and no ensemble has only top actors [...]. Now, there are only three girls in the troupe, and *Twelfth Night* needs exactly three women, and all three roles are prominent ones. I have a very good Viola, a good Mary, but an Olivia[21] who rattles off her lines in an unnaturally high voice and

20 Bennewitz directed Verdi's opera *Don Carlos* in Weimar in 1992, with a set designed by Kristian Panzer, whom he later also worked with on his Mumbai *Faust*.

21 This was Shoba Hegade.

without taking breaths, probably with enormous "feeling." It is as unnatural as the school performances of daughters from the upper or upper middle class; and she also rarely wears any kind of Indian dress, but rather these unbearably tasteless clothes fashioned according to imported taste, with ruffles and frills (something I have never seen in all the years I have been coming to Ninasam), and if once in a while she does wear a salwar kameez [...], then it is an awful "modern version" of this beautiful, simple combination of pants and kurta. So my faulty conclusion from all this was that she must somehow come from the lower middle class (but then how did she acquire this mashed-up city taste? [...]). Surprise: the girl comes from a remote village and from one of the lowest castes or even from below the caste system, her parents are dead, and she didn't feel at home with her brother or sister in the village. So she went to the city and tried her luck as a salesgirl, then as receptionist in a hotel, and then she applied to Ninasam two years ago, where to everyone's surprise she showed up at the selection interview with cut-off hair and make-up (which is already common in the cities, but unthinkable in the rural areas).

Basically, she is a modest girl, not at all vain or arrogant. Probably, those are all attempts to leave her past and her village, which itself is still so far in the past, behind her; and so in her conception of theatre she probably also emulated the clichés of film acting. After I don't know how many fruitless hours I managed to get through this surface to the kernel of her person for five minutes, but right after that it seemed lost again for good, so that yesterday I was already a step beyond the limits of my energy and patience and thought I would not be able to manage with her. I discussed it with Akshara, the director of the ensemble (also a former student of mine from Atul's year in the early 1980s), and when I heard her story, I was moved and also ashamed that I had been rough with her in my impatience. Akshara will work with her separately, and in that way we should manage to not let her fall too far behind the (excellent) others in the show. It is hard to find girls for the ensemble. Just imagine: five months on the road, travelling 8000 km, set up and take down 160 shows yourself under the most difficult living and working conditions, and the girls lend the same hand as the boys. So the Tirugata troupe of Ninasam was happy to get a third girl, even though they knew her experience is limited.

Heggodu, 11 October 1991

Today some big news arrived, i.e., the founder, director, and guru of Ninasam brought it with him from Delhi, and it might be in the news this evening and perhaps in the newspapers tomorrow. I am supposed to be awarded the prize of the all-Indian Sangeet Natak Akademi (the Indian Academy of Arts for music and theatre) – a very rare honour for foreigners. The members of the Academy from all parts of the subcontinent are said to have voted unanimously in favour of suggesting me as recipient of the prize. The announcement is supposed to be today and the prize ceremony in February in Jaipur. I don't believe it yet, and am only telling you for now, and you should also keep it to yourself until I know it from the radio, the newspaper, and the Akademi itself. After that, though, I would like the DNT, the city of Weimar, and the FRG to find out. If it is true, then it would be a beautiful reward for the past twenty years – and yet, the more beautiful reward is the work itself and my experiences in it and through it.

Heggodu, 24 October 1991

The Ninasam Culture Course has been going on since Sunday. You always have to keep in mind that all of it takes place in a village of perhaps 500 inhabitants, not just the theatre institute with its professional training course for actors, a theatre with over 600 seats, a library, audio-visual equipment, and a touring ensemble (with whom I am concluding work today); in addition, every year around this time they hold this Culture Course. More than 200 participants come from all parts of Karnataka, ranging from university professors, authors, students, and journalists to people with an interest in culture from all kinds of professions, including workers. There are lectures and discussions (and what lively ones they are) about politics and culture, literature, music, theatre, film, etc. and in the evenings performances in the theatre. The latter are frequented by the inhabitants of the surrounding villages, who fill the theatre beyond capacity despite often having a long journey back home through the night on foot, bicycle, or scooter.

The opening performance was a solo evening by Sonal Mansingh, the most famous Odissi dancer in India. (Odissi is one of the great classical Indian dance forms.) If only I were a bit more in the reporting mood, I would have liked to describe this to you, though it once again is really indescribable and belongs

Fig. 19 Bennewitz receives the Sangeeth Natak Akademi Prize for Directing from Indian President Ramaswamy Venkataraman and Akademi Chairman Girish Karnad, 1992. Courtesy of Fritz-Bennewitz-Archiv, Leipzig.

> among the events that one rarely encounters more than twice in one's life. The next afternoon I had the unforgettable opportunity to speak with her for an hour here in Prasanna's house [...] (by the way, the fact that she made the trip from Delhi to this southern Indian village is comparable with Pavarotti singing here [...] – that, roughly, is her rank in her art form). For the last two days, the overcrowded theatre has been home to our Tirugata performances, with which they will soon go on tour for five months. This evening, there is the premiere of *Twelfth Night*.

After the premiere of *Twelfth Night*, Bennewitz went to Mumbai for a few days and then back south for a few days rest in Udupi, Karnataka, before continuing on to Mysore for his second production with the Rangayana troupe. B.V. Karanth had chosen Chekhov's *The Cherry Orchard* for adaptation into Kannada with the intent of adding a realistic play to the company's repertoire (Interview Raghunandana). The Kannada translation, under the title *Cherry Thota,* was prepared only shortly before Bennewitz's arrival by H.S. Sivaprakash and was then reworked for the stage by assistant director Raghunandana in collaboration with the actors.

Mysore, 1991: Chekhov, *The Cherry Orchard*

Mysore, 20 November 1991

Yesterday we spent the second day on the *Cherry Orchard,* and beforehand I had worried a bit what they could make out of the Russian Chekhov down here in the Indian south. You cannot imagine it. They had read the entire play for the first time just the night before, and we merely wanted to find out what of it had stuck with them, and then it turned into nearly five hours of the most passionate discussions, with the most intense sympathy for the characters and arguments back and forth about how their behaviour and lives should be judged. I am (probably) doing our actors at home an injustice, but I can't help thinking that they are not capable of sympathizing so passionately with others, and that if they were to get hotly involved with their heads (or even their hearts) at all, it would likely be about what spectacular actions their characters should take. I know I am unjust to them. Otto[22] also thought that my generation would start playing *Faust* under water. I really think without grief or sadness that my time in the theatre is over, and that the next generation has just as much of a right to represent their views and ways of experiencing the world as Otto gave to me – and I will never forget his generosity. It's just that here people still experience the world differently and I experience the world differently through the people.

Mysore, 21 November 1991

Soon, I will go back over to the Kalamandira to work on the *Cherry Orchard,* which after the encouragingly passionate discussions about the play and the characters in the morning was discouraging to the point of despair in the afternoon and evening rehearsals because not one sentence during the reading of the first

22 Otto Lang (1906–84) was Bennewitz's teacher and supervisor as Rector of the Leipzig Theatre Academy (1953–8) and Artistic Director of the German National Theatre in Weimar (1958–73).

Figs. 20 and 21 Bennewitz in a characteristic posture having tea during a rehearsal break – in Mysore in 1991 and as a caricature. Courtesy of Fritz-Bennewitz-Archiv, Leipzig.

act betrayed even the slightest hint of sense and understanding. However, those are the often experienced ups and downs, and later it might be completely different again. We are and I am so dependent on the events and moods of the moment.

Mysore, 24 November 1991

Work is not pure joy at the moment, it just creeps along. But not everything is always a high point in your day-to-day life, either, right? And since I can do nothing else and do not have the imagination for anything else, I keep doing it, because not doing it (any longer) is perhaps even worse than such hours, when I just muddle through. I also can't help myself, I have to try to get to the core of the matter, meaning to the actors' foundations and thus to their centre, where the words are not just recited, but where their lives, experiences, and opinions sit and resonate.

Mysore, 8 December 1991

For me, the *Cherry Orchard* is a grand, unknown experience of unexpected encounters and discoveries. It's just too bad that it entered my life so late; but I probably would not have understood it earlier, anyhow. For the actors here the play is very hard (to play, not to understand, because the characters and situations often seem closer and more familiar to them than to us). I don't know yet whether I will bring it to a public performance by the end of the year.

Bennewitz did bring *Cherry Thota* to a public performance, though actor Prashanth Hiremath, who played Lopahin, is of the opinion that the production was not successful, including for Karanth, who reportedly thought that it did not achieve the goal of creating an Indian form of realism (Interview Prashanth).

Lucknow and Dhaka (Bangladesh), 1992/3

From October 1992 to March 1993, Bennewitz was back on the subcontinent, first for a workshop at the Bhartendu Academy in Lucknow and then to finally follow through on the longstanding wish and invitation from Bangladesh to direct a production there, a Bangla adaptation of Brecht's *Man equals Man* with an ITI-sponsored federation of several group theatres in Dhaka. The passages included here from his letters written during these stays in Lucknow and Dhaka do not speak specifically to the work he did there but rather contain interesting reflections on politics, theatre, and identity.

Lucknow, 5 November 1992

In the last elections, Rajiv Gandhi's Congress Party lost for the first time in the many years since Nehru and Indira Gandhi (who was Prime Minister for all but two years during her long time in government). The elections brought the BJP (something like an Indian People's Party) to power in many Indian states (fortunately not in the central government). This is a fundamentalist, Hindu-chauvinist party which wants to turn India into a Hindu state and which abuses the religious sentiments of Hindus (there are millions, particularly in the rural areas, who are more attached to their gods than to the use of historical reason) to shore up its power. It is also this party that, together with other Hindu sects and organizations, provoked the conflict in Ayodhya, very close to here, where 400 years ago Muslims supposedly built a mosque exactly on the spot where the favourite Hindu god Rama is supposed to have been born. But, my God, who really knows where God was born? [...] This conflict has been going on for years now and militant Hindus had already begun to demolish the mosque, so that the state had to intervene with military force. A year and a half ago, the militants issued a call for *kar seva* (which means something like "volunteer construction hours") for a gigantic temple for Ram, within which the mosque would disappear. At the moment, the central government in Delhi is mediating negotiations between the feuding parties, but the militant temple constructors have already threatened that whatever the outcome of the negotiations, they will continue construction on December 6th and will not stop until the last stone has been put in place.[23]

There is hardly a corner left where the world is not turned upside down – perhaps in my Indian village down south, but I will not get there this year. And in Rembrandtweg 6 there is also relative normalcy still [...]. Enough with the stories about

23 Bennewitz is referring to the Ayodhya dispute, during which the Babri Mosque was destroyed by Hindu fundamentalists on 6 December 1992, and which led to communal riots and court cases for the next two decades.

the temple conflict. But perhaps you can understand that if such people are in power in a state, they want to have their own people in leading positions, especially in cultural institutions. So Professor Bisaria was pushed out of office, even though a considerable number of Indian artists protested and spoke up on his behalf. But the signature of a Chief Minister trumps even the most respectable forums and their protests.

What is interesting is that I had barely arrived here when the representative of the Indian Council for Cultural Relations (ICCR) called and issued an invitation. For good reason, I had been surprised how he could have known so quickly that I was in Lucknow (especially since it must be many years since we met last – I take it he was in charge of looking after me in Calcutta at some point). During my conversation with Prof. Bisaria today, I was able to put two and two together: this man is known as servile to the government and supposedly has connections to the RSS, which is a militant organization of the BJP (like our brigade groups or the SA in former times). Who knows what they want to find out from me? If this is really about more than just the wish to see me again over tea, luckily for me and unluckily for them I am in an unassailable position, and with my Sangeet Natak Academi award I have connections to higher places than they could dream of approaching. It can't be anything else: someone from the Bhartendu Academy must have informed the ICCR man that I had arrived (just as we also had Stasi informers in the German National Theatre), and of course everyone knows I am from the East, and that's how the suspiciously fast invitation must have come about. In a way, this is fun for me.

Lucknow, 14 December 1992

The news says that since yesterday life has normalized everywhere. The government has taken some measures, albeit too late: leaders of the BJP have been arrested and charged with breaching the peace and disrupting the constitutionally guaranteed harmony and tolerance of the various religious communities; militant and extremist Hindu and Muslim organizations have been banned. There remains a smouldering fire underneath, and the wounds of that fateful December 6th, which shame and grief call the blackest day in India since the assassination of Mahatma Gandhi, will not heal quickly, and scars will remain. [...]

The Academy had been closed right after December 6th, like all universities, schools, etc., and will remain closed this week. We should actually not be affected by the curfew, since all but three of our students live in the area of the Academy, but laws cannot bear exceptions. This makes the days very long, and it takes me quite some effort not to abandon myself to the thought that all this is coming at the right time and to get it into my skull that I do not HAVE to be here, as you have often told me. Let's assume my work is (to use a word that is much too grandiose) historically a closed chapter and has to continue having an impact on its own merits, [...] and that I will not achieve anything new anymore. I know this – but I have often named the resulting problem, and you have responded with friendly and considerate understanding: I do not know, and have not had the drive or courage to try it out, how I will feel and behave when I am no longer here, which would leave an open wound. This is the question: should I cut out the wound with the soul surgeon's scalpel, or should I let it heal slowly by itself, so that the need and drive cease by themselves through weaning? It is a similar question as for a smoker – quit from one day to the next and for good, or have one fewer every day? I know that the more radical method is better, but I have to find and make myself ready for it. As yet there is no urgent homesickness. I have been rather successful in getting used to the pattern: when I am here, I am HERE, and when I am there, I am THERE.

Dhaka, 27 January 1993

Bennewitz reports about a reception at the Indian High Commission in Dhaka for Republic Day:

There are many reasons why I feel uncomfortable at such receptions, above all because of the senseless chatting with people one meets or to whom one is introduced, since real conversations are not possible on such occasions. Particularly when it comes to the prominent invitees from politics and high society – where I (not able to suppress the social sensitivity of my imagination) always think of the 50% of the population who live below the poverty line, and of those people I see even in this fancy area, just around the corner, when I go to the post office and the market. They have no roof over their heads, not even a hut slapped together from branches and rags, and the children sort paper and plastic and whatever else from the garbage to sell for a few paisa to the scrap dealer.

Another new sensation I have at such diplomatic receptions is that I am doubly a foreigner there: first, because I do not feel comfortable personally, and second, because I do not feel like I represent a country there; I am careful not to be introduced, deliberately or by chance, to the ambassador of the Federal Republic of Germany. That is also a reason why I don't feel so well and at home abroad anymore (including in India, if I don't happen to be in my village down south, high above the Arabian Sea, behind the Western Ghats) as I did in the years from 1970 up to the last "Days of GDR Culture in India" in February 1990. In those twenty years I was a representative of a country (however rotten it may have been economically, in its leadership, and in spying on its citizens), a country whose humanist international cultural policies based on solidarity and mutual respect I committed myself to and contributed to with my achievements. Then, I was never alone in my own consciousness. And even if generally there was not that much sympathy between me and the GDR diplomats, and I got on just fine without personal contact with them, there were a few among them that became good friends, like our friends the Schades in Berlin, or in Delhi, where I was always invited for potato salad and wieners by the Fischers, and when Dr. Merkel was ambassador in Manila, I enjoyed visiting him and his wife in their home. Today I no longer know what and whom I am representing. My work – as personal an achievement as it was – was essentially always the expression of solidarity between two countries and peoples; and since that no longer is the case, my work has been deprived of its sense and foundational reason, and I should really learn to recognize it as a closed chapter.

Dhaka, 30 January 1993

So far, theatre here has not gotten under my skin and has not even reached my skin. Yesterday, I saw a play with a story from the slums, which of course included a good measure of sensationalism: a lorry driver crippled by an accident lives in conflict with his wife, who is wooed by a rikshaw walla from the neighbouring slum. The cripple divorces her according to Muslim custom with the thrice-repeated phrase: I divorce you, and so the divorced

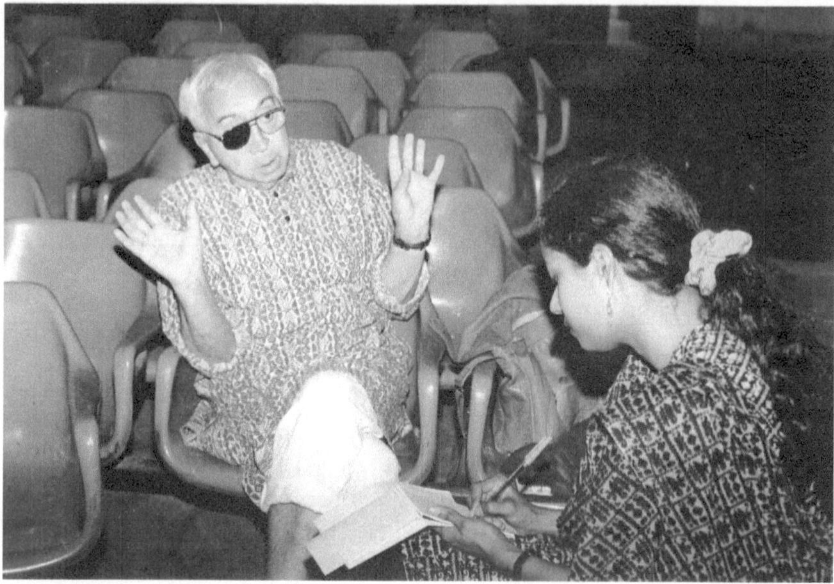

Fig. 22 Bennewitz being interviewed, Dhaka, Bangladesh, 1993. Courtesy of Fritz-Bennewitz-Archiv, Leipzig.

woman has to leave without being able to make any claims [...]. There are all kinds of other slum dwellers and all kinds of conflicts, including political ones, where communists are hunted by the police (the intellectuals here are mostly on the left), and the inevitable Bengali melodrama was also there. However, it was all acted so tightly, genuinely, and well that for the first time during this stay I have seen true Bengali theatre, not pale imitations of their own folk theatre or, worse, of Western theatre.

It is good if each does their own thing well, and they should play *Antigone* how they experience and feel it, and not how they think the Europeans play it – that the Europeans really can do better. What they can do here as their own, the Europeans can certainly not do. And that's why I still believe in the experience and conviction my work has given me that it is DIFFERENCE that counts, i.e., the many colourful, lively differences within the common humanity we all share. Anyhow, these differences will soon go to pot due to the imperialism of the mass media, which knows no borders anymore and will soon penetrate to the most remote jungle village. However, as long as they are not there yet, I'll do my work with conviction, as well as I can – though the inevitable experience of its lack of impact and powerlessness will make this work quixotic some day soon and will give me another reason to retreat beneath the roof of the Rembrandtweg house, something you also wish for. You see: history will do its part for me to grasp and acknowledge my existence as retiree.

Dhaka, 14 February 1993

My work in India does not lend itself to description and explanation and can therefore not be poured into a book and imparted to others that way. What I once said is quite true [...]: my medium is the moment; I have the inestimable and extraordinarily rare fortune that I found a task for life that corresponds to my innermost nature and to my best abilities. That is a blessing and a great boon. Of course, I know – without meaning to be arrogant – that there is hardly a handful of people who do what I do, for various reasons: because they do not want to do it, because it doesn't pay, or because they are not capable of doing it. That does not mean I am one of the greats [...]; I simply am lucky to have the talent necessary for this work, and I am even luckier to have the opportunity to use this talent. Certainly, a particular type of radiance or aura I might exude plays a role, too, but this would be (if I were religious – and perhaps I actually am) a gift from God. However, I believe that aside from a unique talent it is above all a matter of long experience and work – it is no different with any craftsman [...]. Of course, I am not so dense not to know that I live with a certain aura, and yet somehow am the "very normal child" my mother knew me as. With this, the chapter of my so-called greatness is closed and dismissed as nonsense. The blessing and boon are what remains, as is the fact that through the work I enjoyed and still enjoy I have made something of that blessing and boon.

Naturally, I am nevertheless sensitive about slights against me, when something essential is wiped from my biography as with a damp rag, as if those were just a few chalk marks on a blackboard (but this, too, is something I have in common with hundreds of thousands in the colony East Germany). [...] What offends and hurts me is the way in which the new big *Faust* production in Weimar was announced by Mr. Kaufmann, the president of the *Stiftung Weimarer Klassik* (*Weimar Classicism Foundation*) and newly minted artistic director of the *Kunst-Fest* (*Art Festival*) – as if after 1945 there had not been an uninterrupted tradition of *Faust* productions in Weimar of all places, and as if there had never been the unique historical event in the theatre that the same director produced both parts of *Faust* three times over a span of thirty years.[24] To simply pass that over – that is what offends me ... but knowing myself, I will soon have digested that, too. [...] However, I have been thinking that once I am home and have regained a detached and composed attitude (and can consult you, which has always been helpful for such ventures), I might write to the Mayor Dr. Büttner that it takes away from Weimar's justified claim to be an international cultural capital when one of its citizens is not acknowledged even though he has represented Weimar from New York to Manila and has been given the rare honour (which also honours the city) of being the first German ever to receive the Republic of India's highest artistic distinction. I feel very much like writing that letter, and I also think I owe it to my work and that it will help to prevent those achievements of the GDR that have made an historical impact from being thrown out with the trash.

Mumbai, 1993/4

As the previous passage shows, Bennewitz was thinking about his legacy, in a characteristic mix of humility and self-confidence and with a good measure of post-unification bitterness. Goethe's *Faust* plays a central role in this legacy, and so it is likely that Bennewitz saw an invitation by Vijaya Mehta to finally direct an Indian *Faust* in Mumbai as a unique chance to add a crowning achievement to his work in India. After extensive preparation, he worked on this production from September 1993 to January 1994.

---

24 Bennewitz accomplished this in 1965–7, 1975, and 1981, at the Deutsches Nationaltheater in Weimar, the last production running through the year of reunification and into the early nineties. During the same period he also directed *Faust I* in New York (1978), Bombay/Mumbai (1994), Manila (1994), and Meiningen (1995), each in the local language. See John, *Bennewitz*.

Before addressing the production itself, this section about his final stay in India opens with a summative statement of sorts by Bennewitz about intercultural theatre and its relation to his identity, in the form of a paper he gave at a seminar on the topic of "The Actor" held in late 1993 at the Prithvi Theatre, Mumbai.

"Otherness within Togetherness"[25]

I am neither a scholar nor a lecturer – writing and reading a PAPER horrifies me with embarrassment: my medium is the moment. There is too much of a temptation to leave the topic's dead straight highway and roam around into the bylanes and get lost in the jungle, distracted by a beetle or a flower – a welcome excuse to hide behind the privilege of a random selection of rasas, ragas, and talas beating the pulse of that UNDEFINABLE phenomenon THEATRE.

Though quite familiar with India and Indians and Indian artists since 1970, I am still a stranger: familiar by estrangement (which is Brecht's definition of *Verfremdung*). There are cultural patterns and filters moulded by the air we breathe, by hill and brook, by our daily bread and prayers – I am unaware how those subconscious designs define and confine my identity and "otherness."

I am more conscious about the dilemma of a German identity. I am living in Weimar – a small township of 60 000 citizens – synonymous for fame and pride of German culture (Goethe, Schiller, Bach, Cranach, and the Bauhaus to name a few out of the vast field of all arts) – and in almost walking distance from the houses of international reverence, the fascist concentration-camp of Buchenwald has stigmatized the German name with shame. Fifty million victims of war and gas-chambers are a fundamental German identity crisis on the one hand – on the other it creates a different context of reality awareness.

Once I was asked: you have been working with both Asian and European artists for quite some time. Do you notice

25 The title is not Bennewitz's but is a quote chosen from within the paper. Bennewitz wrote the paper in English. It has been very slightly edited for style, with editorial additions indicated in square brackets.

any significant difference in their attitudes towards theatre? Different courses and conditions of history have told stories distinct from each other and songs sung with different tunes. An Indian poet wouldn't address his love with: "You are beautiful like a summer day," but it is a matter of different climate rather than the shared mysteries of love; and German actors rehearsing *Śakuntalā* may have found it rather strange that songs of joy are linked with rain; or in *Mudrārākshasa* that the able Chanakya leaves for the ashram when there was a dire need for such rare statesmen in our country. They all sing the song of man (a footnote would have to make us cautious about the simplification of the statement when coming to the complications of INTERCULTURALISM of sorts).

Theatre as a medium of immediate communication and an open forum to discuss public affairs (even most intimate relations want public attention when brought on stage) knows no difference in ATTITUDES around the world, though attitudes are transformed in response to conditions and structures inherent in the arts by the creative moment of conversion into presentation and dialogue with an audience.

We know and acknowledge those conditions and structures as historical, social, national, regional, cultural, ethnic, religious etc. – differences which time and again meet within the function and functioning of the medium as global community of "Unity in Diversities" – though definitions are not always congruent to realities. It is for the always permanent moment of the respective HERE and NOW to decide on the dialectics of that relation, and our present-day experience tells us: it is the DIFFERENCE that counts and our fractured world may ask for the OTHERNESS within the TOGETHERNESS. Within the scope of these conditions and structures the difference asked for (reduced to a simple denominator) could claim the German artist's approach as analytical by comparison with the Asian artist's (or any other folk-theatre related actor's) spontaneous reaction – in life and on stage – it is a statement with a limping leg like most generalizations; it is a matter of proportion and at least more helpful than the opposites of rational and emotional. A side dish may bring us closer to present realities: many an Indian actor has reduced himself to the monotony of his vocal chords, and the German actor enjoys the discovery of his body by re-emergence of Meyerhold's Biomechanics minus Meyerhold's genius.[26]

To get into a deeper analysis, we could see that statement walking on crutches. Leaving aside the damaging impact of normative aesthetics (like Shdanov's "socialist realism") – there has been a certain homogeneity in the training of actors and the concepts of theatre with border-crossing creative relevance like Stanislavski, Method Acting, not to [mention] Brecht's influence on world theatre.

Post-modernism and global access of the Western world to all corners of the globe have blurred the distinct differences. And I am not referring here to the *Times of India* cultural editorial by Shamlal, who claims that the affluent society has enormous capacity to absorb and neutralize dissent. This explains – he continues – the ease with which business over there can exploit even avant-garde art for commercial purposes. As an American poet has said caustically, "They will wear a Kandinsky, if you make it into a sports shirt or a swimming suit, and if you make it into a sofa, they will lie on it." I mention rather the more creative challenges of pluralism [offered by figures] like Ariane Mnouchkine, Eugenio Barba, the revitalisation of Meyerhold and Tairoff and their Bio-Mechanics, etc.

Aside from the differences predominantly rooted in culture-related conditions and structures there are attitudes toward theatre less "natural" by twists and turns of history, and societies which degrade theatre into an instrument of politics, alienate theatre from the audience by inadequate "insider" repertory and alienating presentation on stage (I am not talking about the sometimes alienating risks of creative experiments), pervert theatre into supermarkets of entertainment-industries, etc. These are global phenomenona, and for the N.C.P.A. clientele *Hotel Motel Patel*[27] is more appealing than Goethe's *Faust*; the dividing lines are drawn in one and the same country, continent, and culture.

---

26 The German-Russian actor and director Vsevolod Emilevich Meyerhold (1874–1940) developed a psycho-physical method of acting which centred on the links between the evocation and performance of emotions and specific gestures and physical expressions.

27 A comedy of the Parsi theatre popular in Mumbai at the time.

The seminar's main topic is THE ACTOR which calls the director to the witness box and before the judge's chair. The director-actor relationship is a highly complex affair and evades scholarly definition. To risk again the simplification of a commonplace: it is similar to the interdependence of captain and crew, but less congruent with (army) captain and soldiers – the snag of the simile is: art knows no order and command. And yet there is (step-)brotherhood in so far as nothing in art can be achieved by voting.

Any creative process is an intimate encounter and needs from the director both a father's loving patience and severe strictness rooted in confidence that any (genuine) actor has deeper depth than he or she knows. A director's authority is nothing but his more convincing suggestion and argument; he should know the route and destination and be able to forget both in the subconscious realms. His concept carries the inspiring ignition spark for the actor, and he should be a good coachman to draw in the reins when things mess up and to give free rein to imagination when the guts respond.

I remember a question often asked: to what extent would you give liberty to your actors? (By the way, I am always caught by a strange feeling when I am asked about "my" actors – they aren't private property.)

I don't think LIBERTY is something which one can give or refuse – what we should aim for is to LIBERATE the actor to his or her artistic self (and often it is a surgical process to liberate them from their mannerisms and the "crimes" – unfortunately (or fortunately for them) not yet articles in the penal code – of anticipation, missing impulses, mindless utterance of words in a meaningful dialogue etc.). It is both intellectual (or rather: intelligent) and sensual guidance of explanation, improvisation, demonstration, a process of mutual trial and error not unlike the way we help and watch a child walk. Alertness and sensitivity tell us the moment when we are at the more receiving end of the process, which means to mould and shape the character of the play from whatever vibrates and emerges from the then liberated actor.

Another case of "liberty" is interpretation. The common case is – often by passionate exchange of arguments – correspondence and agreement to head for the same port. A compromise in

INTERPRETATION is hardly thinkable. In case actor and director differ in principle they should part as partners – it doesn't harm personal friendship and respect for each other, but as said before, neither order nor voting can work in artistic endeavours.

Any play of some stature is a very sensitive organism of its own – dormant in the book and letter only – which meets in a given time at a given place with a group of actors who are likewise sensitive organs of their respective historical, cultural, ethnic etc. conditions and structures.

A director's art in an intercultural encounter should be to initiate the mutual challenge of both (which at the same time is a mutual challenge of play and medium alike), watch and guide the process of integration and assimilation.

How to achieve that "frictional heat" between actor and actor, stage and audience which makes theatre so distinct and irreplaceable even by the most advanced high-tech media [...]? Craftsmanship is a mere precondition of professionalism – no musician, no dancer of some stature goes on stage without rigorous training daily and for years. And no training and skill is an end in itself. Our wealth is imagination and inspiration, which also can be trained by what Brecht calls "the art of observation." [...]

Goethe, *Faust I*

Bennewitz and Mehta agreed on producing *Faust* in Hindi (translated by Ramesh Rajhans and Atul Tiwari) under the auspices of the National Centre for the Performing Arts and the Max Mueller Bhavan/Goethe Institute,[28] and to perform it at the large, prestigious Tata Theatre, with a set designed by Bennewitz's Weimar colleague Kristian Panzer. The production starred the immensely popular Bollywood actors Pankaj Kapur as Faust and Naseeruddin Shah as Mephistopheles. Kapur had

28 There is a historical, perhaps dialectical irony here. Already in 1980, Bennewitz had proposed a production of *Faust* to NSD director B.V. Karanth, in pre-emptive reaction to an offer made to Vijaya Mehta by the Max Mueller Bhavan to direct *Faust* in Mumbai in commemoration of the 150th anniversary of Goethe's death (Arbeitsbericht 16 Sept. 1980–1 Jan. 1981). Neither proposal materialized.

been Bennewitz's student at NSD and had played the lead role in his 1979 *Puntila*, and Shah had also been inspired early in his career by an encounter with Bennewitz; both welcomed the opportunity to work with him, despite their busy filming schedules. However, the resultant drawn-out rehearsal scheduling, along with other problems, severely hampered the production. In his study of all of Bennewitz's German and international *Fausts*, David G. John analyzes this production and its context and reception in depth, concluding that it was unsuccessful as intercultural theatre in contrast to much of Bennewitz's other work in India and other countries (*Bennewitz* 205–31). The letter passages included here complement John's analysis of what turned out to be Bennewitz's last production in India. He went on to direct a much more successful *Faust* in the Philippines and started work on another in the theatre in Meiningen where he had begun his directing career in 1955. Before he could complete his work on this production, he succumbed to the cancer he had been battling for years on 12 September 1995. In the final letter passage included here, he makes one more summative statement about his life and his work in India and muses what should, or rather should not, be included on his gravestone. This passage concludes the chapter and thus, as apparently was so often the case in his life, the loquacious Bennewitz will have the last word in Part I of the book.

> Mumbai, 29 September 1993
>
> Yesterday morning, the technical director was here, and we went through Kristian Panzer's technical drawings; it seems, everything in the stage set can be realized as we had envisioned it. Then I sat with my assistant to prepare for the work with the two women responsible for costumes. After lunch, Atul arrived for our checking and re-translating of his Hindi translation, which is and will continue to be a tough job. It was incomparably easier with Brecht and Shakespeare translations. With Shakespeare, we always have the English original to rely on, and the English translations of Brecht's plays in the American Manheim-Willett edition[29] are nearly as good as the German originals. With Goethe and his *Faust*, the situation is not so advantageous. I went through about five English translations and have arrived at the conclusion that they will just barely do. And apparently Atul

29 Ralph Manheim and John Willett translated most of Brecht's works into English.

(due to whatever personal and professional distractions) has worked a bit superficially, which does not suit Goethe very well. Fortunately I am so much at home in the play that I can interpret the text down to the last comma, and another fortunate circumstance is the fact that the translation will necessarily go through the mill once again when I work with the actors.

But this brings up another problem that is already apparent: the stars (who really are stars but do not at all behave as such) have their film commitments – each in a different production, which means that from tomorrow to October 1st I will be able to work at least half of each day with Mephisto, who will then, however, not be in Bombay for the entire month of October; Faust, in turn, can free up three to four days in October. Such top actors are pushed hard by their producers, and so I can only pray that they will be available for rehearsals in November and December. On October 3rd, I am starting a workshop to get to know the other actors and select the cast for the production. With them, the rehearsal situation won't be much different: while the great ones can hardly reduce their commitments due to demand, the smaller fish have to earn their rice in TV serials. There is one star I do not have scheduling problems with: Nadira Zaheer-Babbar, who as Marthe is in a continuous and not all that large portion of the play. It would not be as simple with the girl who was introduced to me as a candidate for the part of Gretchen, and whom I would take very gladly (even though she is only on her way to her seventeenth birthday), since she is acting in a play that only premieres in early December. Conditions like these have been fairly unknown to me in my twenty-three years in India. During all those years in Delhi at the school and with the Repertory Company, in Bhopal and Mysore, up in my village and also in Lucknow, I had standing ensembles, and was able to work with the actors all day and over the whole production period. I will have to learn to deal with it. After all, there is the great plus that they all go at the work with pleasure and curiosity.

Mumbai, 22 October 1993

When there is meaningful work to be done, I feel no fatigue, though some amount even of meaningful work could have been avoided if I had been involved in the translation from the first line on. I do not want to constantly blame Atul, who certainly has made quite an effort. I see this when the man with whom

I am now checking the text reads Atul's translation to me and re-translates: you can always discern the attempt to give a rhythm and form to the translation, which is precisely part of the problem: [...] Faust-Kapur said to Atul, I can recite your text, but I cannot play it, which means (astonishingly, since Atul has worked with me for more than a decade) that the language has no *Gestus*, and there are too many superfluous formulations and too much complicated grammar. I should bracket out the misunderstanding of some words and passages from this criticism because in that regard the English version already leaves much to be desired. During the hours spent newly translating, I am fortunate that my feeling for and fairly sensuous (not just grammatical and lexical) knowledge of Hindi enables me to work on every sentence until it calls forth action and also sounds good. Of course, what I cannot predict is whether the translation checked and re-worked from three different angles (with Mephisto, with Faust, and with the new translation consultant) will come together as a whole in the end.

Letter to an unknown recipient, Mumbai,
1 November 1993

Working conditions are not favourable to theatre here in Bombay – there is a lot of it taking place, but it does not feed its makers. Film and television use up talented actors by the dozens (times a thousand), and dozens of thousands of actors throw away their talents on the waiting bench for those awaiting their chance. Hindi film (more numerously produced than Hollywood films) does not count – no one fits the professional profile there. Even among the great number of actors demanded by conditions here, there are always only a handful of great ones, who choose and get chosen (the films usually go to international festivals, not into cinemas here), and who sometimes take a side trip into commercial film if they need quick money or for their own peculiar idea of fun – should I be surprised? Even on such side trips into what is unspeakably bad fare, such actors cannot be bad (probably because in a cheerful way they do not take themselves seriously, but still don't work with less energy than they would in *Hamlet* if given the opportunity).

Even a prestigious institute like the N.C.P.A. (National Centre for the Performing Arts) does not pay its actors, and they have a thousand-seat amphitheatre built by an American architect for classical Indian dance, vocal and instrumental music (with foyers that the Alexanderplatz[30] would fit into), where we will perform *Faust* (you see that my "Asian equanimity" is firm in its belief), a modern experimental theatre, an empty cube, in which any audience space and any stage can be constructed, but in which no experiments ever happen, a theatre for modern dance, a chamber theatre, and now an opera house and a concert hall under construction.

A few months ago, my colleague since 1972 [Vijaya Mehta] was appointed artistic director for the complex, and for the first time there is a conception for the next five years, which makes the N.C.P.A. into a producer of its own performances, though not yet with a standing ensemble, but planning two productions per year (normally one Indian and one international) of demanding plays with changing ensembles, among whom the protagonists from the first ranks are supposed to accustom the audience to first-rate theatre experiences. We are making the start, and the big stars, who have come to the play with an enthusiasm that moves me, are living up to their name. Tomorrow we will have a production meeting with the two of them to coordinate the days they have off from their film shoots. Not every role can be cast at that high level, though the actress playing Gretchen is a real "discovery from the street" and a prodigy.[31] The majority of actors are good, and if I can cut through the barriers of mannerisms and bad habits here (which often needs patience beyond all equanimity), they can become better than good (though a gap will remain).

The necessity of unravelling the play through two languages (from English, which also needs double and triple re-translation from Goethe's original text, into Hindi) is also my advantage at work: in a foreign language, I am forced to seek the text in the depth of the actor, on the umbilical cord of truthfulness. And I am not so presumptuous as to be wanting or believing to be able to impart the "world poem." It is only the drama that I am sending into another culture, which is not necessarily the same thing.

Mumbai, 10 November 1993

I know about the difficulties [...] that (aside from our protagonists [...], whose mother tongue is Hindi) all the other actors have, who

---

30 The Alexanderplatz is a famous and storied large square in the centre of Berlin.

31 The role of Gretchen (Margaret) was played by Sharvani Dhond.

speak Hindi because they learned it in school, but whose mother tongue is Marathi. Even when they have fully understood the Hindi text, they have a hard time getting it into the natural logic of that language. The Marathi rhythm runs alongside in their subconscious and infects the Hindi sentence, and so the words come out, but they are not umbilically tied to the inner core of the actor. I am sensitive in an almost physical way to words that seem to come out of the mouth mechanically without thought and are therefore flat, do not electrify the body, and sound like pre-chewed food. And this even though they are all actors of high quality. I have seen them all in their own plays with great pleasure, and thought it should not be difficult to bring the abilities experienced there into this play – but apparently, it is difficult after all and will take time.

[...]

It is astonishing how little foreignness the drama displays in such a different culture (after all, most people reacted to the idea with almost arrogant doubt: *Faust* in India? Is that even possible?!). Goethe was quite right when he wrote in the "Prologue in the Theatre": "Just reach into human life at its fullest – and where you grasp it, it will be interesting ... ." He did reach into it to the fullest, and so through the transformation into another language I make discoveries in the play, its situations and characters, which – even if surely they have been thought before – let me see, discover, and experience what was seemingly familiar in new ways.

Mumbai, 26 November 1993

I wish I could adequately report to you what Faust-Kapur told me this morning about how he finally came to accept the challenge of taking on the role. I think there were four steps: when I came to see him on the day of the bomb attacks,[32] the 12th of March of this year, in order to talk to him for the first time about the project, he was very enthusiastic, even just to have the opportunity to work with me again after fourteen years. The next phase was one of insecurity, because he had last been on stage seven years ago

32 On 12 March 1993, a series of terrorist bombings which caused over 250 deaths took place in Mumbai.

Figs. 23 and 24 Bennewitz during rehearsals for Goethe's *Faust I* in Hindi, with Pankaj Kapur and Naseeruddin Shah (top) and with other members of the cast (bottom), Mumbai, 1993–4. Courtesy of Fritz-Bennewitz-Archiv, Leipzig.

and had since only done television and films, and for a while he thought about withdrawing from the project. He became even more insecure and disappointed, too, after reading the play in translation, because he always saw Mephisto in the foreground and couldn't slip into Faust's skin. But then there was the thought again of working with me and our first conversations, and he read the play again and again [...] – and then, one night, it was like an attack, an illumination, which he put into the simple sentence that there is the same exciting turmoil and restlessness in this man Faust that he feels within himself sometimes. Then he felt connected to the role and cancelled every film shoot for two months [...], which doesn't drive him to the poorhouse but still means foregoing a considerable sum of money, since acting in the theatre is not paid. He also said that the challenge of such a significant play with a character of such hardly comprehensible dimensions – as he by now has discovered himself and experienced in rehearsals with me – does not easily come along twice in the life of an actor – and, if I may write this down, too, he said neither does an encounter with a director like me.

Letter to unknown recipient, Mumbai, 27 November 1993

It is astonishing and somewhat strange that the play is not at all foreign in foreign lands. Of course, Faust does not wander through the myths, legends, and stories here – such a character remains outside of Dharma/Karma/Moksha.[33] Rather, the moving experience of my work here (the play enters my subconscious and makes itself newly unknown to me, which [...] allows almost every day for the sensation of a heretofore undiscovered comma) is that the experience of Faust's otherness opens up his relatedness with all humankind. So, a world poem after all, though that's not what I am putting on stage, but rather the drama.

Mumbai, 27 November 1993

When I am not working and also do not have to think about my work on a "free" day, and am just thinking haphazardly, I think that I am not at all curious about the world and about people anymore. What I mean is that the thought is far from

33 These are key concepts in Hindu spirituality and moral philosophy.

me then that "oh, today I am free, so I could go someplace, see this or that, or visit someone or other" – nothing like that. Have I already had my fill of the world and of people? I feel fine just by myself [...]. It is probably that I have experienced and seen so much already, and always in connection with work; and maybe I also take in enough impressions, consciously or subconsciously, when I take the bus out to the suburbs or walk around the corner to the restaurant, so that at work I can always make thousands of connections at every moment in order to be able to explain a situation in the play or the relationships between characters with reference to life here. [...]

Could the strange state of mind I described above, my lack of curiosity to experience things, also have something to do with the fact that for the past 20 to 25 years I have been living nearly without interruption with Shakespeare, Brecht, Goethe, and Schiller, that I have to try to penetrate into their innards, that I have to make them become alive, comprehensible, and relatable for others? All the things they have written about make up more than a single human life can master – and then there are the images of the old woman sitting in the rubble who has lost everyone and everything in an earthquake and has no more tears left to cry? I do not know.

Mumbai, 30 November 1993

I feel so good when reading your letters, even though each one brings me some homesickness [...]. If things had gone normally, I wouldn't have had to be away for 17 weeks; in that time, I would have done two or even three productions on previous journeys to far-away lands, and here, after ten weeks, I finally had both protagonists together on stage for the first time today, and [...] also for the last time until January 6th. So today I left the house with no drive, because of course I am sometimes assaulted by the thought why this had to happen to me with this of all plays – and then I came back from the rehearsal and am not bothered at all anymore by the problems of time and organization, because even though the two of them, manuscripts in hand, were only taking their first steps on Panzer's wonderful and much-admired installation, I can hear, smell, see and taste the extraordinary quality of these two actors (and also their heartfelt relationship with me, and their – I am not ashamed to say it – love and veneration for me). Naturally, this makes me wish for enough time to work as I am used to, where one discovery already holds the key to the next! Such was the fruitful kind of interplay already at their first shared rehearsal. And then I think, in my nearly unshakeable optimism, that even under these trying circumstances I will manage to create a production, even if it may not bear the final imprint of my handwriting, but it may and even will be recognizable as coming from my spirit.

Mumbai, 5 December 1993

Yesterday evening's rehearsal was routine – Mephisto was not wholly there. Not that he doesn't take it seriously. The role has gripped him (which is not surprising – every Faust has more difficulties) and the play as well. I recognized his lack of concentration by the fact that he was quicker than usual to leave a difficult passage to the translation consultant [...]. This is what makes work here different even with the top actors: they come from film acting, where "work on the role" is a foreign concept – they get their take and two or three tries, and then the scene is shot. (Kapur-Faust is different, he really gets his hands dirty in understanding his role; well, he has not been on stage for seven years, but that alone does not explain it.) Naseer-Mephisto in particular has such a developed actor's instinct and the necessary quick intelligence to master a role very quickly, and for the audience it looks complete, too – but it has not been drawn from the depths. What I mean is that there is no time to really wrestle with the role, and (unfortunately, I sometimes think) Goethe has already made it easy for Mephisto to remain on the surface and still be successful with an audience (that is not overly spoiled).

Mumbai, 21 December 1993

The only thing I am looking forward to is coming home. Though I know that the pleasure of working returns when I'm rehearsing, my enthusiasm about the enterprise is deflated; I will be quite happy to let others bring it to an end. It would hardly be natural if it were otherwise [...] – I am in the 14th week of *Faust*. Let's leave it at that. However, this time I cannot tell myself that this is how I wanted it; I did not know about these conditions beforehand. The only thing keeping me in the game is that all involved, and particularly the two whose meagre rehearsal availability stretches the project to such length, feel that this work is something extraordinary in their lives – yes, I will make this lofty claim (of course, I mean their lives in the theatre, though maybe a bit beyond that, as well). Plus, there is the genuine enthusiasm for Panzer's installation, especially now that they are working within it.

Mumbai, 22 December 1993

I could dance, jump in the air, even pray from gratefulness and joy about Mephisto today! He arrived at rehearsal relaxed [...], and I was able to work with him until we nearly fell into a coma. We went into the two scenes in Faust's study: Mephisto's first appearance, and the wager. I read in English and took over Faust's part. That's what I call WORKING! We had made both scenes nearly ready for performance in less than three hours, and with such new ideas that I no longer need to worry about the production. But how? How can a man live in such extremes?! I had it all behind me already, without pain, because I believed myself exhausted – and then a rehearsal like that comes along. And that was followed by two hours of uninterrupted talking and demonstrating in a lecture at St. Xavier College, without notes and book, citing *Faust* in a mix of three languages – German, English, and Hindi – there were some Germanists in the audience who invited me to show the video of the 1981 production at their university outside of Bombay on January 4th.

Mumbai, 25 December 1993

I am less concerned about the success of the production now, even though the working days with Faust, i.e., Pankaj Kapur, are dwindling, since he has time off from film shoots only from January 6th on. The two to three days with Naseeruddin Shah provided me not only with a rare work experience, but also with the confidence that the production can certainly be a success. The thing I think about rarely and which has just now entered my thoughts is that this is quite a significant cultural experiment (though not yet an event) in its approach: the German *Faust* for the first time in Asia.[34] It had come to America before me. I even seem to remember that Reinhardt

34 This is incorrect. *Faust* had been performed previously in both India and elsewhere in Asian countries. See John, "Goethe's *Faust*" and "Stage Productions" and other essays in the same volume.

himself once tried a German production, and Gründgens' production was there on tour. But I was the first to put it on stage there with African-Americans and Latino-Americans.[35] Even in Europe it has barely crossed German borders: without much success and not understood in England; in Paris in a remarkable production (by Grüber, I think) in a cathedral – other than that, I know of no other productions elsewhere, except for experiments with passages and excerpts in schools and colleges abroad.

What is strange, however, is that while I have this thought that a cultural rarity is happening here in Bombay, the thought does not find its way from my mind to my emotions – there, it remains a work like any other I have done here and elsewhere, but under unaccustomed and sometimes exhausting conditions.

[...]

The numbers are incomprehensible: I have been going out into the world for twenty-four years already, and have been to India twenty-six times in that span. Are they just traces in the sand? No, there is a legacy. Fundamentally, it has been a meaningful life. Is it a finished sentence, or will something come after the comma? Do we ourselves determine where the period goes? Actually, I have always just lived haphazardly, an unplanned life. Things just happened the way they did. That's why it always takes a new effort for me to regard what I have done as an achievement. My God, I hope I'm not starting to write my epitaph – which will, in any case, be silence. Perhaps I should also leave the stone underneath the maple tree as it is. What remains of us is what has come beforehand. There is more to read on a blank stone. I like that thought. Nature writes enough on it through weathering. Emptiness is the true fullness, and the empty stone is not nothing. It is there, the stone. There was, is, and will be something: that's what it says when it remains blank.

35 This is indeed true. See John, "The First Black Gretchen."

PART II

Perspectives on Fritz Bennewitz in India

5 Perspectives from Bennewitz's Partners in India

Fritz Bennewitz: A Character Sketch and Interview

K.V. SUBBANNA

Someone once compared the German personality to a dynamo. As I watched Fritz Bennewitz on stage conducting rehearsals in all his splendour, I was struck by the aptness of the comparison.

An athletic build, the round face wholly changed and reshaped after a disfiguring accident, and yet attractive; a radiant light that springs like a fount through the remaining eye. Watching this silver-haired, sixty-four year old figure moving on the stage like quicksilver is an extraordinary experience indeed.

He lays open a whole spectrum of meanings of every single word in a play, describes and opens our eyes to the character-construct that emerges from these words; discusses the specific social environment that so conditions a character; quotes examples from other plays and directly from life and clarifies; mentions how a certain actor had played that role and explains with analysis, how he had, in that singular "dramatic gesture," succeeded – or failed – in lighting the character and its milieu. And, in the process, he illuminates the relationship between life and theatre, life and art.

Then he starts shaping the actors' movements and speech, design and action. He demonstrates, acting and speaking it out, all himself. At the same time, he says, "I exaggerate everything to the extreme. Grasp only the context from it and then do it in your own manner." Then he adds, "I have two reasons for exaggerating. One, that you should catch the essentials at once. Secondly, looking at my terrible acting, you should detest it and never wish to imitate it." And he breaks into a guffaw.

Until not only the concerned actor, but the whole group grasps the context, he demonstrates it himself tens of times, makes the actors repeat it as many times, until it is certain that everyone has understood.

He shows how to speak the lines, how to pronounce the words loudly and clearly. He works with the actors, moves with them himself, prances, dances, jumps, sits, hums a tune, drums a beat. "Ra ra ra ra ...," he intones, and modulates the rhythm of the scene with it. He jests with the group, jibes at himself, throws a joke among the onlookers and gets his release. He flatters the actors, goads them and feigns impatience to make them more determined. Thus himself enacting a puckish play of sense and nonsense, he fires actors into flaming souls. Working at first vaguely, he finally, gradually shapes a remarkable theatre experience.

As he works with a group of ten, he simultaneously puts himself in a labour ten times the sum total of the whole group. As we sat watching him at work, we were constantly reminded of Dr. Shivarama Karanth's rehearsal sessions.

Working on the first scene of *The Caucasian Chalk Circle*, he elaborated on the hands that appear there in a manner quite unforgettable: The hand of the king who struts, gloating over the inherited royal power that his fist grips; the queen's hand that only moves to parade its pretty fingers and pompous ornaments; the clenched hand of the general, haughty under the illusion that the sceptre it holds for the king is really its own; the hand of the servant that, conditioned to the status-act of holding aloft and displaying the royal child to the masses, moves like a machine; the hand that contemptuously flings a coin at the beggars; the hand that craves to claw out the coin from the filth of the streets; another hand that heartlessly pins the former to the ground and fights; still another hand that despairs of the soullessness of the suppressing hand ... . Thus he described "the drama of hands" contained in that scene. He kept protesting that the actors were not making proper use of their hands, and said, "Do not ever forget that India is the only culture that has developed a unique, distinct performance-language composed solely of hand-gestures."

Some directors emphasise the literary and speech aspects of a play; some others pay more attention to its theatrical possibilities. But Bennewitz achieves a fine balance between the two, without a till on either side; he simultaneously understands and executes in a manner that is truly remarkable. More than all this, for him, the ultimate is not the play or theatre, but life itself, life that takes shape from the sprouting, blossoming, encompassing human relationships. With his basic conviction that theatre is only one among the many meaningful acts of our boundless life, he becomes as important a human being as a theatre director.

Prasanna, who recently saw several plays in Germany, and also dismissed many of them as "mediocre," extolled Bennewitz's production of Goethe's *Faust* as "wonderful." His productions for the National School of Drama, Delhi, and the Rangamandal, Bhopal, have evoked great admiration everywhere. And his *The Good Woman of Setzuan* for our repertory Ninasam Tirugata this year has had an equally enthusiastic reception all over Karnataka. Yet, his rehearsal-sessions sometimes appear more exciting and interesting than his actual productions. Really, Fritz is a treasure-trove for theatre enthusiasts.

During our Film and Theatre Course in October 1989, when he was here on a different assignment, working with our Tirugata repertory troupe on *The Good Woman of Setzuan* by Brecht, he gave a brilliant special lecture on Brecht to the course participants, and then held a rehearsal session in front of them, touching up the production by stopping the actors every now and then, and giving them hints, and at the same time, turning to the participants and explaining in concrete terms, why he wanted it done that way and how that would approximate to Brecht's ideas on theatre and life as a whole. It was the first scene, where three gods, after a long and disconcerting journey through the mortal world, meet Wong, the waterseller at the gates of Setzuan. Wong, aware beforehand that they are gods on a visit to the earth, complains about the inhospitality and ungodliness of his fellow beings, adding that it was this sinfulness that had been the cause of the floods that had ravaged the neighbouring province the previous season. One of the gods is astounded at this reading of the incident, and tries to explain in a commonsensical way that the floods were, in fact, caused by people's laziness in keeping the dam in good repair. Instantly, another god, alarmed that their own existence is put at stake, stops the first god from speaking, so as to leave Wong's understanding stand. Here, Bennewitz stopped the actors, and turning around, said, "This is how social and human calamities are made out to be natural calamities, perpetuating ignorance, illusion, and a sense of powerlessness."

Fritz repeatedly insisted that the actors at first only concentrate on the context and the flow of events, that first their bodies understand the whole situation. Then the right words, in the right way, would naturally follow, he said. During the first stages, he exhorted the actors, using the little fund of Kannada words he had picked up from them, "Put in tumba shakti, tumba tamasha, svalpa artha" (lots of energy, lots of fun, only a little of sense). Then, as the actors improved over tens of rehearsals, and were preparing for a run-through, he said, "Now it has to be tumba shakti, tumba tamasha, tumba artha" (lots of energy, lots of fun, and lots of meaning). It was the sublime process of dynamics evolving into consciousness, taking place right in front of us.

For all his unfathomable active eagerness inside, Fritz is a natural, simple, unassuming person on the outside. "When I am amongst you, I shall be like you. I shall eat whatever you eat, and be one among you all," he indicated the moment he arrived here. "Nothing special for me," he issued a strict order. And he did live like that, on his share of our rice, curry and pickles. When in India, he is a strict vegetarian. He said he liked to have only vegetarian food even in his own country.

He always stuck to a strict schedule in his working and living habits. But whenever during that Film and Theatre Course one of us happened to tell him that a certain film, say, *Pather Panchali*, was to be shown that afternoon or late night, he would immediately shake off his nap or sleep. "I have seen it twenty times," he would say, "I think I will see it again." Later on, he would discuss the films with great interest and understanding, while we would all marvel at his phenomenal powers of concentration and memory.

Fritz is quite loquacious. Once he begins to speak, he goes on and on, linking this with that, and that with this, with the others finding no chance to slip a word in. But when there was a serious discussion on – here, we had a lengthy exchange on the advantages and disadvantages of producing a foreign play in a direct translation or an adaptation from among Satish Bahadur, Kambar, Karnad, Nagraj, Ramachandra Sharma, Ashok, Shoodra Shrinivas and others – he sat there mostly quietly, taking in every word of every one. Then when his turn came, he put forth his own thoughts very clearly. But he also sat listening with infinite interest, as if suggesting that it was more important to learn about others' ideas.

When I gave him Dr. Lohia's works, he sat and read them through with utmost interest. Frankly, unflinchingly, he expressed his disagreement with some of the ideas of this "New Socialist" of India. But otherwise, he discussed his writings with great admiration, and said he had benefited from them.

He was a bit reluctant when I said I wanted to do an interview with him. "I never do well in an interview," he said, putting on the helplessness of a student afraid of taking his exams. "You can pick out anything you like from all that I keep mouthing all the while and write it out.

Won't that do?" he said. I agreed. I received and collected several answers and views of his during the casual exchanges we had now and then. I am only reproducing here as a sample, one of my important questions and his answer to that. I have not recorded his expressions word-to-word, but have tried to retain the tone.

Q: You keep repeatedly stressing, "India, Indians, Indian actors," and so on. I suppose, this is not out of mere courtesy.

A: Absolutely not.

Q: If so – you have seen many countries and peoples – would you clarify your concept of 'Indian' in that background?

A: It's a bit tough. I too have to think it out afresh, explore it anew ... I first came to India in 1970. I only knew the common things about India then. Alkazi at the National School of Drama, Delhi, suggested that I first go round and get a feel of the people and their way of life. I started roaming around Delhi all alone. One evening, I came upon an old man sitting by the roadside. "Must be a beggar," I thought. He looked engaging. I felt an urge to speak with him, and went and sat beside him. Then for more than an hour, together we conducted a "gesture-conversation." It was an exhilarating adventure for both of us. I felt I had discovered the Essence of Humanity through that experience. Don't they say that below and beyond all the enormous differences of nationalities and cultures, there is only one single spring of humanity? I thought I found it out very clearly then. I felt all my hazy, amorphous experiences of humanity closing in to form a clear, crystalline shape then ...

Q: It sounds a bit mystic – very much in keeping with the ethos of India, and probably that of Germany too ...

A: (continuing, unheeding my intrusion): Our production that year received a rave response indeed. But it was only later, when I worked with local adaptations of Brecht's plays that I really felt fulfilled. Thereafter all my productions in India were adapted forms, situated in local contexts, and not direct translations. In such contexts, which they were so familiar with, the Indian actors could so very easily open themselves up. They could create anew and afresh the humanistic elements in the plays, and fully realise them on the stage.

In India, I have discovered that the springs of humanism can be seen so clearly emanating in the "behaviour" of the common people even to this day. This is something so very absent in the Western people. Or even in a country like the Philippines, which is drowned in its attempt at aping the West.

Q: I have a feeling I still have not clearly understood the sense in which you have been using the term "humanism"...

A: I shall give you an example. We were doing *The Chalk Circle* at the Bhopal Rangamandal. The scene was where the maidservant Grusha has to take up and look after the baby abandoned by the queen. Now, the baby cannot do without milk. Grusha goes to a peasant, gets enraged at the exorbitant price he demands, haggles, and finally manages to get a cupful. I suggested that everyone there try to improvise the part directly. One actress did it this way. She skimmed the cream with her finger and ate it herself. Then she fed the baby with the milk. She also saved a drop or two at the bottom of the cup and drank them herself. That she should first taste and test the milk herself; that she should eat the cream because the baby would not digest it; that she first had to sustain herself if she really wanted to save the baby, that, for all this, she should herself have the minimal amount of food to survive – watching all this practical sense and intuition, so natural to a woman, expressed so spontaneously and concretely, I felt was "wonderful." I suppose this example would clarify my concept of "humanism" a bit. This, I hope, is not a mere sentimental or partial view that "man is the most important being." Is it?

Q: No, of course not. You see, India is now undergoing a transition from rural to urban culture. When this process is complete, wouldn't Indians too, like the Westerners, lose their "humanism"? But of course, we cannot say that to retain its "humanism," India should stay where it is now and not move forwards ...

A: I feel India has developed a unique capacity to integrate its past, its history, with its present. This however does not necessarily mean that Indians are different from their Western counterparts. Only India's history is different. That itself might have taught the people here this rare skill of coagulating into the living blood of its today every corpuscle of its entire past.

Fritz answered several other questions of mine with his own elucidation and analysis:

> "I feel that the humanism expressed in Brecht is most important. In this regard, Brecht resembles Shakespeare very much.
>
> "Shakespeare is really the world's greatest. Every single work of his seems to be a complete, total creation by itself. On the other hand, some parts in Brecht may sometimes appear forced and artificial. I would not say that Brecht is equal to Shakespeare.

"The humanistic elements in Brecht's plays and their situations have shone out in all their splendours and new shades when given expression in the local contexts here, both in the actors and the audience. As I have seen it all with my own eyes and been amazed by it, I have no doubt at all as to how relevant Brecht is to India today.

"Indian actors open out slowly and gradually. Once they do, they act with the most natural spontaneity and sensitivity. Bringing out extraordinary nuances in their roles ..."

And so on ... – I only record here the essence of his comments. When, after his ten-day stay with us, we all gathered to bid him farewell, he said, "It would not be so hard if it were a formal meeting. I find it very difficult to speak at a family get together like this. Parting is always painful. You have asked me to come here again. My grateful thanks. I too, would like to visit you again. But, as it is not possible to speak of its certainty, its time, I cannot give you any assurance, any firm word ... I can, for the moment, only say that parting is always painful ..."

Translated by Jashwanth Jadhav

First published in 1986. Reprinted in *K.V.Subbanna Avaru Aaydu Barahagalu*. Ed. T.P. Ashoka. Hampi: Kannada University, 1992.

This version published as "An Interview with Fritz Bennewitz" in *Community and Culture: Selected Writings by K.V. Subbanna. Along with Interviews and Tributes*. Ed. N. Manu Chakravarthy. Heggodu: Akshara Prakashana, 2009, 323–30. Reprinted here with permission.

Interview Responses

Amal Allana

Amal Allana is a prominent theatre and film director and producer and was Chairperson of the National School of Drama from 2005 to 2013. She worked with Bennewitz both in Germany during a training stay there as an NSD student and on several of his productions in India (see also pages 24–5). The following are excerpts from her responses in an interview with Joerg Esleben at NSD on 29 February 2012.

What I really found amazing about Bennewitz was that … the theoretical jargon which was surrounding Brecht was immediately physicalized in his own person by jumping up and demonstrating. He was a great demonstrator and he was a fidgety director.

It was like his second nature to adopt a Brechtian approach to a play.

He was very much an actor's director, because he was very concerned continuously with the physical and body language of the actor. Everything was explained to the actor with a large amount of gesticulation and jumping around, and if any actor actually copied what Bennewitz was doing […] he'd say "no, no, that's all very wrong." Because his excitement about expressing himself was greater than and had nothing to do, really, with what he expected the physical reaction or expression of the actor to be.

His style was always very energetic, and it was restless. People darted across the stage. They were not really still, and the emotions were not internalized. It was highly energized. There was a sense of excessiveness about it. I think that was all part of Bennewitz's personality. It was not bad for Brecht. I think he was somewhat ahead of his time because he was very interested in the physicalization of the actor's body. […] His mind moved so fast that he jumped from topic to topic, and that gave a kind of very peculiar, particular style to his work. It was not conditioned by the visual aspect that much. The visualization was in the actor's body. […] Bennewitz was more spartan in the visualization and in the actors' costumes; it would have to be costumes which lent themselves to ample amounts of movement and would be tight and fitted, not capacious robes hampering movement. His designer, Franz Havemann, created paintings that were a backdrop. There was not too much interconnection – these were the visuals around him, but there was not an engagement of the physical actor with the space. Franz didn't really create spatial sets, I would say, he created sets which were very dramatic, very beautiful, and often very dedicated, made their own comment on the play, rather than creating spatial units within which the physical actor would work. So basically Fritz's actors were unhampered by the set.

There was a large amount of intellectual engagement which was trying to find an expression in the physical. It was a debate with the text which was going on, and he was continuously debating. All his political ideas – he tried to find a means to convey them, because he really believed that theatre would play a very important role in the changing of social attitudes. He was very committed to communism.

Puntila was brilliant. He had finally found an actor who was after his heart, Pankaj [Kapur], because […] Pankaj was a modern actor who had an inbuilt cynicism towards everything, which I think can be translated as that critical distance which is required, because he scoffed and sneered at whatever role. He also had a great comic sense, which a Brechtian actor needs, because he needs the timing and the ability to throw away his lines without thinking that they are lost.

Bennewitz came at a very significant moment in our history; he came at exactly the right point when we said goodbye to Western theatre, or when we wanted to say goodbye to Western theatre. We wanted to debunk Western theatre, where the whole roots movement had by then come into play, and we had said "everything Western is horrible." And once we said "we don't want the three-act form," then we either had the option of going to the Absurdists of the West, or we had the option of going to Brecht. A lot of us opted for Brecht, because Brecht became an easier tool. In some instances, we felt successful – "we understand it!" We felt that we understood this form and structure. We were really not concerned with the content. […] The introduction of this format was a very significant bridge. So in a sense, Bennewitz was the catalyst. His repeatedly coming here for so much time helped matters, because it was with the same person that we were going on this journey. So he became our extension and point of contact with the Western world, with Western drama.

All the productions of Bennewitz, whatever we might say about them now in hindsight, at that moment had a tremendous impact. […] Everybody felt it was exciting. They had never seen productions like these. So it was part of a very avant-garde kind of movement at that time. Nobody who was a serious theatre person would want to miss his productions, so they were very well attended. But though he was very public and open in his rehearsals, he was a very private man.

Samik Bandyopadhyay

Samik Bandyopadhyay is an eminent critic, scholar, and theatre historian based in Kolkata. He was one of two theatre critics banned by the Calcutta Repertory Company from viewing their production of Brecht's Galileo *directed by Bennewitz in 1980, which gave rise to major public scandal (see pages 102–3). The following are excerpts from responses in an interview with Joerg Esleben at Ninasam, Heggodu, on 8 October 2011. They have been edited by the interviewee for purposes of clarification.*

In 1973, Bennewitz came for the first time to Calcutta, and he gave two public lectures: one on theatre of the GDR and one on Brecht. When he talked about Brecht, he talked also about his own experience of working at the Berliner Ensemble, and how it had been quite an unhappy experience of the Brecht cult almost breathing down his neck all the time. Whatever innovations, whatever fresh readings he would have liked to bring to Brecht were being stifled at every point. When he spoke about the theatre of the GDR he was the first person to draw our attention to the work of the Komische Oper. That was quite significant – that was a kind of theatre with which, at least conceptually, even when not having seen it, we could identify a lot, there were continuities and connections that we could feel in our part of the country. It made a lot of sense and sparked off work also in those directions – using the body, using music, using comic spirit in the whole spirit of the carnival. All that became quite useful to us after that first visit. But we didn't have an occasion to see him at work.

In terms of Bennewitz's personality, I was very impressed. It was still the GDR days, and he was on a GDR platform. The local GDR trade agency had organized his visit. His frankness, his honesty, his candour, and the insights that he gave us into Brecht. [...] Brecht was being treated at the time as something that had to be just decoded. There was a single code, and you have to get into it, crack the code, and leave it there. So Fritz, particularly when he spoke about his experience with *Galileo* at the Berliner Ensemble, was opening Brecht in all his possibilities, reading Brecht's theories, his writings, and the ways the writings, his ideas, developed – so there is not one single Brecht, it is not a question of a code which had to be cracked. So the more inventive, the more explorative encounters and negotiations with Brecht – he was virtually the first person who opened that possibility in 1973. And a lot work – even in that other theatre outside the proscenium, which was first critiquing the left from the position of the left, not from the position of the right – was using Brecht, but they could use Brecht only because Fritz had opened up that area, opened that window. Otherwise we would have been bogged down with Willett and Esslin and the cultish Brecht. So he played a very important part in Bengali theatre in that sense. And it is a shame that his two productions in Calcutta didn't succeed.

Fritz made it easier for Indian directors to deal with Brecht and a lot of ideas that grew out of Brecht (not necessarily doing or not doing Brecht), but several possibilities, several ways of dealing with reality in theatrical terms that were there in Brecht could be explored. [...] In the 1970s and 1980s, the time that Fritz came here, there was something happening against which a lot of us were taking an ideological stance – that the state had decided to support in a big way – financially, institutionally – a revival in the cities or a rediscovery from the cities of "folk theatre." So, folk theatres would be torn out of their social and cultural contexts and brought down to the city for city-bred, city-bound theatre directors to "experiment" with the folk forms. So these became completely formalistic exercises, and whatever political bite that the theatre can have was completely blunted, because the supposedly folk element was presented as or conceived to be something so idea-less. It was supposed to be a community just enjoying life, dancing about, singing, with no concerns – there is no poverty, no exploitation, no problem anywhere. It's a happy community. "In the city, don't get bothered with your own problems here, the urban problems, the crises of development, but respond to this wonderful tradition, [the] authentic, in your life." So this was a program that was being constructed by the state with massive state support. Any theatre group which would work with folk elements would have massive funding. So a lot of people were tempted into it, worked their way into it. Whereas Fritz comes into that situation, and he comes as a state guest. [...] So naturally, there was an intention on the part of the government to rope him into this project, and his first work in Bombay was part of that. But somehow Fritz fought against it on his own terms. [...] When we saw the products we could see that he hadn't fallen into that trap. He positioned himself as an outsider. He was not relishing or enjoying it – he was really negotiating with them as an outsider, and that showed that there was that dialectic in the work that he produced. So, he offered an alternative of methodology in handling or negotiating the folk [theatre] at that given point of time, when it had been institutionalized and simplified by the state machinery and the state organizations. That was a very significant thing.

Akshara, K.V.

Akshara K.V. worked with Bennewitz both as a directing student at NSD in the early 1980s (in productions of The Caucasian Chalk Circle *in 1982 and a course on Brecht's* Messingkauf Dialogues *in 1983) and as teacher, director, and company chief at the Ninasam Theatre Institute founded by Akshara's father K.V. Subbanna, during Bennewitz's several sojourns at Ninasam. The following are written responses to interview questions about Fritz Bennewitz.*

JOERG ESLEBEN: How would you describe and characterize Bennewitz? What can you say about his personality, his ways of interacting with people, his politics and values?

AKSHARA K.V.: The first image that comes to my mind when I remember him is his energy and enthusiasm. And, I admired his capacity to be one among the others in extremely different cultural contexts. At NSD and at Heggodu both, one feeling that students felt in his company was that he was "our" man. After a while, his "alien" appearance and language did not matter and students tended to interact with him as an elder from their own community. In Heggodu, this went a step further and many villagers treated him as one of their community. One name that people tagged him with in Kannada was *ajja* (grandfather). The small cottage where he used to stay at Heggodu, is still referred to by people as *Ajjana Mane* (grandfather's house)! He would mix very well with all in the village, but had a sharp eye in understanding people. I remember once, a few days after his arrival in one of the visits, he pointed out to me that a particular shopkeeper in Heggodu is dishonest, and that matched with our own assessment made by several years of acquaintance.

He was a leftist, a sensitive Marxist in his approaches, but a humanist at heart. He was never dogmatic and he never flaunted his beliefs in the form of an ideology. I remember the way he repeatedly conversed with a student at NSD, who had strong rightwing beliefs, and even when he failed to convince that person, he would never get disheartened.

JOERG ESLEBEN: How would you describe and define Bennewitz's way of working as a theatre director? What, in your view, were Bennewitz's core beliefs and principles in theatre work?

AKSHARA K.V.: If I have to describe his method of working on a play in one word, then I would call it "intellectual" in the best sense of that term. He valued the instincts of an actor, he respected the emotional part of the actor's personality, but he insisted that it should all be mediated by a "critical thinking" to become a meaningful performance. One sentence that he would first learn, before he started a rehearsal, to articulate in the language of the actors (in my experience, Hindi and Kannada) is the following: *Tumba shakti mattu svalpa buddhi* (lots of energy; but with a bit of thought!). This was his basic demand from the actors – that they could use all their faculties (and "techniques" that they acquired during their training) with as much energy as they could, but that should eventually be mediated with "critical thinking." Therefore, he would allow the inadequacies of actors in contributing their emotional and experiential energies, but would never allow a "non-thinking" act to happen on stage. I remember several instances when he stopped the rehearsal for long periods just because the actor was not thinking the act.

Another related point is that he would spend a huge amount of his rehearsal time to communicate the thought behind each act. To demonstrate this, he would also act out, in his own way, some bits of the play, with a note saying, "follow my logic; do not follow my action." At every crucial moment, he would stop and ponder over a specific gesture, explaining how a good gesture would incorporate critical thinking on the part of the character and the actor. I vividly remember two instances from *The Caucasian Chalk Circle*: one is when Grusha gets a cup of milk for her child; and she removes the cream before feeding it to the child; then, in the court scene, when the queen's lawyer says – "They say, my lord, that blood is thicker than water." He would show how a Berliner Ensemble actor added a gesture of wiping his lips with a handkerchief with this dialogue; and then would encourage the actors to find such critical gestures. The result of this method was that actors learnt to think, even when they could not actually do an act. Another by-product of this process was that it was informative and useful to watch his rehearsal, without being actually part of his team. Personally, I have learnt a lot from such observation of his work.

JOERG ESLEBEN: What was Bennewitz's contribution to Ninasam?

AKSHARA K.V.: First of all, Bennewitz gave Ninasam some sort of a self-confidence in its work and methods, especially to its theatre Institute and the repertory during its crucial formative years. He was the first non-Indian theatre director to come and work with us and through his work we learnt a lot, not just about the possibilities of "intercultural" exchanges, but also about the ways in which a professional training school could be organized.

Secondly, for people like me he taught a way of delving into a text in a logical manner. This was especially useful to us at Ninasam, as Ninasam has always been a group which gave emphasis on using texts as a base for building theatrical expressions. Ninasam has also been enriched by its connections with Kannada literature (not just dramatic literature, but also poetry and fiction), and therefore, the ways of textual analysis that we learnt from Bennewitz came in very handy when we later started directing our own plays. Bennewitz was, in fact, more than a dramaturge; one could call him a "text-oriented director" who invented theatrical expressions from the text, and most of his rehearsals were devoted to this exploration. This was much more evident when he worked with Shakesperean texts. I am deeply indebted to him for making me understand this process.

JOERG ESLEBEN: If you agree that Bennewitz was highly successful in blending German/European and Indian theatre traditions and styles, how would you explain this success? How would you compare Bennewitz's work with that of other directors doing intercultural or cross-cultural theatre work?

AKSHARA K.V.: In hindsight, it seems to me that the most important aspect that formed the core of Bennewitz's success was that he did NOT have an intercultural agenda; and for that matter, he did not even employ the typical "intercultural method" in building his theatre. For example, he never attempted an exotic blend between elements of cultures; but attempted to create a platform for dialogue. Also, as I have mentioned above, he gave a lot of emphasis on texts and never fancied ways of juxtaposing divergent techniques taken from different traditions. Yes, he interpreted the classical Shakespearean texts for the modern viewer, and he adapted it in some ways for the target audience (belonging to a different culture from his own), but never did a kaleidoscopic collage of diverse elements of the theatrical traditions, as many "intercultural" theatre directors tended to do then, and to some extent even now.

However, in a deeper sense, he was an interculturalist, in the sense that he was creating a conversation between diverse theatre traditions, textualities, and modes of perception and expression. I would argue that this is a more valid way of doing interculturalism, where elements from an alien culture (and its strange mixture) do not become exhibition material, but different ways of seeing and being in the world are made to interact with each other. This approach gives more respect to both the cultures that it handles, and does not objectify any element of cultural expression.

Prasanna

Prasanna is an eminent playwright, director, and cultural activist based in Heggodu, Karnataka. The following are excerpts from his responses in an interview with Joerg Esleben at Prasanna's house near Heggodu on 6 October 2011.

> My personal admiration for him stems from his enormous personal integrity. He was a man with such a simple style of living. He could sleep anywhere, he could eat anywhere. He could work with people of all sorts, [...] especially when he decided to get out of Germany and work in places like India, the Philippines, and Ceylon. I think he knew that he had to work with complete amateurs, which was really extraordinary. As a result, his productions were very uneven. I've seen brilliant productions by Fritz; I've also seen fairly bad productions. But that needed courage, to accept the situation like that. Because if he had insisted on a certain quality and a certain professionalism, he wouldn't have done what he did, which was trailblazing work. I don't know whether it would be an exaggeration to say so, but his contribution is almost like Max Mueller's contribution to Indian philosophy.
>
> His understanding of socialism wasn't a trivialized, ideological understanding. I think he came to India because he really wanted to understand the insides of socialism, which means that he actually wanted to go beyond the ideological aspects of it, to go to poor countries and work with them. His theatre, his style, everything was tuned to that.

> He never came to just give. It was always an equal relationship. He would say "look, I am coming halfway, you have to come halfway."

[About the 1973 Caucasian Chalk Circle:]

> Much, much later I asked Fritz how he managed to communicate so well with the actors, and his answer was "look, I communicate with their common sense. They are craftspeople, as good as anywhere in the world, so they know their skills. So I don't talk to them about Brecht's theories – they are theatre people, they know their skills, they know their crafts, so I try to approach their common sense."

This was a discussion that was happening in connection with what Richard Schechner had just written after coming to India and staying in Benares for about a year or so. He had written something which was hugely publicized, in which he talked of the ritualistic origin of drama. Fritz was not in agreement with that, and a lot of us were not in agreement with it. It is true that there is a ritualistic aspect of theatre, nobody is denying that – but to put the entire emphasis of everything – one's common sense, one's intelligence, one's need to do theatre – just onto a ritual was too much. So we were discussing that, and then I had asked him "how do you approach theatre?" That's when he said, "I approach it through common sense. These are working people, and I am a working person, and it's the communication between two working people, and it is a relationship of common sense."

Bennewitz came with his Bertolt Brecht, with his West, his Marxism, and he wanted India to come with its own experience, and he chose his own India. Richard Schechner chose his India, which was highly ritualistic […]; so he had chosen his side of theatre very carefully, and Bennewitz would choose his side of theatre very carefully. He would always go to the Indian popular theatre, he would always go to Sudra actors, the untouchable actors, the village actors, the actors who were working people. Of course, he also went a great deal to the student actors […]. But even there the basic attitude did not change. I have never heard him talk politics with the actors while directing a play, because first of all it wasn't possible. He never really became comfortable in English. Towards the end of his life, he could speak fairly well in English, but I have seen him rehearse plays, especially in the first phase of his coming here, where it would be completely inarticulate. He would be shouting, screaming, making various noises, trying to goad them to do something, which looked very physical. It wasn't physical – here was a man who was trying to communicate beyond the spoken language. He had to get to the actors and get them to relate. So there was no question of his talking politics to them; he was doing politics. This political question – I believe there is a lot of politics behind his being accepted or not being accepted in Germany. I think it is foolish, because what I have seen of Fritz Bennewitz and his politics, it was very pure.

In terms of his contribution to Indian theatre, I would rate it very high; I would rate it as high as the contributions of Habib Tanvir, Badal Sircar, and the likes of them, for many reasons. One is the massive range. He worked in so many parts of the country. Most of these people actually did that, they actually went to different parts of India and worked there [...]. Fritz did that as much as Karanth did, or Habib did, or Badal Sircar did. And then, there is the vision that he carried with him during that time. That was a time of huge changes in India, when television was catching up. The theatre was going through a terrible crisis, which of course even now we are still going through. At that time for Bennewitz to give that vision was I think very important.

He was building a bridge, and while building the bridge he knew very well that that all bridges are two-way travelling facilities. You don't build a bridge just to cross over, you build bridges in order that you can go there and they can come here. And so it is always an equal participation. In any unequal situation, the first thing that happens is that the bridge is broken, in all wars the first thing that gets destroyed is a bridge. So Bennewitz's attitude was to build bridges. He did not come as the elder brother [...].

People talk about his closeness to the political bosses of East Germany. One doesn't know, really. Of course, whenever he was in Delhi, there was a ritualistic party thrown by the East German embassy. [...] I feel this is trivializing Bennewitz. If he was so politically powerful, there was no need for him to come to India. If he was only using it as a stepping stone, this was the silliest kind to choose. And if he was using some of the embassy connections to enable him to come back again and again to India, Philippines and Ceylon, I say why not? [...] In that sense, Bennewitz was not even as clever as Brecht. [...] Brecht always somehow managed to be on the right side of the fence. Bennewitz did not try that. He was not trying to be on the right side of the fence; he was in fact trying to be on the wrong side of the fence. So I want to go on record and say that the West Germans have committed a huge blunder in neglecting his enormous contribution, because it is a contribution which is a credit to the unified Germany. He is a great German personality who did so much work, and it's already lost. Let's not forget that it's now more than twenty years since he died. They should have done something about it. A whole lot of us offered ourselves, we tried to tell them "look, please do something about it." The problem is also that his work is so scattered – he has gone to so many places and worked there. A lot of it has to be traced from memory; there is not even good documentation available.

Anuradha Kapur

Anuradha Kapur is a prominent practitioner and scholar of theatre. She was a teacher at the National School of Drama during Bennewitz's time there and a close colleague of his, and she was the NSD's director from 2007 to 2013. The following are excerpts from her responses in an interview with Joerg Esleben at NSD on 27 February 2012. They have been edited by the interviewee for purposes of clarification.

> Fritz Bennewitz was able to provide a lens on the Theatre of Roots paradigm, very popular in India at that time, by opening up the debate about the alienation techniques that existed in the traditional theatres of India and those that were put forward by Brecht. He was able to disalign the simple appropriation of Brecht's techniques into Indian theatre historiography. He posited that we ask, as Brecht suggested, what these alienating devices *did to* the audience. And moreover that we look to the past from a position set concretely in our historical present.
>
> One of his most extraordinary working styles was the dialectical nature of teaching, and that he didn't romanticize pedagogy as being inspirational nor did he actually let the actor believe in that – a constant critique via dialogue. Lots of his younger colleagues and students say that they learned this from him: how to edit a text, how to intervene, and how to actually set up a dialogue with the actor. Sometimes he would maddeningly bring the process to a halt by talking – two lines, he'd ask you to stop – but I think it trained our younger people, completely catapulted them outside any self-indulgence.
>
> The failures of *Galileo* and *Faust* had something to do with an established doxa of acting that he perhaps was not able to shift as much as he would have liked to, and which he was able to shift in a very, very large and adventurous, risky fashion with the students.
>
> I think he was successful because he didn't try a blend. […] The adaptation was very much about the materials that were part of the place where he was working. So the objects that he chose produced it. So there was no question of thinking of translation as being a subsumption, it is not subsuming into another culture, it was running parallel, that's why it was interesting. […] What was interesting was that he always started with materials, a certain kind of cooking pot, a certain kind of shoe, a certain kind of cart – that started the adaptation, not saying "this is an Indian play" or "this is a German play in

disguise." This is why *Puntila* was so successful; we always thought, "oh, what a fabulous text has come out," but we never said "this is an Indian text." [His productions] were Indian productions in so far as some of the most interesting aspects of contemporary understanding were right there, but it wasn't clothed in Indianism, there was no Indianness as the most important aspect. He was alert to history. He was able to say "we will use this instead of this. If I bring in a Jeep, it's going to be a certain kind of India," which he did for instance in *Puntila*. And so, when he says, "it's an Indian production," I think it is a form of energy and a kind of collaboration between two theatre-making processes. So when I remember *Puntila* or *Threepenny Opera*, it's not like saying "gosh, it was a revelation about India or Indian theatre" – it is a revelation about theatre languages which are beyond the vernacular references.

Once he stopped working here, the body of work has become obscured in interculturalist discourse. The dominance of the discourse has appropriated this work. For many of us, the fact that it got subsumed in interculturalist discourse was a very saddening thing, because, if he was on the losing side of history, this certainly isn't the winning side in terms of theatre. What it produced has many problems. So that his work seems to be one of the interculturalist experiments within the terms as already defined by Peter Brook; this seems to me saddening, because it takes away the edge of his work, of which there was plenty. He was also wonderfully difficult. He was not role-playing, he was not here as ambassador to anything, not even to Brecht, whom he loved so much. Peter Brook or Ariane Mnouchkine – they are ambassadors of culture. None of that seems to have been at all of interest to him – at least in the way he functioned, I don't know how he saw himself.

We truly admired him. What I really enjoyed was the fact that he was so able to make the contradiction and the dialectic function; it was a great relief: he was able, I think, for many of us to take away the sentimentalizing of the guru tradition, of the acting tradition, of history, of folk, of authenticity – he just taught. It was really liberating; you didn't have to constantly prove with him that you're Indian.

6 Essays on Bennewitz in India

Intersections: Fritz Bennewitz's Biography and His Intercultural Work

ROLF ROHMER

Fritz Bennewitz was born 20 January 1926, and grew up in Chemnitz in Saxony in the eastern part of Germany. His father was a locomotive engineer who loved his profession and hoped his son would follow in his footsteps. Fritz, however, much preferred to read, already writing dramas in school, and encouraging his friends to make theatre. In 1944, shortly before the end of his regular school years, he was graduated early to be drafted into the armed forces and shortly thereafter sent to the battlefield. In 1945 he was taken prisoner of war by the Americans and was made to work in a coal mine. During the evenings in the POW camp he encouraged his fellow prisoners by reading and reciting literary texts, among them Hölderlin's poems and Goethe's *Faust*.

After his return from captivity he re-took the examinations for the *Abitur*, the secondary school degree which qualified him for higher studies. Due to his good results, he was appointed as a "new teacher" and taught as a lecturer at the Pre-Academic Institute for Workers and Farmers in Chemnitz. According to his own testimony, his encounters with his working-class students there led him to decide on his orientation in life. Beginning in 1950, he studied social sciences and humanities for two semesters at Leipzig University under Hans Mayer, among other professors. He then continued his studies at the German Theatre Institute in Weimar. From 1953 to 1955 he was a lecturer on Marxist-Leninist aesthetics at the Theatre Academy Leipzig, the successor institution of the German Theatre Institute in Weimar; at the same time, he was Chair of Art and Literature at the Central School "Rosa Luxemburg" of the ruling Socialist Unity Party of East Germany in Erfurt.

His artistic career began while he was still teaching with guest productions in Stralsund, among other places. In 1955 he left teaching and went to the Meiningen Theatre as director-in-chief. There he achieved his first successes with a young ensemble. His three Brecht productions in Meiningen between 1958 and 1960, the first outside of East Germany's major metropolitan areas, made theatre history. They had an impact far beyond the immediate region, captured the attention and admiration of Helene Weigel, Brecht's widow and the Artistic Director of the Berliner Ensemble, and paved the way to Berlin for some of the Meiningen actors.

In 1960, Bennewitz took over as director-in-chief at the Deutsches Nationaltheater (DNT) in Weimar. He was under contract there until 1991, as regular director only from 1975 onwards. His artistic work gave the DNT a unique profile for decades, especially through productions of plays by Shakespeare and the classic German dramatists, Goethe and Schiller. With evolving interpretations, Bennewitz adapted some of the works to reflect the increasingly critical perspectives on society that were circulating in this era. Furthermore, he threw open the traditional repertoire of the DNT to Bertolt Brecht's plays and explored a wide range of plays from world drama. His artistic reputation also brought him numerous invitations for guest productions on stages in Berlin and elsewhere. For some years, he led a studio at the Weimar theatre where students of the Theatre Academy in Leipzig received practical training. His appointment as professor in this context became permanent in recognition of his artistic and pedagogical achievements.

Bennewitz's productions were based on intensive, ever re-contemplated analyses of the play texts. This helped him understand the actions of the characters in the social and historical conditions underlying the plots. He searched constantly for discoveries and more precise motivations, inspired by new insights from historiography, cultural studies, and social sciences. While he insisted that at first he approached the actors with high didactic demands, he soon learned to incorporate their own artistic initiatives into his directorial work. In this way he eventually succeeded in shaping and promoting the ensemble spirit at the Weimar theatre and in combining it with his own conceptions. Nevertheless, intensity in his work and high demands on others remained dominant traits of Bennewitz as a director – characteristics for which he became known in his later international endeavours.

On the basis of his aesthetic principles and work ethic, Bennewitz achieved remarkable and respected productions. Nonetheless, the reviewers, while acknowledging that his endeavours were aimed at being true to the text, and still intellectually penetrating, occasionally complained that the intellectual claim was not made good on stage in a sensually concrete manner and that the mise-en-scène represented the philosophy of the works and too little of the real actions. Bennewitz was far from rejecting such criticism or answering it with obstinate self-justification; instead, he confronted it with historical and biographical reflection: "You are actually right about that, because philosophy enters the relations between people, and perhaps it is here that the one-sidedness you mentioned makes itself felt. But I think that this problem also has to do with historical context. Since 1945, when the great learning process began, we have neglected the richness of individuality in our striving to represent the social system of coordinates. Today we live in an era of changing functions – not just of the theatre itself, but also of the professions within theatre."

Bennewitz, however, was not an outstanding innovator – and he was quite conscious of this. Nevertheless, he was very attentive to artistic initiatives that he considered to be productive enrichments of traditions in realism and to undermine the cultural-political dogmatism in the GDR. He sought with admirable self-critical effort to let such innovations guide him and endeavoured to make the stimulations gained in this way operative in his work. An example of this was his second production of Goethe's *Faust* in 1975, which, compared to his first in 1965, showed a completely new conception and a new way of acting, provoked by the *Faust* productions by Adolph Dresen (Deutsches Theater Berlin), Christoph Schroth (Schwerin) and Horst Schönemann (Halle).

Given his extremely voluminous artistic work and his participation in related national and international organizations, Bennewitz's abstinence from expressly political activities was striking. Art and culture constituted his field of activity, based on the enlightenment conviction that endeavours in this area would contribute to shaping society in the long run, beyond current political problems and deficiencies. Over time this attitude (along with his attachment to traditions of realism) earned him criticism and a gradual disregard from colleagues in the GDR and especially in historical retrospect after German unification.

However, Bennewitz's directorial work was shaped increasingly by critical reflections on the state of society of the era and in the GDR. Once again, the change among the three *Faust* productions between

1965 and 1981 is characteristic of this – from the idealistic conception of the creative hero anticipating a harmonious "human community" to a critical view of social conditions, perspectives of humanity, and the contradictions of personal engagement. The 1981 *Faust* corresponded to the rebellious mood of a younger generation, was even suspected as being subversive by officials, and continued to have an impact beyond the political upheaval of 1989 and into the 1990s. Some of his other productions were also the subject of intense debate, and his social, cultural, and political sensibility led him to support new critical works such as the plays of Volker Braun.

After the 1960s Bennewitz's artistic career was shaped more and more by activity abroad and international experiences. A study sojourn in London granted him by the International Theatre Institute (ITI) and several guest performances abroad with the Weimar ensemble led to invitations to direct plays and conduct workshops and seminars which, over the next two and a half decades, took him to Romania, West Germany, the USA, Switzerland, Venezuela, and most frequently to India, Sri Lanka, and the Philippines. He was elected as a consultant of the Third World Committee of the ITI, where he gained valuable experience and made contributions that earned him productive partnerships and high recognition. In this context, he went on study trips and to conferences in twenty-seven countries.

Bennewitz went to India for the first time in 1970. He produced Brecht's *Threepenny Opera* with students at the National School of Drama. The production was a success and he realized quickly that "This performance [...] has promoted interest in Brecht and, through the graduates of the school, has had an impact far beyond Delhi as an imparting of methods. Nonetheless, the impact of this work seemed to me to be limited, because it largely remained a production translated from our theatre tradition and our playing habits onto the Indian stage" ("Ajab Nyaya Vartulacha" 1).

This self-critical realization documents a decisive change in Bennewitz's world view and creativity. His life and artistic activity were based on and suffused by historical thinking. In this he always followed, in principle, the Marxist conception of a socialist perspective for all of human society. The existence of socialist states (including the GDR) therefore remained for him the guarantor of a socially progressive future, despite his frequently critical assessment of political practices. However, it was not the political strategies and ideological dogmas that drove him, but rather his views of cultural history and aesthetic theory, which he had gained from the history of the German workers' movement and which were influenced by the writings of Franz Mehring and Clara Zetkin among others. He saw himself and his creative work as being part of an historical process that had begun with secularization in the Renaissance and was bound to lead through the political and social upheavals of the following centuries towards a culturally rich, humanistic society. Three factors were the key points of orientation in his social and artistic praxis: the ideal of a human being as derived from European cultural history, with clear influence from the classical tradition in Germany; a strong Enlightenment impetus; and finally the corresponding conviction that one can contribute to shaping society with artistic endeavours and creativity. Shakespeare, the German classics, and Brecht were aesthetic models for him, because they had been active during great upheavals of history and because their work had provided ideational and methodological directions for engagement in the service of societal progress. It is evident why Brecht, as a contemporary and with a worldview close to his own, became and remained the great role model for Bennewitz.

There had, however, been several turns in Bennewitz's appropriation of Brecht. In the first years of his directorial career, between 1958 and 1960, he had achieved spectacular success at the Meiningen Theatre with three Brecht productions, particularly with the *Threepenny Opera*. With a young, playful ensemble, whose members – like him – had mostly been trained in the Stanislavskian tradition, he approached Brecht in an uncritical and naïve manner, in accordance with the times. Years later he made a self-critical assessment: "The Meiningen *Threepenny Opera* displayed a seeming well-roundedness. I would equate it to surface tension" ("Werkstattgespräch" 5). In 1960 he came to the German National Theatre in Weimar and saw himself confronted with exigencies that he described as follows: "At that time, the Marxist interpretation of the German classics was a historical need ... Weimar as city and preserve of the classics simply had the societal duty of introducing appropriate productions. I directed German classics [and] searched for points of reference that would help work towards their Marxist interpretation. I found them in Brecht and Shakespeare" ("Werkstattgespräch" 1).

Accordingly, he integrated Brecht plays into his repertoire and, in the face of new challenges, also found a new relationship to that playwright: "One has finished training and begins anew, because one clashes with reality and polemicizes against it. Besides, Brecht means eternal training, which one needs in order to stay concrete. I have observed this for years in myself. [...] Only [now] did I make the discovery of the models. They stimulated me to include an overabundance of details. [...] The pendulum swung in the other direction" (Bennewitz, "Werkstattgespräch" 4). With reference to further Brecht productions in later years, he stated: "And then Brecht became unthinkable for me without Shakespeare and vice versa. [...] Much is different than in the model. I try out this method in other productions of Brecht plays as well. Basically, I have said farewell to Brecht in order to approach him" ("Werkstattgespräch" 5–6).

This renewed approach was a result of his work abroad. Based on his experiences in the GDR and his socialist convictions, Bennewitz at first was determined to promote the restructuring of society in countries of the so-called Third World by means of theatre. He argued that theatre in these countries had to be reshaped methodically for this purpose. One can see how strongly he was beholden to the traditions he came from in another version of the self-critical judgment cited above about the *Threepenny Opera* in New Delhi in 1970, which he formulated in retrospect in 1980: "The performance was considered a success by the press and the audience, but *as contribution to Indian national theatre* [author's emphasis] it remained negligible because it was largely a production translated from our theatre tradition and playing habits – a product imported to the Indian stage, not developed from the traditions of that stage" ("Discussion contributions" 149).

Despite experiencing the geo-cultural differences, Bennewitz still frequently returned to the idea that the cooperative exchange of the respective theatre cultures should promote a common strategic goal, not in terms of aesthetics and methods, but in terms of cultural politics. In his view, interculturalism as ingredient and stimulant of global social progress needed such a strategic orientation. He regarded the conception of a national theatre, as it had grown from nationally structured European history since the Renaissance, *not as a final stage* but *as an entry point* for gathering and politically orienting the cultural forces in the various geo-cultural zones, because it seemed to correspond to the struggle for identity in the new states of the decolonized world.

He held the imparting of Brechtian theatre as indispensable for his goals. However, after his own varying experiences with Brecht he neither envisioned a "model strategy" nor the transfer of a "methodological system." Despite his continued ties to inherited patterns of thought he sensed that different geo-cultural conditions necessitated a specific and selective use of Brecht's ideas. In terms of method, he relied above all on the principles of "alienation" and "change" in terms of conceptual and strategic goals. In the spirit of Brecht, he aimed to introduce alienation into the making of theatre in order to discover and make conscious the social background of conditions, characters, and actions; the idea of change aimed at the critical qualification of theatre traditions that he believed to be not yet ready for such a task.

When he returned from India, he was deeply impressed by his experience of the social and cultural life on the subcontinent, an experience which superseded his theatrical ambitions. He was plagued by doubts as to whether Brecht's conception per se represented a standard of theatre practice "in the whole world." One has to consider that although Bennewitz had, by 1970, worked in various European countries and had also travelled to non-European countries for guest performances, he had essentially always been limited to contacts within professional circles that more or less corresponded to his working conditions at home. Now, in India, he had entered a completely different milieu. He was now working in a context without an institutionalized, professional theatre that could or wanted to influence society as a whole. He felt far more entangled in social life and its problems than in theatre affairs. He experienced how closely theatre and every kind of performance is connected to social realities. Though this had been a self-evident thesis for his Brechtian theatre conception and work, he now had to self-critically avow that in Europe, rather than being an actual basis of theatre practice, this attitude had been more of a strategic position as part of the endeavour to regain the social ties and responsibility of theatre that had been lost in the course of European cultural history. He became conscious of the deeper meaning and new kind of challenge posed by Brecht's category of alienation. It now no longer was a question for him of imparting a method, hitherto primarily understood as an acting technique, of discovering and critically illuminating the social background of conditions, characters, and actions with theatre practitioners of a different culture. Rather, he now aimed at experimenting how this method could develop in a theatre culture that had been shaped by the close mutual relations of social conditions, cultural traditions, and performing activities which were based in the actuality of life, as opposed to the "representation" practiced on European stages.

In order to sound out the possibilities, he intensively studied Brecht's appropriation of non-European theatre practices and searched for points of contact between Brecht's theatre aesthetics and the theatre cultures Bennewitz was working in. He found such points of contact above all in the epic traditions of those cultures and Brecht's epic theatre. Here, too, the modifications demanded *objectively* by the respective geo-cultural structures and current situations and *subjectively* by his own personal perception and qualification played an essential role. From the wealth of his ideas and experiments I would like to highlight the principle of the gestic.

Until that point, he had understood *Gestus* primarily as a kind of physical and vocal expression within artistic representation, which was meant to clarify the social status and intentions of a character or action by means of over-playing. In this sense, he also understood *Gestus* as a technical complement of alienation, connected with it in order to illuminate the social context of the plots and to impart critical insights and impulses. To this end, *Gestus* could be acquired by observation and then re-built and mediated in dramatic action. In order to achieve this, Bennewitz accepted formalization and demonstrative clarification if necessary. In short, he understood *Gestus* more as an aesthetic construct rather than as a real experience.

Bennewitz was deeply impressed by experiencing *Gestus* as social reality in India, as everyday expression of social existence and behaviour in accordance with personal identity, as an ability to communicate under any circumstances, and as an immanent disposition to "perform" – which is more than European "representation" or "self-representation." His letters from India contain a wealth of observations and descriptions of this kind. They also make clear that he did not just register facts; he made great efforts to integrate himself into the contexts and conditions. He was able to do so not just by observing social and public life in general but above all by his collaboration with actors and amateurs from non-urban and different ethnic zones. Again and again he expressed his admiration for these partners and their quasi "natural" gestic potentials; he described them as "coming from the basics, from the roots." With this definition, he obviously avoided a social classification like "belonging to lower social classes" or a similar formulation corresponding to Indian social structures. He saw them as immediately connected to "the real shaping and development of social life." Above all, he valued their "natural ability" to not only show themselves in their social identity but also to embody and project a human power beyond that individuality, in a sense a fundamental humanity. For Bennewitz, *Gestus* therefore acquired a new meaning and function. He documented this not through academic definition but through circumscription in his very personal style: "Their gestures are *not acquired* [author's emphasis of this decisive term for his own practice up to that point] but have rather grown from below, from their life experience" (Letter to Ingeborg Pietzsch).

In this way, Bennewitz quickly realized that neither his initial sense of mission nor his original directing concept was adequate to address the conditions in the countries and theatre cultures in which he now worked. He went in search of his own strategy. His efforts were part of global cultural processes of the 1970s and 1980s. They corresponded to the initiatives of many theatre practitioners who were aiming for new cultural strategies and practices in the context of increasing globalization. These included, for example, the cultural- and theatre-anthropological conceptions of Richard Schechner and Eugenio Barba, Augusto Boal's socially and practically oriented and at the same time internationalized "Theatre of the Oppressed," the intercultural methods of appropriation of Ariane Mnouchkine, and many others. The main historical motivation for this development was the fact that after finally overcoming colonialism, many nations, peoples, and ethnic groups, particularly in the Third World, sought a return to their own identity, whereby their respective cultural traditions regained significance. After the Second World War there had been considerable activity in the field of cultural exchange, especially in the area of theatre, with the aim of fostering mutual acquaintance and understanding. However, European and North American models and practices were dominant in this. They were usually imparted with the good intention to provide help to the partners in the Third World in their quest for new cultural self-determination and orientation. New theatre conceptions and practices with a transcultural, internationalized structure were developing, such as those of Peter Brook and Augusto Boal, based on the assumption that this kind of work could foster cultural harmony and anticipate a future global human community. It turned out that such ventures no longer corresponded to the new historical exigencies, so that "international" programs and models were replaced by "intercultural" initiatives.

These new endeavours under the catchword interculturalism remained diffuse. Granted, there were attempts to describe and define what interculturalism is or should be; there was also the conceptualization of specific variants such as a particular "intraculturalism." However, no reliable theory or strategy emerged. This is not surprising in so far as the new historical epoch was determined by the particularities of nations, peoples, and ethnic groups, and thus by their differences. So a strong variation of multiple intercultural initiatives was quite logical and appropriate for the times. Nevertheless, there were (and are) aspects shared by all these endeavours, which justify their being labelled by an overarching term. They all have some degree of a critical relationship to the primarily economic process of globalization as it has developed since the 1970s. Inter*culturalism* stresses cultural forms of existence as a complement or even counterweight to merely economic globalization; it is marked by the endeavour to do justice to the new kinds of mutual relations between cultures, and these are understood as *equally valuable*. *Inter*culturalism searches for appropriate strategies of exchange and cooperation.

Bennewitz recognized the change and renewal of international cultural and theatrical relations happening in the world then (and now) as *the* historical challenge and opportunity. To this end, the aesthetically provocative fury of innovation in Western European theatre seemed to him to be less than helpful, and the creative power of theatre in the East too little open to the world. But his experiences abroad did not only modify his artistic aims, they soon also urged the convinced socialist to adopt a critical perspective on the outdated *political* strategies of internationalism – the "proletarian" kind just as much as the capitalist one. In this, he followed two programmatic approaches. One of them was Jawaharlal Nehru's thesis of "unity in diversity," formulated already in the 1950s at the beginning of the great international process of decolonization and in the context of the constitution of sovereign nations in the Third World. The other approach was Gorbachev's conception of a "global politics" instead of the hitherto dominant political strategy of competition that was geared towards the establishment of *one* specific social order worldwide. Both agreed that the plurality of human and thus societal life praxes would structurally determine the future order of the world and community of peoples, whereby "community" could only be gained within the permanent interplay of the various groups and forces. In favour of this cultural-*political* orientation, Bennewitz deemphasized the critical appropriation of the parallel cultural-*theoretical* initiatives mentioned above and his personal programmatic positioning in public discourse.

In contrast to his contemporaries and despite his voluminous and intensive practical endeavours, he did not work out his own fully developed intercultural conception. There are multiple reasons for this. He certainly did not lack the theoretical abilities to generalize his own endeavours and put them in relation to the relevant discourses. Rather, his reluctance to do so was determined by the fact that in his international encounters he increasingly felt the urge to step out of the biographical ties of his social and cultural political origins. He regarded it as his main task not to design new models and realize them as definitive intercultural contributions, e.g., in India, but rather to orient *himself* in the changing world, to rebuild *himself* with respect to the exigencies he recognized.

From this perspective, he certainly saw fit to keep his distance from conceptions such as those of Richard Schechner and Eugenio Barba, which had achieved recognition as movements with an international impact. In particular, the fundamental idea of a theatre anthropology provoked Bennewitz's criticism. "Theatre anthropology" is interested in *universal* performative modes and qualities and in *universal* origins of theatrical creativity; it searches for continuities and transmissions of this potential in contemporary cultures and endeavours to make them productive as a basis of intercultural interchange in the area of theatre. The merits of theatre anthropology particularly with regard to qualification of the means of performance, acting, and interacting are undeniable – and some of this entered into Bennewitz's praxis as well, apparently without his being conscious of it. However, he worried that in the final analysis the intercultural implications of these conceptions remained beholden to a European view of cultural history and of global relations after all. He agreed in this with colleagues from the Third World like the Indian critic and director Rustom Bharucha or the Nigerian dramatist and Nobel Prize winner Wole Soyinka. The cultural-*anthropological* approach of these theories and practices might with some justification be regarded as an historical overcoming of the dogmas of European or Western cultural and aesthetic conceptions, including all variants of modernity; but Bennewitz saw in them the danger that their orientation towards anthropological constants and historical origins could undermine the specific histories of nations, peoples, and ethnicities, and thus threaten their independent political and cultural self-determination in the present. He suspected a renewed internationalist, even neo-colonialist, conceptualization emanating from and dominated by the West, and given that the globalized world was increasingly shaped by economic interests, he did not see this suspicion dispelled to the end of his life.

In contrast to this, Bennewitz experienced in his process of self-discovery not only the de-territorialization of his social and cultural political ties, but above all a decisive *emergence from European history* into a world in upheaval – a different upheaval than anticipated. He met this challenge by means of extending his historical consciousness.

He endeavoured to understand the historical position of his partners and of the foreign peoples and regions, their historically grown cultural structures and future chances, and to contribute his own history to the cooperation. This necessitated not self-renunciation but a historically modified self-understanding. Shakespeare and Brecht remained the points of orientation for his international work, because in their plays and theatre methods he perceived the realization of a dialectical unity of historical specificity and human universality. In terms of his work with Brecht (and Shakespeare) everything was oriented towards the fundamental aim of "historicizing," to critically discover the social motivations of human action and societal processes in order to make historical perspectives perceptible and bring to bear humanistic values. This he saw as his task. He knew very well that this would be a long process of orientation, of mutual rapprochement, and of practical experiments. Brecht's *Caucasian Chalk Circle* seemed to him a suitable example for a whole series of experiments. He directed it eleven times – in Weimar, New York City, in various regions of India, and in Manila, including three times for children and as a scene study in actor training.

In this sense he was not after the elaboration of new programs. His intercultural endeavours over twenty-seven years took place as constant repetition and variation of practical activities in the form of productions, seminars, and dialogues in many countries. Nonetheless, over time certain working principles did emerge. His central aim was the integration of dramatic offerings from one culture into another, an embedding into an alien context on the basis of "equivalents" that had to be discovered and which necessitated modifications on both sides. He was determined to break open the programmatic theatrical models, methods, and themes he had been trained in and brought with him into the international exchange, in order to enable their new, timely mediation and appropriation. Thus, unlike others, he never again contemplated imparting Brecht's works in the form of programmatic models of theatre aesthetics to his partners abroad. In the context of his Brecht productions abroad he always said that he had not put "the plays" on stage but had rather helped to introduce "the structural principle of the plays" into Indian theatre (or the theatre of the respective region). To this end he worked intensively with the translators in order to achieve the transmission of the works into the linguistic and conceptual worlds of the various cultures. Though he did not know most of the respective languages, he developed a gestic, stylistic, and acoustic sensibility for the appropriate kinds of expression and behaviour. This enabled him to lead and, if needed, correct the actors and to effect changes in the translation in the course of the production process. His collaborators in all countries unanimously confirmed this ability, which astonished them and led them to follow his directions and criticism willingly. In this sense integration became the strategic key concept of his intercultural endeavours. This he wanted to achieve, and he hoped that in future it would happen mutually.

One aspect connected to his understanding of history and theatre remained especially significant for him. Like Brecht, he saw a great socially based, gestic potential particularly in Asian theatre traditions, but at the same time he noticed that due to different historical experiences, thinking and creating in terms of historical developments was under-represented in those cultures. According to his observations, this showed itself in performative practices in the underestimation or neglect of the dramatic texts, in which historical associations are primarily bound up. In the face of the current world political situation at the time he thought the accentuation of this dimension to be indispensable. Therefore, he urged tirelessly that the textual structure and the word should be given more weight in these traditions and in the actors' behaviour. He was convinced that not just any text was suitable for paving the way to interculturalism, and so he chose, in accordance with his partners, such plays as best allowed the realization of his intentions, primarily works by Brecht and Shakespeare, and several times also Goethe's *Faust*.

Bennewitz's journeys through countries and cultures were not free from errors and contradictions, though we need to remind ourselves that both can be occasion for and challenge to productivity. These were numerous in his biography. While his work shaped the profile of the Weimar theatre for decades and his productions always conjured up an ensemble spirit, gradually a mutual alienation between him and the ensemble had crept in. In his intercultural endeavours he vehemently rejected Schechner's theory and practice, but scholarly analysis of his *Faust* productions at La Mama (New York), in Manila, and in Bombay prove the proximity of his directorial practice to certain of Schechner's conceptual and methodological principles. Nehru's thesis of "unity in diversity" remained an indispensable guiding idea for him, even though his Indian partners had bid it farewell long ago, and some of them had never accepted it in the first place.

The most striking contradictions are those that show up in retrospect when communicating with Bennewitz's partners in India, where he enjoyed and still enjoys high esteem. The Indian subcontinent is probably the world's most multi-ethnic and multicultural region. In this context, Bennewitz's strategy of integration did not appear as an intercultural endeavour, as he himself understood it to be. His partners there valued him as an artist who, unlike others, did not act as an emissary or indoctrinator of Brechtian theatre or anything else, but one who combined this anticolonial attitude with a strong work ethic while paying heed to the regional social and cultural conditions. This difference between their pragmatic understanding of his endeavours and his own strategic self-understanding apparently never came to bear during his long career in India, and it only came to light during consultations with his former partners there while researching his biography. It then emerged, too, that his Indian friends had no idea what efforts Bennewitz had to make to master the challenges that his re-orientation in the world outside the GDR and Europe posed, or how his Indian experiences changed his understanding of Brecht and influenced his work at home. With astonishment, they now saw "a completely different Bennewitz" and noted the *productive* errors with regard to Indian conditions that he had made in the course of his learning process and that they had not even noticed in his practical work. What his Indian partners now have to realize in expanding *their* image of Bennewitz is that he was transforming himself in order to undertake the right steps into the very world for which they, due to their historically more favourably structured culture, already have an entrance ticket. They are right that he did not formulate an intercultural strategy or conception, but what he did formulate was the realization that the cultural relations in the world of tomorrow must be different than the strategies of political and cultural internationalism dominant in his time. This was the goal toward which he began to re-orient himself. The principle of integration was the step he was able to take in that direction, and therefore it is not only justified but necessary to claim his endeavours as important for a future intercultural praxis.

In this context we should turn now to certain aspects of Bennewitz's biography that have hitherto not been considered in discussions of his intercultural work. In his work abroad, Bennewitz encountered cultural traditions and forces that had been lost or at least secularized and disciplined in the civilizational history of Europe. In other cultural zones, ancient myths and rituals, the rudiments of a magical worldview, have been preserved to the present day and have a relieving and stimulating impact on the existence of peoples and individuals. While he remained faithful to the traditions of the European Enlightenment to the end of his life, such influences now began to make themselves felt in his life and work as well.

At first, they became tangible in his private life, namely in his vacation experiences on the island of Hiddensee. As few remnants of that magical worldview as there are in Europe, we do have some remaining equivalents in our cultural history, for example, a persistent island myth, the island as refuge for people stressed by civilization, as a place of renewed contemplation of natural, original, and at times also magical forces of existence. The island of Hiddensee was such a place, especially for artists, who had come there since the end of the nineteenth century and had again and again fallen under its spell. Their artistic pathos, driven equally by their "suffering of the world" and their will to shape it, found new impetus here. This was true for Bennewitz as well. On his life paths between Weimar and foreign countries, Hiddensee was a yearly late summer respite. Here he was "a different Bennewitz," fulfilled in experiencing and sensing nature, immersed in a varied circle of friends, often given to boundless sociability, but then again thoughtfully and quietly contemplating the landscape and its inhabitants through the "magical window" in his small dwelling. What he gained there, he took with him out into the world.

Those cultural experiences as well as an increasingly vehement critical stance towards civilization prompted Bennewitz to now include previously unknown elements in his work. This happened when, despite continuing success abroad and at home, his life and work became problematic in the context of societal and political processes in the 1980s and 90s. With increasing resignation he observed the renewed tensions in international relations, the emerging political and social contradictions in the countries of the Third World, the terrorist attempts at their resolution, and the evaporation of ideals for the future. His productions became caught up repeatedly in the maelstrom of political conflicts and his intercultural activities became increasingly difficult due to impeding influences from the new culture industry spreading everywhere. Thus, more and more frequently he posed himself questions about his own place in history and the present, and about his own identity.

In this struggle to come to terms with himself, Bennewitz remembered Goethe's *Faust*; he once again directed the first part of the drama, in Bombay in 1993/4 and in Manila in 1994. He saw the production in Manila as a crowning achievement of his intercultural endeavours and as a new, universal chance for the play. That magical component he had become aware of in the encounter with foreign cultures, and on the island, played a role in this. In the Manila production, the creative power of the doubting intellectual grew from the plebeian shrewdness of a man from the common people, and in Bennewitz's directorial conception Faust's critical appropriation of magical forces played an essential role in his struggle for self-determined, active creativity. In the foreign context, the hope of the beginning was rejuvenated, refined by experiences from three decades and three worlds.

Nevertheless, Bennewitz's biography became more and more marked by tragic elements. He had hoped for an intercultural exchange and thus tried to bring his experiences abroad into his theatre work at home as well. However, his endeavours found no echo there, neither in the official cultural policies of the GDR nor from his critically engaged colleagues. A certain interest in his experiments emerged in Germany for only a short span during the global political upheavals of the 1980s and 1990s. Over time it became clear that his experiences abroad alienated him from conditions at home rather than bringing him closer to coming to critical terms with them. Increasingly there were production problems at home.

He sensed this, but repressed it, too. In his letters only those close to him can catch a hint of it. The unavoidable realization of this problematic situation came over him in the 1990s, when not only GDR history had become desolate for him but he also could not find a basis in reunified Germany: "Until the fall of the Wall I had been a visiting citizen for twenty years, and had identified to a high degree with hopes for a more just world and for the changeability of humankind. I was in the exceptional situation of an intellectual artist who, as it turns out today, made a decisive error. While as an artist I stood in fundamental conflict with any order, I sided with the order instead of with myself. And I had a cosmopolitan experience that I did not translate into demands posed to our reality. My identity might have to find itself anew. But the fertile soil of our lives is and remains our culture."

At the same time he sensed that his work abroad needed new initiatives beyond past successes. With all the variation in his activities he had still followed a basic cultural-political line: the imparting of dramatic texts and thus close ties to literary traditions. Alternatives to this, such as they were being tried out in current intercultural experiments, remained outside of his purview. Six months before his death he described in an interview his experience that "interculturalism has exhausted itself," that it "cannot be upheld in the global world," and that "the worlds are drifting apart culturally." He felt that his integration strategy was no longer effective, and that under the changed geopolitical conditions new intercultural efforts were necessary and possible. The precondition for a participation of Europeans in these efforts, in his firm conviction, was a renewed productive reassessment of their own cultural traditions. He saw first glimpses of this, for example, in the reception of ancient aesthetics by Ariane Mnouchkine and her troupe Théâtre du Soleil, who went back to syncretic structures of ancient theatre in combining the adaptation of literary works with percussion and strongly rhythmic patterns of movement. However, he himself did not feel strong enough to bring something like this into his directorial work abroad. He now had production problems there, as well.

Fritz Bennewitz died, overcome by a cancer he had been battling for years, on 12 September 1995, in the middle of yet another *Faust* production, this time for the Meiningen Theatre. He suffered the fate of an artist who had lost his homeland on his way into the global era, but who could not yet arrive in "the world" for which he longed.

Bennewitz in India: Politics, Brecht, and the Human Touch

DAVID G. JOHN

Politics

Fritz Bennewitz's official assignment in India from the GDR Ministry of Culture was to teach theatre and direct plays, but his mission was at the same time political, to represent and encourage the socialist agenda. He was one of the earliest to join the new GDR's Socialist Unity Party after its formation in 1946, optimistic at the prospect of a new world of equality and harmony, and convinced that international socialism could bring that about. He remained a loyal party member until it was dissolved upon Germany's reunification in 1989, and while by then fed up with the internal politics of his country, never abandoned his commitment to humanistic socialist ideals. "Internal politics," he wrote, "need to be subordinate when it is a question of the survival of mankind" (New Delhi, 6 Nov. 1983, page 161). Only politically trusted GDR citizens were allowed to visit countries freely outside European Socialist borders, which as such Bennewitz did constantly from 1970 until his death in 1995, including India at least twenty-eight times. As director at the German National Theatre in Weimar from 1960 to 1991, the home of German Classicism and jewel in the GDR's cultural crown, he was revered by many as a theatre man – though not by his peer directors in Berlin, the hub of East German theatre – and trusted by his government. While committed to socialist principles, Bennewitz did not proselytize obviously in India or other countries he visited as a representative of the GDR. He became absorbed immediately in his art, the theatre, culture, and the lives and mentalities of his hosts, seized by a desire to understand them and merge his thinking with theirs. He even observed radically socialistic and communist groups in theatre productions and on the streets with scepticism and some disdain, once commenting blandly, "Well, that's not my ideological cup of tea. It's too bad that once again the 'leftists' do so much damage with what they make young people full of good will do ..." (New Delhi, 18 Oct. 1983, page 152). A further important factor in his freedom to travel was his long-time membership in the International Theater Institute (ITI), an organization very important to the cultural branch of the GDR since it provided access to many developing countries open to the concept of socialism, and is still today dedicated to the "power of the performing arts as an indispensable bridge-builder for mutual international understanding and peace" (ITI). During these years Bennewitz was a member from 1969, served as consultant on the ITI's committee on the Third World (1972–84), and as a vice-president from 1984. This ensured that the GDR's voice would be heard in the international theatre community.

While away, Bennewitz was of course carefully monitored by his government, and to this end contributed regular reports, his personal copies of which we can still read in the Fritz Bennewitz Archive in Leipzig, and the tone of which was officious and obedient. His main contact for much of this time was Irene Gysi (1912–2007), an official in the ministry of culture and mother of Gregor Gysi (b. 1948), until recently the leader of the Left Party faction in the German federal parliament. She personally authorized his trips abroad and monitored, in a kindly and supportive way, his activities. Bennewitz's private correspondence to his loyal partner Waltraut Mertes in Weimar was much different, open and personal, as we see in the letters to her translated in this book. While abroad, he had specific duties connected with East German officials, consulates, and offices in India, to which his correspondence often refers. These were of two sorts, attending GDR-sponsored meetings and functions, with which he generally voiced his discomfort, and international social events as part of the GDR delegation, where the cocktail banter was for him mostly "bla, bla, bla" (Bombay, 29 Oct. 1973). Connected with these were his feelings toward the representatives of the rival Federal Republic of Germany, toward whom he developed a phobia: "The External Culture Department of the FRG, the Goethe-Institute ... is always spying on me ... the G.I. not only follows my every step, but also tries to imitate whatever I undertake" (Calcutta, 25 Sept. 1980). He harboured a similar aversion to the United States in the international forum, occasionally advocating a need for "reporting from countries outside of Europe about the global encircling strategy of the USA" (New Delhi, 6 Nov. 1983, page 161). He was no less sceptical about America's great European rival, even if he did support in theory its general political stance. Writing from Bombay in 1973, he effused, "I love our big brother [the Soviet Union] and I don't desire anything other than socialism, or wish for a different kind of socialism to the one we have," but adds that this sentiment was in fact a naïve ideal, for his own experience in Moscow airport during one visit was "the total absence of kindness and friendliness," going on at some length before pulling himself up short: "An uncomfortable thought: if I were to articulate these complaints at an assembly, my relationship with the Soviet Union would become an object of serious concern" (Bombay, 4 Oct. 1973). One thinks of the consequences paid by political dissenters throughout the world at that time and still today. To be fair, however, this should be seen as just one early statement by Bennewitz. He was generally more cautious when voicing opinions on the Russians, as were most other GDR citizens.

In the same letter Bennewitz was surprisingly candid about the disjuncture between the theoretical position of the GDR's humanistic socialism and the consistency of its application. Upon attending the annual celebration of his nation's founding at the Bombay consulate, he reported, "the children barked their pioneer vows into the room and a middle-aged woman whimpered blessings into the blue cloths that had recently been fastened round their necks. ... Everything that is said at such occasions is certainly true – but it's also untruthful, because it's as impersonal as reheated canteen food" (ibid.). Yet he vacillated soon after when attending a meeting of the India-GDR-Friendship-Society in Bombay, reporting impressive speeches in honour of his homeland: "a feeling of pride in the small, yet great GDR brought tears to my eyes" (ibid.). By 1985 he began to distance himself from the formal position of the GDR, as is expressed, for example, in his letter from New Delhi of 10 January 1990 (see page 203). It was socialistic humanism that was the foundation of his belief, always an idealist, rising with dignity above the pragmatics of politics. Resigned to the political failure of his homeland by 1989, he lost much of his optimism for providing a solution for India's economic woes through those politics (see, for example, his letter from New Delhi of 27 Dec. 1989, page 202) He was just as pessimistic that India herself would produce the change. On the very day the Berlin Wall fell, he wrote about a television documentary on the recent murder of Safdar Hashmi, an Indian Communist shot for his ideals, which Bennewitz equated with similar actions by his own government (New Delhi, 3 Jan. 1990, page 203). As far as the reunited Germany was concerned, he wrote, "The German state is of no concern to me – and I need not be their concern. … I have represented the GDR for twenty years; whatever state it had become – I was always proud to represent what it originally was supposed to aim for. Without this state, I could not have done the things I did, which have made an impact and become history here. My works were contributions towards establishing contact between what is proper and unique to here with what is international and proper to humankind" (New Delhi, 8 Dec. 1990, page 221). There is no self-promotion in this claim, just a balanced summary of his accomplishments in India, of which he was justly proud.

India

From his first visit in 1970 until his last in 1994 Bennewitz was at times almost overwhelmed by the country's mass of population and the conditions endured by its poor. Generally eschewing favoured treatment for himself, he usually lived there simply, but to him even this seemed a privileged life compared with the filth and misery he saw all around. He wrote of his deep unease at "tripping over the limbs of the poor in the streets while enjoying the privileges of the rich" (Bombay, 9 Oct. 1973). The images of squalor sometimes assumed nightmarish proportions: "When night falls, they lie in their hundreds on the station platforms – they probably conceive their children there, they give birth to them there, they feed them there and pick their lice there, and they lose them there. … They don't know of doctors and they die as they are born – both events often not even noticed by society and bureaucracy" (ibid.). His initial horror gave way in time to a gradual self-distancing from such scenes and emotions, similar to that which native Indians of higher socio-economic standing and seasoned visitors there developed, a necessary defence. Yet even amid the dense traffic of the cities streaming alongside abject poverty, his keen eye saw "almost unnoticed ... the steady trickles of moving, bustling people who draw themselves along through this unmoving knot of tin and wood like bloodstreams, the supply lines of life." This image of humanity, the human mass, was for him in the end an overwhelmingly positive sign despite the economic inequality and squalor. "In our pallid sentimentality," he wrote, "we only see their capacity for suffering rather than the TENACIOUS VITALITY they represent," and because of this, the misery became acceptable (Calcutta, 1 Oct. 1980, caps his; see also Tatlow 357). His inextinguishable optimism, like that of the Indian people, shone through. Only when the blight was caused by external forces of profiteers did he rail against its injustice, as for example in the devastation caused by the environmental catastrophe in Bhopal (7 Jan. 1985, page 177). Such experiences led to reflections on economic and social inequality, and by contrast the equality and relative prosperity he perceived in his homeland, but he did not make it a point to preach against the injustice of India's fundamental social structure and paid only scant attention to its caste system. He grew to accept Hinduism as a way to deal with these ills, and Hinduism's theology of reincarnation as a palliative to the misery of the present. Deeply touched by the anguish of many, he was nevertheless confident that his work in the theatre could make a difference, for his art was always connected to the human lot, and the question of how to improve it.

Indian Theatre

"Theatre in our sense of the word doesn't exist here," Bennewitz wrote from Delhi in 1970 while directing Brecht's *Threepenny Opera*, his first play there, and one highly praised at the time (10 Mar.). Still, despite using Indian actors and playing a translation in Hindi, it was later generally acknowledged to be more of a transplanted German than an Indian production. This jarred his European anchor. In the next two and a half decades in India he adjusted to many fundamental differences between the theatre he knew and what he learned there. He was well-served by the venue and facilities in such arenas as the National School of Drama (NSD) in Delhi and the National Centre for Performing Arts in Bombay, but in many others the practicalities of theatre space and lack of infrastructure were constant problems for many of the companies he worked with. They usually had to rent space for performances and rehearsals both, lacked a standing stock of scenery, props, and costumes, and had few resources to fill the gaps (Calcutta, 25 Oct. 1980, page 96). Constantly frustrated, he nevertheless delivered many productions of high quality. He learned soon to recognize the important distinctions among professional schools of drama, independent acting companies, and amateur groups. He moved among and worked with all three: the NSD which was India's primary training ground for professional actors and his professional home base; Bharat Bhavan's Rangmandal in Bhopal, the permanent acting company with which he had his most continuous cooperation in India and for which he held the highest regard for bringing classical and contemporary Indian drama to the stage; many groups in small towns and villages who had no formal training but were talented and rich in the traditions of Indian folk theatre; and individual artists everywhere, singers, dancers, actors, whose spontaneous acts of performance in public spaces carried on ancient traditions of the Indian people and became increasingly important in his mind as time went on. The degree to which the actors he directed were formally trained before joining his casts caused in him reactions ranging from disappointment to elation; he did not praise the sophistically trained alone, but was often enthralled by raw talent, which he himself could then mould; he was, by contrast, disappointed by actors with years of superior training and impressive reputations on the stage, who now lacked dedication or flair (Calcutta, 25 Oct. 1980, pages 97–9). For Bennewitz it was the actors who made the show.

Indian Actors

The most fulfilling and enriching aspect of Bennewitz's many stays in India was his contact with these actors. This intimate, professional, often deeply appreciative and affectionate relationship is well documented in the surviving correspondence between them. The process of teaching and directing in India – his two primary assignments as a representative of the cultural ministry of his homeland – were rife with problems he had never imagined. Because his first *Threepenny Opera* in New Delhi gave him access to actors trained by the NSD, there were no major problems, but the move to Bombay and the staging of *The Caucasian Chalk Circle* with Marathi players in 1973, and other venues later on, brought different circumstances. There, for example, he was forced to switch actors for parts in mid-rehearsal. He lacked the time to train a potentially excellent candidate from the popular theatre for the main role of Azdak and was forced to replace him. The actress of Grusha had to be replaced well into rehearsals because her husband simply made her stay at home. Typhoid fever struck another actor's five children and necessitated a further substitute (Bombay, 19 Oct. 1973). His directing partner Vijaya Mehta, who shouldered the great part of the personnel burden like a "real work horse," was his saving grace, as Esleben has shown in convincing detail (Bombay, 25 Oct. 1973, Esleben, "From Didactic to Dialectic").

In every one of Bennewitz's productions in India the director, cast, and crew were under enormous time pressures. He himself tended to overpack his travel schedule with commitments to direct abroad alongside productions at home in Germany, all of which resulted repeatedly in inadequate time for translation, rehearsal, and production. A vivid example of this pressure can be seen in his Calcutta *Galileo* of 1980. The translation of the play into Bengali had not been completed by the time the short rehearsal period began. No orientation or blocking could take place until it arrived. The German text was translated first into English, then to Bengali, and then back and forth between the two and numerous translators to have it fine-tuned, and then it still had to go to the scribes who manually made copies for distribution individually to the players. To this were added the costume designing and fitting, set building, and musical accompaniment, freshly composed for the Indian adaptation, all this in a blistering schedule of four weeks before opening night. Here, and in many other productions, the whirlwind of chaotic activity swirled around Bennewitz at the focus, with a crowd of people working simultaneously in his own living space for up to thirteen hours in a row. Actors had many "ingrained habits to unlearn," he wrote (Calcutta, 28 Sept. 1980), and complained generally that the level of talent just wasn't sufficient for his purposes, so he had to rehearse around the part of the Philosopher and also work hard on the part of the Mathematician (Calcutta, 30 Sept. 1980). But there were always bright spots. "Our Galileo is simply a grand actor," he wrote jubilantly (Calcutta, 28 Sept. 1980), and on a later occasion, "do you also know what a great, deep joy it is to see their heart and mind shine from their faces and their gestures when they have found themselves in the beauty of simplicity?" (New Delhi, 6 Nov. 1981, page 110). Reading his letters, one becomes accustomed to jumps from one extreme to another, a characteristic trait and way of thinking that pointed to the dialectical thought process that underpinned his approach. Bennewitz's personal interaction with his actors was also often impeded by their different tongues. He complained that about eighty per cent of them came from the lower classes and could not speak any language well, especially English. He overcame this problem remarkably through his ability to absorb some of the local languages himself, working with those on site who knew English, and communicating a great sense of empathy to all those with whom he interacted, even if awkwardly across linguistic boundaries. He, his actors, and technical assistants strove in unison to produce their plays, but nobody harder than the director himself. He gained a permanent reputation for this dedication and energy, and his tolerance of the Indians' lot and their ways. He even learned to enjoy the rituals they insisted on conducting before rehearsals, a symbolic religious spiritualism completely foreign to his materialistic mind, yet accepted by him as part of the process of creating theatre together (Bombay, 19 Nov. 1973; see too Bennewitz's essay "Otherness" in this volume).

Bennewitz, Brecht, and India

The main links between Bennewitz's brand of humanistic socialism and India were Marxism, the theatre, and Brecht. From 1949 to 1953 he studied German literature and philosophy in Leipzig and, in tandem, theatre at the German Theatre Institute in Weimar. During this time he became chief instructor of the Socialist Unity Party's (SED) Central Party School for Art and Literature Rosa Luxembourg in Erfurt, and from 1953 to 1955 he held the position of lecturer on aesthetics and theatre at the University of Leipzig. He completed his studies in culture, literature, and philosophy there and afterward pursued theatre studies at the German Theatre Institute in Weimar and the Hans Otto Theatre Institute in Leipzig, while continuing to lecture in aesthetics and theatre at the latter (John, *Bennewitz* 19–20). Bennewitz was not just a theatre director, he was from the beginning a teacher, and what he taught was based on Marxist political philosophy and aesthetics, so it should come as no surprise that this was the foundation of what he taught in India as well. The vehicles to convert this theoretical knowledge and conviction to the stage in Germany, India, and many other countries were Brecht's theory and practice, in which Bennewitz was well steeped.

While our concentration in this volume is on his activity in India, we should be reminded that this activity was constantly intertwined with his directing work at home and in other countries. Between 1970 and 1994 he directed some thirty times in India: five complete and several excerpted Brecht plays, seven complete and several excerpted Shakespeare plays, and three plays from the works of Braun, Chekhov, and Goethe. During the same period he also directed productions of Brecht, Shakespeare and other authors in East Germany and in many other countries besides India at least as frequently. These productions included almost all of the same plays he directed in India during the same period (John, *Bennewitz* 278–84). His East German and international productions laid the foundation for those in India, and while he did indeed learn over time to adapt those models substantially for Indian actors, audiences, and their culture, and rejoiced in the nuances he discovered with and for their audiences, the starting point and impetus for them was nevertheless the same as for those in his homeland.

Bennewitz's Brecht productions in India added momentum to a trend that began there more than twenty years earlier. Amal Allana, Chairperson of the NSD from 2005 to 2013, daughter of Ebrahim Alkazi, first director of the NSD, and herself an outstanding director of many productions, including Brecht, was a close colleague of Bennewitz when he worked in India. In her contribution to the recent volume *Brecht in/ and Asia*, she describes the importance of Brecht in the process of India's nation building after the end of British rule in 1947 ("Brecht"). She traces his influence in the new post-colonial culture of India, which paralleled similar influences in Latin America, Egypt, and parts of Africa in their peoples' struggles against colonial rule (see also Silberman). The introduction of Brecht's work was spearheaded by the young Indian playwright and director Balwant Gargi and director Habib Tanvir as a result of their experiences at the Berliner Ensemble just before and after Brecht's death in 1956 (Allana, "Brecht" 28–9). Further important steps to introduce Brecht to India were taken in an international east-west seminar on the playwright in Delhi in the early 1960s, organized jointly by the International Theatre Institute and Bharatiya Natya Sangh, which led to the establishment of cultural exchange programs between India and the GDR (Allana, "Brecht" 31). Left-leaning theatre practitioners in Bengal led the Brecht charge thereafter with translations and productions of his works, one of the earliest being *The Life of Galileo* in 1964, followed soon after by *The Caucasian Chalk Circle*. At this time the Indian Brecht Society was also founded (Allana, "Brecht" 32). In 1968, Ebrahim Alkazi participated in the "Brecht-Dialog" in East Berlin, organized by the ITI. With the latter's support, there were Brecht productions at the NSD directed by Carl Weber (*Caucasian Chalk*

Circle, in Hindi, 1968) and then Bennewitz (*Threepenny Opera* in 1970). Bennewitz had been chosen because of the spectacular success he had enjoyed with this play in Meiningen and Berlin in 1958 (Erck 176; John, *Bennewitz* 52). From that point he never looked back, and he was joined by many Indian directors who released a flood of Brecht productions over the next twenty years (see also *Change the World* 22–3).

The enthusiasm lasted well into the nineties, as evidenced by two noteworthy testimonials to Brecht co-published by India and the GDR. The first was on the occasion of an exhibition at the Brecht Centre in Berlin in 1982, which moved to the NSD in November 1984, entitled *Change the World. It Needs It!* and included a booklet with text, pictures and illustrations of Brecht's biography and works. It further contains a list of the eleven Brecht productions mounted at the NSD between 1968 and 1984, five of which were by Bennewitz, one by Carl Maria Weber, the other six by Indian directors, several of which were never attempted by Bennewitz. It is instructive to note that his Brecht productions in India were limited to just five plays, *The Threepenny Opera, The Caucasian Chalk Circle, Galileo, Puntila and his Servant Matti, Man equals Man*, and *The Good Person of Sichuan*, all but one repeated in remounted productions; a modest offering, given the possibilities. (In the mixed program "Brecht on Trial," made up of scenes from several plays, some from *Arturo Ui* and *Mother Courage* were also included.) In the eighties he focused much more on Shakespeare, but that is another subject. There are scene shots in this booklet from some of these productions, including those of Bennewitz, some productions at the Berliner Ensemble in the GDR, and brief articles by Werner Hecht (9, 32–4) and Manfred Wekwerth (27) of the GDR. There is also a valuable, extended "Bibliography of Brecht Literature and Theatography of Brecht Performances in India" which includes a mixture of titles from the holdings of the Brecht-Archive in Berlin, some of which refer to Brecht in India, and translations of his plays into Indian languages, showing a much larger range than the previous list above (24–5). The theatography includes information on thirty-seven Brecht productions in India between 1960 and 1980, some performed in English, others in Indian languages, with many details on the place of production, language, directors, and actors (26). Bennewitz's contribution actually represented only a small part of the activity on Brecht (see also *Change* 22–3, and Allana, "Brecht").

The other noteworthy publication, *A Tribute to Bertolt Brecht 1993*, is a collection of essays on Brecht productions in India and Germany from a strongly Indian perspective (Nissar Allana). In addition to an introduction by Nissar Allana, spouse of Amal Allana, editor of the volume and distinguished stage designer and producer of many Brecht and other plays as well as ten scholarly essays, the book contains many scene shots and a valuable bibliography of 85 productions of Brecht plays in India from 1970 to 1993 with details of translators, adaptors, directors, and performance languages (87–8), hence a continuation of that in the work described above, though the list is not complete. There is a huge range, twenty-six different titles and six others which were selected scenes or whose English titles leave the original unclear. Almost all the directors were Indian, with only eight exceptions. The only one of these who directed more than once is Bennewitz, who is listed nine times, so for a third of all the productions. This demonstrates that although not a director of the first wave, he was without question the most prominent foreign director of Brecht in India during the long period from 1970 to 1995. The languages of his productions are also included: Bengali, Hindi, Marathi, and Urdu, but it was even more complicated than this, as he learned when dealing with translations of the *Chalk Circle* into Bundeli in Bhopal, as well as *Puntila, The Chalk Circle,* and the *Good Person of Sichuan* into Kannada for productions in Bangalore and Heggodu (John, *Bennewitz* 279–80, 283): "... what I had not been fully conscious of is that there are hundreds of dialects in Kannada, and some are as different from each other and as mutually unintelligible as Bavarian and northern low German. So they have to reach a shared Kannada in which they can express as much of themselves as in the dialect they grew up with and in, and that process takes time" (Heggodu, 2 Oct. 1989, page 198). Bennewitz, with assistance, directed in all of the languages above, which suggests that he was also in tune with regional Indian differences. Finally, it is noticeable from this bibliography that the volume of Brecht productions in India declined gradually during the eighties and early nineties, a pattern which paralleled Bennewitz's own activity there. With the political changes throughout Eastern Europe then, Brecht and his message moved into the shadows. In the sixties there were ten Brecht productions in India, in the seventies forty-two, the eighties twenty-five, and from 1990 to 1993 just eight. Brecht's heyday in India was over, as was Bennewitz's there and at home (see also Ghosh).

Among the many subjects addressed in Brecht's political and theoretical writings, two concepts stand out as crucial for our understanding of Bennewitz's teaching and directing activities in India: dialectics and history. These at the same time comprised the essential foundation of the Marxist political philosophy and process. In his "Dialectical Dramatics," written in 1931, Brecht extols "... the revolutionary effect that the dialectical process has everywhere it penetrates, through which it manifests its role as the best gravedigger of bourgeois ideas and institutions" (Brecht, *Werke* 21, 432 / trans. DGJ). He leaves no doubt that his dramaturgy has as its guiding principle the effecting of fundamental social change. So he argues in his "Short Description of a New Technique of Acting which Produces an Alienation Effect" (*Werke* 22/2, 641–59 / trans. Willett 136–47) that the purpose of the alienation technique is "to make the spectator adopt an attitude of inquiry and criticism in his approach to the incident" (*Werke* 641 / Willett 136). Later in the same treatise he emphasizes that "this criticism of the world is active, practical, positive. Criticizing the course of a river means improving it, correcting it. Criticism of society is ultimately revolution ..." (659 / Willett 146). The central image here, changing the river and its course, is ironic, and certainly problematic in the present context, for it amounts to challenging Nature herself, something that would appear ridiculous to the Indian Hindu mind, as would the advocacy of revolution in a society built on passivity, which Bennewitz himself described as "...the habitual, moulded attitude of ACCEPTANCE ... (New Delhi, 25 Nov. 1984, page 171). Additionally, dialectics for Brecht were much more than a historically-oriented concept. They were fundamental as well to his concept of acting technique. In his theory of acting he was fond of inserting examples of dialectical argumentation, as in the "Dialog about an Actress in the Epic Theatre" (*Werke* 22/1, 353–5) and "The Exchange" (Brecht, *Werke* 22/2, 670–2), which consist of discussions between Brecht (the Ich) and an actor, or an actor and an audience member, about various aspects of performance. He essentially sets up the questions or counter-arguments to himself through these personae and then replies in instructive fashion, an artificially structured didacticism which reached its highest form in the *Lehrstücke*. In the "Appendices to the Short Organum" of 1948 he offers concrete examples of how actors must show their understanding of the world and humankind by playing their roles as constant dialectical inquirers, always reflecting this frame of mind (*Werke* 23, 292–4; Willett 279–80).

The foundation of Brecht's theory is history, the history of humankind, through which the dialectical process works. In the "Brief Description of a New Technique of Acting" he refers to "the historification of everyday life" as "a decisive technical feature" and requires that "the actor must play the events of a play as historical events. Historical events happen once for all [time] and are over. They are bound up with particular epochs" (*Werke* 22/2, 646 / Bentley 40). Through this the definition and development of the social classes, and particularly the proletariat, become clear, the class which for the first time called into question the validity of the social system which preceded its emergence (Brecht, *Werke* 22/1, 17). It is instructive to notice that the *Short Organum*, Brecht's most detailed and definitive piece of writing on the theory of theatre (*Werke* 23, 65–97 / Willett 179–205) is based not on artistry but on history. After a few introductory paragraphs it begins to recount the history of civilized mankind, starting with Aristotle and moving on to the Ages of Scientific Discovery and Industrialization, the acceleration of and control over industrial production, the suppression of the workers by the bourgeois class, and a set of questions as a result (Secs. 4–21). Then come the answers, which of course are that a new class of workers must emerge and take control (Secs. 22–32) and that the theatre must play a leading role in making this happen: "We need a type of theatre which not only releases the feelings, insights and impulses possible within the particular historical field of human relations in which the action takes place, but employs and encourages those thoughts and feelings which help transform the field itself" (Sec. 35); and further: "The 'historical conditions' must of course not be imagined (nor will they be so constructed) as mysterious Powers (in the background); on the contrary, they are created and maintained by men (and will in due course be altered by them) …" (Sec. 38, Willett 190). With this historical foundation and the setting of the task for theatre to continue to develop the perspective of the new proletarian class, the remainder of the *Short Organum* could then deal with more artistically focused matters such as *Gestus* (see Rohmer 295–6), *Fabel*, music, choreography, and design, all of which were also points of concentration for Bennewitz's directing in India.

Bennewitz was an invited participant in the Berlin "Brecht-Dialog" in 1968, a kind of international Brecht summit sponsored by the GDR Ministry of Culture, Academy of Fine Arts, and the Brecht House, with international representation (*Brecht Dialog*). The conference discussed and reaffirmed participants' commitment to Brecht's socio-political and aesthetic principles and their resolve to apply them vigorously to their artistic fields. That Bennewitz was one of the invited number attests to his status as a director in the GDR and loyalty to this line of thought. In the full range of his Indian letters, not just those translated here, he refers to Brecht frequently, and the most important Brecht concept emphasized is the Hegelian-Marxist idea of dialectical process. Yet as he began to apply Brecht's theory to his directing in India, Marxism's fundamental concept of history, and the importance of history itself, immediately made the task problematic. The entire historical panorama was a western and European one. Its historical sweep ignored Asia. But India's history did not include feudalism as a distinct age, nor the Renaissance, nor the Enlightenment which signalled a breakthrough to modernity and a turning over of social classes, nor the American and French revolutions, nor the rise of the proletariat and toppling of the aristocracy throughout Europe and the Russian revolution which set the course for international socialism. Yet these structures and events were the very historical backbone of the Marxist concept of history and dialectical materialism. India did not have historically the same social groups and classes as Europe either, nor did most Indians have a sense of what those were, and they were anyway largely foreign to their own caste system. Most Indians were Hindus (over eighty per cent), with an inbred sense of accepting their history, linking it with reverence to their religion, and not being inclined to challenge or attempt to change its course. Hindus believe in reincarnation. Trying to change one's life in the greater sense is contradictory to that philosophy and perceived as futile. So Bennewitz's attempts to produce Brechtian theatre were faced with an almost impossible attitudinal challenge (see also Revermann 286). He was further dealing for the most part with post-independence Indians, the young generation who had been taught to look ahead, not back, even if they practiced the Hindu faith. He realized and wrote of the disjuncture as early as 1973, linking it to religion and the Indian concept of good and evil: "the juxtaposition of GOOD and EVIL is still static like that between Rama and Ravana, not dynamic and dialectical, just like historical consciousness is static rather than dynamic and dialectical; there is no thinking and experiencing of historical processes" (Bombay, 19 Nov. 1973, page 59). He complained that this audience had "not yet learned to think in terms of historical processes, but only in terms of far distant pasts that are not related to the present or in terms of immediate undialectical parallels" (ibid.; see also Bhave 13–14).

The point of departure for Bennewitz's first production of *The Chalk Circle* in 1973 was a liberal translation which made generous accommodations such as adjusting the place of action from the Caucasus to India's Western Ghats, Christian allusions to Hindu, and the costumes, props and scenery to Indian mores. But such concessions, he pointed out, had their limits since it was impossible to adapt the uprising of the carpet weavers to Indian circumstances since "Indian history does not know such uprisings, and comparisons with uprisings during the struggle for independence from British colonial rule do not provide the social context needed for the play. [see also Bhave, 14, col. 2, and Silberman] They are also not so alive in the consciousness of the masses, and generally you cannot count on a developed historical consciousness at all here" (Mumbai, 10 Nov. 1973, page 48). He was amused when for his Delhi *Galileo* in 1983 volumes of Karl Marx's *Capital* were used as props on stage, but were nowhere to be found in the library of the school (New Delhi, 2 Nov. 1983, page 160). Wrestling further with the problem, he wrote: "I can help them understand *what* they can do with the play – but I must help them so that *they* find and fill in the *how*, that they bring their daily and historical life into the play" (New Delhi, 6 Nov. 1981, page 111). Specifically with regard to the *Chalk Circle*, he wrote in 1973 that the character of Irakli was incomprehensible to the Indian audience of the time since the concept of the good robber who gains our sympathy by stealing from the rich and giving to the poor had no models in their minds, unlike English audiences who would think at once of Robin Hood, or German ones of Schinderhannes or Schiller's Karl Moor. His Indian audience had been schooled by Gandhi specifically not to use violence and such means against their oppressors (Bombay, 10 Nov. 1973). He himself too saw India's main historical task at the time not as rising up in revolt, but – and here he went beyond Gandhi – "the unification of all national powers for the preservation of national independence and for the construction of a stable democratic order, even in its bourgeois form, as the basis for a possible socialist revolution later" (ibid.).

In contrast, Bennewitz was impressed by the farces of actors trained in the Indian popular theatre tradition of Tamasha, and he later integrated their techniques into his own productions, calling it "Total Theatre," a theatre that includes the means of expression provided by a combination of acting, music, and dance (ibid.), and an essential feature of Marathi theatre which became important for him when he produced with Vijaya Mehta in Bombay. He described the Tamasha actors' challenge to be that of moving between their traditional improvisation of the spoken text and delivering Brecht's scripted text on stage (ibid.), but when integrating Tamasha, he referred to a "loss of ideological orientation ... by which the fun has degraded itself to mere entertainment, where once the unity of entertainment and enlightenment perfected in Brechtian theatre was surely present at least in a vague way but definitely as an ideal possibility" (ibid.). Brecht's steady insistence on the combination of entertainment and enlightenment was constantly in Bennewitz's mind – at least at this early stage of his Indian experience – a yardstick for the value of the Indian forms he encountered. There was progress toward this goal. Gradually, he taught his actors to transfer Indian historical experiences to Brecht's work to make them understandable to themselves and their audiences.

He was equally troubled about the handling of dialectical structures. He feared that Brecht's frequent dialectically constructed dialogues between characters, for example between Azdak and Schauwa at the end of the *Chalk Circle,* might not be truly understood by "even the most dialectically trained audience" (Bombay, 10 Nov. 1973, page 51) let alone an audience in India. So as time went on, he modified his stance with regard to Brecht's style, feeling that he was facing an impossible task. Writing from Delhi in 1979, where he was staging *Puntila* at the NSD, he lamented, "... there is hardly any prior training for Brecht, at least no practical training. The adaptations of the last years (initiated by Vijaya Mehta and myself!) have gone to seed, and have been adapted away from Brecht, so that most often hardly more than his name is left" (New Delhi, 12 Oct. 1979, page 65). He commented on directing *Arturo Ui* in the same year, "Fundamentally, my training program is to show that there is no *Brecht style,* that the style is inherent to the play and dependent on conditions of location and time (and of course on individual imprint – but that only in the very last place)" (New Delhi, 23 Oct. 1979, page 67). In letters soon following he rejoiced in the success of this more flexible application of Brecht's style which minimized attempts to develop awareness of the dialectical historical process and emphasized instead parallel historicism in the plays' central story. Such were the scenes of war in *Mother Courage* which could be played as instructive correspondences to stages of Indian history of which the actors and audiences were aware: the British army's relationship to Indian peasants or the questions of patriotism in the *Chalk Circle;* human dignity in *The Good Person of Sichuan;* or the use of parody in the *Threepenny Opera* to unmask the social exploitation of commercial film (New Delhi, 4 Nov. 1979, page 70). By 1980, when directing *Galileo* in Calcutta, Bennewitz stretched his notion of dialectics to an almost unbelievable degree of elasticity by referring retrospectively first to 1973 when the dialectic "had to be translated into a morally rigid emotional system, where *good* and *evil* oppose one another instead of existing one within another," and then to later insights into Indian mythology through the stories of the *Ramayana* in which the understanding of dialectics is less of a contradiction than it might have appeared for those who have grown up with these stories, i.e., not under the yoke of the Christian dualism of God and the devil, but with Indian gods who are both good and evil at the same time. The most striking image for dialectics, he concludes here quite spectacularly, is a three-headed Shiva representing the god of threefold unity as creator-preserver-destroyer (Calcutta, 30 Sept. 1980, page 91). He had abandoned the dialectic process and replaced it with Indian mythology. The dialectic *process* connected originally to socialist structural change had been adjusted to mean simply the highlighting of social and political issues. Bennewitz's continued use of the word "dialectic" thereafter should be understood in this sense, much less charged than it was originally in the early Indian years. These changes, one might suggest, were a product too of time and dislocation, similar to those experienced by the model he was trying to emulate, as Marc Silberman has cleverly described when writing of Brecht's years as a refugee abroad: "The fifteen year migrancy put everything in his life into flux, providing an existential encounter that became his own personal 'alienation effect,' so to speak, and bringing him into proximity with the diasporic writing of postcolonial subjects" (Silberman 244).

Synthesis

We return to the final portion of the commentary on Brecht's *Short Organum* above, and the more artistically focused matters such as *Gestus, Fabel,* music, choreography, and design, all of which were prominent in Bennewitz's directing in India. Given present constraints, we shall focus on one of these, music, as this is, in the author's view, the most revealing for an understanding of Bennewitz's synthesis of Brecht with his own Indian style. In 1940/1 Brecht wrote a short piece entitled "Music" which referred to musicality in language – the tonal dimension inherent in different patterns in all spoken languages – rather than formal composition or song. He warns strongly against musicality in spoken dialogue as "dangerous because among other distortions it also causes the actor to perform from the very beginning as if he has already read the end of the play" (*Werke* 22/2, trans. DGJ). In other words, pronounced and intended tonal musicality in language detracts from the primary purpose of dialogue which is to develop the dialectical argument of the action. Full focus should be on this aspect of language, not on the actor as performer or singer. From this Brecht turned to develop, with Kurt Weill, their new style of music designed not to beautify but to serve as part of the dialectical argument of the language and hence to instruct. This he described in the commentary "On the Use of Music in Epic Theatre," (*Werke* 7, 472–82 / Willett 84–90) and its first application in the *Threepenny Opera*. He explained there that "the music, just because it took up a purely emotional attitude and spurned none of the stock narcotic attractions, became an active collaborator in the stripping bare of the middleclass [*sic*] corpus of ideas" (7, 474 / Willett 85–6). This new type of music, he continued, served to expose human and social relationships, show them as changeable, and as dependent on economic and political influences and relationships. In plays in which this new music was featured prominently, Brecht linked it further to his discussion of *Gestus* in the *Short Organum* and the actors' duty not just to play, but to show and instruct (7, 697 / Willett 203).

As time passed and his experience in India deepened, Bennewitz was ever more captivated by Indian music and the cultural heritage it represented. Music was traditionally much more part of theatre in India than in European culture, and the longer he stayed the more he was drawn to it as a dramatic form. He wrote of the grand theatrical festivities surrounding annual feasts such as Dasara, the ten-day Hindu festival celebrating the god Rama's victory over his evil counterpart Ravana, which was acted out in the Ramlila, and which, although amateurish, impressed him with its use of song and mime, and the fact that it was able to psychologically transform audiences of thousands (Bombay, 7 Oct. 1973, page 39). He was moved by a child's naïve song-like narration with classical hand gestures of the *Ramayana* in the street, the Hindu legend of the birth of the gods, performed ritualistically in Old Hindi in traditional melodic structures which reflect the practice of every traditional Hindu family to recite the entire work annually in twenty-four hours (New Delhi, 4 Oct. 1979, page 64). That such events occurred in open public places he soon realized to be an essential part of Indian theatrical tradition, as or even more important than the formal stage. He became increasingly aware of the importance of meeting the expectations of regional audiences instead of forcing upon them a foreign style. That was the key to unlocking the possibility of changing attitudes and social structures (Bombay, 10 Nov. 1973). The incident of the boy's chanting the *Ramayana* in the street opened an entirely new realm of theatrical experience for him and one which became essential for his own Indian productions. He wrote of other scenes similar to that of the child, a market in Bhopal where vendors grouped themselves and shouted rhythmic offers to potential buyers, which were then complemented by a neighbor's different melodic approach, then a third to produce a syncopated overture. Further along, in the higher-priced market section, the rhythms and melodies became more complicated, harmonized, and juxtaposed, like fugues, as opposing vendors sparred with their neighbors for business advantage, until this goal seemed subsumed by the musical process itself. Bennewitz related this to something in the back of his mind, Brecht's borrowing of melodies from street vendors he had overheard (letter to Ulf-Ingo Westphal, Bhopal, 8 Jan. 1986), so the way to Brecht became for him through Indian theatre instead of the reverse (see also Chandavarkar). In Bhopal in 1983 he began to better understand how Indian music related to life, including his own. In the Indian "original folk tone" he noted the "repetitions, which turn the sung sentence around in a circle at least three times," and extrapolated, "there it is again: thinking and living in circles, cyclically […]. And despite this great narrative tradition with and through song [...] – the circle is a return of the line to itself, and the line is not even a line sent out from a beginning into infinity, existing in a space that because of the infinite goal also becomes infinite in extension, but the line as circle is endless because the beginning and end can be set arbitrarily an infinite number of times, so space is circumscribed finiteness, which does not end only because the circle is the movement of the line" (Bhopal, 23 Sept. 1983, pages 143–4). This thought would dwell within him to the end of his Indian experience.

Bennewitz's second Indian *Threepenny Opera* in 1989 was staged nineteen years after his first in New Delhi, during which time he had learned to think like an Indian and work with Indians to make Indian theatre. Babukodi Venkataramana (B.V.) Karanth (1929–2002), distinguished composer, theatre director, film-maker, and director of the NSD from 1977 to 1982, joined him to re-compose all the music for the production. But Bennewitz stressed that the songs were not to be learned: "the music has to take root in the heads and in the vocal chords … it is not written down in notes … it is committed directly to memory, … that's how pieces passed through generations from mouth to ear survive …" (Bhopal, 26 Aug. 1989). He connected that idea with his colleague Atul Tiwari's singing passages of the *Ramayana*, as the child in the street described above. He had heard Atul recounting the Hindu legend of the birth of the gods in Old Hindi with the same traditional melodic structures, representing his family's Hindu practice.

Bennewitz explains in the same letter that it is difficult for Indians to sing Brecht songs generally because of the primacy of the lyrics, but when transformed to Indian music and giving it precedence over the text, the problem is overcome and they become Indian (ibid.), as does the work.

In the same year, nearing the end of his years in India as well as of his life, and in the last year of the German Democratic Republic, Bennewitz wrote a beautiful, tender description of a sixteen-year-old boy masterfully playing the sitar in dialogue with another traditional instrument, the tabla, alternating between passionate monologue and dialogue. He was moved by a host of intercultural parallels with Goethe's archetypical plant in his poem *The Metamorphosis of Plants*, and the scientist's provocation of God in his *Faust*. This boy, he continued, had begun to play the sitar at the age of four and was the fourth generation to do so: "the sitar must have grown into his hands at a very young age, completely naturally and organically" (Bhopal, 30 Aug. 1989). Music remained one of the keys to Indianize the plays that Bennewitz directed there. At the same time he had cause to question the historical course of socialism, even if he remained loyal to the theoretical concept, but now showed signs of replacing that concept with what India had taught him. Instead of believing wholeheartedly in the inevitable socialist dialectic, he began to think "in cycles (cyclical movements that return to themselves and thus have no beginning and end) here in Asia and India, as opposed to our Enlightenment structures of a rising line or at least spiral" and he began to see this as "easily transposed into one's own life" (New Delhi, 3 Dec. 1990, pages 217–18; see also Revermann 286).

Conclusion

From the beginning, with the Delhi *Threepenny Opera* in 1970, Bennewitz was aware of his socio-political and artistic assignments in India: "it's not a private pleasure trip or a holiday," he insisted repeatedly, but added "(what I get out of it for myself, inwardly, is another matter entirely)" (New Delhi, 6 Apr. 1970). What he did get out of it for himself was twenty-five years of personal satisfaction as an artist and human being. He grew to love India with all his heart, and India him. Already by 1973, with the Bombay *Chalk Circle* and partnership with Vijaya Mehta, he was beginning to realize how deeply the Indian experience was affecting him: "I … think about what that means for me and maybe generally: at home. I'm at home here, too. I'm not a stranger in a foreign country. ... And yet I am an other and not at home, but at home I am an other, too" (Bombay, 9 Oct. 1973, pages 39–40). His "otherness" had begun to apply in both places, but from this point on seems to have lessened with respect to India, and deepened with respect to the land of his birth. He never again felt completely at home in Eastern Germany, let alone in its reunited form. Yet his idealism rose above all that he rejected in it: "In those twenty years I was a representative of a country (however rotten it may have been economically, in its leadership, and in spying on its citizens), a country whose humanist, international, cultural policies based on solidarity and mutual respect I committed myself to and contributed to with my achievements" (Dhaka, 27 Jan. 1993, page 237). He could rejoice in having achieved his own goals, those of his personal convictions both socio-political and aesthetic, in having planted "tender shoots" in the world "that have now become forests" (New Delhi, 15 November 1982). In 1990, in recognition of his work in India, he learned that he was to receive "the prize of the all-Indian Sangeet Natak Akademi (the Indian Academy of Arts for music and theatre) – a very rare honour for foreigners," calling it "a beautiful reward for the past twenty years – and yet, the more beautiful reward is the work itself and my experiences in it and through it" (Heggodu, 11 Oct. 1991, page 239). India's President Venkataraman personally presented him with the award, only the second non-Asian to receive it, a distinction he would carry with great satisfaction for the rest of his life. In his final years Bennewitz bade farewell to India not through Brecht and Shakespeare, but through the classic of all German dramas, Goethe's *Faust*. For a final time he collaborated with Vijaya Mehta to direct part one of the tragedy in Mumbai in 1994, and then again, both parts, with Alfred Pasch, in Meiningen in 1995, but died before he could witness the première. His life in India had been fulfilled and he had returned to rest forever as a German director in his troubling homeland.

Chronology of Bennewitz's Stays and Projects in South Asia and of His Indian Projects in Germany

19 February–16 April 1970 New Delhi, National School of Drama	Bertolt Brecht, *The Threepenny Opera* in Hindustani; title: *Teen Take Ka Swang* Urdu translation – Surekha Sikri Songs translated by Sheila Bhatia Costumes designed by Amal Allana, executed by Roshen Lal, assisted by Malavika Thapar, Rita Puri Sets by E. Alkazi, Goverdhan Panchal, Krishna Jena, B. Raghunatha Rao Music composed by Vanraj Bhatia, assisted by Sushil Chowdury and Naima Khan Assistant director – Amal Allana Cast (selection): Macheath – Manohar Singh Peachum – M.K. Raina / S.K. Sawhney Celia Peachum – Nadira Zaheer Polly – Uttara Baokar Tiger Brown – Madhav Khadilkar Lucy – Suhasini Kale Ginny Jenny – Meena Walawalkar (For a complete list of on-stage and off-stage roles, see *Rang Yatra: Twenty-Five Years of The National School of Drama Repertory Company*. Ed. J.N. Kaushal. New Delhi: National School of Drama, 1992, pages 66–7.)

	Premiere in the Open Air Theatre at Rabindra Bhavan on 13 April 1970.
20 January – 19 February 1971 India	Bennewitz accompanied the NSD tour with various productions including the *Threepenny Opera* to Mumbai, Pune, Hyderabad and Bangalore.
3–10 December 1971 Mumbai	Brief stay for discussions about the India-GDR cultural exchange agreement, including with Maharashtra government officials about a possible production of Brecht's *Caucasian Chalk Circle.*
25–6 November 1972 Mumbai	Participation in the First Asian Theater Conference held by the Natya Sangh in Mumbai; first meeting with Vijaya Mehta.
4 April–20 November 1973 Mumbai, Marathi Sahitya Sangh	Brecht, *The Caucasian Chalk Circle* in Marathi; title: *Ajab Nyaya Vartulacha* Co-directed with Vijaya Mehta Marathi translation – C.T. Kanolkar Music composed by Bhaskar Chandavarkar Songs – Aarti Prabhu Dance – Harish Pitale Costumes – Ram Gothaskar Lighting – Sudhir Thakur Cast (selection): Village Chief in prologue – Madhav Khadilkar King (Georgi Abaschwili) – Bal Karve Queen (Natella Abaschwili) – Kusum Naik Tundiltanu (Arsen Kazbeki) – Baba Parulekar Hansi (Grusha) – Bhakti Barve Sahadev (Simon) – Madhav Khadilkar Laxman (Grusha's brother) – Bal Karve Sister-in-law (of Grusha) – Meera Dabholkar Emperor – Janardhan Parab Ajabdas (Azdak) – Suhas Bhalekar Shiva (Schauwa) – Kamalakar Kulkarni Laxmi (Ludovica) – Sanjeevani Bidkar/ Archana Palekar Old Woman – Sulabha Ghanekar

	Premiere at the Sahitya Sang Mandir on 16 November 1973.
21–7 November 1973 Kolkata	Lectures on Brecht and the theatre of the GDR, encounters with leading theatre practitioners.
27–30 November 1973 Kathmandu, Nepal	Discussions about a possible theatre cooperation.
30 November–3 December 1973 New Delhi	Guest performance of *Ajab Nyaya Vartulacha*; discussions with GDR diplomats and Indian government functionaries about a guest performance of the production at the Berliner Festtage and further cooperations.
September–October 1974 GDR/Switzerland	Guest performances of *Ajab Nyaya Vartulacha* at the Berliner Festtage, at the German National Theatre in Weimar, in other cities in the GDR, and in Zurich, with Vijaya Mehta, C.T. Khanolkar and Bhaskar Chandavarkar in attendance.
28 November 1974–2 January 1975 India	Lectures and discussions concerning the cultural exchange agreement between India and the GDR in New Delhi, Mumbai, Pune, Ichalkaranji (Maharashtra), and Trivandrum (Kerala).
29 November–19 December 1975 India	Travel to New Delhi, Mumbai, Pune, Cochin, among other places, together with set designer Franz Havemann in preparation for the production of *Mudrārākshasa* in Weimar.
June–October 1976 Weimar	Visakhadatta, *Mudrārākshasa* in German; title: *Mudra-Rakschasa oder Der Siegelring*

Co-directed by Vijaya Mehta (lead) and Fritz Bennewitz
German translation by Wolfgang Morgenroth, performance script by assistant director Wolfgang Mach
Sets and Properties – D.G. Godse (lead), Franz Havemann, Ingrid Rahaus
Choreography – Guru Krishnan Kutti
Music – Bhaskar Chandavarkar

Cast (selection):
Tschandragupta – Detlef Heintze
Tschanakja – Victor Dräger
Rakschasa – Fred Diesko
Malajaketu – Hans Radloff
Bhagurajana – Hasso Billerbeck
Scharangarawa – Peter Berg

Premiere at the German National Theatre in Weimar on 6 October 1976.
Guest performance at the Berliner Festtage

The production was recorded by GDR television and broadcast on 16 October 1976 (again on 7 September 1981).

5–19 November 1978
India

Seminars and lectures on Brecht and international cooperation in the theatre in New Delhi, Mumbai, Bangalore, Hyderabad, and Kolkata.

May 1979
Weimar

Guest performance of *Mudra-Rakschasa* during the World Sanskrit Conference in Weimar.

2 October–14 December 1979
New Delhi, National School of Drama

Brecht on Trial
Production with students of a scene collage from *The Caucasian Chalk Circle, The Threepenny Opera, The Good Person of Sichuan, Life of Galileo, Mother Courage, Arturo Ui*
In Hindi and Urdu

Presented at Bahawalpur House Lawns, 9–14 November 1979.

Brecht, *Mister Puntila and his Man Matti* in Hindi; title: *Chopra Kamaal – Naukar Jamaal*

Production with the NSD Repertory Company
Adaptation by Anil Choudhury
Sets and Props by Robin Das
Costume design by Madhu Malti Mehta
Lyrics by Anil Choudhury
Music by B.V. Karanth, assisted by Raghuvir Yadav and Gyan Shivpuri

Cast (selection):
Phoolmati – Madhu Malti Mehta
Judge – Anang Desai
Chopra – Pankaj Kapoor
Waiter – Amitabh Srivastava
Jamaal – K.K. Raina
Laveena – Anila Singh
Gulati – Vijay Kashyap
Champa – Uttara Baokar
Veterinarian – Virendra Razdan

(For a complete list of on-stage and off-stage roles, see *Rang Yatra: Twenty-Five Years of The National School of Drama Repertory Company*. Ed. J.N. Kaushal. New Delhi: National School of Drama, 1992, pages 119–20.)

Premiere at the Gandhi Memorial Hall on 12 December 1979.

13–14 October 1979 Chandigarh	Lectures at the Department of Theatre, Panjab University.
29 November – 3 December 1979 Waltair, Visakhapatnam	Lectures and discussions during a seminar organized by the NSD at Andhra University.
7–14 January 1980 Mumbai	Discussions with Vijaya Mehta in preparation of the production of Kālidāsa's *Śakuntalā* in Leipzig.

June 1980 Leipzig	Kālidāsa, *Abhijñānaśākuntalam* in German; title: *Shakuntala oder Der entscheidende Ring* Co-directed by Vijaya Mehta (lead) and Fritz Bennewitz German performance script based on the translation by Georg Forster Sets and Properties – D.G. Godse (lead) and Franz Havemann Choreography – Rohini Bhate Music – Bhaskar Chandavarkar Cast (selection): Shakuntala – Ellen Hellwig Dushyanta – Gottfried Richter Kanva – Werner Godemann Gautami – Eva Mayer Vidushaka – Fred-Arthur Geppert Anasuya – Ramona Hennecke Priyamvada – Christine Reinhold The ballet dancer Gabor Zsitva played a number of movement-oriented roles. Premiere at the Schauspielhaus Leipzig on 29 June 1980. Guest performance at the Volksbühne during the Berliner Festtage 1980. The production was recorded by GDR television in a performance without audience in May 1982 and broadcast on 22 January 1983.
17–21 September 1980 New Delhi and Mumbai	Discussions at NSD and with Vijaya Mehta, including plans for a possible production of Goethe's *Faust* in India.
21 September–26 October 1980 Kolkata, Calcutta Repertory Theatre	Bertolt Brecht, *Life of Galileo Galilei* in Bengali; title: *Galileor jeeban* Bengali adaptation by Mohit Chattopadhyay Set Design – Jochhan Dastidar Costumes – Sona Adhikary Lighting – Tapas Sen

Cast (selection):
Galileo – Sombhu Mitra
Virginia – Saonli Mitra
Andrea – Dwijen Banerjee
Signora Sarti – Swatilekha Chattopadhyay
Sagredo – Bibhash Chakravarty
Cardinal Barberini – Ashok Mukhopadhyay
Cardinal Inquisitor – Rudraprasad Sengupta
Old Cardinal – Biplabketan Chakravarty

Premiere at the Academy of Fine Arts on 18 November 1980.

22 October–1 December 1981
New Delhi, National School of Drama

Shakespeare, *A Midsummer Night's Dream*
in Hindi; title: *Bagaro Basanta Hai*

Production with students in the third year.
Translation – J.N. Kaushal
Assistant director – Raghunandana

Cast (selection):
Theseus – Chander Mohan
Hippolyta – Sunderashree
Philostrate – Kartik Awasthi
Egeus – Waman Kendre
Demetrius – Mipam Othsal
Hermia – Vibha Mishra
Lysander – Bahar Uddin
Helena – Diana Thakor
Peter Quince – G.K. Nairy
Francis Flute – B.M. Vyas
Nick Bottom – Ashok Banthia
Snug, a joiner – Golam Sarwar
Tom Snout – Chidamba Rao
Robin Starveling – Ashok Mishra
Puck or Robin Goodfellow – Haren Bhattacharya
Fairy – Bani Sharad Joshi
Oberon – R.K. Bumma
Titania – Hema Sahay

Premiere in the NSD's Circulation Unit Room on 28 November 1981.

	During this stay, Bennewitz also gave a lecture in the Department of Theatre, Panjab University, Chandigarh.
2–6 December 1981 Mumbai	Discussions with Vijaya Mehta about further cooperation, including plans to produce a contemporary Indian play in the GDR.
6–21 December 1981 Sri Lanka	Lectures, discussions, and workshops (with scenes from Brecht's *Caucasian Chalk Circle* and *Good Person of Sichuan* in Sinhala) in Colombo and at Peradeniya University.
27 August–30 September 1982 Bangalore, Prayoga Theatre Group	Brecht, *Mister Puntila and his Man Matti* in Kannada; title: *Shriman Puttappana Aalu Somanu* (alternate title: *Donku Desai Naukara Shahi*) Adaptation – Chandrashekhar Kambar Producer – T.S. Ranga Music – Janardhan Poems – Siddalingaiah Assistant Director – Raghunandana Cast (selection): Puttappa (Landlord) – Sundar Raj Soma (Slave) – Suresh Shetty Puttappa's Daughter – Poornima Vyasulu In further roles: Umashree Mallige Nagaraj Suvarna Nalina Murthy Premiere at the Rabindra Kalakshetra Theatre on 26 September 1982.
1–3 October 1982 Mumbai	Discussions with Vijaya Mehta about plans to produce Girish Karnad's *Hayavadana* in the GDR.
4 Oct–20 November 1982 New Delhi, National School of Drama	Brecht, *The Caucasian Chalk Circle* in two versions, one for adults in Hindi, one for children in Hindustani. Title: *Insaaf ka Ghera* Productions with students in the third year.

Version for adults:
Adaptation – R.G. Bajaj
Translation of songs – Vallabh Vyas
Music composed by Mohan Upreti
Assistant Director – Atul Tiwari

Cast (selection):
Singer – Vallabh Vyas
Karinda – Manjul Kishore Verma
Raja Vaitaladitya – Sundarlal Meetoo
Rani – Sushmita Mukherjee
Tondi Lal – Ravindra Khanwilkar
Banke Bahadur – Satish Gautam
Mainavati – Madhushree Dutta
Ajabdas – Vinay Pande
Chibban – Jayaram Tatchar
Grand Duke – Manjul Kishore Verma
Poor Old Peasant Woman – S. Malathi
Kallan Daku – Satish Gautam

Premiere in the Circulation Unit Room on 16 November 1982.

During this stay, Bennewitz also held a seminar with Brecht's *Messingkauf Dialogs*.

21–6 November 1982 Mumbai	Discussions with Vijaya Mehta.
27 November–6 December 1982 Ujjain	Participation in the Kālidāsa Sanskrit Theatre Festival and conference; lectures and opening of an exhibition on Sanskrit theatre in the GDR.
8 December 1982–14 January 1983 Sri Lanka	Workshop production of Brecht's *Mother Courage* in Sinhala (in collaboration with Somalatha Singha) with students at the University of Colombo; lectures and discussions at the Universities of Kelaniya and Peradeniya.
7 August–28 September 1983 Bhopal, Bharat Bhavan, Rangmandal troupe	Brecht, *The Caucasian Chalk Circle* in Bundeli; title: *Insaaf Ka Ghera*

	Adaptation – Madan Soni Assistant Director and Performance Script – Atul Tiwari Music – B.V. Karanth Stage Design – Jayanth Dheshmukh Lighting Design – Vipin Kumar Sharma Costumes – Arun Varma, Chandra Saxena, Mahendra Raghuvamshi and Govind Dixi Cast (selection): Singer – Dwarika Prasad Ajabdas (Azdak) – Dwarika Prasad Raiya (Grusha) – Vibha Mishra Ramna – Vipin Varma King – Alakhnandan Queen – Saroj Sharma General – Arun Varma Thondilal (Fat Prince) – Rajkumar Kamle Vaidhyaraj (Physicians) – Jayanth Dheshmukh and Mangilal Sharma Architects – Asheesh Kothwal and Javed Zaidi Elder Brother – Javed Zaidi Sister-in-Law – Chandra Saxena Ghappoo – Mangilal Sharma Captured King – Pradheep Goswami Old Lady – Chandra Saxena Decoit Kalandhar – Amar Singh Premiere at the Antaranga Theatre on 27 September 1983.
29–30 August 1983 New Delhi	Bennewitz attended a performance and discussion of Vijaya Mehta's pilot production of *Hayavadana*; he also met and had a discussion with Peter Brook.
29 September–4 December 1983 New Delhi, National School of Drama	Shakespeare, *Othello in* Hindi

Production with the Repertory Company
Hindi verse translation – Raghuvir Sahay
Set, Properties and Costume design – Robin Das
Lighting design – G.S. Marathe
Music and Sound – Vasant Josalkar and Suneel Sinha
Assistant Directors – Vageesh Kumar Singh and Atul Tiwari

Cast (selection):
Othello – G.P. Namdev
Desdemona – Himanti Bhatt
Iago – Yuvraj Sharma
Roderigo – Basu Patil
Cassio – Lalit Mohan Tewari
Brabantio – Lalit Behl
Emilia – Uttara Baokar
Bianca – Dolly Ahluwalia

(For a complete list of on-stage and off-stage roles, see *Rang Yatra: Twenty-Five Years of The National School of Drama Repertory Company*. Ed. J.N. Kaushal. New Delhi: National School of Drama, 1992, page 146.)

Premiere on 24 November 1983.

Brecht, *Life of Galileo* in Hindi

Production with students in the third year
Translation by V. K. and Dinesh Aggarwal
Assistant Director – K.S. Rajendran
Sets and Properties – C. Basavalingiah
Costumes – Salim Arif
Music and Sound – Ram Murti and Mahavir Bhullar

	Cast (selection): Galileo Galilei – Kiran G. Kulkarni Andrea (child) – Abhinav Kaul Mrs. Sarti – Renuka Israni Ludovico Marsili – Anand Wardhan Priuli – Afsar Hussain Sagredo – Chander Mohan Virginia – Sima Biswas Federzoni – C. Basavalingiah The Doge – Salim Arif Cosimo-de-Medici – Man Mohan Singh The Little Monk – Surender Sharma The Cardinal Inquisitor – Chander Mohan Cardinal Barberini – Afsar Hussain Andrea Sarti – Jitendra Shastri Premiere on 27 November 1983.
4–13 December 1983 Mumbai	Discussions with Vijaya Mehta regarding the production of Girish Karnad's *Hayavadana* in Weimar; discussions with leading theatre personalities (Jennifer Kapoor, Naseeruddin Shah, Pankaj Kapur, Nadira Zaheer Babbar).
22–5 February 1984 New Delhi	Discussions about the production of Girish Karnad's *Hayavadana* in Weimar.
May–June 1984 Weimar, German National Theatre	Girish Karnad, *Hayavadana* in German; title: *Hayavadana oder die vertauschten Köpfe* Directed by Vijaya Mehta in collaboration with Fritz Bennewitz German translation by Christa Schuenke based on Girish Karnad's own English translation Choreography – Ramesh Purav Music – Bhaskar Chandavarkar Costume assistance – Ingrid Rahaus Masks – Johannes Ohla Set design collaboration – Franz Havemann Assistant Directors – Roselinde Lange and Cordula Alwardt

Cast (selection):
Prinzipal (Bhagavata) – Hasso Billerbeck
Actor I – Hansgerd Sonnenburg
Actor II – Christoph Heckel
Hayavadana – Christoph Rauch
Devadatta – Detlef Heintze
Kapila – Thomas Schneider
Padmini – Elke Wieditz
Kali – Regina de Reese
Child – Alexander Deibel
Chorus – Ernst Eichholz and Katherina Brey

Premiere at the German National Theatre on 26 June 1984.

6 January–18 February 1985
Bhopal, Bharat Bhavan, Rangmandal

Shakespeare, *A Midsummer Night's Dream* in Hindi; title: *Bagaro Basant Hai*

Translation – Raghuvir Sahay
Music – B.V. Karanth
Assistant Director – Atul Tiwari

Cast (selection):
Theseus – Rajkumar Kamle
Hippolyta – Shobha
Egeus – Pradeep Goswami
Hermia – Vibha Mishra
Lysander – Jitender Shastri
Helena – Abha Mishra
Demetrius – Mahendra Raghuvanshi
Titania – Saroj Sharma
Oberon – Arun Verman
Fairy – Anita Dube
Fairy Matarfool – Arti Deshpande
Philostrate – Jayant Deshmukh
Bottom – Dwarika Prasad
Peter Quince – Amar Singh
Snug – Javed Jaidi
Flute – Kamal Sharma
Snout – Mangilal Sharma

Premiere in February 1985.

25–8 January 1985 Mumbai	Discussions with Vijaya Mehta about a next production of an Indian play in the GDR.
18–21 February 1985 New Delhi	Discussions about projects at NSD.
18 September–2 November 1985 New Delhi, National School of Drama	Brecht, *Man equals Man* in Hindi; title: *Maina ikvalsa Maina* Production with students in the third year Translation – Sudarshan Juyal Design of Sets, Costumes, Properties and Lighting – Franz Havemann Music – Mohan Upreti Cast: Galy Gay – Piyush Mishra Galy Gay's Wife – Vibha Sahota Jesse Mahoney – Dinesh Khanna Jeraiah Jip – Yeshwant Nikose Polly Baker – Gajendra Nayak Uriah Shelley – Vijay Deepak Chhibber Wang the Monk – Abdul Latif Khatana Sergeant Fairchild – Hergurjit Singh Widow Begbick – Alka Srivastava Sacristan – H. Janardhana Soldiers – Ishan, Janardhana, Malkani, Jugindro Sudarshan Premiere on 1 November 1985.
21–6 September Chandigarh	Guest of a festival of North Indian theatre.
31 December 1985–19 February 1986 Bhopal, Bharat Bhavan, Rangmandal	Shakespeare, *King Lear* in Hindi; title: *Raja Lear* Translation – Atul Tiwari Music – B.V. Karanth Assistant Director – Atul Tiwari

	Cast (selection): Lear – Amar Singh Goneril – Vibha Mishra Regan – Shobha Cordelia – Saroj Sharma King of France – Sharad Shabal Duke of Burgundy – Trasheesh Kotval Duke of Albany – Jayant Deshmukh Duke of Cornwall – Mahendra Singh Raghuvanshi Edgar – Jitendra Shastri Edmond – Arun Verma Oswald – Mangi al Sharma Curan – Raj Kumar Kamle Old Man – Pradeep Goswami Doctor – Govind Dikshit Fool – Dwarika Prasad Premiere in February 1986.
11–17 January 1986	Guest performances of the 1983 Bhopal *Caucasian Chalk Circle* in Jabalpur, Lakhnadon, and Bislapur, and of *A Midsummer Night's Dream* in Ujjain.
18–21 January 1986 Mumbai	International seminar on East-West relations in the theatre, guest performance of *Caucasian Chalk Circle.*
19–22 February 1986 Mumbai	Discussions with Vijaya Mehta about their next collaborative production of an Indian play in the GDR.
22 February–23 March 1986 Sri Lanka	Workshop on a children's version of Brecht's *Caucasian Chalk Circle* in Sinhala (in collaboration with Somalatha Singha) with students of a newly established theatre academy; further workshops and lectures in Colombo, Kandy, and at Peradeniya University.
3 October–3 November 1986 Heggodu, Ninasam	Brecht, *Caucasian Chalk Circle* in Kannada Production with students of the Ninasam Theatre Institute

11 August–20 September 1987 Bhopal, Bharat Bhavan, Rangmandal	Shakespeare, *The Taming of the Shrew* in Bundeli; title: *To Sana Purusa Na Mo Sama Nari* Translation – Madan Soni and Navneeta Sarkar Music – B.V. Karanth Sets – Franz Havemann Cast (selection): Karan – Anita Dubey Saint – Rajkumar Kamle Vareena (Katherina) – Vibha Mishra Bianca – Saroj Sharma Lunco – Sanjay Mishra Besta – Gopal Dube Petruchio – Dwarika Prasad Horetensio – Kamal Kumar Biondello – Rajkamal Nayak Grumio – Jitender Shastri Vincentio – Javed Jaidi Curtis – Omprakash S. Maurya Nathaniel – Govind Dikshit Peter – Ganesh Chaurasya Panda – Amar Singh Tailor – Rakesh Sahu Cap Seller – Anoop Joshi Officer – Ganesh Chaurasya Premiere at the Antarang Theatre on 18 September 1987.
18 February–24 March 1987 Sri Lanka	Preparatory discussions for the production of Brecht's *Threepenny Opera* in Colombo and lecture-demonstrations about Shakespeare's *A Midsummer Night's Dream* at Peradeniya University.
21 September–10 November 1987 Colombo, Sri Lanka	Brecht, *The Threepenny Opera* in Sinhala; title: *Andi Rale Nadagame* Presented by the Bertolt Brecht Arts Circle Translation and Assistant Director – Ranjit Dharmakirti Music – Sena Jayantha Weerasekara Lyrics – Ariyawansa Ranaweera Sets – Winston Suludagoda

Cast (selection):
Macheath – Neil Alles
Peachum – Jayalath Manoratne
Celia Peachum – Somalatha Subasinghe
Polly – Chintanee Hindurangala
Brown – Elson Divituragama
Lucy – Deepanie Silva
Ginny Jenny – Lalanie Pushpamala
Ballad Singer – Suminda Sirisena

Premiere on 12 November 1987.

11 November–12 December 1987 Kolkata	Work on a production of Brecht's *Mother Courage* with Utpal Dutt and Sova Sen (production not completed).
11–14 September 1988 New Delhi	Preparations for the NSD production of Volker Braun's *Great Peace*.
15–18 September 1988 Bhopal and Mumbai	Discussions about projects at Rangmandal and with Vijaya Mehta.
18 September–17 November 1988 Kolkata, Padatik	Shakespeare, *King Lear* in Hindi; title: *Raja Lear* Translation – Akshay Upadhay Design – Franz Havemann Music – Chandan Roy chowdhury Cast (selection): Lear – Shyamanand Jalan Goneril – Chetna Jalan Regan – Sanchaita Bhattacharya Cordelia – Shampa Ghosh King of France – Pramod Ranjan Prasad Duke of Burgundy – Balmukund Hada Duke of Cornwall – Kunal Padhi Duke of Albany – Mehmood Alam Earl of Kent – Pradip Ray Earl of Gloucester – Shakeel Khan Edgar – Arun Sharma Edmund – Ashok Walia Oswald – Balmukund Hada Fool – Rajaram Yagnik Premiere at Gyan Manch Auditorium on 5 November 1988.

6 August–18 September 1989
Bhopal, Bharat Bhavan, Rangmandal

Brecht, *Threepenny Opera* in Hindi; title: *Paisa Phenk -Tamasha Dekh*

Translation – Atul Tiwari
Music – B.V. Karanth
Sets – Jayant Deshmukh
Costumes – Vibha Mishra
Lights – Satyavrat Rayut

Cast (selection):
Krishna Rampuria (Macheath) – Dwarika Prasad
Police chief – Raj Kumar Kamle
Bodhan (Peachum) – Amar Singh
Mrs. Bodhan – Meena Sidh
Pallavi/Pauli (Polly Peachum) – Vibha Mishra
Thakur – Balram Singh
Juhi – Saroj Sharma
Yadav Constable – Gopal Dubey
Pandit Poojanram – Govind Dikshit
Rattiram – Sanjay Mehta
Bheema the wolf – Alok Chatterjee
Raka the pick-pocketer – Javed Jaidi
John – Ravilal Sangde
Kaliya – Ganesh Chaurasiya
Ranga – Rajneesh Jhanji
Narrators – Anoop Joshi and Umesh Tarksvar

Premiere at the Bharat Bhavan on 13 September 1989.

18–21 September 1989
Mumbai

Visit with Vijaya Mehta.

21 September–29 October 1989
Heggodu, Ninasam, Tirugata troupe

Brecht, *The Good Person of Sichuan* in Kannada; title: *Sezuan Nagarada Sadhwi*

Translation – K.V. Subbanna
Music – B.V. Karanth

	Cast: Devaru (God) 1 – Prakash Garud Devaru 2 – Ganesh Prasad Devaru 3 – Gopal Rao Manvi Wang – Siddaraja Kalyanakar Shen Te/Shui Ta – Rajanibhat Kerekai Yang Sun/Atthige – Krishnamurthy Kavathur Mr. Shu Fu/Thamma – Mahaveer Jain Policeman – Gajanana H.C. Ganda (Husband) – Bangarappa M.B. Aliya (Son-in-Law) – Ramesha Dhu Sangolli Ajja (Grandfather) – Garuraja Marpalli Nirudhyogi/Huduga (Unemployed/Boy) – Nagaraja Dongre Badagi (Carpenter) – Subbu Holeyaar Mrs. Shin – Padmavathi M.A. Mrs. Mi Tzu/Sose – Padmini G. Mrs. Yang/Hendati (Wife)/Mudhi Soole (Old Whore) – Susheela M.A.Vaadhya Kaara – Ramachandra Hegade Premiere at the Shivarama Karantha Rangamandira on 26 October 1989.
29 October–5 November 1989 Mumbai	Discussions with Vijaya Mehta and Vanraj Bhatia.
5–11 November 1989 New Delhi	Planning meetings at NSD for the production of Volker Braun's *Great Peace*.
16 December 1989–25 February 1990 New Delhi, National School of Drama	Volker Braun, *Great Peace* in Hindi; title: *Mahashanti*

Production with the NSD Repertory Company
Adaptation – Ram Gopal Bajaj
Set design – Bapi Bose
Costume design – Dolly Ahluwalia
Properties – Swaroopa Ghosh and Motilal Hare
Masks – Kriti Verma
Lighting – G.S. Marathe
Music – Bhaskar Chandavarkar
Movement – Khalid Tayebji
Combats – Neelmani Singh

Cast (selection):
Wang – Ravi Khanwilkar
Kau-Tzu – Jitendra Shastri
Fan-Fei – Himani Shivpuri/Seema Biswas
Spirit of Revolution – Ashok Lokhande/ Kuldeep
Hu-Hai – Dinesh Khanna
Eunuch – Akhilesh Khanna
Chao – Anupam Shyam
Wei – Abhijit Lahiri
Chu-Yuan – Shrivallabh Vyas
Queen – Pratima Kazmi
Pao-Mu – Hema Singh/Nutan Surya
Hsien – Ashok Lokhande
Chu-To – Amit Banerjee
Hsi Kang – Ram Gopal Bajaj/Lokendra Trivedi

(For a complete list of on-stage and off-stage roles, see *Rang Yatra: Twenty-Five Years of The National School of Drama Repertory Company*. Ed. J.N. Kaushal. New Delhi: National School of Drama, 1992, page 196–8.)

Premiere on 12 February 1990 as closing event of the "Days of GDR Culture in India."

Shakespeare, *Twelfth Night* in Hindi; title: *Barahavin Rat*
Production with students in the third year
Translation – Rameshwar Prem

	Cast (selection): Sir Andrew Aguecheek – Vishweshwar Holikarimath Maria – Bhagirathi Bai Sir Toby – Baharul Islam Malvolio – Anup Hazarika Premiere in the Circulation Unit Room on 22 February 1990.
25 February–1 March 1990 Mumbai	Visit with Vijaya Mehta.
1–4 March 1990 Bangalore	Guest performance of Bennewitz's Ninasam production of *The Good Person of Sichuan*.
5 March–2 April 1990 Heggodu, Ninasam	Shakespeare, *A Midsummer Night's Dream* in Kannada Production with the students of the class of 1989–90 at the Ninasam Theatre Institute Translation – K.S. Nissar Ahmed Music – Prathishkumar and T.R. Srinivasa Murthy Cast: Theseus/Oberon – Mahabal Dheeran Egeus – Vivekananda Aliger Lysander – Vijay Kulakarni Demetrius – M.P. Belliyappa Philostrate – Shridharachari Peter Quince – H.S. Nandakumar Bottom – Shi Nagendraprabhu Tom Snout – Ismail Francis Flute – Krishna Bhat Robin Starveling – Ganapathi B. Heggade Snug – T.R. Srinivasa Murthy Puck – Prathishkumar/Bharamanna/Nagaraj/Natesha Hippolyta/Titania – P.R. Rajeshwari Hermia – Lakshmi Kabberalli Helena – N.N. Veena Fairies – Phaniamma/Bhagya/Lakshmi/Sandhya

	Premiere at the Shivarama Karantha Rangamandira on 31 March 1990.
30 October–28 December 1990 New Delhi, Shri Ram Centre Repertory Company	Shakespeare, *The Tempest* in Hindi Translation – Amitabh Srivastava Music – B.V. Karanth Songs – Subodh Lal Set – Jayant Deshmukh Lights – Girdhari Lal Cast (selection): Prospero – Manoj Sharma Miranda – Vani Singh Ariel – Girish Bhai Antonio – Vibhanshu Vaibhav Alonso – Aditya Narayan Srivastava Gonzalo – Pawan Kumar Sebastian – Kannan Iyer Ferdinand – Zulfiqar Caliban – Kali Prasad Mukherjee Premiere at the Shri Ram Centre on 22 December 1990.
29 December 1990–15 January 1991 India	Workshop in Bhopal and guest performances in New Delhi, Lucknow, Shimla.
15 January–24 February 1991 Lucknow, Bhartendu Academy of Dramatic Arts	Brecht, *Life of Galileo* in Hindi Translation – V.K. Sharma Costume design – Nargi and Alok Music – Ainbar Sadik Co-Direction – Raj Bisaria

Cast:
Galileo – Yogesh Pathak
Andriya – Priyanshu Mishra/Narendera Gupta
Sarti – Shelja Kapoor/Sheela Chaurasiya
Ludovico – Vijay Shukla
Vice Chancellor/Singer/Gaffone – Aibnar Sadik
Sagredo – Suneel Jayasval
Senator/Philosopher/Old Cardinal – Abhijeet Kumar Mandal
Spy/Renouncer/Announcer – Sushil Bhole
Senator/Pope – Suresh Kala
Virginia – Nishi Pandey/Chitra Singh
Grand Duke – Ajeet Kumar Singh
Federzoni – Tapan Das
Obese Monk – Alok Mohan Aggrawal
Scholar/Guard – Anoop Shukla
First Renouncer – Ratan Vahnray
Scholar/First Clerk – Prabesh Yati
Father Christopher Clavius – Mohammad Shafiq
Renouncer – Lalit Singh

Premiere at Ravindralaya Auditorium on 19 February 1991.

1–22 March 1991
Mysore, Rangayana

Shakespearege Namaskara
(collage of scenes from *Hamlet, King Lear, Midsummer Night's Dream*) in Kannada

Translation – K.S. Nisaar Ahmed (Mechanicals scene from *A Midsummer Night's Dream*), Ramachandra Deva (scene from *Hamlet*), and H.S. Shivaprakash (scene from *King Lear*)

Teaching Staff:
Shankaranarayana Jois
Yoganarasimha H.K.
Anju Singh
Srinivas Bhat
H.K. Dwarakanath
P. Gangadharaswamy
Raghunandana
C. Basavalingaiah
Jayatheertha Joshi
B.V. Karanth

Cast:
Mandya Ramesh
Jagadeesh Manevarthe
B. Krishnakumar Naarnakaje
Hulugappa Kattimani
Arunkumar
N. Mangala
K.R. Nandini
Noor Ahmed Sheikh
Maheshwar C. Hiremat
Basavaraj Koduge
Pichalli Srinivas
M.C. Krishna Prasad
K.C. Ragunath
Vinayaka Bhatta Hasanagi
S. Ramanath

21 September–October 1991 Heggodu, Ninasam, Tirugata troupe	Shakespeare, *Twelfth Night* in Kannada; title: *Habbadi Hanneradane Ratri* Translation – N.S. Lakshminarayan Bhatta Music – Devadaasa Rao K. and Bhushan

Cast:
Sir Toby – Ismail
Malvolio – Gajanana H.C.
Sir Andrew – Gajanana V. Hegade
Fabian/Captain – Ganapathi Hegade
Antonio – Ganeshaprasad H.K.
Adhikaari (Officer) 1 – Devadasa Rao K.
Adhikaari 2 – Dharmendrakumar H.K.
Maria – Padmavathi Prasad
Valentine/Sebastian – Panduraja
Nakali – Badami Y.D.
Curio – Bhushan
Duke Orsino – Mahabala Dheeran
Viola – Shailashree S.D.
Olivia – Shoba Hegade

Premiere at the Shivarama Karantha Rangamandira on 24 October 1991.

11 November–
December 1991
Mysore, Rangayana

Chekhov, The Cherry Orchard in Kannada; title: *Cherry Thota*

Translation – H.S. Shivaprakash
Lights and Stage Design – Tapas Sen
Music – B.V. Karanth
Assistant Director and Script Adaptation – Raghunandana

Cast:
Mandya Ramesh
Jagadeesh Manevarthe
B. Krishnakumar Naarnakaje
Hulugappa Kattimani
Arunkumar
N. Mangala
K.R. Nandini
Noor Ahmed Sheikh
Maheshwar C Hiremat
Basavaraj Koduge
Pichalli Srinivas
M.C. Krishna Prasad

	K.C. Ragunath Vinayaka Bhatta Hasanagi S. Ramanath Ramesh Birvaa S. Raamu Saroja Heggade Pramila Bengre M.S. Geetha Manjunath Belekere Santhoshkumar Kusanur Mahadev B.N. Shashikala Premiere in late December 1991.
February 1992 Leipzig	Girish Karnad, *Nāga-Mandala* in German; title: *Naga-Mandala – Stück mit einer Kobra* Directed by Vijaya Mehta in collaboration with Fritz Bennewitz Translation – Eva Walch from Girish Karnad's own English translation Sets – Gerhard Roch and M.S. Sathyu Music – Bhaskar Chandavarkar Cast (selection): Rani – Gislén Engelmann Appanna/Naga – Guido Lambrecht Kurudavva – Ellen Hellwig Kappanna – Paul-Dolf Neis Part of the Indien-Festspiele 1991–2 Premiere in the Kellertheater of the Schauspielhaus Leipzig on 29 February 1992. Performed at the Maxim-Gorki-Theater in Berlin on 3 and 4 March 1992.
22 October–27 December 1992 Lucknow	Workshop and seminar.

29 December 1992–14 March 1993 Dhaka, Bangladesh Centre of the ITI	Brecht, *Man equals Man* in Bengali; title: *Loka Samana Loka* Translation – Asaduzzaman Noor Set Design – Quamruzzaman Runu and Kazi Sayeeda Light Design – Quamruzzaman Runu Costume Design – Kazi Sayeeda Music – Shankar Sajwal Masks – Golam Sarwar and Rashedul Huda Rashed Associate Director – Salek Khan Cast (selection): Galy Gay – Asaduzzaman Noor Galy Gay's wife – Rokeya Rafique Baby Jesse Mahoney – Fazlur Rahman Babu Jeraiah Jip – Golam Sarwar Polly Baker – Azizul Hakim Uriah Shelley – Shankar Sawjal Charles Fairchild – Azad Abul Kalam Leokadia Begbick – Sara Zaker Mr. Wang – Md. Abdullah Al Faruk Mah Sing – Abdullah Al-Baki (Rana) Premiere at the Mahila Samity Auditorium on 28 February 1993.
18 September 1993–13 January 1994 Mumbai, National Centre for the Performing Arts	Goethe, *Faust I* in Hindi Co-directed by Fritz Bennewitz and Vijaya Mehta Translation – Ramesh Rajhans and Atul Tiwari Set, costume and lighting design – Kristian Panzer Costumes – Bharati Jaffrey and Anisha Agarwal Music – Conrad Aust and Baskar Chandavarkar Masks – Banoo Batliboi and Dilshad Faroodi Choreography – Dodo Bhajwala

Cast (selection):
Faust – Pankaj Kapur
Mephistopheles – Naseeruddin Shah
Margaret – Sharvani Dhond
The Lord – Kishore Kadam
Student – Sagar Arya
In further roles:
Shubhangi Kerkar
Girija Katare
Vaishali Thakker
Ganesha Yadav
Nandu Madhav
Jamil Khan

Premiere at the Tata Theatre on 8 January 1994.

Glossary of Theatre Terms, Institutions, and Cultural References

Alienation, Alienation Effect Alienation is a key concept in Bertolt Brecht's theory of Epic Theatre. An Alienation Effect (*Verfremdungseffekt, V-Effekt*) is achieved by various means that disrupt theatrical illusion and allow the viewer to take a critical stance towards the events and issues depicted on stage.

Azdak Azdak is one of the main characters in Bertolt Brecht's *The Caucasian Chalk Circle*. The simple but savvy village scribe is made into a judge by the upheavals of civil war and passes judgments in favour of the poor and against the ruling class. The character was particularly important to Bennewitz due to his subversive, critical potential.

Berliner Ensemble (BE) Originally "Theater am Schiffbauerdamm," founded in 1949 in East Berlin by Bertolt Brecht and Helene Weigel, still thriving as the home of Brecht's plays and other left-leaning works and interpretations.

Bharat Bhavan The Bharat Bhavan is a multi-arts centre in the city of Bhopal, Madhya Pradesh. It was built in the form of several interconnecting terraces by Charles Correa and inaugurated in 1982. It houses an art museum, centres for poetry, music, and cinema, several theatres, and the Rangmandal ensemble, with whom Bennewitz worked in his productions in Bhopal.

Bhavai Bhavai is a folk theatre form from Gujarat that honours the goddess Amba. It is characterized by its penchant for social satire and strong humor that is even directed at deities.

Dasara Or Dashahara, Dussehra, and similar names, a Hindu festival on the tenth day of the half moon in the Hindu month of Ashvina, or the beginning to middle of October in the modern calendar. It is the last day and climax of a ten-day festival with variants in other parts of India.

Dasavatar A Marathi and Konkani folk theatre form about the ten avatars of Vishnu, which contains songs and invocations to deities as well as moral and satirical elements.

Deutsches Nationaltheater (DNT) The theatre in Weimar has a long and highly politicized history. It originated as court theatre in the Duchy of Sachse-Weimar-Eisenach, where Goethe and Schiller played key roles in shaping it and producing some of their own key plays. This classical legacy was politicized in conflicts over culture between conservative and progressive forces during the eras of the German empire and of the Weimar Republic, for National Socialist propaganda during the Third Reich, and for a socialist agenda in the GDR. Bennewitz worked here from 1960 to 1991, as chief director until 1975 and as regular director thereafter.

Epic Theatre Epic Theatre is the name most commonly given to Bertolt Brecht's conception of a socially activist theatre developed against a theatre of illusion and emotional catharsis usually associated with Aristotelian ideas.

Faust The two parts of Johann Wolfgang von Goethe's drama about the scholar Faust, whom legend held to have made a pact with the devil, were written over a span of sixty years between 1770 and 1830. They belong among the most important German literary texts and contributions to world literature. They were of particular significance to Bennewitz, who staged them numerous times in Germany as well as in the USA, India, and the Philippines.

Ganesh, Ganesha The elephant-headed god is one of the most popular in the Hindu pantheon, and probably Bennewitz's favourite. He is revered as the remover of obstacles, the god of intellect and wisdom, and the patron of arts and sciences. He is often invoked at the beginning of rituals and performances.

German National Theatre see Deutsches Nationaltheater (DNT)

Gestus *Gestus* is a key concept in Bertolt Brecht's theory of Epic Theatre. It refers to the way in which an actor shapes her/his role in order to reveal and lay open for critical thought the social roles, attitudes, and relations of the character depicted.

Grusha Grusha is one of the main female characters in Bertolt Brecht's *The Caucasian Chalk Circle*. She rescues a child of noble birth during revolutionary upheavals, brings him up as her own, and, in Azdak's eponymous judgment of the chalk circle, is rewarded custody of the child over the biological mother due to her more genuine love and care.

International Theatre Institute (ITI) The ITI was founded in 1948 under the auspices of the United Nations Educational, Scientific and Cultural Organization (UNESCO) with the aim of fostering the development of theatre and international exchange through theatre. There are national ITI Centres in numerous countries, and the organization maintains a number of committees. Bennewitz was active in the GDR Centre of the ITI and in its Third World Committee, later renamed the Cultural Identity and Development Committee.

Kathak Kathak is a classical Indian dance form originating in Uttar Pradesh. It includes influences from ritual and temple dances, Persian and Central Asian dances, and the bhakti movement.

Kathakali A highly stylized dance form originating in the seventeenth century and performed mainly in the southern state of Kerala. It is cast primarily with mythical figures in extravagant costumes and make-up, and uses intricate movements and mime.

Mahābhārata One of two major Sanskrit epics of ancient India, along with the *Ramayana*. The *Mahābhārata* tells the story of the struggle between the two royal clans of the Kauravas and the Pandavas, and it contains much philosophical reflection, particularly the central *Bhagavad Gita*.

Mudrārākshasa *Mudrārākshasa* (*Rakshasa's Signet Ring*) is a historical play in Sanskrit written by Visakhadatta probably in the fifth century AD. It "is a *nataka* in seven acts, on the reconciliation of Rakshasa, minister of Nanda, the late king of Pataliputra, with Chanakya (or Kautilya), Brahman minister of emperor Chandragupta Maurya (reigned c. 321–297 BC), who overthrew Nanda." (Lal 519)

National School of Drama (NSD) The Indian National School of Drama in New Delhi was founded in 1959 under the aegis of the national performing arts academy Sangeet Natak Akademi. The NSD comprises a theatre school and the professional NSD Repertory Company (inaugurated in 1968 and fully established in 1976) as well as a Theatre-in-Education company and regional centres. The directors of the NSD have been Satu Sen (1959–61), Ebrahim Alkazi (1962–77), B.V. Karanth (1977–82), B.M. Shah (1982–4), Mohan Maharishi (1984–6), Ratan Thiyam (1987–8), Kirti Jain (1988–95), Ram Gopal Bajaj (1995–2001), Devendra Raj Ankur (2001–7), Anuradha Kapur (2007–13), and Waman Kendre (2013–present).

Natyasastra Also *Natya Shastra*, the most important source of knowledge about ancient Indian theatre traditions. The ancient treatise is thought to have been written by Bharata between the second century BC and the fourth century AD and was expanded by commentary from Abhinavagupta and other authors. In over thirty chapters, it addresses a vast range of aspects of performance, including theatre architecture, music, acting styles, language use etc.

Ninasam Ninasam is a theatre institute in the small village of Heggodu in Karnataka. It was founded as a theatre group by K.V. Subbanna's father in 1949 and expanded by Subbanna with a view to bringing theatre, cinema, and art to rural Karnataka and involving the local community in these art forms. The institute comprises a theatre school, the Tirugata ensemble, and a publishing house. It holds numerous seminars and workshops and hosts the annual Culture Course with lectures and performances. Bennewitz produced four plays with the Tirugata troupe between 1986 and 1991 and had a particular fondness for the place, which he often referred to as "my village."

Ramayana After the *Mahābhārata*, India's second most important epic poem of legends and myths. Its main characters are Rama, the seventh incarnation of the god Vishnu; Sita, wife of Rama, model for Hindu women and avatar of Lakshmi; Lakshman, brother and avatar of Rama; the demon Ravana, primary antagonist in the *Ramayana*; Hanuman, god in the form of anthropomorphized monkey.

Rangayana Rangayana is a theatre institute in Mysore, Karnataka, founded in 1989 on the initiative of B.V. Karanth. It houses a theatre training institute and a standing theatre troupe that performs plays in Kannada. Bennewitz produced two plays with Rangayana in 1991.

Rangmandal Rangmandal is the theatre ensemble of the Bharat Bhavan cultural centre in Bhopal, Madhya Pradesh. Bennewitz worked with this ensemble in his productions in Bhopal.

Sadhu, Sadhvi A Hindu holy man (Sadhu) or woman (Sadhvi), usually itinerant, who is seeking to attain the liberation of moksha through asceticism and meditation.

Śakuntalā The classical Sanskrit drama *Abhijñānaśākuntalam* (usually shortened to *Śakuntalā*) was written by Kālidāsa, who is thought to have lived during the reign of the Gupta dynasty in Northern India in the fourth century A.D. It tells the intricate mythic love story of king Duşyanta and Śakuntalā, the foster daughter of a Brahman hermit, involves failed recognition due to a spell, a lost token ring that breaks the spell when found, and divine intervention. The play was produced by Vijaya Mehta in Leipzig in 1980.

Sangeet Natak Akademi The national academy of India for the performing arts, established in 1952. It confers the prestigious Sangeet Natak Akademi

Award in a number of performing arts categories. Bennewitz won this award in the Theatre Direction category in 1991 as the first German recipient, only the second time it was given to a foreigner.

Stanislavski, Stanislavskian The Russian actor and director Constantin Sergeyevich Stanislavski (1863–1938) developed a highly influential theory of acting and system of acting instruction. The Stanislavskian method relies on actors using memories, imagination, and physical actions to access and portray emotions.

Sutradhara A central character in Sanskrit theatre with directing and commentating functions.

Tamasha Tamasha is a folk theatre form from Maharashtra blending dance, songs, erotic humour, and subversive social satire.

Verfremdungseffekt, V-Effekt See "Alienation"

Yakshagana A folk theatre form from Karnataka, blending simple and highly codified and conventional performance elements.

Bibliography

FBA = Fritz Bennewitz Archiv, Leipzig

Abhinav. "Brecht in Bundeli." Publication venue and date uncertain (perhaps *Economic Times*, October 1983). FBA. Print.

Agiman, Denise. "L'Approche Interculturelle au Théâtre." PhD diss. Université du Québec à Montréal, 2006. TS.

Allana, Amal. "Brecht: A Participant in the Process of Nation-Building." Wessendorf and Weidauer 27–43.

Allana, Nissar, ed. *A Tribute to Bertolt Brecht*. [New Delhi, India]: Theatre and Television Associates, [1993]. Print.

Bajeli, Diwan Singh. "*Othello* in Hindi." *The Evening News*, 30 Nov. 1983: 6. Print.

Bandyopadhyay, Samik. Interview with Joerg Esleben at the Ninasam Theatre Institute, Heggodu, Karnataka. 8 Oct. 2011.

Barba, Eugenio. "The Legacy from Us to Ourselves." In *Theatre: Solitude, Craft, Revolt*, 216–25. Aberystwyth: Black Mountain Press, 1999. Web. 6 Aug. 2012.

Bhardwaj, Suresh. Interview with Joerg Esleben at the National School of Drama, New Delhi. 27 Feb. 2012.

Bengre, Pramila. Interview with Joerg Esleben at Rangayana, Mysore. 19 Mar. 2012.

Bennewitz, Fritz. Letters from India. FBA, various binder locations. Cited with place and date of writing. In contextual commentary and essays, citations include page references to the present work if the passage concerned is printed herein. TS and MS.

– Arbeitsberichte. Work reports about Bennewitz's activities in India and other countries sent to various institutions (mainly GDR Ministry of Culture, ITI Centre GDR), 1971–90. FBA. TS.

– "Teaching and Learning – Prof. Fritz Bennewitz interviewed." Interview by Karin Karlsson. 1972. Bibliographic provenance unknown, probably published by the GDR Ministry of Culture. FBA. Print.
– "Erfahrungen mit Brecht im Ausland." *Theater der Zeit* 5 (1973): 41–2. Print.
– "Ajab Nyaya Vartulacha." Article in the program notes for the 1974 guest performances in the GDR of *The Caucasian Chalk Circle* with Vijaya Mehta. Also filed as typescript with hand-written notes by Bennewitz, 3 pp. FBA. Print.
– "Ein indischer Kreidekreis." *Theater der Zeit* 29 (1974): 44–7. Print.
– "Internationale Co-operation auf dem Theater. Bericht über Arbeitserfahrungen im Kulturaustausch DDR-INDIEN." 3 pp. FBA. TS.
– "Werkstattgespräch mit Fritz Bennewitz – aufgezeichnet von Ingeborg Pietzsch." Typescript with two versions of an interview between Bennewitz and Pietzsch and hand-written notes by Bennewitz. Citations are from the second version. FBA. TS.
– "Mit *Puntila* kontra ethnisches Show-Theater – Notizen zur Brecht-Rezeption in Indien." *Notate: Informations- und Mitteilungsblatt des Brecht-Zentrums der DDR* 1 (February 1980): 1–2. Print.
– Discussion contributions to the Brecht-Tage 1980. *Brecht 80 – Brecht in Afrika, Asien und Lateinamerika – Dokumentation*. Ed. Werner Hecht, Karl-Claus Hahn and Elifius Paffrath. Publications of the Brecht-Zentrum of the GDR, Volume 2. Berlin: Henschelverlag Kunst und Gesellschaft, 1980. 95, 149, 162, 164, 176. Print.
– "An Interview with the Director." Interview with Diana Thakor. Program Notes for *A Midsummer Night's Dream*, National School of Drama. New Delhi, 1981. Print.
– Letter to Ingeborg Pietzsch. 10 Aug. 1982. FBA. TS.
– "Theatererfahrungen in der Dritten Welt. Gespräch mit Fritz Bennewitz." Interview with Ingeborg Pietzsch. *Theater der Zeit* 5 (1983): 42–6. Print.
– Interview, Kolkata 1988. 4 pages. FBA. TS.
– Interview, *Jugantar* 1988. FBA. TS.
– Interview, *Theater Quarterly*. 1990 or later. 6 pp. FBA. TS.
– "Director's Note" on *Mahashanti*. NSD, 1990. In *Rang Yatra: Twenty-Five Years of The National School of Drama Repertory Company*. Ed. J.N. Kaushal. New Delhi: National School of Drama, 1992. 196–9. Print.
– "Theatre can be defined only in its social context." Interview with Shamsul Islam. *The Times of India*, 14 Feb. 1990. Print.
– "Director's Note" on *The Tempest*. Program of the production, Shri Ram Centre. New Delhi, 1990. FBA. Print.

– "Some notes on experience and methods of intercultural cooperation on stage with my Indian counterparts." *C.I.D.C. Theatre Quarterly* 3 (Dec. 1992): 3. Print.

– Paper for a seminar at the Prithvi Theatre, Mumbai. Typescript in English, November 1993. 3 pp. FBA. TS.

Bentley, Eric, trans. "A New Technique of Acting, by Bertolt Brecht." *Theatre Arts* 33/1 (Jan. 1949): 38–40. Print.

Bhanja, Niren. "Brecht unlearnt." *The Hindustan Standard*, 5 Dec. 1980. Print.

Bharucha, Rustom. *The Politics of Cultural Practice: Thinking through Theatre in an Age of Globalization*. Middletown, CT: Wesleyan University Press, 2000. Print.

Bhave, Pushpa. "Brecht in Maharashtra." N. Allana, *A Tribute* 11–15. Print.

Brecht, Bertolt. *Werke. Große kommentierte Berliner und Frankfurter Ausgabe*. Ed. Werner Hecht et al. 25 vols., plus Registerband. Berlin and Weimar: Aufbau; Frankfurt/M.: Suhrkamp, 2000. Print.

Brecht-Dialog 1968. Materials Folder for Participants in the "Brecht-Dialog 1968." Berlin: n.p., 1968. Print.

Brecht-Dialog 1968. *Theater der Zeit* 2, 1968. 34 + VIII pp. Print.

"Brecht in Bengali." Rev. of Bennewitz's 1980 production of *Life of Galileo* in Kolkata. *India Today*, 2–15 Feb. 1981: 129. Print.

"Brecht not the monopoly of intellectuals – Bennewitz." Newspaper report in the FBA on Bennewitz's production of Brecht's *Mr. Puntila and his Man Matthi* in Bangalore, 1982. Newspaper title unknown. 25 Sept. 1982. Print.

Chandavarkar, Bhaskar. "An Approach to Music for Brecht." N. Allana, *A Tribute* 17–22.

Chander, Romesh. "Excellent production by Bennewitz." Rev. of *A Midsummer Night's Dream* at NSD, 1981. *Times of India*, 14 Dec. 1981: 4. Print.

– "Simplicity marks Brechtian director's *Othello*." *Times of India*, 25 Dec. 1983. Print.

– "*Mahashanti*: A revolution foretold." *Times of India*, 22 Feb. 1990. Print.

Change the World. It Needs It! Brecht exhibition of the Brecht Centre of the GDR. Presented at the National School of Drama, 20 Nov. 1984. Supported by: the Embassy of the German Democratic Republic; Werner Hecht, Director, Brecht Archive; and the Ministry of Education and Culture, Government of India. Designed by Gopi Gajwani. New Delhi: Rajinder Paul at Pauls Press, [1984]. 36 pp., unpag. Illustr. Print.

Dalmia-Lüderitz, Vasudha. "To be more Brechtian is to be more Indian: On the Theatre of Habib Tanvir." *The Dramatic Touch of Difference: Theatre, Own and Foreign*. Ed. Erika Fischer-Lichte, Josephine Riley, and Michael Gissenwehrer. Tübingen: Gunter Narr, 1990. 221–35. Print.

Dalmia, Vasudha. *Poetics, Plays, and Performances: The Politics of Modern Indian Theatre*. New Delhi: Oxford University Press, 2006. Print.

Dasgupta, Samir. "Brecht comes to Calcutta." *Amrita Bazar Patrika*, 26 Dec. 1980. Print.

"Direktive für den Aufenthalt eines Regie-Teams aus der DDR an der National School of Drama." Memorandum for Bennewitz's first stay in India. Berlin, 30 Dec. 1969. FBA. TS.

Duve, Freimut. "Teen Take Ka Swang: Die *Dreigroschenoper* in Neu-Delhi." *Die Zeit*, 15 May 1970. Print.

Erck, Alfred. *Geschichte des Meininger Theaters*. Meiningen: Südthüringisches Staatstheater, 2006. Print.

Esleben, Jörg. "From Didactic to Dialectic Intercultural Theater: Fritz Bennewitz and the 1973 Production of the *Caucasian Chalk Circle* in Mumbai." Wessendorf and Weidauer 302–12.

– "East meets East: Fritz Bennewitz's Theatrical Journeys from the GDR to India." *Kindred Spirits: Transcultural Encounters between Germany and India in the 19th and 20th Centuries*. Ed. Joanne Miyang Cho, Eric Kurlander, and Douglas T. McGetchin. New York: Routledge, 2014. 203–14. Print.

– "*Śakuntalā* in the GDR: Gender Dynamics in Vijaya Mehta's Leipzig Production of Kālidāsa's Play." *Gendered Encounters between Germany and Asia: Transnational Perspectives, 1800–2000*. Ed. Joanne Miyang Cho and Douglas T. McGetchin. New York: Palgrave Macmillan. Forthcoming. Print.

Fischer-Lichte, Erika. "Staging the Foreign as Cultural Transformation." *The Dramatic Touch of Difference: Theatre, Own and Foreign*. Ed. Erika Fischer-Lichte, Josephine Riley, and Michael Gissenwehrer. Tübingen: Gunter Narr, 1990. 277–87. Print.

Garud, Prakash, and Rajini Garud. Interview with Joerg Esleben at Ninasam, Heggodu. 17 Mar. 2012.

Ghosh, Dharani. "Brecht Productions in Bengal." N. Allana, *A Tribute* 5–9. Print.

Gilbert, Helen, and Jacqueline Lo. *Performance and Cosmopolitics: Cross-cultural Transactions in Australasia*. Basingstoke: Palgrave Macmillan, 2007. Print.

Grover, Anil. "The Theatre of Conflict." *Probe India*, April 1981: 6-9. Print.

Guenther, L. "The Development of the Friendship Movement: India-GDR." *India-GDR Relations: A Review*. Ed. Diethelm Weidemann and N.L. Gupta. New Delhi: Kalamkar Prakashan, 1980. 199–218. Print.

Gupta, Abhijit. "Raja Lear: Royal Letdown." Rev. of Padatik's 1988 production of *King Lear*. N.p. December 1988. Print.

Gupta, Anand. Interview with Fritz Bennewitz. *Dinman* 1983. FBA. Print.

Guttal, Vijaya. "Translation and Performance of Shakespeare in Kannada." Trivedi and Bartholomeusz 106–19. Print.

Hiremath, Prashanth. Interview with Joerg Esleben at Rangayana, Mysore. 13 Mar. 2012.

Huber, Anneliese. "The Development of Cultural Relations Between the GDR and India." *India-GDR Relations: A Review*. Ed. Diethelm Weidemann and N.L. Gupta. New Delhi: Kalamkar Prakashan, 1980. 77–97. Print.

ITI – International Theatre Institute: World Organization for the Performing Arts. Web. 24 Feb. 2012. http://www.iti-worldwide.org/iti.php.

Jain, Kirti. Interview with Joerg Esleben at the National School of Drama, New Delhi. 29 Feb. 2012.

John, David G. "The First Black Gretchen: Fritz Bennewitz's *Faust I* in New York." *Monatshefte für den deutschen Unterricht*, 94/4 (2002): 441–57. Print.

– "Goethe's *Faust* in India: The Kathakali Adaptation." *International Faust Studies: Adaptation, Reception, Translation*. Ed. Lorna Fitzsimmons. London, New York: Continuum, 2008. 161–76. Print.

– "Stage Productions of Goethe's *Faust* in India." *Orient und Okzident. Zur Faustrezeption in nicht-christlichen Kulturen*. Ed. Jochen Golz and Adrian Hsia. Köln, Weimar, Wien: Böhlau, 2008. 129–51. Print.

– "Fritz Bennewitz's Islamic *Chalk Circle* in the Philippines." Wessendorf and Weidauer 313–26.

– *Bennewitz, Goethe, Faust. German and Intercultural Stagings*. Toronto: University of Toronto Press, 2012. Print.

Kapur, Anuradha. Interview with Joerg Esleben at the National School of Drama, New Delhi, 27 Feb. 2012.

Karanth, B. V. *Here, I Cannot Stay; There, I Cannot Go. Autobiography of B.V. Karanth as told to Vaidehi*. Trans. C.N. Ramachandran and Padma Sharma. New Delhi: National School of Drama, 2012. Print.

Kazmi, Nikhat. "Shakespeare anew." Preview of *The Tempest*, 1990. *The Sunday Times*, 23 Dec. 1990. Print.

Knowles, Ric. *Theatre & Interculturalism*. Basingstoke, New York: Palgrave Macmillan, 2010. Print.

Kulick, Holger. "Volker Braun und das Stasi-Theater." *Spiegel Online*, 26 Oct. 2000. Web. 19 June 2012. http://www.spiegel.de/kultur/literatur/ddr-schriftsteller-volker-braun-und-das-stasi-theater-a-99987.html.

Kumar, Kanti. "A complex theme skilfully handled." *Times of India*, 10 Jan. 1991. Print.

Lahiri, Urmimala. "Brecht in Bengali." Rev. of Bennewitz's 1980 production of *Life of Galileo* in Kolkata. *Indian Express*, 15 Feb. 1981. Print.

Lal, Ananda, ed. *The Oxford Companion to Indian Theatre*. New Delhi: Oxford UP, 2004. Print.

Lo, Jacqueline, and Helen Gilbert. "Toward a Topography of Cross-Cultural Theatre Praxis." *TDR, The Drama Review* 46.3 (2002): 31–53. Print.

Manmohan. "Indian actors are sensitive and talented." Newspaper preview of *Taming of the Shrew*, Bhopal, 1987. N.p., n.d. FBA. Print.

Mehta, Vijaya. Interview with Joerg Esleben in Mumbai, 16 Apr. 2012.

Misra, Satish. *India-GDR: Three Decades of Relations*. New Delhi: Patriot, 1986. Print.

Nagpal, Kavita. "Poor Theatre at its best." Rev. of *A Midsummer Night's Dream* at NSD, 1981. *Hindustan Times*, n.d. FBA. Print.

– "Peace only after liberation." Rev. of Volker Braun's *Mahashanti* at NSD, 1990. *Business Standard*, 25 Feb. 1990. Print.

Nathan, Archana. "From the corridors of cinema." Interview with M.S. Sathyu. *The Colloquium* 1.1 (2010): 26–31. Web. 6 Mar. 2012.

Ninasam Tirugata: An Overview of 28 Years. Web. 26 Oct. 2015. http://www.ninasam.org/pdf/Ninasam__tirugata_Consolidated_report_2013.pdf.

NSD Graduates. Online list of graduates of the Indian National School of Drama from 1961-2013. Web. 28 Oct. 2015. http://nsd.gov.in/delhi/wp-content/uploads/2014/09/NSD-GRADUATES1.pdf.

Patil, B.S. Interview with Joerg Esleben at the National School of Drama, New Delhi, 1 Mar. 2012.

Peters, Julie Stone. "Intercultural Performance, Theatre Anthropology, and the Imperialist Critique." *Imperialism and Theatre: Essays on World Theatre, Drama, and Performance*. Ed. J. Ellen Gainor. London: Routledge, 1995. 199–213. Print.

Pflaum, Hannelore. "Ursprüngliches Volkstheater. Fritz Bennewitz inszenierte in Indien." *Thüringische Landeszeitung*, 29 Nov. 1983. Print.

Pietzsch, Ingeborg. "Theatererfahrungen in der Dritten Welt. Gespräch mit Fritz Bennewitz." *Theater der Zeit* 5 (1983): 42–6. Print.

Raghunandana. Interview with Joerg Esleben via Skype, 11 May 2012.

Ray, Sankar. "Re-creating Brecht." Rev. of Bennewitz's 1980 production of *Life of Galileo* in Kolkata. *Capital*, 5 Jan. 1981: 24. Print.

Regus, Christine. *Interkulturelles Theater zu Beginn des 21. Jahrhunderts: Ästhetik – Politik – Postkolonialismus*. Bielefeld: Verlag, 2008. Print.

Revermann, Martin. "Brecht's Asia versus Brecht's Greece: Cultural Constructs and the Explanatory Power of a Binary." Wessendorf and Weidauer 276–89. Print.

Rohmer, Rolf. "Annäherungen an den Interkulturalismus mit Brecht: Fritz Bennewitz' Theaterarbeit in Asien." Wessendorf and Weidauer 290–300. Print.

Sahay, Hema. "The Interpretation of 'Dream'." *Financial Express*, 26 Sept. 1982. Print.

Sharma, Tripurari. Interview with Joerg Esleben at the National School of Drama, New Delhi. 28 Feb. 2012.

Silberman, Marc. "A Postcolonial Brecht?" Wessendorf and Weidauer 240–7. Print.

Sinha, Gayatri. "Memorable *Othello*." Newspaper review. N.p., n.d. FBA. Print.

Stephan, Erika. "Am wichtigsten ist der Dialog." Interview-article on Fritz Bennewitz. *Die deutsche Bühne* 4 (1995): 14–17. Print.

Tatlow, Antony. "Brecht's East Asia: A Conspectus." Wessendorf and Weidauer 352–68. Print.

Trivedi, Poonam and Dennis Bartholomeusz, eds. *India's Shakespeare: Translation, Interpretation, and Performance*. Newark: U of Delaware P, 2005. Print.

Trivedi, Poonam. "Introduction." Trivedi and Bartholomeusz 13–43. Print.

Trivedi, Poonam. "'Folk Shakespeare': The Performance of Shakespeare in Traditional Indian Theatre Forms." Trivedi and Bartholomeusz 171–92. Print.

Wessendorf, Markus, and Friedmann J. Weidauer, eds. *The Brecht Yearbook/ Das Brecht Jahrbuch* 36. *Brecht in/and Asia/Brecht in/und Asien*. Madison: U Wisconsin P, 2011. Print.

Wikipedia: The Free Encyclopedia. https://www.wikipedia.org/.

Index

www.ingramcontent.com/pod-product-compliance
Lightning Source LLC
LaVergne TN
LVHW040153080826
844660LV00014B/944/J

* 9 7 8 1 4 8 7 5 0 0 3 8 2 *